The Battle for the Maginot Line, 1940

The Battle for the Maginot Line, 1940

The French Perspective

Clayton Donnell

Pen & Sword
MILITARY

First published in Great Britain in 2017 by
Pen & Sword Military
an imprint of
Pen & Sword Books Ltd
47 Church Street
Barnsley
South Yorkshire
S70 2AS

Copyright © Clayton Donnell 2017

ISBN 978 1 47387 728 3

The right of Clayton Donnell to be identified as the Author of this Work
has been asserted by him in accordance with the Copyright, Designs and
Patents Act 1988.

A CIP catalogue record for this book is available from the British Library

Typeset in Ehrhardt by
Mac Style Ltd, Bridlington, East Yorkshire
Printed and bound in the UK by CPI Group (UK) Ltd,
Croydon, CR0 4YY

Pen & Sword Books Ltd incorporates the imprints of Pen & Sword
Archaeology, Atlas, Aviation, Battleground, Discovery, Family History,
History, Maritime, Military, Naval, Politics, Railways, Select, Transport,
True Crime, Fiction, Frontline Books, Leo Cooper, Praetorian Press,
Seaforth Publishing and Wharncliffe.

For a complete list of Pen & Sword titles please contact
PEN & SWORD BOOKS LIMITED
47 Church Street, Barnsley, South Yorkshire, S70 2AS, England
E-mail: enquiries@pen-and-sword.co.uk
Website: www.pen-and-sword.co.uk

Contents

Preface and Acknowledgements

I've wanted to write this account of the battle for the Maginot Line since 1988, perhaps even as early as 1964, when I saw my first concrete bunker resting quietly in an open French field. I was fascinated from the very beginning and my curiosity about the origin and construction of the Line and the role it played in the Second World War has never been satisfied. So in this book I have taken the opportunity to describe the layout of the Line, its marvelous technical features and the thinking behind it. I have presented a detailed account of the defence mounted by the French when the Germans and then the Italians invaded in 1940. I've also looked at the way the Germans used parts of the Line as they tried to slow the Allied advance in 1944. Finally I have added much thought and discussion that hopefully persuades the reader who holds such an opinion, to reconsider whether the Line deserves an unfortunate reputation as a military failure.

I would not be writing books at all if not for my friend Joe Kauffmann, who introduced me to my editor at Pen and Sword. Marc Romanych, a fellow Maginot Line author with a great interest in the Line, provided me with several great photos to use in the book, as well as some excellent source material from his website – digitalhistoryarchive.com. John Calvin runs wwii-photos-maps.com and he also sent me some photos of German troops you'll find in the book. If you want First and Second World War archival photos, maps and documents, visit these two sites. Jean-Yves Mary, author of many excellent books on the Maginot Line, provided several great vintage photos. Hans Vermeulen, a long-time friend, from the Ouvrage du Fermont, was a huge help to me in finding answers to questions and also contributed some excellent photos from his collection. Thanks to Michel Grami from our Maginot Line Facebook site – *Ligne Maginot Nord-Est* – for the use of his beautiful photo of the Reibel twin machine gun from Casemate Oberroedern Sud (sorry I had to be make it grayscale). Pascal Lambert of wikimaginot.eu permitted me to use several photos. You can get lost for days in this website. I have. I want to thank my family – my wife, who has put up with my grumbling over the past eighteen months; my artist, who is also my daughter Erin, who optimized the photographs and built the maps from scratch; and my brother who always encourages me to look at the glass as half full. Finally, there are several photos in the book from my old friend Dan McKenzie who is now no longer with us but who will always be with us and who I miss every time he comes into my thoughts. Thanks to his wife Alison who has graciously allowed me to use some of Dan's excellent photos. I dedicate this book to him.

Abbreviations

A	*Ouvrage*	Military designation, as in A19
AA		Anti-aircraft
AC	*Anti-char*	Anti-tank
AC47	*Anti-char 47*	47mm anti-tank gun
AM	*Armes-Mixtes*	Mixed arms turret or cloche
AP	*Avant-Poste*	Advanced post
AR		Artillery Regiment (German)
BAF	*Bataillon Alpin de Forteresse*	Alpine Fortress Battalion
BCA	*Bataillon des Chasseurs Alpins*	Light Alpine Infantry Battalion
BCC	*Brigade de Char de Combat*	Tank Brigade
BCHM	*Bataillon de Chasseurs de Haute Montagne*	Light Alpine Mountain Infantry Battalion
BCM	*Bataillon de Chasseurs Mitrailleurs*	Light Infantry Machine-gun Battalion
BCP	*Bataillon de Chasseurs à pied*	Light Infantry Battalion
BCPyr	*Bataillon de Chasseurs Pyrénéens*	Light Pyrenean Infantry Battalion
BEF		British Expeditionary Force
BM	*Bataillon Mitrailleuse*	Machine-gun Battalion
C	*Casemate*	Military designation, as in C24
CAF	*Corps d'Armée de Forteresse*	Fortress Army Corps
CDF	*Commission de Défense de la Frontière*	Commission for the Defence of the Frontier
CDT	*Commission de Défense du Territoire*	Commision for the Defence of the Homeland
CEC	*Compagnie d'Équipages de Casemates*	Casemate Crew Company
CEO	*Compagnie d'Équipages d'Ouvrages*	Fortress Crew Company (French)
CEZF	*Commission d'Étude des Zones Fortifiées*	Commission for the Study of the Fortified Zones
CM	*Compagnie de Mitrailleuses*	Machine-gun Company
CORF	*Commission d'Organisation des Régions Fortifiées*	Commission for the Organization of the Fortified Regions
CSG	*Conseil Supérieure de Guerre*	Supreme War Council
DBAF	*Demi-Brigade Alpin de Forteresse*	Alpine Fortress Half-Brigade
DBMC	*Demi-Brigade de Mitrailleuses Coloniaux*	Colonial Machine Gun Half-Brigade (French)
DCA	*Défense Contre-Avions*	Anti-air defences

DI	*Division d'Infanterie*	Infantry Division (French regular)
DIF	*Division d'Infanterie de Forteresse*	Fortress Infantry Division
DIM	*Division d'Infanterie Motorisée*	Motorized Infantry Division (French regular)
DINA	*Division d'Infanterie Nord-Afrique*	North African Infantry Division
DLC	*Division Légère de Cavalerie*	Light Cavalry Division (French)
DLM	*Division Légère Mécanisé*	Light Mechanized Division
DM	*Division de Marche*	Marching Division
EH	*Entrée d'Hommes*	Troop (men's) entrance
EM	*Entrée de Munitions*	Entrance for munitions and supplies
FCR	*Fortification de Campagne Renforcée*	Reinforced field blockhouses
FM	*Fusil-mitrailleuse*	Automatic rifle
GA	*Groupes d'Armées (GA1, GA2, etc.)*	Army Groups (French)
GFM	*Guetteur-Fusil-Mitailleuse*	Cloche for sentry with automatic rifle
GO	*Gros-Ouvrage*	Large artillery fort
GQG	*Grand Quartier Général*	General Headquarters (French)
	Groupe de Reconnaissance de Corps d'Armée	Corps Reconnaissance
GRDI	*Groupe de Reconnaissance de Division d'Infanterie*	Divisional Reconnaissance
GRM	*Garde Républicaine Mobile*	Mobile Republican Guard (French border)
ID		Infantry Division (German)
IR		Infantry Regiment (German)
IRGD	*Infanterie-Regiment Grossdeutschland*	Grossdeutschland Infantry Regiment (German)
JM	*Jumelages de Mitrailleuses*	Paired machine guns
LG	*Lances-Grenades*	Grenade launcher cloche
M	*Magasin (M1, M2, M3)*	Munitions magazines
MAC	*Manufacture d'Armes de Chattelerault*	
MF	*Maison Forte*	Fortified dwelling
MLR	*Ligne Principale de Resistance* (LPR)	Main line of resistance
MOM	*Main d'Oeuvres Militaire*	Military construction
NATO		North Atlantic Treaty Organization
NCO	*Sous-Officier*	Non-commissioned Officer
O	*Observatoire*	Military designation – observatory, as in O12
PA 1, 2, etc.	*Points d'Appuis*	Strongpoints – forward outposts

PAF	*Points d'appui fortifiés*	Fortified strongpoints
PAL	*Position Avancée de Longwy*	Advanced Position of Longwy
PC	*Poste de Commande*	Command Post
Pi.		Pioneer (German)
PJ	*Panzerjäger*	Tank Hunter (German)
PO	*Petit-Ouvrage*	Small infantry fort
R	*Raccourci*, as in 75mm *Raccourci*	Gun with shortened barrel
RA	*Régiment d'Artillerie*	Artillery Regiment
RAC	*Régiment d'Artillerie Coloniale*	Colonial Artillery Regiment
RAF	*Régiment d'Artillerie de Forteresse*	Fortress Artillery Regiment (French)
RALA	*Régiment d'Artillerie Lourde d'Armée*	Heavy Artillery Regiment
RAM	*Régiment d'Artillerie Motorisée*	Motorized Artillery Regiment (Mobile)
RAMF	*Régiment d'Artillerie de Forteresse Motorisée*	Motorized Fortress Artillery Regiment (Mobile)
RAP	*Régiment d'Artillerie de Position*	Positional Artillery Regiment (French)
RATT	*Régiment d'artillerie tous terrains*	Artillery Regiment – All Terrain
RDP	*Régiment de Dragoons Portés*	Dragoon Regiment (Motorized)
RF	*Région Fortifiée*	Fortified Region
RI	*Régiment d'Infanterie*	Infantry Regiment (French regular)
RIC	*Régiment d'Infanterie Coloniale*	Colonial Infantry Regiment
RIF	*Régiment d'Infanterie de Forteresse*	Fortress Infantry Regiment (French)
RM	*Région Militaire*	Military Region, as in a type of blockhouse
RMIC	*Régiment de mitrailleurs d'infanterie colonial*	Colonial Machine-gun Regiment (French)
RMIF	*Régiment de mitrailleurs d'infanterie de forteresse*	Fortress Machine-gun Regiment (French)
RRT	*Régiment Régional de Travailleurs*	Regional Labour Regiment (French)
S	*Section*	120mm interval field artillery battery in SF Haguenau, S1, S2, etc.
S/S	*Sous-Secteur*	Sub-Sector of a SF
SAA	*Schwere Artillerie Abteilung*	Heavy Artilley Detachment (German)
SD	*Secteur Défensive*	Defensive Sector
SES	*Section d'Éclaireurs skieurs*	Ski patrols in the Alps
SF	*Secteur Fortifié*	Fortified Sector
SFBR	*Secteur Fortifié Bas-Rhin*	A type of blockhouse along the Rhine – Type SFBR

SRA	*Service de Renseignements d'Artillerie*	Artillery information service
SRI	*Service de Renseignements d'Infanterie*	Infantry information service
SRO	*Service de Renseignements d'Ouvrage*	Ouvrage information service
STG	*Section Technique du Génie*	Engineering Technical Section
TM	*Tourelles Mitrailleuse*	Machine-gun turret
TSF	*Transmissions sans fils*	Wireless radio (French)
UEC	*Unités d'Équipages de Casemate*	Casemate Teams (SF Vosges)
VA	*Vorausabteilung*	Advanced Detachment (German)
VDP	*Vision Direct et Periscopique*	Cloche for periscope and direct vision
VP	*Vision Periscopique*	Cloche for periscope

MAP KEY

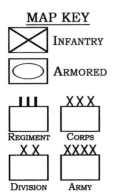

INFANTRY

ARMORED

REGIMENT   CORPS

DIVISION   ARMY

Introduction

At 35 minutes past midnight on 25 June 1940 the armistice between France and Nazi Germany went into effect and the Battle of France came to an end. The river valleys of the Marne, Somme, Aisne, Moselle and Meuse, ancient bulwarks that guarded north-east France from invasion, were now quiet. French villages were empty, smoking ruins. Fighting in Champagne and Artois and Lorraine had ended several days before. The French army, fighting in retreat since 10 May, was pushed back into an ever-solidifying German trap stretching from the Vosges Mountains to the Swiss border. The trap was closed when General Heinz Guderian's Panzers reached the Swiss frontier. Except for a few holdouts, France's main armies surrendered on 22 June. The Belgian Army had surrendered at the end of May. The British were long gone, having miraculously escaped from the beaches of Dunkirk in early June, and German troops and administrative units began the occupation and subjugation of conquered territory.

On 13 June, as the front collapsed, French troops augmenting the defences of the Maginot Line were pulled out of the intervals between the forts to join the army moving to the south. The remaining fortress troops were ordered to sabotage and abandon the Maginot Line forts by 17 June and head south, but fate and military circumstance intervened. First, the Line was now surrounded by Germans so the fortress troops were trapped. Second, the French high command saw in this situation an opportunity to tie up a few German troops while the main army made its escape. The new mission of the crews of what remained of the Maginot Line was to hold out *à l'outrance* – to the limits of their ability. Thus, they did so for the next eight days, undergoing a terrible onslaught from German siege guns and assault troops while the regular units fought rearguard actions to the south. After 22 June, the only French forces still fighting were the fortress troops of the Maginot Line, holding the fortified sectors along the now non-existent border that stretched from Alsace to Longuyon. The Army of the Alps held the southern bulwark of the Line against a massive Italian invasion. The electric motors that powered the forts still hummed. The ventilators pumped fresh air in and shell smoke out. Observers continued to report targets to the artillery and infantry commanders. Orders were shouted and the incredibly engineered French fortress guns fired thousands of shells and bullets until the very last moment.

At 0035hrs on 25 June 1940 Commandant Braye of the Ouvrage du Fermont reluctantly and despairingly gave the order to '*cessez le feu*' – 'cease fire'. With that the guns of Fermont fell silent. Braye looked around his small command post located in the depths of the fort, 30m below ground, at the men he had worked with and laughed with and shared meals with for the last ten months. Some were visibly dejected, weeping; some were glad the nightmare was finally over. But, there were still duties to be attended to; final issues to be taken care of; and to await the dreaded instructions on the disposition of the men and handover of the fort to the Germans.

A few moments later the ringing of the telephone in the command post broke the silence. Braye was handed the receiver. It was one of the fort's observers reporting the sound of machine-gun fire coming from the east in the direction of the Casemate de Beuville. Was the casemate still firing? Did they not receive Braye's order to cease fire? Were they ignoring the order? Braye was patched through to Lt. André Renardin, chief of the casemate. 'What the hell's going on?' Renardin replied that a German machine-gun crew was shooting at them from Blockhouse 318 – Bois de Beuville Est – and it looked like they were preparing for an assault on the casemate – the sentry had spotted 'shadows' moving in the barbed wire. Were they German soldiers or yet another hallucination? The last thing Braye wanted to do was restart hostilities but the machine-gun bullets were real and if the Germans were planning an attack on the casemate he needed to send a message they would understand.

Sub-Lt[1] Bourbon, commander of Fermont's Bloc 5, was notified of the continuing gunfire to the east. The bloc's 81mm mortar crew was in the process of shutting down the operation of the turret, their job apparently done. Suddenly an alert sounded and the crew was notified of a new target. The *Chef de Tourelle* (Chief of the Turret) instinctively shouted commands to his crew. Hearing the coordinates, he moved the dials on the Teleflex device that passed orders on to the gun crew in the small gun chamber overhead. The gunners climbed the ladder into the gun chamber on the top level, and the aimers took their position in the centre. Each man instinctively played his part. In an instant, the 82-ton turret cylinder began to lift along its piston shaft into the firing position; the entire structure then pivoted in a smooth motion to the given *gisement* – bearing and elevation. The mortars' F.A. Model 1936 shells were lifted from storage racks into the small hoist that delivered them up to the gun chamber. There, within the sealed, claustrophobic compartment, two mortar crewmen lifted the freshly-delivered

81mm mortar turret on display at Fermont Museum. The cap has been removed to show the layout of the small gun chamber. (Hans Vermeulen)

shells into the breeches of the two grey mortars. A wheel was turned to adjust the gas pressure in the two cylinders on top of each gun to set the range to the target. The command to fire was given and in a matter of seconds Bloc 5's mortar rounds landed on the wire perimeter of Casemate Beuville. The rounds landed in front of Blockhouse 318 but the German crew continued the firefight for another hour. Maybe the Germans had not had word of the Armistice from their commander or they wanted to get in a few more shots before the war was over. No one knew. At 0140hrs the German gunfire finally stopped and the Maginot Line fell silent.

On 12 June, the French army was reeling. The Germans had launched *Fall Rot* – Case Red – on 5 June and troops and tanks poured across the French border towards the Seine and the Somme. In a few days, the German army crossed the Seine and Paris was surrounded. General Freydenberg's Second Army was barely holding out on the Aisne River. XXI, VI, XX, XIII Army Corps, XLII, XLIII, XLIV CAF and 102 *Division d'Infanterie de Forteresse* (DIF – Fortress Infantry Division) fell back towards Alsace, hoping to either rally there or hold out until the armistice and be permitted to head south into the zone of Free France. General Prételat, commander of Second Army Group, fearing for his left flank in the event the Second Army front collapsed, discussed with General Weygand, commander of all French forces, the option of pulling his troops out of the Maginot Line and moving them to the south. If that decision was made, he said, the fortifications would have to be destroyed and abandoned by their crews.

Prételat's fears were realized on 11 June and the sector commanders of the Maginot Line received orders stipulating that, beginning on 13 June, interval troops and supporting artillery batteries were being pulled out of the Line to join the main army. Even some of the fortress troops were being turned into marching divisions. The fortresses of the Line were to be rendered unusable then abandoned in a series of three phases from 14 to 17 June. The reaction of the fortress troops to this announcement was one of disbelief, shock, anger, sadness and despair. Men cursed distant generals and politicians; others wept or consoled those who wept. Nearly to a man they couldn't believe they were being asked to destroy and then abandon their ship. The amount of money spent to build the Maginot Line was not their concern, although it was certainly a question that would be asked; more significant was the countless hours of training to learn how to use it and the confidence the people of France placed in it; all for nothing. But, as it turns out, only a handful of casemates and forts were sabotaged and abandoned. The majority remained operational and proved to be powerful machines of precision and engineering genius, commanded by inspiring and respected leaders of talented specialists and technicians. In the final days of the war the guns of the Maginot Line inflicted heavy casualties on German troops, forcing them to abandon dozens of attacks.

The combat that took place in and around the Maginot Line is mostly absent from historical accounts of the Battle of France. This is not really a surprise. Alistair

Horne discusses the Maginot Line in about twenty pages of his marvellous book – *To Lose a Battle – France 1940* – including two pages about the Line 'during the battle' [for France], one mention of 'morale', and one mention of the Line being 'encircled and abandoned'. Apparently, in Horne's mind, that was the extent of the function of the Maginot Line and many would agree, but it's not this author's intention to point out what was missing from a particular work, but to add the account to the historical inventory.

The Maginot Line was and continues to be surrounded by myth and misconception and opinions that it was a huge waste of money – a white elephant – one of history's greatest military blunders. Some of the notoriety is perhaps rightly earned and if one doesn't dig below the surface, it's easy to be in agreement. The simple, strategic fact is that the Line was outflanked, France fell in six weeks and there was nothing the fortifications did to stop that from happening. To accept that simple summation is justified, depending on the angle at which you are looking at the Battle of France. Does one look at the Maginot Line from the gross perspective of the rise of Germany and the conquest of Europe, or from a more focused perspective of the timeless role of fortification as an instrument of war? If one is of the former school, then hopefully this account will enlighten them to the valiant role played by the men who served in the Line. If the latter, then it will fill in some of history's missing pieces and introduce a new set of compelling characters that brought some light to a very dark chapter of French history.

Regardless, the Maginot Line has received some well-deserved vindication since the dark days of May and June 1940. Several of the forts were refurbished by the army after the war and used as NATO command centres. Some forts were upgraded mechanically and strengthened against nuclear, biological and chemical attack. Many others remained abandoned, like La Ferté, where 107 men died inside the fort on 18 May 1940. In the 1960s, after Charles DeGaulle withdrew France from NATO, the French army began, in a sense, to 'board up' the Maginot Line. When that happened, interest in its history and technical features was piqued. Word spread in newspapers that certain of the former top-secret forts could be visited. Land containing bunkers or casemates or entire forts was put up for sale. All across the Line the concrete bunkers were abandoned to nature, exposed metal destroyed by scrap-metal salvagers, or opened as museums by local associations. Still much of the military property remained just that, '*Terrain Militaire*', off limits to the casual passer-by or fortophile.[2]

With French Army interest in and military necessity for the forts waning there came a renewed interest in rehabilitating not only the abandoned forts but also the Line's reputation. In the 1970s a detailed account of the fighting along the Maginot Line was written by Roger Bruge in his excellent three-volume set,[3] taken mostly from letters and interviews of the men who fought and served there, both French and German. Commandant of Artillery of Ouvrage du Hochwald, René Rodolphe, wrote an account of the fighting in the Fortified Sector of Haguenau

Modified entrance to Ouvrage Hochwald's former Munitions Entrance – Bloc 8 of the Ouvrage Hochwald Est. (Dan McKenzie)

in Alsace.[4] Claude-Armand Masson was an observer in Casemate Crusnes Ouest, also known as C24, in the Fortified Sector of Crusnes and he wrote a book about his experiences.[5] Philippe Truttmann, a former army engineer who served in the Line, Jean-Yves Mary and Jean-Bernard Wahl produced tremendous volumes that demonstrated the technical details and history of the forts and fortified sectors and the men who served there. Other veterans provided short personal accounts. Unlike Horne's, these accounts gave life to the combat experiences of the fortress troops and revealed that their story was no less harrowing than that of the regular soldiers who fought in the field. They were hit by the same tanks, shelled by the same heavy guns, attacked with grenades, rifles and machine guns and bombed by the same aircraft as the field army. Just because they were behind a concrete wall didn't make the experience any less terrifying or deadly.

The troops of the Maginot Line never had the luxury of simply closing up the armoured doors and blinds and sitting out the war. From the moment Rommel's 7th Panzer Division crossed the Meuse River at Houx in Belgium on the night of 12/13 May the bunker crews experienced war in all its brutality. Unable to respond with artillery, because they didn't have any, the crews in the Sedan bunkers were blown to pieces or forced to surrender as tank shells and Flak guns tore holes in the concrete and smashed the guns and the men inside. Sedan experienced its worst debacle since September 1870 when the thin line of bunkers guarding the Meuse was easily breached and tanks poured across the river and headed west to encircle the Allied armies fighting in Belgium. There was a momentary opportunity for the French to rally on the hills below Sedan but they did not act swiftly enough and panic ensued.

In 1914 German 210mm, 305mm and 420mm siege guns were used to destroy the forts of the Western Front. In 1940 the 88mm Flak gun operated by Luftwaffe crews tore apart the reinforced concrete of the strongest construction materials ever used by military engineers. The 88's high velocity anti-aircraft shells, designed to shoot an aircraft out of the sky, chipped away from close range at the concrete and the steel reinforcing rods, piece by piece and tearing the thick steel walls of the observation cloches to shreds. Even the tons of bombs dropped by Ju-87 Stuka dive bombers did not cause the same degree of damage as that done by the anti-aircraft guns. The Stuka bombs were terrible. They shook the ground and drove the men deep underground, but they were nothing compared to the relentless 88 shells that tore apart the blocs. Bunkers and casemates that were meticulously planned out and built over a decade with some of the finest and strongest construction materials became unrecognizable.

Unidentified armoured cloche showing damage from German 88mm shells. (NARA)

Construction of the Maginot Line did not become fact until the late 1920s. After intense debate that included discussion of the types of construction materials, technical materials and armaments to be used in a new fortress system, plans were finally drawn up and presented to the Minister of Defence. The decisive debate over funding the Line was held in 1929 when the issue was finally brought to the Chamber of Deputies and the Senate. The Deputies argued back and forth. The government at the time was leftist and had different priorities and from the beginning it looked like all of the work of the defence committees and commissions was going to be for naught. The future hung in the balance until André Maginot stepped up to speak to the assembly in January 1930. Maginot served as Minister of War from 1922 to 1924 and again from 1929 to 1932. He was a man of Lorraine who fought and was wounded at Verdun. He was a nationally-recognized war hero and he spoke passionately to the deputies about Lorraine and the dire need to defend it in the coming war and he cajoled and twisted the necessary arms. Many acknowledge his role and passion as the decisive spark that persuaded the deputies to pass the budget that funded André Maginot's line.

Construction had already started in the Alps prior to the aforementioned events, as a result of Italy's new dictator Mussolini bragging of his intention to return the lost provinces of Nice and Savoie to the Italian people. Hitler was still a footnote in history at the time, waiting for his rise and fall. In 1928 ground was broken at the Ouvrage de la Madeleine above the village of Rimplas in the Alpes-Maritimes Fortified Sector. The future Ouvrage du Rimplas was the first of the absolutely amazing and unique forts of the south-east front. The combat blocs of this eagle's nest guarded the Valleys of the Tinée, Roubion and Valdeblore with 75mm and

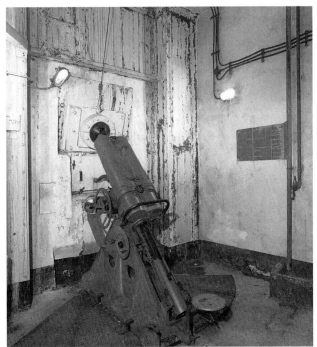

81mm casemate mortar from the Ouvrage du Barbonnet, Alpes-Maritimes. (Dan McKenzie)

81mm mortars, 75mm howitzers, grenade launchers and machine guns. In the north-east along the German border, ground was finally broken in the summer of 1929 at the forts of Rochonvillers, Hackenberg and Hochwald and dozens of construction sites sprang up along the frontier in the first phase of construction – *Première Urgence* – in *Région Fortifié* (RF – Fortified Region) Metz and RF Lauter. When the budget passed, enormous plans for an enormous system were underway but, just as quickly, the money ran out.

As the months and years passed, plans were scaled back not only in the size of the Line but in its strength. Multi-bloc artillery forts became small infantry forts. The latter became casemates joined via tunnel to a second casemate. The paired casemates became single casemates. The single casemate was cancelled altogether and a weak blockhouse without armoured embrasures was built at the last minute to replace it. This continuous erosion left a fractured line that not only lacked cohesion but also lacked depth and firepower. Forts were left without any artillery cover from adjacent forts. The 75mm shells of Simserhof could only provide artillery support to the Ouvrage du Welschoff in *Secteur Fortifié* (SF – Fortified Sector) Rohrbach if a good wind was blowing towards the west. These holes in the firing plots along with gaps in the fortress line at several locations allowed the Germans to surround and neutralize the weaker blocs, resulting in the fall of SF Maubeuge and the defences of the Ardennes, the Meuse, Sarre, the Vosges Mountains and later the mighty Rhine River herself.

The Montmédy sector was evacuated in early June, opening up SF Crusnes to flank attack and gradual encirclement from the west. The toughest battle was fought for the Fortified Sector of the Sarre, a 20km front that was captured after a two-day battle that cost the Germans heavy casualties and their first true setback of the campaign, but opened up a gap through which German units moved and turned to the west to roll up the SF Faulquemont and east to outflank SF Rohrbach. A successful attack through the lower Vosges opened another gap in the Line and the Germans moved through and to the south to chase the main armies, leaving a few regiments behind to mop up.

The weak blockhouses along the banks of the Rhine were fired at from the German side for months and the river was easily crossed on 15 June. Three lines of defence were breached in a short battle and the troops guarding the Rhine pulled back over the Vosges Mountains. The Rhine defences, void of interval troops, were too weak to stop German assault troops from crossing the river and punching their way through the thinly-held line of casemates that guarded the foothills of the Vosges and from where they completed the pincer movement that hastened the surrender of the Armies of the East.

The Battle of France was one French debacle after another but the purpose of this book is to highlight the small victories of the troops of the Maginot Line. In the south, there was complete victory. The Army of the Alps fought and defeated wave after wave of Italian tanks and infantry attempting to break through the narrow mountain passes and strike out for Nice. Nine men of the tiny guard post of Pont Saint-Louis on the French-Italian border at Menton blocked all Italian attempts to move along the narrow coastal highway. The artillery of the Alpine Maginot Line was magnificent, landing pinpoint strikes against Italian forces at every turn. Not a single major fort fell. The defenders of the most isolated outposts experienced unending terror at night or in the fog, but time after time their attackers were chased off by the guns of a nearby fort. This was how the Maginot Line was supposed to work; a triad of excellent gun design, swift communications and observation working together to counter every enemy move. The tactical situation in the Alps was much different from that of the north due to the terrain but it did not diminish the valour and tenacity of the fortress troops, who time and again came to the rescue of the forward posts.

In the north, the Ouvrage du Fermont fought off multiple attacks. The casemates of Aschbach and Oberroedern were pounded and German pioneers stood outside the entrance, but the guns of the nearby forts of Schoenenbourg and Hochwald drove them back and caused them to cancel all further attacks. In late June Michelsberg and Mont des Welches became the focus of ill-conceived attacks and the adjacent guns of the forts of the Boulay sector blocked all attempts by German pioneers to move forward. In SF Faulquemont, the forts of Bambesch and Kerfent were pounded into submission. While they surrendered their neighbours, Laudrefang and Téting, in no better condition, held out until the armistice, never raising the white flag. From the smallest bloc to the largest fort, there are similar stories to tell.

There is a certain nature about troops defending a fortress that is incomparable to the infantry man, not to diminish their role in any way. This nature was exhibited vividly by the troops of the Maginot Line in May and June 1940. A man defending a static structure like a concrete casemate or underground artillery fort cannot fall back to the next position. His duty is to defend the block of concrete he has been assigned to defend. The fortress troops of France lived under the creed of Verdun's military governor during the First World War, General Coutanceau, who coined the phrase which was carved into the walls of the forts that 'it is better to be buried in the ruins of a fort than to surrender it'. Many of the men who served in the Maginot Line were killed inside the concrete chambers by German shells and fumes. Several of the forts surrendered but of those that did not, many of their commanders were outstanding leaders their men would follow until the means to defend was exhausted. Did their heroics make a difference in the outcome of the Battle of France? No, it did not. But telling their story should bring some grandeur and honour back to the entity known as The Maginot Line.

Part I

Pre-War – Development and Initial Deployment, 1919 to May 1940

Chronology 1922–1940

August 1922	The French Supreme War Council establishes the *Commission de Défense du Territoire* (CDT) to study the current state of French defences.
December 1925	The *Commission de Défence de la Frontière* (CDF) is established to further study a frontier defensive system.
20 September 1927	After the CDF publishes its findings the *Commission d'Organisation des Régions Fortifiées* (CORF) is established to study the technical details of the new system.
1928	Construction of prototypes begins in the Alps as a result of threats by Mussolini and in certain locations in the north.
14 January 1930	The French government allots funds to build what will be called the Maginot Line.
1934	Construction of an extension of the Line to the north-east begins – called the New Front.
7 March 1936	Germany reoccupies the Rhineland. French troops move into the Maginot Line for the first time.
March 1938	The Line goes on alert when Hitler annexes Austria.
1 September 1939	Germany invades Poland and France orders general mobilization.
9 September 1939	Abortive French offensive into the Sarre region of Germany. The guns of the Maginot Line fire their first shots.
12 April 1940	General alert order in the north. Called off on 21 April.
9 May 1940	Heavy German activity spotted along the Luxembourg border.

Chapter 1

Development of What Became Known as the Maginot Line

When the First World War came to an end it appeared that France was among the clear winners in every respect. The lost territories of Alsace and Lorraine were returned along with significant reparation payments from Germany for many years to come. But all was not as it appeared. Germany, though clearly the vanquished, was in several respects in better shape than France. The war had not reached Western German territory, in particular the Ruhr and the Saar industrial regions, and Germany was still capable of producing goods. On the other hand, France's industrial base and the entire northern part of the country – hundreds of thousands of square miles – were devastated by the war. The land was polluted with chemicals from poison gas and millions of unexploded bombs and mines remained in the fields and woods and would continue to kill and maim for decades. Hundreds of French villages were destroyed. Entire forests were levelled and some areas, identified as the '*Zone Rouge*', were declared to be such total losses and so dangerous to humans they would never be settled again, even to this day. France, the victor, needed to rebuild the entire northern part of the country.

Germany did not require any such rebuilding programme nor was she as seriously affected demographically as France. German army losses were high – in the millions – 9.8 per cent of the male population. France lost 1.4 million dead, or 10 per cent of the population, but it was a population that did not flourish and this statistic would reach a crisis point in the 1930s. In 1935, as a direct result of war losses, France would have the smallest pool of recruits from which to fill the ranks of the army. The army had to come up with a solution and it had to be done before then.

France carried a huge war debt. Reparations awarded in the Versailles Treaty amounted to 165 million marks but this was not enough to rebuild the country and Germany was notorious for missing payments. Finally, the Lausanne Accords of 1932 placed a moratorium on the remaining debt and Germany was off the hook.

The treaty also redrew the border. France recovered Alsace and Northern Lorraine. The Rhineland was declared a demilitarized zone and France was given the right to occupy it for fifteen years. This period of time could be extended if debt payments were not made, which became a moot point. Germany was also prohibited from building fortifications and her army was reduced to 100,000 men. On the surface, the Versailles treaty looked to be a fair deal for France, but underneath lurked a plethora of problems. As the years went by, things would get worse.

Meanwhile, Italy was quickly becoming a threat. Mussolini, during one of his bombastic balcony speeches in Rome, boasted of recovering the territories of Nice and Savoie[1] from France. This opened up the possibility of an entirely new war front. Finally, France's existing fortifications were old and heavily damaged and while the provinces of Alsace and Lorraine were returned, the restored territory needed to be defended. The choice of the nature of the defence for the military planners of the French command was between a sword and a shield. To use a strong and victorious army that was unfortunately weary of fighting and would be at its weakest in the late 1930s, or to build a shield and block the frontier. The debate was long but in the end France chose the shield.

The 1871 to 1918 Franco-German border was defended by the powerful but obsolete Séré de Rivières forts. This system, begun in the 1880s, consisted of a line of forts, interval gun batteries and troop shelters that stretched along the Belgian and former German border. It was a system of entrenched camps – cities surrounded by a ring of forts – connected by a thin line of isolated 'arresting forts'. The main camps were located at Verdun, Toul, Épinal and Belfort. The forts were modernized in the years prior to the war with the addition of a layer of concrete poured over the masonry, installation of armoured gun turrets and construction of underground concrete barracks that afforded a greater degree of protection to the garrisons. However, the most powerful fort in the system, Manonvillers, that guarded the Charmes Gap, was destroyed in a matter of hours by heavy German siege guns and for this reason many of the forts were disarmed in 1915. After the successful defence of Verdun and the role the forts played in that victory, however, the concept of permanent fortification as a reliable means of defence experienced a renaissance.

The resistance of Verdun was a major factor in the post-war decision to undertake the construction of a new system of permanent defences. Marshal Philippe Pétain, one of France's greatest military heroes, declared that the fortifications of Verdun had fulfilled their role. General Descourtis, commander of engineers for Second Army, stated that the concrete forts held out well. Permanent fortification, initially condemned in the early years of the war, had reaffirmed its value.

A number of treatises on the organization of territorial defence were published in the early twenties. Colonel Becq, in his *Conférence sur l'organisation défensive du territoire* of March 1923 proposed several solutions for defending the frontier:

- Field fortifications consisting of strongpoints on a continuous front.
- Observatories; shelters with machine guns and anti-tank guns; command posts; gun batteries.

He compared the ideal solution to the Cherisey position built by the Germans south of Metz, with a 12km front and 3–4km in depth, equipped with 2,500 shelters protected by 1.5m thick concrete walls, interconnected by trenches.

Becq's solution included two phases:

- 1st phase: reforestation of the frontier to camouflage a series of military roads and 60cm railway lines with observatories, barracks, shelters and command posts. The forest would be a minimum of 10km in depth.
- 2nd phase: the wooded area being insufficient in itself, France must return to concrete. German technology within 50 years[2] would be such that we must create a veritable Wall of China. While 2.5m of concrete withstood the 420mm guns in the First War, a future counterscarp should be double that in thickness. The forts, 1,000–2,000m apart would contain underground facilities with electrical generation, ventilation and water. Finally, the guns would be protected in steel turrets.

Colonel Birchler, in his résumé of 2 October 1922, proposed armoured casemates and turrets for machine guns, combat shelters, armoured observatories and underground shelters for troops. Artillery for interdiction would include gun turrets and Bourges-type casemates for flanking fire. 75mm guns would be used for long-range coverage and the 155mm howitzers for ravines and dead ground. The main elements would be connected by tunnels.

General Normand, in his *Essai sur la défence de France*, noted that certain zones needed to be covered by fortifications and others through certain destructions:

- Those used for mobilization or concentration.
- The capital.
- Industrial areas (mines, industry).
- Essential lines of communication.

Fortification must play an active role to:

- Mask the movement of troops.
- Support the entry of field troops into the line.
- Guard all outlets from the frontier.
- Facilitate troop manoeuvres.
- Provide supply centres and strongpoints for advancing troops.
- Serve as a refuge for retreating troops.
- Force the enemy to commit significant forces to protect its rear as it passes by the fortress.

In June 1922, the *Conseil Supérieure de Guerre* (CSG – Supreme War Council), with Pétain as Vice-Chairman, created a sub-commission that reported to the CSG, the *Commission Chargé des Études d'Organisation de la Defence du Territoire*, chaired by Marshal Joseph Joffre. Two opposing viewpoints arose very early in the discussions. Pétain favoured a battlefield organized along the frontier to carry the war to the enemy. Joffre favoured vast fortified regions. The opposing viewpoints were so strong that the group was disbanded only fifteen days after its creation.

On 3 August 1922, a new commission – the *Commission de Défense du Territoire* (CDT) – was created with General Adolphe Guillaumat, Inspector General of the Army and member of the CSG, serving as President. It held only two meetings and on 27 March 1923 closed out its mission with a 36-page *Rapport au Ministre sur les principles de l'organisation défensive du territoire*. This report drew two conclusions: the defence of France should be based on the development of fortified regions with a dual purpose – defence of the frontier and as a place to launch an offensive by the armies; and it should be based on a system of permanent fortifications built along certain parts of the frontier. General Henri Berthelot, former military governor of Metz, identified the most dangerous potential invasion routes:

- Via the north-west massif of the Hunsrück and along the right bank of the Moselle, then through Luxembourg.
- Across the plateau of Lorraine.
- Between the Vosges and the Rhine.
- Through the Belfort Gap.

The commission concluded that it would be necessary to build permanent fortifications from Longwy to Basel via Lauterbourg, leaving the Sarre devoid of defences.[3] The trace was to consist of three *Régions Fortifiées* (RF):

- RF Metz.
- RF Lauter.
- RF Belfort.

Aside from making some general suggestions, the commission was not tasked with laying out the exact trace of the Line, or providing technical specifications. These required further study by the commission or its successor.

The commission's report was not immediately acted upon due to objections from the army high command. No funding was authorized to advance further studies and discussion was tabled until it was brought up in September 1925 by General (and later Senator) Adolphe Messimy. He raised the alarm with Paul Painlevé, the new Minister of War, of the lateness in beginning the study requested by the commission. On 15 December 1925, the CSG, with the help of Gaston Dumergue, President of the Republic, persuaded Painlevé to accept the creation of a commission to further study a frontier defensive system. On this date the war minister created the *Commission de defence de la frontière* (CDF) with General Guillaumat in charge. He was joined by Generals Berthelot, General Marie-Eugène Debeney, former Chief of Staff to Pétain, General Jean Degoutte, commander of the French Army of the Rhine until 1925, General Louis Maurin, an engineer, General Etienne-Honoré Filonneau, also an engineer, and Colonel Frederic Culmann, an artillery expert.

The first meeting of the CDF was held in February 1926. Nine months later the commission published its findings: *Rapport No. 171F du 6 Novembre 1926*. Guillaumat: 'Inspired by the hope to create a grand resistance to positions proposed on each of our frontiers, the Commission has studied the types of *ouvrages* [which will be] entirely new and in the projected ensembles to be incorporated into the ancient places of Metz and Belfort which have retained a certain valour. Also, it [the commission] has conceived of a system that is solid and deep and favours an obstinate struggle of long duration.' The document was 105 pages long and included maps and plans.

The CDF report, like the CDT's, did not provide in–depth technical details except to specify the general features of a 'principal' fort: about 170m in length with four turrets, two flanking casemates, six machine-gun casemates and two observatories. An 'intermediate' fort was smaller with two turrets and two machine-gun casemates; not much different from the modified forts of 1916–17.[4]

In 1923, Lieutenant-Colonel M.[5] Tricaud, in the *Révue du Génie*,[6] proposed what he called a *fort palmé* or 'webbed' fort in the form of dispersed structures spread out like a spider's web. It was a design somewhere between the 1916–17 modified French forts and the German *Festen* of Metz/Thionville. The forts' 'combat blocs' were dispersed rather than being grouped together in a mass, to provide maximum protection to the garrison. Tricaud appeared before the CDF in 1927 to defend his idea, but he failed to do so because of some inherent technical flaws. However, later in the year the idea resurfaced. Pétain got hold of the study and was impressed and Tricaud's *fort palmé* became the model for further studies.

The CDF's discussions continued into 1927 even after publication of its findings. The details of the new system had to be decided upon. Painlevé authorized the CDF to study the technical aspects of the fortifications in terms of construction materials, armaments and the design of the permanent fortifications. On 30 September 1927, the *Commission d'Organisation des Régions Fortifiées* (CORF) was created to carry out the studies and to develop the final designs.

The CORF presented a detailed report to the war minister on 12 March 1928. The report was sent to the government for funding approval. It outlined the organization of the fronts and their technical details including communications and electrical equipment. It outlined twelve types of forts to be built, from heavy forts to small shelters for local reserves. The CORF left some leeway to the engineers, knowing that terrain would determine the final configuration of each fort. In September 1928, the CORF presented their armaments recommendations: to develop a rapid-fire gun – the *canon-obusier de 75mm* based on the 75mm Model 1897.

General Belhague took over the presidency of the CORF from General Filloneau after his death in 1928. He quickly added his fingerprint to the development of the future Line and it was a large print. He proposed the following concepts for armament:

- Addition of an 81mm mortar to strike dead ground.
- Turrets to house two howitzers each.
- A short-barrelled 75mm gun (75R – *raccourci*).
- A 75mm mortar.

The tried and trusted 75 was the primary gun selected, to be adapted for use in the fortress, installed in casemates in groups of three for flanking fire and in turrets in pairs that could fire in all directions. The Model 1929 and 1932 guns were shortened versions of the Model 1897. The Model 1929 gun had a very similar operation to the Model 1897 from which it was derived. The barrels and breeches and recoil system were similar in function. The barrel was mounted on a fortress-specific carriage with a ball affixed to the mouth of the barrel to form a tight seal against the embrasure fitting. Casemate versions protruded beyond the ball by 1.5m, making it vulnerable to enemy fire. Only thirty models were installed in casemates, fourteen in the north-east, twelve in the Alps and four in Corsica.

The 75mm Model 1932 (75/32) gun was an improved model that did not extend beyond the embrasure opening, which could be closed off by a shutter. The barrel length was 30cm, supported on a newly-designed carriage. Twenty-three guns were installed in 1940.

81mm mortars were installed at a fixed angle with breech-loading capability. The range was controlled by adjusting gas pressure inside two cylinders located on top of the weapons. They had a range of 2,800m.

The 135mm Model 1932 *Lances-bombes* (bomb thrower) for turret or casemate, was developed by the CORF as a high-angle weapon to reach dead ground. The gun

Twin 75mm guns. The set, with two 75mm barrels and a scope in the centre, were mounted inside a 75mm Model 1933 gun turret. This pair is on display at Ouvrage du Michelsberg. (Hans Vermeulen)

was developed to strike targets up to 6,000m away that could not be reached by the 81mm mortar. The result was a very powerful gun unique in the French inventory with no equivalent field pieces. Shells could be set to fall from 27° to 90° depending on the type of projectile used. The bomb thrower had a short tube with a semi-automatic breech and a ball attached to the mouth to protect the embrasure opening. The piece was mounted in a casemate or in pairs in turret. It had many flaws during testing including twisting tubes and inaccurate targeting. Testing ended in 1934 and no further corrective measures were taken. The gun performed very well in 1939 to 1940. A total of forty-three pieces were installed, thirty-four in turrets and nine in casemates. Standard features:

135mm Lances Bombes *howitzer. Casemate version located inside the Ouvrage d'Agaisen in the Alpes-Maritimes.* (Dan McKenzie)

- Barrel length: 1.145m
- Weight: 288kg
- Maximum range: 5,600m
- Rate of fire: 6 shots/minute
- Turret firing angle: 9° to 45° degrees
- Casemate model firing angle: 0° to 40°

The 13.2mm paired Reibel MAC 31 machine gun was the infantry workhorse. It was designed in the late 1920s to replace the 8mm Hotchkiss Model 14 used in French tanks. It used the 7.5mm ammunition, same as the FM 24/29 Model D. The gun was first tested successfully in the Casemate Bois de Kanfen Est. It was used in the Maginot Line in pairs, assembled as a single unit and mounted on a support. In case of intensive gunfire, the guns were to be alternated to allow one to cool while the other was in use. The unused barrel was sprayed with water from a Vermorel spray tank located nearby. Three models were developed for the Maginot Line: Model F 31 for casemate embrasures and cloches (AM and M); Model T 31 for machine-gun turrets; Model 31 TM for mixed turrets or cloches. Standard features:

- Overall length: 1.05m
- Barrel length: 60cm
- Weight: 10.7kg (F), 10.3kg (TM), 10.4kg (T)

- Maximum rate of fire: 750 rounds per minute
- Muzzle velocity: 694m/s

The automatic rifle – *fusil-mitrailleuse* (FM) Model 24–29 was used in small embrasures in the casemate facades and cloches for close defence. The gun was produced by the *Manufacture d'Armes de Chattelerault* (MAC) from 1927 to 1957. Almost 200,000 FM 24–29s were produced, including 2,512 D-type used in Maginot Line fortifications. The D-Type was produced from 1934. It was also paired in casemates and blocks with the Reibel MAC 31. Standard features:

- Cartridge: 7.5mm Type 1929C
- Overall length: 1.7m
- Barrel length: 0.5m
- Weight: 8.93kg
- Maximum range: 3,100m
- Maximum rate of fire: 450 rounds per minute
- Muzzle velocity: 820m/s

Belhague's structural ideas included powerful forts (*ouvrages*), with intervals organized as follows:

- A line of casemates about 800m apart.
- Small forts (*petits ouvrages* (PO)) every 3km in the form of infantry forts for machine gun and mortar turrets and forts for the 75R model guns.
- The forts would all be designed in the *palmé* or webbed style.

Each fort was different as it was adapted to the surrounding terrain. Each location required a detailed reconnaissance by the CORF and a *plan de masse* created and approved by the Minister of War, along with a detailed implementation plan. By the end of the year most of the plans were ready to go. The only thing needed was funding.

André Maginot (1877–1932) served in several cabinets of the Third Republic. He became War Minister for the second time on 3 November 1929 and inherited the responsibility begun by his predecessor Painlevé for funding of the Maginot Line.[7] The requested funding would provide France with the most powerful fortification system in its history, but approval of the funding was not assured. The deputies argued that the work of the CDF was not conclusive and perhaps other regions of the country also needed to be defended. Lorraine was to receive 52 per cent of the budget and an attack through Lorraine was not a foregone conclusion. 'What about the Rhine or Paris?' 'What about an airborne invasion – are the walls going to be high enough to stop that?' These questions were compelling, but Maginot was able to persuade the deputies of the necessity to 'defend the frontier and to prevent the violation of our territory by an enemy army'. Not only were his arguments persuasive but he was able to get the desired result thanks to a clever 'hallway campaign', some arm-twisting and decisive support from other elected deputies from Lorraine. The matter went to a vote in the lower chamber and passed with a show of hands. In the Senate, the measure passed by voice vote 270 to 22 and was signed into law on 14 January 1930 by President Gaston Doumergue.

Construction of *première urgence* began in the north in the summer of 1929 at three locations – Rochonvillers on the plateau of Aumetz, Hackenberg which blocked the Moselle Valley and Hochwald, the cornerstone of the defence of Alsace. By the end of 1930 twenty-one construction sites were in operation in the north-east and seven in the Alps. The main sites included:

Jumelages de Mitrailleuses *(JM)* – *a twin Reibel MAC 31 machine gun currently on display inside the Casemate d'Oberroedern Sud, SF Haguenau. Note the Vermorel water canister in the corner, used to cool the gun barrels. The circular piece on the side is the magazine.* (Michel Grami)

US Army infantry patrol from 410 Infantry Regiment, 103st Infantry Division approach Bloc 13 of Ouvrage Hochwald Ouest, SF Haguenau, on 15 December 1944. (NARA)

- RF Metz:
  - Large forts/ensembles: Rochonvillers, Molvange, Métrich, Hackenberg, Anzeling.
  - Medium-sized forts: Soetrich, Kobenbush, Galgenberg, Billig, Mont-des-Welches, Michelsberg.
  - Infantry forts: Immerhof, Bois-Karre, Oberheid, Sentzich, Mont-du-Coucou, Bois-de-Bousse.
- RF Lauter:
  - Ensembles: Simserhof, Hochwald.
  - Medium: Schiesseck, Grand-Hohékirkel, Otterbiel, Four-à-Chaux, Schoenenbourg.
  - Infantry: Lembach.

In addition, 143 casemates were under construction in the north-east and fifty-three in the Alps. Factories were manufacturing 220 steel cloches, 500 armoured embrasures and twenty turrets.

The second phase of construction – *deuxième urgence* – started in 1931. It was a continuation of the work already started and included modifications based on lessons learned in the first phase. Funding restrictions reduced the scope of several projects and this would become a familiar pattern in the years to come.

The second phase included the extension of the RF Metz:

- Left wing: extension of the forts from Rochonvillers to Longuyon, the result of political pressure from regional deputies to protect the industrial basin of Longwy-Briey.[8] It included three artillery forts – Fermont, Latiremont and Bréhain – and four infantry forts – Ferme-Chappy, Mauvais-Bois, Bois-du-Four and Aumetz – plus two casemates, six observatories and twenty-four shelters.
- Right wing: extension of the Line from Anzeling to Téting that included twelve forts – Bovenberg, Denting, Village de Coume, Annexe Nord de Coume, Coume, Annexe Sud de Coume, Mottenberg, Kerfent, Bambesch, Einseling, Laudrefang and Téting. The most powerful armament in these forts was limited to six 81mm mortars, two at Annexe Sud de Coume (Bloc 3) and four at Laudrefang (Blocs 1 and 3).

Extension of RF Lauter:

- In the centre of the Lower Vosges, thirty-three casemates and blockhouses were added between Biesenberg and Lembach. From Schoenenbourg to the Rhine a line of casemates was added near the towns of Oberroedern, Hunspach, Kauffenheim, Aschbach and Hoffen.

Rhine: the third line of villages, consisting of heavy casemates, was added.

North: Twelve casemates were built in the Forêt de Raismes and thirteen in the Forêt de Mormal. The addition of defences in the north was also due to local political pressure.

In 1933 the army acknowledged the necessity to extend the Line to the north, an elongation of the RF Metz towards Montmédy in order to guard against a German invasion through Luxembourg and Belgium. Engineers marked out the northern frontier with points (*môles*) of resistance to block the main invasion routes and guard French industrial interests. Plans were approved in July 1934 for what became known as the 'New Front' and the CORF was given only 140 million for 24km of the future Montmédy bridgehead. This included two ouvrages each with a 75mm turret (Velosnes and Le Chénois), two POs – La Ferté and Thonelle – and twelve casemates.

There were numerous glaring gaps in the New Front construction, both geographical and technical. While they may have presented in the planner's minds excellent points of departure from which to launch attacks, the French army lacked the mobility to do so and instead the Germans used them as invasion routes.

The two 81mm casemate mortars in Bloc 3 of PO Coume-Sud and four in Blocs 1 and 3 of PO Laudrefang were the only heavy weapons placed in the New Front. The two POs of the Plateau of Rohrbach – Haut-Poirier and Welschoff – were equipped with a 'mixed arms' turret, the 75R05 model modified to hold a 25mm anti-tank gun and paired machine guns, the *Tourelle pour deux armes mixte*. In the end, this was woefully insufficient to counter enemy artillery batteries. Haut-Poirier had no artillery support at all from adjacent forts.

The way events turned out, the French could have saved the money they sunk into the bridgehead. Here the Maginot Line terminated on a ridge overlooking the Chiers River at the PO La Ferté, whose crew waited for an attack from the north that would instead come unseen from the west from the direction of Sedan. It was 30km from La Ferté to Sedan at the mouth of the Ardennes forest. A line of blockhouses was built along the Chiers and Meuse, but it was not a true fortified line or barrier. The army had high confidence in France's ability, or absence of necessity, to defend this region. Pétain famously remarked: 'The Ardennes Forest is impenetrable if some special facilities are undertaken.[9] Consequently, we consider this to be a zone of destruction. This front has no depth; the enemy will not commit to it [*ne pourra pas s'y engager*]. If they do, we will cut them off at the forest exits. Thus, this sector is not dangerous.' He was marvellously wrong.

Gamelin, in a confidential note written to the war minister on 16 February 1936, wrote:

> The Ardennes region cannot be regarded as threatened just as Lorraine and Alsace. Even in case of sudden attack of the enemy, France would obviously, for its part, take all measures to effectively cover its own borders. The line of the Meuse is important militarily only in case of an absolute surprise in which the opponent suddenly invades Luxembourg and Belgium with motorized forces which cannot be slowed down. But these forces are not capable of a systematic attack on an organized line of the Meuse.

It if were possible, Gamelin was even more wrong than Pétain.

Components of the Maginot Line

The main component of the Maginot Line was the infantry or artillery fort, called an *ouvrage*.[10] It comprised what was known as the 'Main Line of Resistance' (MLR). Those elements designated as ouvrages were broken down into two types:

- *Gros-Ouvrage* or large ouvrage – a multi-bloc fort equipped with artillery weapons of at least 75mm calibre.
- *Petit-Ouvrage* (PO) or small ouvrage – a multi- or single-bloc fort equipped with infantry weapons up to 81mm mortars.

On the surface the ouvrage was composed of a varying number of concrete casemates, also identified as a 'bloc'.[11] These casemates, either combat or entrance blocs, were connected to the underground tunnels of the fort by staircases and lift shafts of varying depths, averaging 30–35m.

The ouvrage was protected by early warning outposts placed between the MLR and the frontier. The line of advanced posts (AP) guarded the roads that led towards the MLR. Their mission was to raise the alarm[12] in the event of an attack and to delay enemy forces for as long as possible. The units manning the outposts were expected to mount a fighting retreat, covered by friendly infantry or artillery fire, and to help slow the advance of the attacker by destroying roads and bridges and important crossroads.

Further back from the border the MLR was protected by permanent obstacles designed to block tanks and infantry. Germany's use of tanks in the Polish campaign raised very real concerns that they would be used against the French and anti-tank defences became a priority. Upturned train rails were implanted in the ground four to six rows deep to block the movement of tanks. The steel rails were 3m in length and placed 60cm to 1.5m apart.[13] Barbed wire was strung between them. Each separate casemate or surface bloc attached to an ouvrage was also surrounded by a dense field of barbed-wire entanglements strewn with mines and booby traps. Both the anti-tank rails and barbed wire obstacles were covered by overlapping anti-tank and machine-gun fire.

The first phase of construction by the CORF included powerful casemates of varying styles – single, double, etc. (able to flank in one or two directions). They were built on the main line of resistance and provided continuity of fire between the larger forts. They also served as observation posts. Casemates were equipped with machine guns and anti-tank guns, a power generator, telephones and small barracks. The guns of the casemates were protected by armoured embrasures and both casemates and combat blocs were defended by *cloches*, shaped like a bell and made of solid steel of varying thicknesses. There were several types of cloches. The GFM – *guetteur-fusil-mitrailleuse* or *cloche de guet* was the standard cloche with embrasures to hold an episcope for viewing. It was armed with the FM and

Barbed-wire entanglements. Identified on reverse as SF Boulay. (Marc Romanych)

a 50mm mortar. Casemates with observatories were equipped with a cloche *vision periscopique* (VP) paired with a GFM. There were many modifications to the cloches, including the cloche Model 1930 for the *Jumelage de Mitrailleuses* (JM) – the paired Reibel machine guns.

To assure a continuous defence in depth and to provide for mobility, interval troops were placed between the casemates and the ouvrages. They lived in shelters with trenches and in small blockhouses. The interval troops, also equipped with field artillery, provided an additional level of support to the forts in advance of the Line and covered any dead ground that could not be reached by the guns of the forts. They also provided cover in case of an attack from the rear if the enemy was able to penetrate the main line of defence. Interval troops were specialized units made up of infantry, artillery and engineers. Without interval troops, the Maginot Line would be severely weakened.

The Ouvrages – the Forts Palmé

The initial CORF plans envisioned two entry blocks, one for the troops that led directly to the underground barracks – *Entrée d'Hommes* (EH) – and one for the delivery of munitions and supplies – *Entrée de Munitions* (EM). The design of the entrance blocs varied from one ouvrage to the next, depending on the layout of the terrain. Entrances were to be located to the rear of the fighting blocs on the rear slope of a hill out of the reach of enemy artillery fire. As funding dried up, they were combined into a single mixed entrance. In the New Front infantry forts the entrances were located in one or more of the actual fighting blocs. The forts in the Alps did not have a dual entrance concept (men and munitions). Rather, they had a single, combined entrance but some forts had an additional entrance accessible by cable car.[14]

Mixed entrance to Ouvrage de Monte Grosso, SF Alpes-Maritime, S/S Sospel. Note the drawbridge common to the Alpine Maginot Line forts. (Dan McKenzie)

The munitions entrance was large enough to accommodate trucks or small locomotives that pulled wagons on 60cm rails, loaded with supplies or munitions carried from depots to the rear of the Line. The track continued inside the entrance and continued to the underground magazine that could be reached either by lift or along a sloping tunnel that led to the lower level.[15]

Each ouvrage had two main levels – the surface and the underground zones. All of the combat blocs and entrances were located on the surface. The underground zone, located an average of 30m below the surface, provided maximum protection to the troops and munitions. It included four main sub-zones: munitions storage, living quarters, power production and ventilation, and command and control. The largest forts had a main magazine identified as the M1, located along the main

Technicians load caissons of shells on to a wagon inside Ouvrage Hackenberg's Magazine M1. This photo was taken in 1940. (Jean-Yves Mary)

The Atelier *or tool room of Ouvrage d'Agaisen, adjacent to the power station.* (Dan Mckenzie)

tunnel. Small forts did not have an M1. Instead, munitions were stored at the base of each combat bloc – M2.

During wartime or alerts the fortress troops lived in underground barracks that consisted of dormitory-style rooms for the troops and single rooms for the officers, toilets and wash rooms, a kitchen, water storage tanks supplied by underground wells and a small infirmary. A power-generating station and repair shop (*usine*) for maintaining the motors and equipment, such as the turrets, guns, ventilation equipment, radios, etc., were located along the main corridor. Each fort was equipped with one or more diesel-powered motors to generate electricity. During peacetime, the forts were connected by underground cable, through reinforced concrete sub-stations, to the external power grid. If power from the outside was cut, the forts switched to their generators to produce electricity for the operation of the lifts, ventilation, lighting, heating and the revolving gun turrets. In case of an attack with poison gas and to remove fumes produced by the guns, the forts were equipped with ventilation systems to circulate air throughout the fort. Air was drawn from the outside through filters where it was scrubbed of toxins and then released into the fort. The forts were sealed from the outside by airlocks and by forcing the air to blow outside the fort through vent shafts or gun embrasures in the observation and defensive cloches.

The fort's *raison d'être* was its guns. The combat blocs that housed either turret or casemate guns were located on the surface. Each bloc was accessed by an offshoot tunnel from the main trunk of the fort. Each offshoot had a double set of armoured doors that were sealed off when the bloc was in combat mode. The guns were reached by a staircase for the crew that wound around a lift used to move munitions up to the gun level. The staircase/lift shaft opened on to the lower level of a two-storey casemate. In turret blocs, the lower level housed the drive mechanisms to raise and lower and rotate the turret and storage of replacement barrels, repair equipment

*Gun crew at work on
the intermediate level
of the 75mm Model 33
turret of Bloc 2, Ouvrage
du Hackenberg. The
man second from left is
adjusting the directional
indicator located on
the inside of the ring
surrounding the turret.*
(Jean-Yves Mary)

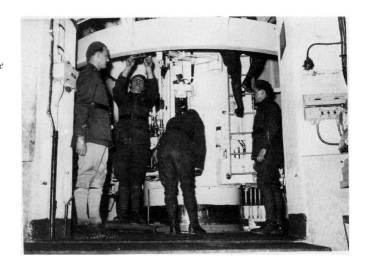

and a ventilator. The upper level contained a small dormitory room for the watch shift and latrines for the gun crew and officers. The upper level contained the main controls to move the turret guns by revolving the turret to the proper target and to raise it into the battery position or lower it for protection. In casemates, the guns or mortars were located in the upper levels. Extra ammunition for the guns were stored in magazines (M3) on the surface level and passed up on a hoist to the gunners at the top of the turret or in the casemate.

Electric motors to power the turret were located in a central cylinder and allowed the crew the move the guns with the push of a button. The turret could also be moved by hand if power failed and the mechanics were such that this did not take a great deal of strength to do. A 75mm gun turret had a crew of seventeen. Twelve men were responsible for getting the munitions from magazine to barrel.

A ladder gave access from the intermediate level to a trapdoor in the floor of the firing chamber, a small enclosed capsule located at the top of the turret. The interior of a 75mm turret was 2m in diameter and the walls and ceiling were 30cm thick. The turret's twin guns were located, side-by-side, in the firing chamber. Two crewmen were assigned to tend the guns. The ideal crewman was small in stature due to the cramped nature of the capsule. Despite the physical difficulties of working in this environment, being a gunner carried with it considerable prestige.

Artillery and Observation

The strength of the Maginot Line was in the triad of an excellent gun design, swift communications capabilities and observation. Observation posts, either adjoined to the ouvrage or stand-alone, were equipped with sophisticated and highly-precise periscopes that could be raised through the top of the observation post's thick steel cloche.

Observation cloche at Ouvrage du Simserhof. (Marc Romanych)

Observers were in direct contact with the command post. Each infantry and artillery fort had a command post to direct combat. The entire frontier was plotted out in advance. Every possible target and coordinate was identified and the gunners and observers knew precisely where everything was located. Detailed panoramas – photos or paintings – of the surrounding terrain as it would look from their viewing portal or periscope were placed inside their observation post. Potential targets could easily be located on a quadrilateral map. If the enemy was spotted next to a building, all they had to do was find the building on the sketch or photo and pass that information on to the artillery command post.

The infantry commander directed the activity of the following:

• Infantry blocs (flanking casemates with 47mm anti-tank guns, JMs and FMs for defence of the approaches from enemy infantry attacks). The infantry blocs worked in conjunction with the interval casemates to provide covering or interdictory fire.
• Machine-gun turret blocs.
• Observation cloches (GFM) to keep watch over the surface of the fort. These were equipped with machine guns and 50mm mortars to cover the barbed wire and anti-tank obstacles.
• If necessary, the infantry commander also directed combat inside the fort if the enemy gained access.[16]

The duties and responsibilities of the artillery commander were more complex. He reported to the fortress commander. Observers passed information and target coordinates to the artillery commander who decided which weapons to use against the target.

The infantry or artillery command post was broken up into two sections, the *Service de Renseignements d'Artillerie (Infanterie)* (SRA/SRI – Information

Service) and the *Poste Central de Tir* (Central Firing Post). The former consisted of a bank of telephones manned by operators connected to each of the fort's observation posts.[17] Each operator had a chalkboard on which to write target information reported by the observers. To the rear of the operator was a table occupied by recorders (*Secretaires*) and target plotters and behind them was the Information Officer. On the opposite wall from the telephone operators were panoramic photos depicting what could be seen from each observatory. An orderly passed messages to other command locations in the fort. Information from the SRA/SRI was passed on to the artillery or infantry commander located on the other side of the room and from him through the *Directeur de Tir* (Fire Director) to the combat blocs.

Based on the information received from observers, the commander made the decision which blocs would be used to engage the target. The coordinates were passed on to the bloc commander via telephones or order transmission devices paired up with similar devices located in the combat bloc. These were used when the noise of the guns firing made it difficult to communicate by telephone and visual communication was necessary. The transmitters were used in the artillery blocs and a device was installed in the bloc PC; the second in the firing chamber (casemate) or on the side of the turret. There were several types[18] but the main transmitter used in the Maginot Line in 1940 was developed by *Société Carpentier*, an electromechanical system composed of three elements, two transmitters and a battery power supply. Transmitters were used in pairs; the master box was situated in the PC, the second in the combat bloc in proximity to the middle level of the turret. The boxes were for the most part identical. Each had a circular dial with identical indicators and a double needle that was adjusted by a knob at the base of the transmitter that was synchronized with the second machine. The operator

Telephone switchboard operators. (Jean-Yves Mary)

in the PC placed the black master needle of the transmitter on the selected order. This in turned moved a red needle in the receptor box to the prescribed order. The operator then pressed a button that lit up a red light on the transmitter. A red light lit up on the receiver in the bloc and an alarm bell sounded indicating there was an order. The operator of the receptor box turned his black needle in alignment with the red needle indicator. He then pressed the activator button on the receptor which shut off the red lights in both boxes.

The *Transmetteur d'ordres Téléflex* was a mechanical device used locally to pass orders from the *Chef de Tourelle* in the middle level to the gunners in the upper level. It was composed of two cylindrical bronze housings with identical indications on the front. A handle connected to a steel cable was connected to a handle in a second box, moving it to the same position and displaying the same information on both boxes.

The Maginot Line was laid out so that only in rare cases did the range of the guns permit them to fire on enemy territory. The guns were strictly defensive in nature. The forts had few guns but they were rapid-fire and could respond quickly at the moment of assault in any direction. Anti-aircraft guns were few and far between and only deployed to the rear of the fortified line. Despite these drawbacks, the fortress guns were extremely efficient, capable of laying down powerful suppressing fire. The observatories performed an excellent job in locating distant targets. In cases where the system worked, and we will see some examples in future chapters, the Germans were unable to advance against such heavy resistance. The crews were equal to the quality of the guns, drilled to perfection on the same terrain they would defend in 1940 and which they would come to know very well.[19] When war came, they were ready.

Between PO Chappy and Anzeling there were fifty-nine 75mm guns with thirty-eight in turrets (the rest in casemates); twenty-five 135mm howitzers with twenty-two in turrets; and thirty-four 81mm mortars, twenty-eight in turrets. Between Simserhof and Schoenenbourg there were twenty-four 75mm, fourteen in turrets; fourteen 135mm, ten in turrets; and seventeen 81mm mortars, fourteen in turrets. These were few guns for such a long front but quality compensated for quantity.

Such was the ouvrage. Hundreds of men living together underground where the lighting was either dark or harsh, the air and the concrete was damp, with a constant, pervasive noise – droning, clanging, shouting, the boom of guns. The men were called *équipages* (crews), rather than garrisons. They were specialists, much more like sailors on an underground battleship than soldiers. They worked and trained in close quarters and their commanders ruled the roost. Commandant Rodolphe, artillery commander of the Haguenau Fortified Sector summed it up as follows: 'They had the last word, after God, like the captain of a ship.'

German map showing the fortified sectors from the Channel to the Mediterranean. (Denkschrift)

Chapter 2

The Maginot Line Sectors as They Were in 1940

It would be impossible to chronicle the entire order of battle of the Maginot Line from 1939 to June 1940. Units were moved about on a daily basis from sector to sector. The names of the sectors changed as a result of internal army reorganization. The following is a snapshot of the sectors of the Line where the most intense fighting took place as of 10 May 1940.

First Army Group (GA1) was commanded by General Gaston Billotte.[1] It included the zones of the French Seventh Army under General Henri Giraud, the British Expeditionary Force (BEF), commanded by General Gort, First Army under General Georges Blanchard, Ninth Army under General André-Georges Corap and Second Army under General Charles Huntziger. This encompassed a very extensive region that stretched from Dunkirk to Longuyon. It was, however, defended along its entire length by only two 75mm gun turrets at Ouvrage Le Chesnois and Ouvrage de Velosnes. It also included a small number of POs – Eth, Les Sarts, Bersillies, La Salmagne, Boussois, La Ferté and Thonnelle – plus dozens of CORF, *Fortification de Campagne Renforcée* (FCR) blockhouses – sometimes called *Blocs Billotte* – designed by the *Section Technique du Génie* (STG)[2] and casemates and blockhouses built between mobilization and the German attack.

General Giraud's Seventh Army had command over the SF Flandres that stretched from the North Sea to Armentières. A number of FCR and STG casemates were built in 1939–40, centred on Hondschoote, Mont-Noir and Mont-Cassel. This included six FCR Type A4 blockhouses, six STG flanking blockhouses and nine STG type A double blockhouses and one STG Type B simple blockhouse. The blockhouses around Mont-Cassel were built by the *Commission d'Étude des Zones Fortifiées* (CEZF). General Robert Barthélémy was the sector commander.

The SF Lille was commanded by General Bertschi[3] with troops from 16 *Régiment Régional de Travailleurs* (RRT – Regional Labour Regiment). It was defended by sixty-five blockhouses of various types too numerous to name, twenty-three *abris de tir* (shelters equipped with small arms)[4] and nine *Tourelles-démontables*.[5]

The SF l'Escaut fell within the zone of General Blanchard's First Army. A line of twelve CORF casemates was built on the edges of the Forêt de Raismes. These were powerful infantry casemates with JM and 47mm anti-tank (*anti-char* – AC47) guns and mixed arms cloches. The casemates were part of 108th *Compagnie d'Équipages d'Ouvrages* (CEO), created from 1st Battalion of 57th *Régiment d'Infanterie de Forteresse* (RIF) and commanded by Captain Desmoulins. To the north of the forest were a number of FCR and STG blockhouses and casemates built inside the old Fort de Maulde, called the *Ensemble de Maulde*. 107th CEO, commanded by Captain Michelet, manned the ensemble's defences – Blockhaus Sud-Ouest de Maulde 1, 2 and 3; STG artillery casemate Ouest du Fort de Maulde with two 75mm Model 97/33 guns in casemate; the Observatoire du Fort de Maulde; two artillery casemates, one with 155mm GPF guns,[6] the other with two 75mm Model 97/33 plus two blockhouses. The 107th occupied thirty-two blockhouses and *abris de tir* and one CORF double casemate, Talandier, equipped with JM, AC47 and a mixed arms turret. 106th CEO (Captain Saudo) commanded a moderately more powerful sector that included the CORF Casemate de Jenlain and the westernmost infantry fort, the PO d'Eth. The zone of the 106th also had twenty-four blockhouses and shelters. The *Avancée* (forward defences) *de Valenciennes* fell under the responsibility of 106th CEO and consisted of fourteen FCR blockhouses and, on a second line, six STG blockhouses built by the CEZF.

The SF Maubeuge was another disappointment in a long list of poor decisions made in the 1930s. The CORF built a line of thirteen casemates across the northern edge of the Forêt de Mormal, south-west of Bavai. The casemates, part of the second phase (*deuxième urgence*) of the project, were not incorporated into the final trace and served as a secondary line. The army studied the Maubeuge salient but there were no plans to upgrade or add new defences. Urgent appeals by local representatives in the senate persuaded the army to construct defences. A plan was developed to construct an artillery fort at Bavai plus seven casemates. Maubeuge was to receive four artillery and two infantry forts, plus thirty-six casemates. However, despite the pleas of the senators and Generals Weygand and Gamelin, the CSG rejected this plan and cut the proposals to pieces. The result was the construction of four infantry forts on top of existing Séré de Rivière's forts,[7] a line of Type *1ere Région Militaire* (RM),[8] STG and FCR blockhouses and seven CORF casemates. When one views a range chart of what was and what might have been, the results are stark: four 75mm turrets would have reached across the Belgian border, easily covering the northern and western approaches to the position and could have seriously hampered the progress of German tanks and infantry to the south, behind the Line, after their breakthrough in the Forêt de Trélon.

General Corap commanded Ninth Army and the fortifications of the *Détachment d'Armée des Ardennes*, the XLI *Corps d'Armée de Forteresse* (CAF) and the 102nd *Division d'Infanterie de Forteresse* (DIF) (formerly *Secteur Défensif des Ardennes*). This section of the Line stretched from SF Maubeuge to SF Montmédy. It was the scene of the German crossing of the Meuse north of Charleville-Mézieres and where Rommel easily broke through the Trélon-Anor defences. The light fortifications here were built in and around the wooded terrain of the Ardennes, difficult for the movement of an army, especially motorized units and even more so across the valley of the Meuse between Charleville-Mézières and Givet. As we have seen, Pétain himself declared this zone to be impassable if certain special modifications were made, such as blocking roads, destroying bridges, etc. The Ardennes was not perceived to be dangerous and it would be a zone where field fortification equipment[9] would be stored and used when needed and the destruction of roads and bridges carried out if deemed necessary. However, in 1935 light defences were constructed by troops of the Second Military Region under General Barbeyrac,[10] after whom some of the defences were named. They were constructed by the – *Main d'Oeuvres Militaire* (MOM) – military personnel and in 1937 civilian contractors were hired to build casemates and fortified houses (*Maisons Fortes*). The line of defences ran through the Forêt de Saint-Michel and through the ancient fortress of Rocroi to the Meuse River. The left bank of the river was guarded by STG casemates and blockhouses while the right bank was placed under surveillance by mobile units whose mission it was to destroy all access routes to the river.

The region between Trélon and Rocroi was designated the XLI CAF, commanded by General Emmaneul-Urbain Libaud with a contingent of artillery troops. The line from Trélon to Anor was guarded by four FCR and twenty-seven 1st RM type blockhouses and augmented by twenty dismounted tank turret emplacements and four observatories. Twenty-nine casemates for machine guns and anti-tank guns covered the western part of the Forêt de Saint-Michel and guarded the road to Hirson. The eastern defences of the forest and the *Avancée de Rocroi* included fifteen FCR and twenty-one STG blockhouses, eighty-five Barbeyrac-type shelters with small arms defences (*abris de tir*) and four observation posts. Sixty-five Barbeyrac shelters followed the course of the Meuse.

The zone of 102 DIF (formerly *Secteur Défensif des Ardennes*) followed the line of the Meuse between Anchamps and Pont-à-Bar. Two artillery casemates were built in 1938 at Nouzonville and Flize. Eight additional casemates were built in 1939 around Charleville-Mézières (*Tête de Pont de Charleville*). 102nd Division was commanded by General Françoise-Arthur Portzert and included 42nd and 52nd *Demi-Brigade de Mitrailleuses Coloniaux* (DBMC – Half-Brigade of Colonial

An STG casemate built by the CEZF, located in the second line, Sedan sector. (Marc Romanych)

Machine Gunners), 148th RIF and 160th *Régiment d'Artillerie de Position* (RAP – Positional Artillery Regiment). The defences were as follows:

- *Sous-Secteur* (S/S) *de Sécheval*: 42 DBMC (Lt-Col Pinsun) to guard three *Maisons Fortes* (MF1, 2 and 3), twenty-seven *abris de tir Barbeyrac* and one observatory.
- S/S d'Étion: 52 DMBC (Lt-Col Barbe) with four MF; eight STG and one *abri de tir* in the *Tête de Pont de Charleville*; the STG 75mm artillery casemate of Nouzonville flanking to the left; forty additional *abris de tir Barbeyrac* and two observatories.
- S/S Boulzicourt: 148 RIF (Lt-Col Manceron) with two STG blockhouses, one in the old Fort des Ayvelles and one STG 75mm artillery casemate flanking to the left; forty *abris de tir Barbeyrac* and three observation posts.

The SF Montmédy fell under the control of Second Army, commanded by General Huntziger, and was comprised of two very different types of defensive schemes as a result of the incorporation in 1940 of the Montmédy Bridgehead (*Tête de pont de Montmédy*) and the Meuse Front (*Front de la Meuse*). It was a mix of CORF construction in the former and STG in the latter, which included the *Secteur Défensif de Marville*.

The Montmédy Bridgehead was begun in 1934 with the construction of two artillery works, the Ouvrages de Velosnes and Thonelle (where only the infantry blocks were completed) and twelve casemates out of a total of twenty-two planned. Ouvrage du Vaux-les-Mouzon was never built. In 1938 the *Tête de pont de Montmédy* was reinforced by a line of small blocks (rectangular blocks with two embrasures with a flat façade) and several *tourelles démontables*. The purpose of the strengthening was to alleviate some of the problems created by dead ground. The bridgehead also included four artillery casemates similar in design to the Meuse Front to provide flanking fire. The front included a small flooding zone along the frontier at Grand-Verneuil, fed by the Chiers River and located near the casemate of Saint-Antoine. In 1939 to 1940 a second set of blocks was built. These were type GA1 (simple and double casemates) with an embrasure to the front. Construction was mostly completed by 10 May, but none of the armour components (cloches, embrasures) had been delivered. A second line of STG casemates was started on the line of Poix – Terron – Mont-Dieu. This too was incomplete when the fighting began.

Construction of the *Front de la Meuse* began in 1935 with small *Blocs Barbeyrac* in a variety of designs and forms. This was followed in 1937 to 1938 with several casemates built by the STG and six artillery casemates for the 75mm Model 1897/1933 gun. During the phony war the position was extended with the construction of larger blocs (*Blocs Billotte*, or type FCR), also of numerous varieties. On 10 May, most of these were incomplete and out of all of the larger blocks, only the Casemate Palleto (No. 61) had received its armour components (embrasures, observation and sentry cloches).

The *Secteur Défensive de Marville* (Defensive Sector of Marville) was attached to the command of the *Région Fortifiée de Metz* (RFM – Fortified Region of Metz). It included two lines of defences. Several small blocks and *tourelles démontables* were built along the Chiers River. A line of blockhouses of the standard RFM Model 1936, modified by the STG for a 25mm anti-tank gun, were built along the plateau de Marville. In 1939 several STG casemates with armoured cloches (STG Type B1) were added. The principal line of defence followed the Chiers to Flaberville where it then crossed the Bois Lagrange. After this the position rejoined the Chiers downstream from Charency-Vezin where it then climbed once again to the plateau. As in the other sectors, no armoured components were installed.

A tourelle demontable *located near Trelon.* (Bundesarchiv)

Second Army Group (GA 2) commanded by General André-Gaston Prételat under Third Army commanded by General Charles Condé, had the most powerful sector of the Maginot Line under its jurisdiction. The RF Metz was created to defend the industrial basin of Thionville and Briey and the railway junction of Metz. It included S/S Marville (peeled away and transferred to the SF Montmédy in late 1939) and the fortified sectors of Crusnes, Thionville, Boulay and Faulquemont. The RF Metz was dissolved on 18 March 1940 and its organic elements folded into the new XLII CAF.

The SF Crusnes was not on the original plans of the CORF until Senator Lebrun insisted it be added to protect the industries of Briey. Because of this it gained an advantage of receiving the earlier CORF technology but for the same reason it also suffered from the first set of funding restrictions and cuts or reductions to the scope of the project. Ten GOs were planned but later cancelled or reduced in size.[11] General Gaston Renondeau was appointed commander of XLII CAF on 27 May 1940. His command included 149, 139 and 128 RIF, each with three battalions and the artillery of 152 RAP. The sector was reinforced by 51 and 58 DI (B series reserve) and 20 DI (A series reserve).

The SF Thionville was part of the first phase (*première urgence*) of construction and it received all of its planned components. As of 1 January 1940 the sector was commanded by General Poisot and included under his command 167, 168 and 169

RIF and artillery of 151 RAP.[12] The *Corps d'Armée Coloniale* (CAC), 56 DI (series B reserve) and 2 DI (Series A reserve) were in reserve.

The SF Boulay was very strong on the left where it received practically all of its components, while on the right flank, which was developed after 1931, it was much weaker. There were no artillery forts, observatories or interval shelters on the Plateau de Coume, only small infantry forts. A position called the *Barrage de Metz* was originally planned to have three artillery ouvrages but after a visit by Pétain the plan was cancelled. The sector underwent several realignments after mobilization. It was commanded by General Besse and included 164, 162, 161 and 160 RIF and artillery of 153 RAP and 23rd *Régiment d'Artillerie de Forteresse* (RAF). Reinforcements came from General Loiseau's VI Corps, the British 51st Highland Division,[13] 42 DI (active) and 26 DI (series A reserve).

The SF Faulquemont was conceived to protect the city of Metz and local industries from German guns and to block a German attack from the Sarre region. Despite the original plans the sector lacked depth and suffered from cancellations. It was as weak as the right flank of SF Boulay. Once again, artillery forts were reduced to infantry ones and there was not a single 75mm turret in the sector. The most powerful guns were 81mm mortars in combat blocs. The entries were located in the combat blocs rather than to the rear. General Girval became sector commander as of 29 April 1940. Defending units included 160, 146 and 156 RIF, plus artillery support from 163 RAP. 47 DI was in reserve.

General Edouard Réquin's Fourth Army was in command of the SF Sarre.[14] The Sarre gap was never meant to have permanent fortifications. The Sarre region was placed under the control of the League of Nations until 1935 at which time a referendum was held to determine if the citizens living in the region wanted to rejoin Germany. In January 1935, they voted to do so and suddenly the French needed to find a way to defend the gap. Already discussed as early as 1930, the engineers came up with the idea to create a flood zone by building dams along the Sarre, Albe and Moderbach rivers to join together a series of small ponds (*étangs*) that dotted the wooded area between Sarralbe and Saint-Avold.[15] The western flank that was anchored by the Nied River was not included in the flood zone and instead received a number of blockhouses for anti-tank guns and machine guns located in advanced posts and fortified strongpoints – *Points d'appui fortifies* (PAF). Four artillery casemates were added in 1936. In 1938 a line of large STG casemates was started, but too little too late because it was never finished. The CEZF built a second line between Faulquemont–Sarralbe–Sarre-Union–Diemeringen on the course of the Albe. In October 1939, the sector lost two sub-sectors (Lixing and Leyviller) to SF Faulquemont but gained S/S Sarralbe and Kalhausen. SF Sarre included three forward positions – *Avancées* – Biding, Barst-Cappel and Holving to slow an attacker's progress. A fourth, the *Avancée de Puttelange* was added in March 1940. Colonel Dagnan commanded the sector troops which included 69, 82 and 174 *Régiment de mitrailleurs d'infanterie de forteresse* (RMIF – Fortress

Machine Gun Regiment), 41 and 51 *Régiment de Mitrailleurs d'Infanterie Colonial* (RMIC – Colonial Machine Gun Regiment), 33 RIF and artillery support from 66 RAP. 11 DI and 82 DIA, two active units and 52 DI (series B) were in reserve.

Fifth Army under General Victor Bourret commanded the former RF Lauter which was dissolved on 5 March 1940 and became XLIII CAF. The sector connected the Sarre to the Rhine. It ran across the lower Vosges Mountains and was strictly defensive in nature. Several of the elements originally planned were not built and construction ended west of Rohrbach. In 1934 the plateau of Rohrbach received funding and the connection to the Sarre was completed with the 'New Front' extension, as it was called – ten casemates and three infantry forts. The most powerful fortification was the *Ensemble*[16] of Hochwald on the far right flank. The *Ensemble de Bitche*, with the powerful artillery forts of Simserhof and Schiesseck, guarded the left flank. XLIII CAF was commanded by General Louis Lescanne.

The SF Rohrbach was a very powerful sector, weak on the left but stronger in the centre. It was commanded by General Chastanet and included 51 RMIC, 133, 166, 153 and 37 RIF and artillery support from 150 RAP and 59th *Régiment d'Artillerie de Forteresse Motorisée* (RAMF – Motorized Fortress Artillery Regiment). 24 and 31 DI Alpine[17] were in reserve.

The SF Vosges became the XLIII CAF in March 1940. The sector was broken up into two in terms of the character of the defences. From Main-du-Prince to Windstein the Schwarzbach creek served as the main defensive feature. Twelve dams were built to raise the level of the creek. The flood zone was protected by thirteen infantry casemates and two MOM artillery casemates at each end and it fell within range of Ouvrage du Grand-Hohékirkel's 75mm/33 gun turret in Bloc 4. The other end of the sector was defined by the terrain of the lower Vosges whose deep valleys and twisting passes were defended by blockhouses and the turrets of Ouvrage du Four-à-Chaux. The flanks were quite strong but the centre was weak. Three additional artillery ouvrages were planned but not built. Colonel Senselme commanded the sector and had under his command 37, 154 and 165 RIF and artillery support of 168 RAP and 60 RAMF. 30 DI Alpine was in reserve.

The SF Haguenau also had a disparity in style from one flank to the other. The western flank was the location of one of the largest forts of the Maginot Line, the Ouvrage du Hochwald, with two demi-forts, three entrances and an anti-tank ditch defended by a number of flanking casemates. On its left was Ouvrage du Four-à-Chaux and on the right Ouvrage du Schoenenbourg, two powerful forts in their own right. Between Schoenenbourg and the Rhine additional artillery forts[18] were planned but they were reduced to casemates. Lt-Col Jacques-Fernand Schwartz commanded the sector and under his command were 22, 79, 23, 68 and 70 RIF, plus the artillery of 156 RAP and 69 RAMF. Two reserve divisions, 70 DI and 16 DI, served as reinforcements.

The Rhine Defences[19]

It would seem, geographically and in the mind of the planners, that defending against a crossing of the Rhine River was not simple, but certainly the river was a major obstacle to a swift penetration through the Line. First of all, there was the river itself, averaging 200m in width along its course through Alsace. After crossing the river, the attacker was confronted with a line of heavy, marsh-filled woods defended by interlocking fire from blockhouses and casemates. The original concepts envisioned the Rhine as the primary line of defence of Alsace and all that was needed were some passive shelters along the banks while the main defences were placed on the line of villages (Herrlisheim, Gambesheim, Plobsheim, Erstein, Gerstheim, Obenheim, Boofzheim and Diebolsheim). Strasbourg was to be an open city.

The final layout of the Rhine defences consisted of three lines. The first line of machine-gun casemates was built on the banks of the Rhine. They were weak and cramped with only a single level and the façade was exposed to direct enemy fire from the opposite bank. About fifty blockhouses of various types were built.[20] Casemates were armed with Reibel and Hotchkiss 13.2mm machine guns. Type G casemates, also of varying design and named after General Garchery, inspector-general of 7th RM, were built 800m to 1,000m apart and mixed in with the other first-line casemates. Also weak, these were armed with FMs or 8mm Hotchkiss machine guns. Bridges were guarded by blockhouses.

The second line was 1km behind the first. It was called the 'line of sustainment' or 'line of shelters' and consisted of light structures, mostly large shelters plus three casemates that guarded the roads leading inland from the river. This line was also very weak with no depth and little defensive value. The marshy Rhine forest, 2–3km in depth, lay behind the second line. Small MOM blockhouses were built at the exit points of the forest.

The third line, called the *Ligne des Villages* (Line of Villages), began 2–3km from the river. It was built along the road that linked the villages on the western edge of the forest. It included type SFBR[21] casemates – heavy double casemates with a GFM cloche and some with machine-gun cloches. The line of villages was supported by field artillery units. None of the three lines had flanking artillery casemates.

The SF Bas-Rhin was designated the 103 DIF in March 1940. General Valée was in command of the sector that included 70, 172 and 34 RIF, plus 237 RI and artillery of 155 RAP. 62 DI (B series) was in reserve.

The zone of Third Army Group (GA 3) of General Antoine Besson and that of Eighth Army (General Marcel Garchery) included the sectors to the south of Strasbourg, including the following: The SF Colmar became 104 DIF on 16 March 1940. It was commanded by General Edouard Cousse and included 42 and 28 RIF and 242 RI. 54 DI (B Series) was in reserve. The SF Mulhouse was designated 105

DIF on 16 March 1940. It was composed of two types of defensive areas; one like the SF Bas Rhin to the north, with a dense line of casemates covering the region of the Pont de Chalampé, and a more open area further south of Hombourg. The main feature of the sector, besides the river, was the Hardt Forest, very thick and difficult to penetrate. It was organized with several strongpoints and a light line of defences around Basel. A small number of MOM blockhouses were built between Hombourg and Kembs. The sector was commanded by General Pierre Didio with 10 RIF and 159 RAP.

The SF Altkirch was located to the south of SF Mulhouse. This book will not describe this sector in detail as no serious fighting took place there, but here is a brief description of the sectors and defences: XLIV CAF was formed on 16 March 1940 and commanded by General Julien Maurice Tence. It included the *Secteur Défensif*, renamed on 16 March 1940 the SF Altkirch, commanded by General Joseph Salvan, with 12 and 171 RIF; 67 DI in reserve. The S/S Franken was manned by 171 RIF and included five STG artillery casemates and twenty-seven STG blockhouses. The S/S l'Ill (Durmenach) of the 12 RIF was equipped with two STG artillery casemates, three STG blockhouses and four heavy artillery batteries (Willerhof – four 155mm L Model 16; Breitenhaag – two 240mm Saint-Chamond; Eichwald – four 155mm L 1916; Strengwald – two 240mm Saint-Chamond), Finally, the defences included twelve blockhouses for machine guns and two observatories. It also included the *Secteur Défensif*, renamed on 16 March 1940 SF Montbéliard, with the old Séré de Rivières forts of Montbart and Lomont.

XLV CAF was created originally as the Army of the Jura. It was an autonomous unit commanded by General Marius Daille with VII/400 Pioneer Regiment and it served between the Army of the Alps and SF Central Jura. The SF Jura, renamed the SF Jura Central, included several MOM and STG blocs plus the forts of Larmont, Joux and Saint-Antoine. Defences other than the forts included:

- Barrage of the roads on the Doubs: one blockhouse for 47mm anti-tank guns; three guard posts with road mines.
- Passages of the Doubs: four fortified posts, three with blockhouses for 47mm guns.
- CEZF Line:
  - S/S Nord (Morteau): four casemates.
  - S/S Centre (Pontarlier): three casemates.

The Alpine defences will be described in detail in a later chapter.

Chapter 3

1936 to May 1940

On 7 March 1936, without any French resistance, German troops reoccupied the Rhineland. The fortress troops, however, were ordered to immediately report to their positions inside the Maginot Line. This brief tour of duty pointed out numerous defects in the forts, especially the living conditions. Sleeping quarters were unfinished, groundwater leaked through and ran in streams down the walls and across the tunnel floors, the heaters didn't work and the lighting was dull and often not working at all. Nevertheless, it was a good learning experience for the troops and the engineers used it to make improvements.

The Rhineland alert came to an end and the troops moved back to peacetime camps to resume training. This included learning to operate and fire the fortress guns and support equipment, and command and control procedures. Training exercises resulted in significant improvements to the organization of the various fortress facilities and the rules and regulations for combat. During this period, improvements were made to the physical layout of command and control, including physical changes and improvement of the lighting and communications equipment. Manuals for all of the crews assigned to duty in the forts were reviewed and combat procedures were tested and modified. Officers and NCOs were sent to observe how naval crews operated in environments similar to the forts.

In March 1938 Hitler's *Anschluss* of Austria brought the crews back into the forts on a full alert that lasted into early May. In September, the crisis in the Sudetenland came to the forefront and once again the forts were occupied by the crews. Tensions remained particularly high until the Munich agreement of 30 September 1938 resulted in a return to calm.

In March 1939, the Germans sent soldiers to occupy Bohemia and Moravia. In August Hitler started talking about establishing a 'Danzig corridor', a veiled threat to Poland. On 15 August, a partial French mobilization was ordered. By the 24th the crews of the forts were in place and on 25 August, the claxons sounded at 0200hrs to enact *Mesure 41* and three hours later the fortress troops' families were evacuated from the local army camps within range of enemy fire and sent into the interior of France. Covering forces were mobilized on the last week of August 1939. From 26 August, the works of the Maginot Line received their wartime contingents.

On 1 September, the first day of general mobilization, observers in the SF Vosges and SF Haguenau reported that German civilians were being evacuated from villages adjacent to the border. They also watched as French villages began to empty of their inhabitants. The evacuation of Grande-Roselle was accompanied by military music while that in the vicinity of Wissembourg was much quieter, almost stealthy. Families carried suitcases, walked to the crossroads, climbed into cars and drove away. From Bloc 6 of Four-à-Chaux, which looked out over the Sauer valley, observers reported the evacuation of Lembach village. It was completely without fanfare; no cars; people moving on foot or on bicycles. Everything except what they could carry was left behind. Lt René Lurat of II/242 RI, upon reaching the village of Neuf-Brisach, found everything abandoned, dogs wandering the streets, meals left on the table, dresser drawers and armoires left open; 'families leaving behind their cherished memories and secrets'.[1]

In the rear of PO Welschoff, Singling village received evacuation orders on 1 September at 1600hrs. Gros-Rederching's population of 1,039 packed up and walked off in a convoy, some going in cars, others in wagons, trains or bikes. Those who walked had to go 18km behind the Maginot Line to find shelter. Roppersviller evacuated its total population of 317, and Bliesbruck 900. Ipling was located in front of the advanced posts of the SF Sarre. Two gendarmes from Grosbliederstroff delivered the evacuation order to the town at 1600hrs. In the Sarre region a group of villagers walked south all night and at 0600hrs crossed over the anti-tank rails and barbed wire that formed the edge of the AP of Puttelange. Exhausted, they finally found themselves safely behind the Maginot Line. Sarralbe's 3,800 inhabitants were ordered to evacuate the large town by 2200hrs on 1 September. Their first destination was Nouvel-Avricourt where they were to catch a train to Angoulême. Nouvel-Avricourt, south of the Marne-Rhine Canal, was a 50km walk.

On 3 September, the following communication was sent out to the fortress sector commanders: 'State of War not confirmed. Avoid frontier incidents. Block any violation of the border but if the enemy penetrates, chase him off with rifle [fire].'

Villagers evacuate the frontier – September 1939. (John Calvin – wwii-photos-maps. com)

Nothing unusual was reported on the German side of the border. The territory between the main line of defence and the frontier was now empty of its civilian population. At 0900hrs on 3 September the *Garde Républicaine Mobile* (GRM)[2] in the Forbach salient was ordered to cut the phone cable that linked France to Sarrebrücken. An hour later the gendarmerie at Stiring-Wendel received orders to shut the barricades across the roads at the border blockhouses. The GRM was a strictly defensive unit and at Vieille-Verrerie and Grande-Roselle they were ordered not to open fire at any of their German counterparts. Contact with the Germans continued and relations remained cordial. Conversations took place and cigarettes and wine were exchanged across the barricades. This ended on 13 September when a GRM lieutenant grew tired of seeing the cross-border banter and fired a shot over the heads of the German border guards. They disappeared into their customs post and were not seen again.

On 6 September, the message: 'State of war confirmed. Increase vigilance', was sent by the French High Command. In SF Haguenau, Hochwald was given the order not to open fire without orders from the sector commander.

On 9 September, the French launched their hapless Sarre 'offensive', hardly worth much of a mention but it nevertheless revealed the first sign of the coming French defensive spirit. Fourth Army under General Réquin, reinforced by 9 *Division d'Infanterie Motorisée* (DIM – Motorized Infantry Division), 23 DI and three R35 tank battalions, advanced into Germany to capture the heights of Sarrebrücken, the first fighting to take place there since 1870 and this particular foray's results were not much better. 2 DI of General Paul Arlabosse crossed the Sarre and 21 DI of General Marie-Camille-Charles-Raymond Pigeaud took the ridges north of the Blies. French chasseurs and cavalrymen penetrated the Bois de Saint-Arnaud and the Forêt de Warndt. Further east the French 41 DI launched an attack and captured the German village of Schweigen, about 1km across the border from Wissembourg. A group of 75mm guns were installed at Rott to support 3rd Battalion 4 RTM.

The 75mm turret guns of Hochwald Est's Bloc 7bis[3] supported the operation. The guns opened fire at the prescribed time, the first shots of the war fired by Hochwald. After several rounds one of the turret guns malfunctioned. The crew doubled the rate of fire of the remaining gun to make up for the loss of the other barrel. The attack was short-lived. Not finding any enemy in Schweigen, or getting any response from German forces, the French quickly pulled back.

German territory was inundated with anti-personnel mines and by 14 September the French were ordered to establish a defensive line along the captured territory. General Prételat's orders of 14 September – 'to organize on the conquered terrain' – revealed that he had no intention of engaging in a major battle for Sarrebrücken, or for any other territory out of reach of the safety of the Maginot Line. The fortress line was created to force the enemy to attack it, not to place French troops 10km ahead of it. On 4 October French divisions pulled back to the intervals of the Maginot Line.

The Germans were not concerned with minor French actions; their attention was fixed almost completely on the battle in Poland. The French border was of little concern at the time. German aircraft went on frequent missions into France and several were shot down. On 26 September German 150mm guns responded to French fire in the vicinity of Schweigen. Two days later all of the bridges over the Lauter were destroyed, clearly indicating to the Germans that the French no longer had any intention of launching an attack on their territory. French and German patrols often crossed paths north of Wissembourg but this was the extent of hostile activity.

On 15 October, a French commando group from 3rd Hussar Regiment led by Captain Marc Rouvillois conducted a night operation to chase German observers from the border town of Windhof. The town was searched under cover of the 75mm turret guns of Hochwald but no Germans were found. An ambush was set up overnight but not a single German was spotted.

From October 1939 interval infantry and fortress troops improved the border defences. Regular army division commanders took charge of building defences in their sectors, often imposing their personal points of view in regards to the construction of blockhouses and shelters, rather than deferring to fortress engineers. Each commander had his own theory on the organization of the terrain and designed blockhouses that fulfilled his personal concept of static defence. Infantry units frequently transferred from one sector to another. In some cases, they were ordered by the new commander to abandon the work of their predecessor and start over building something they deemed to be better. The result was a hodgepodge of blocs of all types of designs. In the spring of 1940 the territory of Fifth Army had more than fifty blockhouse types, making it impossible to supply them with standard armoured fittings such as doors and embrasures. Fittings were manufactured to standard dimensions, but with so many different designs the result was that most of the fittings were left un-mounted or jury-rigged to fit the openings. All of this at the expense of the most critical defences, such as anti-tank ditches and anti-personnel obstacles.

The autumn weather of 1939 was beautiful but it turned into one of the coldest and snowiest winters ever. The boredom of what became known as the 'Phoney War' set in for the troops living in the tunnels and underground chambers of the Maginot Line. The experience was worse for the men in the advance posts who waited and watched for an enemy that was hardly seen or noticed. The night brought with it a sense of foreboding and paranoia. The Germans started sending out more and more night patrols, small formations of special troops with a mission to infiltrate and harass the forward posts. The French were constantly jumping at every shadow, waiting for an attack to come out of nowhere. Alerts to possible German attacks became a frequent occurrence, grating on the nerves of the forward observers. Machine-gunners, warned of attacks that never came, fired their guns at a phantom enemy. By early December German infiltration of the Line was becoming more and more frequent. French patrols found footprints in the snow around the perimeter of the forward positions. The French were warned not to patrol in front of the Line alone or without weapons. Each night anti-tank barricades were rolled across the roads.

Men killing time in the autumn of 1939 inside the barracks room of Ouvrage Hackenberg. (Jean-Yves Mary)

Christmas arrived, but the church bells were silent. The villages were dead and empty. Snow covered the rooftops and only the footprints of small animals or French patrols passing through on rounds appeared on the unploughed streets. The patrols were looking for, but hoping not to find, the enemy inside one of the houses or hiding behind a garden wall. The Germans celebrated Christmas on the other side of the border and all was calm that night. Inside the Maginot Line the troops gathered around Christmas trees cut from the nearby forests and sang carols, thinking about their families far away. Midnight Mass was celebrated in the large central gallery at Hochwald and similar celebrations took place inside forts across the Line. The holiday passed by and the troops celebrated the arrival of the dreadful New Year.

As 1940 approached for the troops guarding the Rhine, the intensity of machine-gun and small-arms fire back and forth across the Rhine escalated. The Germans fired on anything that moved, French work crews in particular. Workers building new blockhouses on both sides of the river were forced to put up camouflage to hide construction work. In March Captain Malet of I/42 RIF ordered a gun in

Men of Ouvrage Hackenberg at Mass inside the M1 Magazine – 1939–40. (Jean-Yves Mary)

Blockhouse G12 to fire on the embrasure of a German bunker, silencing a gun that was tormenting French soldiers working along the river bank. Malet received a Croix de Guerre for his act. The Germans targeted the FM and MG embrasures of the cloches, damaging or destroying the guns. Replacement of the guns often took several weeks and with the guns removed, large openings were left in the embrasures. German snipers targeted the open embrasures and their bullets ricocheted around inside the blocs.

Cramped quarters and boredom began to take its toll. The men lived in close proximity to each other in claustrophobic conditions that became worse as the days passed. It took great leadership on the part of the officers and NCOs to break up verbal arguments and keep them from descending into physical altercations. Commanders kept the men busy with daily drills to hone their skills. The greater enemy was the terrible winter of 1939/1940. Rain poured down and in December the ground was frozen, making work impossible. In February, it snowed practically every day of the month.

Despite all of the difficulties experienced by the fortress troops during the winter, they succeeded in placing the majority of their automatic weapons under concrete cover. I/82 RMIF built seventeen blockhouses in April alone, including several concrete platforms for the Renault 37mm tank turret of First World War vintage. Two hundred and fifty blockhouses were constructed in SF Sarre but unfortunately none of the camouflage and protection was completed and the blocs stood out like sore thumbs. Most of the work was incomplete by May 1940.

Fourth Army of General Réquin completed more than 400 blockhouses between September 1939 and May 1940. Of thirty-one large STG casemates planned in 1938, twenty-eight were finished. Six rows of anti-tank rails traversed most of the Maginot Line. Entire forests were cut down to create fields of fire and obstacles to block the roads and tank routes. All of the communication lines were buried.

The night of 27/28 March was ominous; there was no moon and the sky was further darkened by thick rain clouds. Casemate de Chalampé Berge Nord was located on the bank of the Rhine, just a few metres from the river's edge. Sentries patrolled the perimeter of the casemate twenty-four hours a day. A second sentry kept watch from the claustrophobic steel cloche. On this particular night, the sentry in the cloche could see nothing at all through the embrasure and could hear only the sounds of the river a few metres away and the sounds coming from the men inside the casemate below. The second sentry patrolled the rear of the casemate where the road passed by. A few steps; stop and listen; turn; his back to the woods, the outline of the casemate a few feet away, slightly but not much darker than the sky behind it. It was late winter and the woods were devoid of night sounds – no birds or insects; only a slight rustling in the branches from the wind. In the cloche, darkness, the sentry trying to block out the occasional noises made by a couple of men in the casemate tunnel below, wandering around at night, unable to sleep, rustling papers or the scrape of a metal coffee cup, the smell of tobacco wafting up and out of the cloche embrasure. Outside was nothing but blackness and perhaps the sound of the sentry's feet shuffling, pausing, turning. Just before midnight the sentry on the perimeter heard the sound of machine-gun fire off to the north – another casemate firing on a German patrol, or on a ghost. The sound lasted a few minutes then again silence. Suddenly there was a snap of branches coming from the tree line. The sentry froze and shouted '*Halt la!*' and demanded the password as it might be a French patrol passing by. He was answered by a rifle shot and someone shouting '*Prisonnier, prisonnier*'. He ran back towards the casemate, activated an alarm, then jumped into a trench. The crew in the casemate rushed to their positions and the gunners opened fire on the woods with automatic rifles and machine guns. The German patrol, if that's what it was, ran off and most likely headed back across the river.

The next morning Sub-Lieutenant Péter, commander of C 11/1, spoke with the sector commander Lieutenant Colonel Thiervoz, who asked if what the sentry heard might have been a hallucination. Péter told the commander that his men found two German helmets and three hand grenades left behind in the woods. It was determined that a German patrol had crossed the Rhine and attempted a surprise attack on the outpost. The shouts of '*prisonnier*' were possibly an attempt by the German patrol to convince the sentry to surrender. Further investigation revealed that the Germans had probably crossed on what was left of the Roppenheim Bridge. The bridge had been blown up the previous autumn but the job was incomplete and a small but intact support that spanned the length of the river was left standing. Other, similar incursions took place along the river and demonstrated that the river was not the obstacle it was thought to be.

In the north, the 3rd *Division Légère de Cavalerie* (DLC – Light Cavalry Division) of General Robert Marie Édouard Petiet (1880–1967) guarded the border of Belgium and Luxembourg from its location in the *Position Avancée de Longwy* (PAL). Petiet's mission, if and when the Germans attacked Luxembourg, was to move 3 DLC into the Grand Duchy between Mersch and Bettembourg and demolish factories, bridges, railroads and electrical plants. This would delay the Germans but only by about twenty-four hours – possibly, however, enough to make a difference in the ability of the German spearhead to cross the French border. There was no question of conducting a pitched battle in Luxembourg, only actions to slow the German advance towards the Maginot Line. Petiet had to get into Luxembourg first. Two to three hours could make a difference, perhaps even less.

At 1600hrs on 12 April Third Army transmitted a general alert order.[4] As a result, at 1930hrs General Petiet gave the order to his men to seek shelter but be prepared to move to their jumping-off points. The French expected an attack at dawn. At 0530hrs the order to advance was called off but the cavalry and motorized units were ready to move. The next few days passed by but the execution order never came. Finally, on 21 April the alert was cancelled. On 25 April, several officers of 3 DLC were given leave to visit their families. The calm of the 'Phoney War', returned to the front, but not for long.

Part II

The Initial German Attacks, 10 May to 12 June 1940

Chronology 10 May to 12 June 1940

10 May, 0435hrs	Execution order given for the invasion of Luxembourg. Opening of the Battle of France.
12 May	German 1st Panzer Division attacks the line of fortified houses north of Sedan. Three Panzer divisions move towards Sedan and cross the river at night.
12 May	Rommel's 7th Panzer Division crosses the Meuse near Dinant and heads towards Maubeuge.
13 May	The Advanced Position of Longwy falls to the Germans and they move ahead to the Chiers River valley.
13 May	The Sedan defences collapse.
14 May	The French abandon the defences of the Chier, exposing the small infantry fort of La Ferté
16 May	Rommel's panzers attack the weak border defences at Solre-le-Château. The tanks quickly blast their way through the French blockhouses. A 20km breech in the frontier opens the way to an advance on Maubeuge.
18 May	Casemate Ostergnies, south of Maubeuge, is attacked by German 88mm guns, quickly reducing its defences. The Germans envelop Maubeuge.
16 to 19 May	Ouvrage La Ferté is attacked by German pioneers who systematically destroy the fort's defences, resulting in the suffocation of the entire crew of 109 fortress troops. La Ferté is the first Maginot Line fort to be captured.
20 May	Gamelin replaced by General Maxime Weygand.
22 to 23 May	The forts of Maubeuge are pounded by German artillery and surrender one by one.
26 May	Weygand meets with General Gaston Prételat who suggests abandoning the Maginot Line.
22 to 27 May	German attack and reduction of SF Escaut.
29 May to 6 June	Outposts of SF Sarre are attacked.
5 June	The German army launches Case Red, phase 2 of the Battle of France.
5 to 12 June	French forces retreat from the Somme and Aisnes as the front collapses.

Chapter 4

The Invasion of France

Fall Gelb (Case Yellow) – preparatory code word passed to German Corps commanders to signal the imminent invasion of France and the Low Countries.

Augsburg – second word to execute the invasion but not to cross the border.

Danzig – word of execution.

10 May 1940, 0435hrs – *Danzig*

Fall Gelb called for a massive invasion of Luxembourg, Belgium and Holland. Generaloberst Fedor von Bock's *Herresgruppe* (Army Group) B with Sixth and Eighteenth Armies headed into Belgium. General Gerd von Rundstedt's Army Group A,[1] with Fourth, Twelfth and Sixteenth Armies moved into Luxembourg and northern France through the Ardennes where they would cross the Meuse. The spearhead was *Panzergruppe* Kleist[2] with five panzer divisions, three motorized divisions and a Flak corps. Army Group C[3] under General Wilhelm Ritter von Leeb, with First and Seventh Armies, faced the Maginot Line. Meanwhile, France's best fighting units of First Army Group of General Gaston Billotte advanced into Belgium.

The Germans did not expect the French to mount a campaign in open country. Instead they believed and feared that the French would use the Maginot Line as a place from which to manoeuvre and launch attacks, or to await an attack. The Germans were also concerned the French would attack their southern flank from the Maginot Line while it moved through Belgium. If the French counter-attack failed, they could return to the cover of the forts. To counter this, von Rundstedt sent General Ernst von Busch's Sixteenth Army in as a flank guard to take up a position along the French border from Sierck-les-Bains to Mouzon and thus screen the panzers as they moved through the Ardennes. Sixteenth Army would face General Condé's Third Army. Von Busch's main problem was how to cross Luxembourg before the French could bring up motorized units to block his advance. General Petiet's 3rd DLC[4] (Third Army) was waiting to do just that. The Germans had to count on secrecy and speed of execution.

Hitler's idea was to use Fieseler-Storch Fi-156 aircraft to land troops behind the lines. General von Busch was not enthusiastic about using airborne troops, mainly because the small aircraft held only five passengers so the operation would require either a large number of aircraft or numerous round-trips from Germany to the landing points, or both. He preferred to cross Luxembourg with a fast motorized force before the French had time to move up their cavalry. He wanted to send in six *Jagdkommando* (Hunter Commando) units. Each *Jagdkommando* group was composed of forty men with six machine guns and one anti-tank gun. Following behind these were two *Vorausabteilung* (VA – Advanced Detachments). The VA were composed of a battalion of machine gunners, a rifle company, a *Panzerjäger* (PJ – tank hunter) company, a pioneer detachment and a radio team. The VA used motorized vehicles – trucks and armoured personnel carriers. Each VA had sixty machine guns, eighteen mortars, sixteen anti-tank guns and twelve 20mm anti-aircraft guns.

Hitler was not satisfied with this arrangement, fearing the two motorized groups could be held up by obstacles and demolitions. He got his wish for an airborne assault and ordered the creation of *Luftkommando* units that would be transported to the border by air. As a result, von Busch modified the composition of the *Jagdkommandos*, reducing them in size. Their mission now was to rapidly cross Luxembourg to reinforce the *Luftkommando* units. They were designated VA-A and VA-B. VA-A was commanded by Major Freiherr von und zu Aufsess and would move along the axis Luxembourg-Longwy. VA-B, commanded by Major Freiherr von Dobeneck, pushed along the Luxembourg border between Esch-sur-Alzette and Bettembourg. Another small scouting detachment under Major Joachim von Hellermann with two cavalry squadrons and bicycle troops would move between the two. Sixteenth Army would follow behind.

Oberleutnant Werner Hedderich of 80th Infantry Regiment (IR) of 34th Infantry Division was chosen to lead the *Luftkommandos*. One hundred and twenty-five men volunteered for the mission. They were to be flown into Luxembourg in five waves of twenty-five aircraft each. In April, Hedderich and his men were sent to Trier from where the aircraft would depart. On 9 May, the *Luftkommandos* were placed on alert. Twenty-five Fi-156 aircraft arrived at Trier-Euren field. Hedderich

Germans approach a Fieseler-Storch Fi-156 aircraft, the type used to carry Luftkommandos *into Luxembourg in May 1940.* (Bundesarchiv)

assembled his officers and reviewed maps and charts of the landing zones and the points to be seized.

On 9 May observers in various locations in Luxembourg reported the following activity:[5]

- Stoltzemburg – Intense German troop activity on the German side of the Our River, however, it could be part of a shooting tournament scheduled for 10 May. The group included several cars, 200 men and cavalry.
- Roth by Vianden – Afternoon of 9 May – patrols the length of the frontier and a large assembly of German troops and equipment spotted from Roth.
- Born – 9 May, 1500hrs – motorized column halted across from Born. Officers in uniform inspected the bank of the Sûre. Thirty minutes later they got back in their cars and headed towards Henkel. They were followed by twenty trucks carrying boats and bridging equipment. The officers pulled up to the river near Wintersdorf; the trucks remained in the woods.
- Wasserbillig – On the afternoon of 9 May, an inhabitant of Wasserbillig reported he came across two Germans at Langsur and during the course of the conversation the two men informed him that since morning, trucks carrying military equipment were at the Chateâu de Langsur. In the afternoon bridging equipment was spotted at Oberbillig on the Moselle. In the evening the sound of horses, motors and vehicles could be heard.
- Rémich – Towards the end of the afternoon suspicious movement taking place on the German side, possibly troop assembly. Flares and optical signals were spotted in the German villages of Palzem, Nennig and Desch.

Overnight, small German units crossed over into Luxembourg by boat and raided several of the gendarmeries located on the Luxembourg side of the Moselle and Sûre Rivers. At Grevenmacher, Bous and Moestroff, through which 1st Panzer Division would pass, some shots were fired but there was no major resistance. 2nd Panzer Division's route took it through Vianden. At 0350hrs a group of commandos approached the Vianden customs house. The gendarmes and a small militia force occupying the post quickly surrendered. A report from Hosingen detailed the crossing of the Ours River by German troops in boats. 10th Panzer Division's vanguard waited opposite Echternach to cross over. At 0330hrs German powerboats began to make their way across the Moselle downstream of Echternach. At dawn hundreds of German soldiers were crossing the bridge at Stolzemberg.

France's wireless radio system – *Transmissions sans fils* (TSF) – began to broadcast messages from observers in Luxembourg to the French Army's Intelligence Agency, the *Deuxième Bureau*. The messages were noted but not deemed important enough to pass on to army division headquarters. At 0415hrs the *Services de Renseignments* (Information Service) of Longwy received a message from Luxembourg that large numbers of German fighters and bombers were flying overhead. General Petiet

Operators of the TSF – Transmissions sans Fils – radio used inside the forts of the Maginot Line. (Jean-Yves Mary)

was awakened at 0300hrs by the sound of aircraft. He rose and dressed, but still could not find out for certain what was going on. This was unfortunate because if this was a full-fledged German invasion then decisions had to be made very quickly. The trigger of the starting pistol had to be pulled but no one was ready to pull it. Finally, at 0415hrs, Third Army Headquarters at Fort Jeanne D'Arc north-west of Metz sent an alert message to Petiet and General Sivot, commander of XLII Fortress Corps[6] at Briey,[7] detailing the action taking place to the north. The French realized too late that they had been taken completely by surprise.

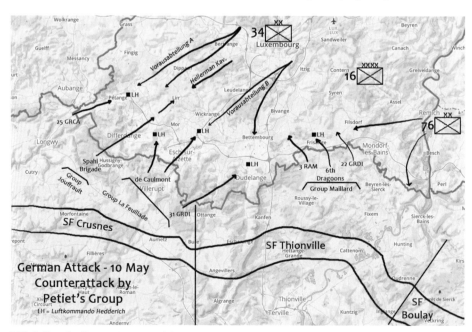

Fall Gelb – *the German invasion of the West, showing movement through Luxembourg on 10 May and the belated counter-attacks by Petiet's four groups.* (OpenStreetMap)

Even so, the reaction was still horribly slow. It took until 0517hrs for XLII Corps to alert 58 DI at Longwy that an invasion of unknown scope was in progress. 51 DI of XXIV Corps (Gen Fougère) and 160 RI (Col Fortet) were notified at 0600hrs, 201 RI (Lt Col Rougier) at 0615hrs. The most serious problem was the delay in alerting Petiet's men. Furthermore, since the downgrade of the April alert, the cavalrymen were scattered in different locations and some of the men were on pass. The division was reported at 15 per cent effectiveness. At 0600hrs 3 DLC was finally ordered to begin its movement into Luxembourg but Hedderich's *Luftkommandos* had already won the race.

At 0425hrs, the twenty-five Fi-156 aircraft took off from Trier-Euren field and followed the course of the Moselle at low altitude. Below, the commandos could see thousands of German vehicles – tanks, trucks, artillery pieces – moving along every road. At Wasserbillig the pilots crossed the border into Luxembourg and followed the railway line. At Luxembourg City, the five groups split up and headed to their assigned target destinations. The initial waves were dropped off and the aircraft took off immediately to pick up the next group.

Hedderich's men dug in at their location at Soleuvre, about 2km north of the French border and 7km from the Ouvrage du Bréhain, to block the road to Luxembourg City. They used farm equipment and set up machine-gun positions. Hedderich's men had the pleasure of stopping the vehicles of the Crown Prince of Luxembourg and later staff from the French embassy. They were instructed to turn around and were informed that all roads into France were now under German control.

Another group (identified only as being led by 'Lt W') seized the intersection of Bomich between Pétange and Bascharage on the Route de Longwy. Lt Steffen's group was in place between Bettembourg and Dudelange above Ouvrage Rochonvillers. Lt Lauer and his men dropped next to the Thionville-Luxembourg road, close to the village of Hau, several hundred metres from the border village of Frisange. Lauer blocked the road with trees and sent a patrol towards the border. There was no activity at all on the French side. Lt Oswald's men guarded the crossroad of Foetz, 3km north of Esch-sur-Alzette.

Meanwhile, Sixteenth Army was on the move across the Moselle into Luxembourg. The main bridges had fallen to the Germans intact, but the roads were blocked by concrete barricades with steel rails running between them and topped with barbed wire. The obstacles blocked Sixteenth Army's vanguard at several locations and the men waited for pioneers to clear them out of the way. In some places ramps were built over top of the barricades to permit the motorcyclists to cross over. Temporary bridges were hastily built to accommodate the huge influx of vehicles and troops. With the roadblocks being removed and bridges going up over the Moselle, the pace quickened and German troops fanned out across the small Grand Duchy.

The first German attacks of *Fall Gelb* on French territory came from the air. Around 0500hrs, German bombers struck the Metz-Frescaty airfield and other airfields in the north-east. At 0500hrs, the French Third Army was still unsure what was happening to the north but the bombing was a sure sign that a major operation was taking place.

The *Jagdgruppen* moved ahead quickly, Dobeneck's men clearing the way for the *Vorausabteilung*. Major von und zu Aufsess's VA-A crossed the Moselle further to the south. Hellermann's cavalry, the centre guard for the two *Vorausabteilung*, crossed a temporary bridge over the Moselle near Wormeldange. At 0630hrs, motorcyclists of *Jagdgruppe* A of Hautpmann Brede caught up with Oswald's airborne group at Foetz. The two units moved ahead towards Esch-sur-Alzette.

Finally, at 0655hrs General Condé gave the order of execution to Petiet's troops to move into Luxembourg. By this time, however, Hedderich's troops were already in control of the key points across the border and Sixteenth Army's vanguard was quickly catching up. Von Busch was still cautious, expecting to encounter resistance from Petiet's troops at the French frontier, but nothing was there.

Several other French cavalry units were in positions from the Meuse River at Nouzonville to the Moselle waiting to move into Belgium and Luxembourg when hostilities began. 5 DLC was positioned between Sedan and Carignan with the objective to move to La Roche-en-Ardenne. 2 DLC manned the Line from Margut to Allondrell and would move in the direction of Arlon and Bastogne. The following units were attached to the light cavalry divisions and also tasked with cross-border patrols: three independent cavalry brigades – 3rd Brigade of Spahis[8] in the region of Nouzonville; 1st Brigade of Cavalry in front of Carignan; and 1st Brigade of Spahis facing Luxembourg between Saulnes and Hussigny. Several GRCA and GRDI[9] units were located along the same frontier.

Petiet's cavalry troops advanced in four groups between the Moselle and Longwy. General Maillard's group, consisting of 4th Hussars and 6th Dragoons, reinforced by 22 GRCA of Colonel Leclerc[10] and 63 GRDI of Commandant Oudar,[11] along with 45 GRDI of Lt Col Kéranget, composed the right wing and acted as the pivot for the groups on the left. Kérangat's 45th made it no further than the frontier. 22 GRDI[12] crossed the border at Aspelt, north-west of Mondorff, only to find the valley already occupied by the Germans. 6th Dragoons moved along the Thionville-Luxembourg road where Lauer's troops barred the road at Hau. Col Jacottet's dragoons brought with them H35 tanks and motorcyclists of 63 GRDI, greatly outnumbering Lauer's small squad. The French attacked the roadblock, killing Lauer and three of his men, but the French did not push the attack. On the left 3 Mobile Artillery Regiment (RAM) of Commandant la Motte-Rouge moved 5km inside the border where they were stopped by Lt Steffen's group between Crauthem and Bettembourg.

The second Petiet group was commanded by Colonel Lafeuillade and moved in three columns. 31 GRDI, commanded by Lt Col Watteau, was on the right and included three armoured cars. It moved towards the frontier post of Rumelange. The post was still under Luxembourg's control and Watteau set up his command post at the railway station in the town. A patrol from 31 GRDI reported they had come across a German roadblock 3km away at Tétange and that one of the armoured cars had been destroyed by a 37mm Pak.

The centre column of the second group was unable to move out of Esch-sur-Alzette because Oswald's *Stosstrupp*, now reinforced by the *Jagdgruppen*, blocked the northern exits of the town. At 0940hrs Lt Col Couteulx de Caumont, part of the second group, arrived with the bulk of his column that included a platoon of H35 tanks. The column attempted to move towards the barricade but the tanks became stuck in the mud. They were then sabotaged and abandoned. The French greatly outnumbered the sixty Germans blocking their way but the Germans were occupying excellent high ground.

Five kilometres west of Esch-sur-Alzette the third column of Group La Feuillade passed through the border town of Belvaux. Six kilometres further on at Ehlerange they were notified that the Germans were 3km away at Monderchange. Fifteen minutes later three armoured cars found the Germans and were blocked by anti-tank fire. There was no chance of moving forward.

Petiet's third group included the Spahi brigade of Colonel Jouffrault, comprised of 6th Algerian Spahis (Col Goutel) and 4th Moroccan Spahis (Col Roman-Amat), supported by 6th Battery of 46th *Régiment d'artillerie* (RA) (Capt Petit), plus elements of 61 GRDI. These men moved mostly on horseback. The first cavalrymen that entered Luxembourg around 0800hrs were preceded by three armoured cars,[13] fifteen motorcyclists and a platoon of H-35 tanks of 3 RAM. The group hoped to move quickly into Luxembourg and their path was the one that passed between *Vorausabteilung* A and B, into which Hellermann's men were now moving. Fortunately for the Germans, Hedderich's men blocked the road 500m north of Soleuvre. The leading armoured car was hit by anti-tank fire. The tanks were reluctant to move around the blockade, fearing they might run into a minefield. The Spahis on horseback moved out to the east and west to outflank the Germans. Sensing they were about to be hit hard by the French, Hedderich's men pulled back. This was the first French victory and the horsemen moved ahead into the gap where they would soon run into Hellermann.

The Spahis advanced through Sanem and were now about 15km from the capital. Captain de Saint-Quentin's platoon rode to the top of a ridge east of Limpach that overlooked the Messe Valley. Below him was an astonishing sight. All the roads were packed with convoys of German troops – infantry and artillery. The German 34 ID, commanded by General Hans Behlendorf, was now pouring through Luxembourg towards France. The Spahis could go no further and turned back.

The same scenes played out across Petiet's path further to the west. While 34 ID approached France on the *Route de Longwy* General Behlendorf was hit by

French fire and had to be evacuated from the field. He was temporarily replaced in command by Lieutenant General Werner Sanne.[14]

The fourth Petiet group consisted of 25 GRCA (Lt Col Lesage) and the divisional reconnaissance group, 70 GRDI (Commandant Viennet). Lesage's mission was to cross the border at Longlaville and move in the direction of Luxembourg City. The 6th Spahis were to his right. At 0830hrs 70 GRDI crossed into Belgium and headed towards the Meuse River north of Messancy Belgium. They made contact with 2 DLC around 1000hrs. To the south they spotted and clashed with German motorcyclists. Several French were killed and 70 GRDI turned around.

25 GRCA moved out of Longlaville, east of Longwy, at 0530hrs. The recon group consisted of thirty-six officers, eighty NCOs, 800 men, 400 horses, 107 motorcycles, eighteen cars, twelve machine guns, thirty-two FMs, four 25mm anti-tank guns and three 60mm mortars. At 0840hrs they reported the presence of a light German unit occupying the foundry south-west of Athus, the railway station of Rodange and several other locations. Upon entering Luxembourg Captain Martin's squadron was hit by machine-gun fire from the top of a ridge. One man was killed and the rest of the men dove into the ditch along the road. At 1005hrs Lt Col Lesage radioed that 25 GRCA was pinned down and German armour was moving towards the frontier. He awaited orders from Petiet to pull back towards Longwy.

Throughout the day the main German divisions advanced all across the front, pushing the French back across the border. At 2030hrs on 10 May, Petiet received new orders from General Condé – to protect the security of the Army Corps engaged west of the Moselle and to cover the PAL. Operations in Luxembourg came to an end. The long retreat had begun. 25 GRCA headed south towards the Maginot Line. By 12 May they were 5km behind Ouvrage du Fermont and Ouvrage du Latiremont.

2 DLC, commanded by General Berniquet, moved in the direction of Arlon, where the division met the vanguard of the German 10th Panzer Division, commanded by Lieutenant-General Ferdinand Schaal. A minor skirmish took place and both sides held their ground. 2 DLC placed roadblocks at Vance and Étalle where 10th Panzer and *Infanterie-Regiment Grossdeutschland* (IRGD) were approaching after having surrounded Arlon. The French were rapidly pushed back out of Vance. 2 DLC put up a better fight at Étalle, supported by 2 Armoured Car Regiment (RAM), 3 Dragoon Regiment (RDP) and 16 GRCA, which had moved up and seized the perimeter of the village. The Germans broke through this position but were held up in other places. By nightfall 10th Panzer Division had reached the day's objective.

On 11 May, 2 DLC continued its delaying mission and engaged with troops from the German XIX Army Corps.[15] 2 DLC received support from the 75mm guns of Bloc 5 of Ouvrage de Velosnes, which was covering units operating near Virton. 5 DLC was also engaged with XIX Corps. They held on as long as possible on

10 May but were forced to retreat when attacked by 1st and 10th Panzer Divisions at Suxy-Neufchâteau. They were no match for the armour and all cavalry troops retreated towards the Semois River and attempted to regroup.

The Metz-Longwy road makes a sharp curve and climbs a steep rise in the Bois Lemone. It was guarded at the top of the hill by the Casemate de Crusnes Ouest, designated C24. Tanks of diesel fuel, boxes of supplies, munitions, medical supplies, ventilation filters and black cylinders containing the cloche periscopes were scattered across the floor of the casemate. The men had spent the winter here and there was a very heavy weight on their shoulders and the bad odours of closed-in humanity. Nearby, the interval troops slept in barns or shelters open to the elements. 'From 10 May', remarked Masson, 'we were a colony of snails living in the same shell, shut off from the outside. We lived in a perpetual *qui-vive* – who goes there? Endless alerts, isolation and the demoralizing impression of being buried alive.'[16]

The casemate routine consisted of a six-hour watch, six-hour rest and six-hour picket duty; over and over. There were no longer any days of the week. It was an unending cycle.

- Watch – Each man performed his specialty in the cloches, fire room, radio post, telephone.
- Picket – The men were at the ready to reinforce the watch. They spent time clearing trenches, repairing or putting up additional barbed wire, cleaning up inside the casemate. At night the men slept in their clothes, just in case.
- Rest – Sleep as much as possible. At night the surroundings of the casemate were dark and silent.

The announcement of the German invasion of Belgium, Holland and Luxembourg was passed on to the crew. Calm gave way to busy activity. Infantrymen greased the automatic weapons and filled up the circular machine-gun magazines; engineers tested the motors and the ventilation; the transmission crew uncovered the TSF antenna; the artillerymen plugged in the telephones; observers took out and installed the heavy periscopes into the roof of the cloche VP. The long wait was over – for good or bad.

Position Avancée de Longwy – PAL – 11–13 May

According to the initial project of 1930, the town of Longwy was to be fortified by the CORF. It was part of the northern wing of RF Metz. The plans included construction of eight ouvrages and a small number of casemates. The original trace of what would have been the main line of resistance ran from a few kilometres west of the Ouvrage de Bréhain and north-west to the town of Longwy. It then followed a south-westerly trace to the northern edge of Longuyon. All of this was cancelled after Pétain's survey of the Line in 1930. The main line was pulled back to the Chiers. A few blockhouses were built and some concrete positions were added to the old fortress of Longwy. Even so, the PAL did not collapse right away; French resistance there was tough.

Fighting at Longwy continued for the next two days. The battle progressed through the Bois de Chadelle and against the walls of the Citadel at Longwy-Haut which was destroyed by German heavy guns in 1914. The valiant siege of Longwy did not repeat itself in 1940 although 227 RI fought an incredible battle.

On 11 May 1940, the mission of the German 17 ID under Lieutenant General Herbert Loch was to capture Longwy. 3 DLC was tasked with covering the approaches to the former fortress and to delay the movement of 17 ID. By the end of the day, however, some elements of 3 DLC were still in Luxembourg fighting the 17th's lead elements. The French were pulling back to the PAL but did not have the time to set up a strong defence, nor did they have adequate forces to do anything more than skirmish with the Germans.

During the night of 11/12 May the French situation deteriorated and by 0800hrs the leading elements of 17 ID appeared on the hills overlooking Longwy. For the first time the Germans could be seen in the scopes of the Maginot Line observers. At 0803hrs the 75mm turret of Ouvrage du Fermont opened fire on III Battalion, 55 IR of 17 ID as it moved out of Gorcy between Villers-la-Chèvre and Tellancourt. At 0612hrs on 13 May observers at Ouvrage du Latiremont spotted German infantry moving along the *Route Nationale* (RN) south of Longwy. The Germans had arrived in range of the main guns of the Maginot Line. Despite the intervention from the artillery of the Maginot Line the Germans continued to surround the PAL and drove towards the city of Longwy. It was chaotic and gaps began to open up in the French line. Around 1100hrs the German 21 IR attacked the Redoubt, a section of the ancient fortress of Longwy, which was finally captured at around 1600hrs. At 1930hrs the French 3 RAM launched a counter-attack against the redoubt using Hotchkiss H35 tanks but supporting infantry units failed to follow up and the attack ended.

There was no change in the situation as 13 May dawned but the German attacks were clearly taking a toll on the French defenders. In the morning Lexy was surrounded. In the afternoon, the defenders of the Citadel were chased back towards the Chiers River. Small pockets continued to fight but the defence was now collapsing everywhere. It was at this juncture that General Condé made the decision to abandon the PAL. In the evening of 13 May, under cover of the guns of the Maginot Line, in particular the 75mm turret of Fermont, 51 and 58 DI pulled out of the salient towards the main line of resistance. By the morning of 14 May, the PAL and the major industrial plants of Longwy were in German hands.

The loss of the PAL was not in itself a terrible catastrophe. Troops were only sent into the PAL to slow down the German advance towards the Maginot Line. The French fought well, especially at Longwy-Haut and the Plateau de Saulnes, but they were quickly overwhelmed by a much more powerful German force that had initially fought rather sloppily but managed to win the day. Had the French launched a flank attack out of Longwy with a significant force they might have done some damage to XIX Corps, but this was never considered. There was never any thought of a French victory at Longwy and the position was, as expected, abandoned.

On 11 May observers in SF Haguenau reported heavy aerial activity – flyovers but no bombing. The ouvrages and anti-aircraft units received a permanent order to open fire on all enemy aircraft. Haguenau airfield was bombed and several French convoys were strafed by German aircraft. A train moving along the 60cm military railway was attacked, suffering multiple wounded and killed. On 12 May German aircraft passed out of range of the turrets, heading west. In SF Vosges, the observatory of Schaufelstal was attacked and captured late in the day despite the support from interval and fortress artillery. The 75mm turret of Four-à-Chaux's Bloc 2 fired 500 rounds, causing heavy German losses. The TSF announced combat on the Meuse at Sedan:

> From the Commander-in-Chief: Enemy attack that we have expected since October took place this morning. It is a fight to the death between the Germans and us. The order for all the allies is calm, energy, confidence. As Marshal Pétain said twenty-four years ago: 'We shall get them [*Nous les aurons*]'.

In SF Crusnes, the 75mm turrets of Blocs 4 and 6 of Ouvrage du Bréhain opened fire but their range was too short to reach into Luxembourg. Bréhain covered 10km of front with numerous observation cloches in the fort itself and in neighbouring casemates and observatories. C24 kept watch on the Bois de Butte and the Bois d'Ottange and alerted Bréhain to enemy activity. 'We were like guard dogs warning the master of the approach of thieves.'[17]

Chapter 5

Collapse of the Meuse and Sedan

General Burtaire was in command of SF Montmédy. His units included 147, 136, 155 and 132 RIF, 4 BM, 1/169 RAP. 10 CA (General Grandsart) with 55 DI (series B) and 3 *Division d'Infanterie Nord-Afrique* (DINA – North African Infantry Division) (General Chapouilly) and 18 CA (General Rochard) with 3 DIC (A reserve) and 41 DI (A reserve) were in reserve. The defences were organized as follows:

- S/S Sedan: 147 RIF (Colonel Pinard) – eight *Maisons Fortes* (MF 8 to 15), eight FCR blockhouses and one STG artillery casemate for 75mm Model 1897/33 flanking left. It also included fifty-eight *abris de tir Barbeyrac* and nine observation posts. The role of the *Maisons Fortes* crews was to defend the roads and to carry out demolitions on the roads leading from Belgium.
- S/S Mouzon: 136 RIF (Lt-Col Vinson) – seven *Maisons Fortes* (MF 16 to 22). On the main line of resistance were eight FCR blockhouses, three STG 75mm artillery casemates flanking to the right, nine STG blockhouses of various type, 104 *abris de tir Barbeyrac* and four observation posts. The second line along the Meuse included fourteen *abris de tir Barbeyrac*. The second position (CEZF Line – 1940), was equipped with eleven STG type A and B blockhouses.

The Sedan defences looked strong on paper – forty-three armoured anti-tank casemates in various stages of completion. These were large STG or FCR casemates built along the Wadelincourt-Remilly and Donchéry-Flize roads. The field troops carried automatic rifles, heavy machine guns and 25mm and 37mm anti-tank guns. However, the Casemate de Vaux-Dessus, located between Sedan and Donchéry, was the only 75mm 1897/1933 artillery casemate in the Sedan sector capable of firing on the German axis of attack. The other 75mm casemates were not oriented to fire in that direction. Due to continual delay and procrastination, there was no effort to improve the defences of Sedan before the war. The defences in front of Sedan were poorly organized. The line within Sedan itself lacked depth and there was no second line established behind the town. The army left a 3,000-metre gap between the Casemate de Pépinière-Creplet and Casemate de Côte-du-Prés-de-Meuse. The 1st and 10th Panzer Divisions would soon pour through this gap.

A line of *Maisons Fortes* was built along the Belgian border between the Semoy and the Chiers. The idea of turning houses into blockhouses came from the former Prime Minister Édouard Daladier who was impressed by the defensive capabilities of ordinary villages during the Spanish Civil War. In 1939 the town of Villy was turned into a stronghold in itself.[1] The *Maisons Fortes* were blockhouses with what appeared to be a regular house built on top. The blockhouse section had embrasures for 25mm or 37mm anti-tank guns, plus machine guns and FMs. Twenty-two were built close to the border.

On the night of 11 May, 5 DLC was ordered by General Huntziger to pull back to the line of fortified houses north of Sedan. Establishing a defence there was practically impossible. Not only were the French troops in disarray but there was no time to establish a strong defence. The French had too few men and their weapons were not powerful enough to stop the German armour that was fast approaching the frontier. General Grandsart, commander of the French cavalry, requested artillery support from batteries to the rear of the forests north-east of Sedan, but no support was forthcoming.

XIX Motorized Corps, led by General Heinz Guderian, faced the Maginot Line defences of Sedan. The Panzer Corps consisted of 1st Panzer Division under General Kirchner, 2nd Panzer Division, commanded by General Rudolf Veiel and 10th Panzer Division under Schaal. The *Grossdeutschland* infantry regiment followed behind the armoured spearhead.

The Sedan defenders included elements of 147 and 136 RIF plus 55 DI, a poorly-trained 'B' division made up of unseasoned troops who were now being counted on to hold the Meuse River against a massive armoured attack. 71 DI, another 'B' division, guarded the rear of the Sedan position. Both of these divisions came under General Huntziger's Second Army.

On 12 May, the main German attack by 1st Panzer Division fell on the western group of *Maisons Fortes*. German XIX Corps approached the blockhouses which were just a few kilometres from the Meuse. 1st Panzer Division, moving in the

German Panzers pass through the village of Sugny in early May 1940, on the way to Sedan. (John Calvin – wwii-photos-maps.com)

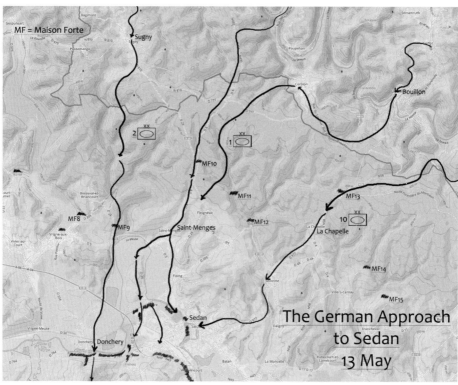

Three German Panzer divisions crossed the Meuse River and advanced on Sedan to quickly cut through the weak, thin defences. (OpenStreetMap)

direction of Saint-Menges, ran into 5 DLC who put up a strong fight at the *Maison Forte de Saint-Menges*. The Germans lost two tanks. On the French side, Lt Boulanger of 78th *Régiment d'Artillerie Tous Terrains* (RATT – 'All Terrain' Artillery Regiment) of 5 DLC and four gunners were killed in the house. Despite the strong resistance of 78 RATT, 1st Panzer Division pushed through the main line of resistance by early afternoon. 15th Dragoons also fell back and suffered heavy losses. The Germans pushed their way through the forest and broke out in view of Sedan and the Valley of the Meuse.

At 1000hrs, the Luftwaffe bombed the blockhouses in front of Sedan, destroying communications and blinding the sub-sector's observers. At 1400hrs 1st Panzer's tanks, plus Pak and AA guns opened fire. French counterbattery fire coming from Bulson, located behind Sedan, had little effect. German 88mm Flak guns zeroed in on the French gun embrasures in the blockhouses. Without armour protection the embrasures were torn to pieces. The shells now exploded all around the blocks, the fumes suffocating the defenders.

At 1600hrs, German tanks moved forward and established a bridgehead at Iges. Troops from Grossdeutschland Regiment and I and II Battalions of *Schützen-Regiment* (Rifle Regiment) 86 of 10th Panzer Division crossed the Meuse at

Wadelincourt in small inflatable boats and approached the line of blockhouses. These were taken out one by one. Blockhouse 48 of Bellevue was captured without a shot fired. Troops from 1st Panzer Division and IRGD moved into the gap caused by the capture of the blockhouse and came in behind the Casemate de Vaux-Dessus.[2] This casemate blocked the passage of 2nd Panzer Division and was quickly silenced.

On 13 May the Luftwaffe's *Luftflotte* 3 and *Luftflotte* 2 flew hundreds of sorties against the Sedan bunkers and Marfee heights behind Sedan. The Stukas cut phone communications and shot radio antennae from the tops of command posts. Five hundred Ju-87 missions were flown in a five-hour period. Many of the gunners in the bunkers abandoned their positions as a result of the air sorties.

By the evening of 13 May it was still possible for the French to mount a counter-attack on the bridgehead since no tanks had yet crossed the Meuse. The Germans were delayed in bringing their armour across the river and for a few hours they were vulnerable. However, the French suffered their own doubts and delays. False reports came in that the Germans had crossed the river and passed through the Sedan defences. Because of this and the Luftwaffe action, at 1830hrs the gunners at Bulson abandoned their guns for fear of being outflanked. This in turn caused a panic that spread from unit to unit of 55 and 71 DI and they began to withdraw. The citizens of Sedan and the civil authorities also fled, resulting in further chaos. Overnight the engineers of 1st Panzer Division built a pontoon bridge at Gaulier and the tanks of 1st and 2nd Panzer moved uncontested across the Meuse. 10th Panzer built a bridge near the Pont du Bouillonais and moved its tanks across during the night.

On 14 May, the French tried but were unable to coordinate a defence. General Huntziger sent 3 DIM and 3 DCR towards the Meuse. General Grandsart pushed two battalions of light tanks along with 213 RI towards Bulson, but he was unable to fully engage the Germans. In the beginning of the afternoon the 1st and 2nd Panzer Divisions reach Chémery where they split up and headed west. 10th Panzer moved to capture the Heights of Stonne where they set up a good defensive position to fight off a French counter-attack.

On the night of 12/13 May, lead elements of Rommel's 7th Panzer Division crossed over the Meuse at Houx in Belgium, between Dinant and Namur. General Corap's Ninth Army was tasked with blocking the crossing. Corap, believing the German force was insignificant, was fully confident of pushing Rommel's forces back across the river. He soon discovered otherwise. By noon on 13 May the German bridgehead was holding and the French were now involved in a major battle.

Meanwhile, at 1430hrs on 13 May, 6th Panzer Division, commanded by General Werner Kempf, attempted to cross the Meuse north-west of Sedan. The S/S Sécheval centred on the small town of Monthermé and was defended by 42 DBMC (Lt Col Pinsun), who were protected by about a dozen blockhouses

A German Panzer III tank of the type used during the Battle of France. (John Calvin – wwii-photos-maps.com)

to guard a 15km front. The region known as the 'meander of the Meuse' was heavily wooded. Rather than attempt to cover the entire length of the river, which stretched as far north as Givet, the defences were set up along the base of the meander, from Nouzonville to Revin. The first phase of the crossing went well for the Germans, but they ran into heavier resistance along the second line of defence on the plateau of la Rova. The initial German attack was stopped by the colonials of 42 DBMC. The tanks of 6th Panzer had not yet crossed over.

The attack continued the following day and the colonials held their strongly entrenched positions. In the evening German engineers completed a bridge over the Meuse and 6th Panzer's tanks moved across. 42 DBMC held out overnight but on 15 May the French were dislodged and pushed back by superior forces. By evening Kempf's Panzers reached Montcornet.

The fall of S/S Sécheval proved to be the end for 102 DIF. 42 DBMC was broken up during the fighting on the isthmus. 52 DBMC, holding the Charleville bridgehead, was now threatened by 6th Panzer Division which had moved to the rear of its position. 148 RIF, with 2nd Panzer Division moving on its right, was in a precarious position. All that remained of the regiment's defences was II Battalion in the area of Villers-Semeuse. A remnant of I Battalion was left at Flize. III Battalion no longer existed.

In the evening of 14 May, General Huntziger was concerned that the breach opened up in his line would allow the Germans to flank the Maginot Line. He decided to abandon the line of the Chiers and its fortifications and take up a position on the line of Iner-Malandry. In reality, there was no defensive line of Iner-Malandry except on paper. The result of this decision was to increase the size of the breach. Huntziger hoped to organize a counter-attack and to create a new line hinging on the PO La Ferté, located about 25km east of Sedan. In the middle of the night of 14/15 May the blockhouses along the Chiers River between Sedan and Villy were abandoned. A large amount of equipment was left behind, including artillery and anti-tank guns. On the morning of 15 May General Eugen von Schobert's VII Army Corps attacked. As a result, the fall-back position behind the Chiers was evacuated.

The breach of the Meuse had dire consequences for the future conduct of operations. At Sedan and Monthermé, the combat blocks built to guard the Meuse were too few in number, were unfinished, poorly located and of questionable defensive value. At Sedan, many negative factors contributed to a rapid breakthrough of the defences by the Germans. It did not help matters that the defenders at Sedan were among the weakest French units while the best troops were fighting to the north-west in Belgium. However, the major contribution to the collapse of the Meuse line was the predetermined weakness of the defences which led the Germans to choose to attack there.

SF Haguenau observations: On 13 May at 0500hrs a large formation of German aircraft was spotted heading west. It returned two hours later. The Ferme du Litschof (SF Vosges) was surrounded by a German patrol but the garrison escaped with the help of French artillery fire. Heavy German losses were reported by the infantry. At 1900hrs GAF2 requested fire to the north of Niederschlettenbach against enemy movement; S1 fired twenty rounds and also on German infantry to the west of Rechtenbach. Hochwald's Bloc 7bis fired forty rounds. Observatory 07 reported German infantry was scattered and dispersed. The TSF radio reported the German attack on Sedan and Longwy

C24 observations: On 13 May the crew of C24 was shocked to discover French troops positioned between the Maginot Line and the border region of Villerupt and Audun-le-Tiche pulling back. It was an excellent place of defence. The entire area was guarded by trenches, anti-tank rails and blockhouses constructed since the autumn of 1939. There would be many more shocks in the days to come.

Chapter 6

Breakthrough and the Battle of SF Maubeuge

General Hermann Hoth's XV Army Corps[1] was tasked with crossing the Meuse and breaking through the line of fortifications from Solre-le-Château to the south of Fourmies near Trélon. This action would bring Hoth's Panzers in behind Maubeuge and in contact with Ninth Army's II and XI Army Corps.[2] The attack target zone lay between the SF Maubeuge and the *Secteur Défensif d'Ardennes*, which was occupied by 102 DIF. A weak 60km zone separated the boundaries of the two sectors and it was through this the Germans would attempt to pass.

It was weak for two reasons: 1) the fortifications were Type 1 RM blocks reinforced by GA1 blocks; and 2) it was not manned by any fortress units. The RM blocks were built in 1937 but the line had no depth. These were double blocks (fire cover in two directions) defended by a narrow anti-tank ditch and a thin belt of barbed wire. There were also a number of dismounted tank turrets positioned along the line in close proximity to the blocks. Their mission was to stop enemy tanks. The main weakness of the position was that tanks could get very close to the turret blocks without coming under their fire, enabling the tanks to neutralize them while the infantry moved up to neutralize the infantry blockhouses. Finally, the position had no supporting field or fortress artillery.

The Trélon-Anor position had been occupied since March 1940 by 4 DINA, which organized the defences and had all of its equipment in place along a 20km front. However, 4 DINA was ordered to move into Belgium on 10 May, leaving their former position undefended. General Billotte, commander of GA1, knew there was a gap and ordered it to be defended. 101 DIF was ordered to extend its front southward beyond Trélon. 101 DIF had five training battalions at its disposal that were scheduled to join the division on 16 May. General Billotte also made 1 DINA available to Ninth Army if necessary. 1 DINA was in reserve behind Valenciennes, in the vicinity of Avesnes when it received orders to move to the south of Maubeuge and occupy the gap in the defences at Trélon between the blockhouses of Fourneau and Étang-de-la-Galoperie. The first units of 1 DINA arrived on the morning of 16 May and took up their positions in the blocks, joining up with 101 DIF to the north and 22 Infantry Division at Amorelles. Unfortunately, 1 DINA's artillery had not yet arrived. 4 DINA occupied the defences around Anor. This sector also suffered from a lack of depth. The road from Belgium at the Passe d'Anor was held by two GA1 blocks. Several light blocks were built on the outskirts of Anor and that was it.

Two battalions of 84 RIF held the blockhouses in the vicinity of Solre-le-Château. This area was defended by four blockhouses – Perche-à-l'Oiseau, Trieu-du-Chêneau, Ferme-aux-Puces and les Aunieaux. Blockhouse La Gobinette was unfinished. This made up the first line of defence; the second line and the route de Felleries was guarded by the blockhouse of l'Épine (site of a proposed artillery ouvrage). Artillery support was provided by 301 *Régiment d'Artillerie Coloniale* (RAC – Colonial Artillery Regiment) and the 1st Group of 104 *Régiment d'Artillerie Lourde d'Armée* (RALA – Heavy Motorized Artillery Regiment) was returning from Belgium, but they had only ten rounds per gun.

On 16 May Rommel's 7th Panzer Division attacked the battalions of the 84th at Solre-le-Château. At noon, Rommel made contact with the blockhouses held by III/84 near Clairfayts. Around 1630hrs the Germans attempted to break through the line but were blocked by anti-tank guns mounted in the blocks, plus artillery support from behind the line. The anti-tank ditch that ran between the blocks was effective in keeping the tanks on the road. Rommel was forced to use the road that ran between the blockhouses of Trieu-du-Chêneau and Ferme-aux-Puces. The Germans began their attack on the blocks around 1730hrs but the French held out and the tanks were unable to pass. Sadly, the 301st and 104th ran out of ammunition and were no longer able to provide artillery support. Blockhouse Les Aunieaux ceased firing around the same time, perhaps also running out of ammo. Ferme-aux-Puce's embrasure was struck point-blank by a tank shell and the block was put out of action.

Around 2100hrs, Rommel ordered 25th Panzer Regiment to move along the road and to keep up a continuous fire on the blocks. Perche-à -l'Oiseau's anti-tank gun was hit and destroyed. This opened up a gap in the line. Blocks Épine and Hérelles were hit by machine-gun fire from the tanks and the crews of the blocks were unable to stop their progress down the road. 7th Panzer now moved to the rear of the line and did not pause until it reached Landrecies south of Maubeuge.[3]

The following morning, 17 May, German infantry conducted mopping-up operations along the line. The tanks, however, were not finished. 5th Panzer Division, led by Lieutenant General Max von Hartlieb-Walsporn, now approached the frontier from Belgium, moving parallel to 7th Panzer towards Solre-le-Château. The tanks crossed the border at Hestrud and moved quickly past the blockhouses between the border and Solre-le-Château. II Battalion of 84 RIF put up a strong defence but they were no match for the German tanks. At 1030hrs Blockhouse Malakoff and the dismounted turret were silenced, followed by Blockhouse Groëz. Lt Pamart's blockhouse of Solre-le-Château fell at 1100hrs. Pamart was killed by a blast through the embrasure. The block of Ferme-de-la-Folie was silenced. 5th Panzer then broke through the line. An hour later they met up with 7th Panzer Division at Berlaimont on the Sambre River. Since crossing the border 5th Panzer Division had moved 16km into France and was now to the rear of the forts of Maubeuge.

III/84 fought to the north of Solre-le-Château. The Germans moved out of the Bois de Belleux and to the rear of the blocks defended by 84 RIF. Lt Pinchon's Blockhouse de Garennes was attacked from behind. It was equipped with a 37mm TR Model 1916 anti-tank gun. The crew repulsed the initial attacks but as more tanks moved up the block was quickly overwhelmed and Lt Pinchon was killed. Blockhouse Bois-des-Nielles fell at 1600hrs. Perche-à-l'Oiseau held out a little longer but the crew ran out of ammunition and surrendered at 1800hrs. To the south the Germans moved towards Liessies, attacking the defenders from the flank and rear. Blockhouse Beaux-Sarts fell at 1500hrs and Beaux-Monts later in the evening. By 2000hrs the position north of Liessies had collapsed.

Around 1900hrs, while some units and blockhouses continued to hold out, General Béjart gave the order for 84 RIF to pull back and to set up a new line of defence on the Sambre River between Jeumont and Maubeuge. The evacuation order failed to reach all of the crews in the blocks. II/84 moved several of its units. III/84 lost contact with II/84 and instead attempted to move south towards the Oise River. Most of III/84 was captured on 18 May.

The fall of the frontier line was devastating to French defensive capabilities and there was no time to move in reinforcements. The French command could do only what they had so far successfully been able to do – fall back. On the night of 16/17 May XI Army Corps, on which the units defending the border depended for support, was withdrawn to the Sambre. XI Corps was positioned to face southeast to protect the rear of SF Maubeuge. This was done to keep Maubeuge from being captured, but it had the ominous effect of opening up the road to Le Cateau to the German tanks. There was nothing to stop them.

The Meuse River and the Line of defences along the Belgian border centred on Solre-le-Château could have stopped the Germans. However, the French abandoned the border defences to defend the Meuse. The defence of the border was left to only three battalions of 84 RIF. The slow pace of the move into Belgium not only failed to block the Germans from crossing the Meuse, but the French were unable to pull back quickly enough to defend the border. The result was a virtually undefended 20km gap behind Maubeuge. When the Germans broke through this line the fall of Maubeuge was only a matter of time.

Observations in SF Haguenau from 14 to 18 May

SF Haguenau was composed of:

- S/S Péchelbronn: 22 RIF (Chef de Bataillon Fabre), with 1st and 2nd *Compagnie d'Équipages de Casemates* (CEC – Casemate Crew Company) of SF Haguenau: Casemate Schmeltzbach Est; (E 700) – Ouvrage du Hochwald (Lt-Col Miconnet); Abri Walkmühl, Abri Birlenbach, Casemate Drachenbronn Nord and Drachenbronn Sud (connected by underground tunnel), Casemate Bremmelbach Nord and Sud (connected by underground tunnel), Casemate Breitnacker Nord and Sud (connected by underground tunnel); (O 800) – Ouvrage du Schoenenbourg (Commandant Reynier); Abri Grasserloch, Abri Schoenenbourg, Casemate Ingolsheim Ouest and Est.

- S/S Hoffen: 79 RIF (Lt-Col Rethoré) with 3rd CEC and 4th CEC of SF Haguenau: Casemate Hunspach Village, Hunspach, Hunspach Station, Moulin d'Hunspach Ouest, Moulin d'Hunspach Est; Abri Buchholzberg, Abri Hoffen; Casemate Hoffen Est, Bois d'Hoffen, Aschbach Ouest, Aschbach Est, Oberroedern Nord, Oberroedern Sud, La Seltz; Observatoire Hatten.
- S/S Soufflenheim: 23 RIF (Lt-Col Lefèvre), with 5th and 6th CEC of SF Haguenau: Casemate Hatten Nord, Hatten Sud, Hatten, Bois de Rittershoffen 1, 2, 3, 4, 5, 6, Koenigsbrück Nord, Koenigsbrück Sud; Abri Sauer, Koenigsbrück, Donau; Casemate Kauffenheim, Abri Heidenbuckel, Casemate Heidenbuckel, Rountzenheim Nord, Abri Soufflenheim.
- S/S Sessenheim: 68 RIF (Lt-Col Blanoeil), with 7th and 8th CEC – Casemate Rountzenheim Sud (connected to Casemate Rountzenheim Nord by underground tunnel underneath the railway line), Casemate Auenheim Nord and Sud; Advanced Posts (MOM) Climbach, Rott (Scherhol), Rott (Hannenacker), Rott (Roetzmuehle), Steinseltz Nord, Steinseltz Sud, Riedseltz Nord, Riedseltz Centre, Riedseltz-Oberdorf, Riedseltz Voie-ferrée, Riedseltz Sud, Oberseebach Nord, Oberseebach Sud, Trimbach, Niederroedern Nord, Niederroedern Sud; 2nd Line: eight STG casemates – line of seventeen *Maisons Fortes*.[4]

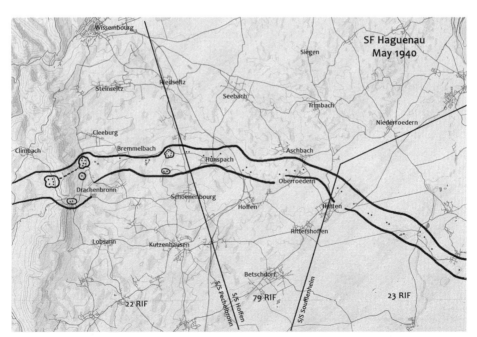

SF Haguenau in May 1940. The left flank contained the powerful forts of Hochwald and Schoenenbourg, the right a thin line of heavy CORF casemates stretching to the Rhine. (OpenStreetMap)

On 14 May at 0300hrs, heavy enemy machine-gun and artillery fire was reported from the direction of the Moulin de Saint-Rémy on the Lauter. Schoenenbourg's Bloc 3 fired eighty rounds on the target. The Germans fired around 600 artillery shells throughout the day on the villages in front of and on the main defensive line.

At 1147hrs Bloc 7bis of Hochwald fired twenty rounds on German infantry at Rechtenbach. S2 fired twenty rounds on the village of Schweigen. Bloc 7bis fired thirty rounds and S2 twenty rounds on the Bois des Maronniers where German troops were assembling. Shortly thereafter observers spotted a German observation post on Hill 417 north-west of Weiter and requested it be shelled. Throughout the afternoon and evening S2 and S4 fired on the Mundat forest and Germanshof where German infantry also appeared to be assembling for an advance. The Germans fired back and hit a stock of ammunition near a small depot behind S4.

The Germans crossed the Lauter and chased the light French advance elements out of Mundat with the goal of surrounding the Geisberg hill, south of Wissembourg. It was not a powerful German advance but French units holding the advance posts of S/S Hoffen were chased back to the line of fortified APs. Schoenenbourg shelled enemy formations moving south-east of Mundat. A German 280mm gun fired thirteen shots on Schoenenbourg, the heaviest calibre yet deployed. West of Hochwald, observers attempted to locate the gun's exact position north-west of Muhlenkopf where earlier, French patrols heard the sound of tractors and chains.

On 15 May fortress infantry troops were anxious that a German attack might take place along the entire sector front at any moment. From 0440hrs to 0640hrs all of the turrets were placed on alert for a possible defence of the Col du Pigionnier, but nothing came of it. German artillery was quiet until the afternoon when 200 shots from a German 105mm howitzer were fired at Hunspach, Geisberg and Altenstadt.

Bloc 4 of Ouvrage du Schoenenbourg with 75mm turret retracted, cloche GFM on the left and cloche VDP on the right. Ouvrage Hochwald is located on the ridge in the background. This photo is taken looking west.
(Dan McKenzie)

The steeple of the church of Altenstadt was blown off. Around 1100hrs, German infantry was spotted 1,800m west of Schleital. Three 75mm turrets responded with 240 shots and the Germans were dispersed. German infantry also moved toward Altenstadt but were chased off by Bloc 7bis.

Around 1500hrs German 280mm guns in the Bundesthal fired twenty shots on Schoenenbourg causing minor damage to the anti-tank rails on the perimeter. The heavy shells left craters 6m in diameter and 2.5m deep. The guns were out of range of any French guns. At night Bloc 7bis fired shots into the German rear and along lines of advance towards the villages of Oberotterbach, Rechtenbach and Schweigen.

May 16th was a calm day. German infantry attacks were suspended but artillery fire continued. 105mm guns shelled Schoenenbourg. Bloc 7bis responded. Around 0940hrs a heavy gun, probably a 280mm, opened fire on Observatory 01 of Hatten.[5] Of twenty-three shots fired only one struck the rear of the observatory, causing minor damage to the concrete. By evening 16 DI abandoned the line of the Lauter and pulled back to a position along the line of advance posts. Troops of 70 DI in Wissembourg and Altenstadt were evacuated. The new line ran as follows: Ferme Boesch – Climbach, Tour-de-Scherhol – Scherhol Forest House – Hill 290 – 276 – 249 – 243 – German monument of Geisberg – Château-Geisberg – Hill 182.4 – Ferme de Geitershof – blockhouses of Oberseebach, Trimbach, Kuhbenmühl.

German artillery was very active during the night of 16/17 May. German guns were moved closer to the Lauter. Fire continued virtually non-stop on Steinseltz, Oberhoffen-les-Wissemberg, Riedseltz, Hunspach and to the rear of the Maginot Line against the heavy artillery positions east of Soultz-sous-Forêts. At 0120 the blockhouses of Oberseebach fired red signal flares, indicating an attack was taking place. The turrets of Schoenenbourg and Hochwald responded, Blocs 3, 4 and 7bis firing 240 shots in ten minutes. At 0230hrs the commander of the advance posts of Geisberg radioed to say that the Germans were in front of the anti-tank rails, moving towards the blocs. Bloc 7bis fired in front of the blockhouses. It was later reported that this was not a serious incursion, simply a German reconnaissance patrol testing the perimeter defences.

On 17 May 279 RI of 70 DI captured four prisoners on Geisberg, part of the recon patrol from the previous night. They were being hit by French fire and tried to regroup by the railway tracks but were unable to regain their lines. During the day, fire continued against all German infantry units, particularly west of Mundat. The guns of the Maginot Line responded to every German shell that was fired. The sound of artillery continued throughout the night and the French poured harassing fire on Rechtenbach, Altenstadt and Saint-Rémy. Nine hundred and sixty-two shots were fired throughout the day.

May 18th began with a relatively quiet night and morning. An NCO from a German patrol was captured near Geishof. At 1400hrs sixty shots were fired on Bobenthal and Chateau Saint-Paul by one of the 120mm interval batteries, identified as '*sections*'. These were Bange Model 1878 long-barrelled (L) guns with a range of about 9,000m. These guns were very accurate and efficient. The Germans also shelled Rott, Camp de Drachenbronn and Altenstadt. Two hundred and twenty-five shots from Bloc 7bis landed on the Lauter crossings between Weiler and Wissembourg. The French later learned these rounds severely affected German movement and caused serious casualties. French radio reported German attacks in the direction Avesnes, Vervins and north of Rethel.

In SF Crusnes, on 14 May French divisions pulled back from in front of the Maginot Line, taking with them their 105mm and 75mm field guns and howitzers pulled by tractors. On 15 May, the rearguard of the covering troops passed by the Maginot Line which was now the primary defensive line. The men remaining behind in Casemate C24 waited for the enemy to appear in the woods. 'Each sound of snapping branches or rustling through the brush was amplified against the silence of the countryside.'[6]

The Battle of Maubeuge – 19 to 21 May

After the breakthrough at Solre-le-Château, 7th Panzer Division continued on to Le Cateau to begin the process of trapping Allied forces in Belgium. 5th Panzer Division was tasked with crossing the Sambre River and fighting through the Forêt de Mormal towards Le Quesnoy.

General Billotte ordered French forces currently on the right bank of the Sambre to pull back to the river and establish a defensive position in front of Maubeuge. The French First Army held the line from Charleroi to Berlaimont. It was sparsely defended and had several prominent gaps. 4 DI was sent to reinforce 101 DIF. 43 DI held the Line from Jeumont to Maubeuge. What remained of 84 RIF was positioned from Maubeuge to Berlaimont to hold the bridges over the Sambre. The course of the river from Berlaimont to Landrécies was guarded by Ninth Army. XI Army Corps, commanded by General Julien Martin, was tasked with holding the Forêt de Mormal. The defences sounded quite strong numerically but the units never had the time to organize and establish a firm defence.

On the afternoon of 17 May, the Germans reached the Sambre and in the evening the French were already under attack in several locations. On the morning of 18 May 5th Panzer Division approached the Forêt de Mormal from three directions, cutting off several XI Corps units near Jolimetz. The town was occupied by 1 *Division Légère Mécanisé* (DLM – Light Mechanized Division) of General Picard, who wanted to launch a counter-attack against the flank of the German XXXIX Corps. However, General Martin decided on a different course of action, using Picard's division to defend the roads leading into the forest from the east. 1 DLM fought all day long, especially at Jolimetz. On 21 May, the Germans captured several casemates in the Forêt de Mormal. With the support of tanks, they were able to move up close enough to toss grenades at the embrasures.

In the evening XI Corps and 1 DLM lost contact with each other and headed west out of the forest towards Valenciennes and Le Quesnoy. 3rd Panzer Division moved in to clear out the Forêt de Mormal.

On the evening of 18 May, the defences along the Sambre between Maubeuge and Charleroi were abandoned. French units formerly in that position turned to form an arc around Maubeuge. The Maubeuge salient was now in danger from both flanks. The Germans threw General Erich Hoepner's XVI Corps with 3rd and 4th Panzer Divisions and 20th Motorized Infantry Division into the breach opened up by 5th Panzer Division. XVI Corps units reached the Sambre on 20 May.

The fortress of Maubeuge is steeped in history, remembered for the valiant fourteen-day stand by Colonel Fournier's men in 1914. The outcome of the 1940 Battle of Maubeuge was unfortunately settled from the start, due to the fact that it was already outflanked and surrounded before the first shot was fired, as it had been in 1914. The speed of the collapse was shocking and occurred not only as a result of German tactics, even though they were coolly and soundly executed, but due to engineering flaws of the Maginot Line forts. Even the Germans must have been surprised at how quickly these supposedly powerful, unassailable concrete vaults were put out of action and the crews surrendered. Such a simple thing as blocking the ventilation shafts did the trick.

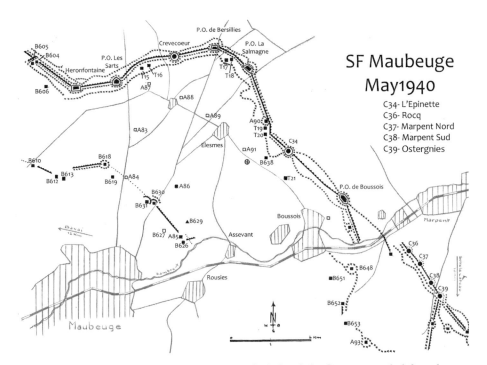

SF Maubeuge in May 1940. The line here was outflanked and the Germans attacked from the rear, pounding the concrete blocs and casemates to pieces with 88mm Flak guns. (Deutsche Angriffe ...)

In May 1940 SF Maubeuge was designated the 101 DIF. It was commanded by General Béjard.[7] Infantry troops included 84 and 87 RIF, 18 and 19 RRT, I *Bataillon Mitrailleuse* (BM – Machine Gun Battalion) and II and III Battalion of 161 RAP. The fortifications were defended as follows:

- S/S Hainaut: 87 RIF (Lt-Col Corbeil), with four FCR and twenty-five 1 RM type blockhouses; 105 CEO (Captain Fagot): Casemate Héronfontaine, Ouvrage des Sarts and two FCR blockhouses; 104 CEO (Captain Pujade): Casemate Crèvecoeur, Ouvrage du Bersillies; 103 CEO (Captain Brichard): Ouvrage de la Salmagne plus two FCR blockhouses and a *ligne d'arrêt* along the border of the SF Escaut and the S/S Thiérarche consisting of six FCR, two STG and twenty-eight 1st RM type blockhouses; 6th and 7th Companies of 87 RIF: thirteen CORF casemates of the Forêt de Mormal, plus nine observatories
- S/S Thiérarche: 84 RIF (Lt-Col Marchal), with two FCR blockhouses; 102 CEO (Captain Bertin): Casemate l'Épinette, Ouvrage de Boussois and three 1 RM type blockhouses; 101 CEO (Captain Cariou): four CORF casemates (Rocq, Bois-de-Marpent Nord, Bois-de-Marpent Sud, Ostergnies), three FCR, one STG and forty-six 1 RM blockhouses.
- Second position: two STG and two FCR blockhouses.

The main fortifications consisted of the CORF casemates and infantry ouvrages. The casemates were simple or double, with a combination of one or two JM/AC47 embrasures, an additional JM embrasure and a variety of cloches GFM Type B and mixed arms cloches. Casemate Héronfontaine could be considered a monobloc ouvrage as it was equipped with a mixed arms/50mm mortar turret, plus a mixed arms cloche.

Ouvrage Les Sarts had two blocs; Bloc 1 was a simple casemate with one JM/AC47 and one JM embrasure, cloche AM and cloche GFM B. Bloc 2 was equipped with a mixed arms turret plus a mixed arms and two GFM B cloches.

Ouvrage Bersillies had two blocs; Bloc 1 a simple casemate with one JM/AC47 and one JM embrasure that flanked to the north, plus mixed arms cloche, GFM B and a *Lances-Grenades* (LG – grenade launcher) cloche. Bloc 2 was equipped with a mixed arms turret plus two mixed arms cloches and two GFM B.

Ouvrage La Salmagne's two blocs include a mixed arms turret, mixed arms cloche and GFM B in Bloc 1 and a simple casemate for JM/AC47 and JM flanking east, plus GFM B and LG.

Ouvrage de Boussois had three combat blocs. Bloc 1 was a simple casemate with JM/AC47 and JM flanking west, cloche AM and GFM B. Bloc 2 was equipped with a mixed arms turret and GFM B. Bloc 3 was a simple casemate flanking east with JM/AC47 and JM embrasures, a mixed arms/50mm mortar turret and two GFM B.

The attack on Maubeuge began early in the morning of 18 May. 28 ID[8] was tasked with reducing the works of the Maginot Line. Stage one of the assault was to silence the CORF casemates on the right bank of the Sambre. These included Casemates Marpent Nord, Marpent Sud, Roq and Ostergnies.

Casemate Ostergnies, commanded by Lt Michel, was a simple flanking casemate with one JM/AC47 plus two mixed arms and one GFM B cloche. It was located on the extreme right flank of SF Maubeuge, south of the Sambre River. At 1030hrs on 18 May German troops moved in behind the casemate, occupying positions formerly held by French interval troops. The Germans brought forward 37mm and 47mm anti-tank guns and opened fire on the casemate's JM/AC47 embrasure, knocking out the guns. Things were then quiet until around 1500hrs when the embrasure was hit with tremendous force. The Germans had set up an 88mm anti-aircraft gun[9] along the Quatre-Bras–Jeumont road, out of the range of French guns. The shells were aimed directly at the gun embrasure. The impact of the high-velocity rounds tore away chunks of the concrete façade, destroying the framework for the armoured embrasure. Several crewmen inside the gun chamber were wounded and the casemate filled with thick smoke. The mixed arms turret in Bloc 2 of Ouvrage de Boussois attempted to intervene but did little to hamper the German attack. Powerful 150mm howitzers also pounded Ostergnies and its neighbouring casemates. The crews continued to suffer under the onslaught of the 88s. When it was apparent they could no longer hold out, they sabotaged their equipment, tossing the pieces down the wells. By 1800hrs the casemates south of the river had fallen.

In the meantime, the Germans focused their artillery on the forts. Bloc 3 of Ouvrage de Boussois, a casemate with JM/AC47 that flanked towards the west, was hit by 88s and 150s which the Germans were able to move to within just 1,500m of the fort. At this range, these guns were devastating. Bloc 1 was also targeted.

German action was also taking place north-west of Maubeuge. A line of small FCR and Type 1 RM blockhouses of varying designs, called the *Ligne d'Arrêt*, were built between Bavay and Maubeuge. It didn't do a very good job of stopping anything. On the morning of 19 May, the German VIII Corps, now deployed to the rear of Maubeuge, moved north-west and struck the line from the rear. Several blockhouses were captured by 8 ID which was able to approach the rear of the blocks because the French anti-tank guns were facing towards the front. On the evening of 19 May the line came under heavy attack and many of the blockhouses fell. 8 ID reached Bavay. Fort Leveau was captured in the morning of 20 May. 158 RI counter-attacked but failed to recapture the fort. However, the blockhouse of Ferme-aux-Sarts, surrounded by the Germans, was relieved. The blockhouse of Plantis was abandoned at 1830hrs after the crew had put up a strong fight. The blocs of Pavillon, Saint-Joseph and le Feignies fell.

On 20 May, 8 ID continued its advance towards Longueville, Audignies and Mecquignies, heading in the direction of the SF Escaut. The road was covered by several small blockhouses, also FCR and Type 1 RM. Blockhouse Ferme Fréhart fell at 1000hrs, Audignies and Bois-de-Louvignies at noon. The road to Mons was covered by Maison-Rouge, Faubourg-Ouest-de-Mons, Faubourg-Est-de-Mons and Pont-Allant and each of these was attacked. The crews, having no support to the rear, attempted to escape but several were killed and wounded; all of the blocks were captured. The following day, 21 May, was the end of resistance for the small blockhouses of Maubeuge:

- Quêne-Luquet (Lt Polvent) and La Belle-Hôtesse (Lt Fontaine), north of Bavay had their rear façades pounded full of holes by 88mm shells and surrendered around 1300hrs.
- La Raperie (Lt Reignoux) and Saint-Hubert (Capt Henry) fell around the same time.
- The crew of Ferme-Cambron evacuated the block under heavy fire at 1500hrs.
- Le Pissotiau (Lt Stievez) and Moulin-Rametz surrendered around 1500hrs.
- The blockhouse of Cimitière de Saint-Waast-la-Vallée was the command post of General Béjart. It was attacked at 1600hrs and pounded by 88s; the garrison was evacuated after the block became untenable. The general escaped to the main French lines.

On a very sad note, Captain Baillif, commander of 7th Company of II/84 RIF, which had recently fought and survived the panzer onslaught along the frontier, was killed in the blockhouse of Perche-Rompue, along with three of his men.

The Fall of Maubeuge – 22 to 23 May

The pounding of Ouvrage de Boussois continued after the fall of the casemates and the attack was nearing a desperate climax. Most of the fort's guns had been put out of action; there was no ventilation and the crew was overcome by fumes that seeped down into the combat blocs and underground quarters. Bloc 3's turret guns attempted to hit dead ground along one of the approaches to the fort but could only reach it with the 50mm mortar in the observation cloche. Around 0900hrs Stukas dropped 500kg bombs on the blocks while troops of 2nd Company of 49 Pioneer Battalion under Oberleutnant Langenstrasz crept closer and closer to the fort. As soon as the bombing and shelling stopped the pioneers attacked. Their plan was to cross the ditch surrounding the fort, head towards the blocs and neutralize the ventilation shafts. The air inside was bad enough but this would put an end to any chance of continued resistance. The crew did just that for a short time but the quality of the air worsened and around 1100hrs Captain Bertin raised the white flag over Bloc 3. A few moments later the crew stumbled out into the daylight, trailing a thick, acrid smoke. While the Ouvrage de La Ferté was the first Maginot Line fort to fall on 19 May, Boussois was the first to raise the white flag and surrender.

The next target was the Ouvrage de la Salmagne, commanded by Captain Brichard. It was attacked by 49 IR soon after the fall of Boussois. Salmagne provided artillery support for Boussois but was also bombed by Stukas and shelled by German artillery. The situation deteriorated when the blockhouse of Élesmes[10] (Lt Petot) fell on 22 May. This allowed German gunners to bring up a battery of 88mm guns to within 150m of the fort. At that range the job was done quickly. The high-velocity shells were aimed at the embrasures of Bloc 2 which were shattered to pieces and the 47mm gun inside was destroyed. The German guns then turned on Bloc 1, firing on the entry door and the unique caponier jutting out from the bloc. Around 1500hrs Captain

Bloc 1 of Ouvrage de Boussois, SF Maubeuge. (Pascal Lambert – wikimaginot.eu)

Brichard evacuated his men from Bloc 2 to Bloc 1, but the loss of ventilation made the journey along the smoke-filled underground tunnel a very dangerous one. By the time the evacuation took place German pioneers from 3rd Company, 49 IR were on top of Bloc 1. The pioneers attacked the mixed arms turret with an explosive charge and the turret was destroyed. Salmagne now had no weapons. At 2030hrs Captain Brichard surrendered.

Ouvrage de Bersillies (Captain Pujade) was attacked by the Germans from daybreak on 22 May. The German guns concentrated on the rear façade and on Bloc 2. The following morning the onslaught continued and the mixed arms turret was put out of commission. At 0915hrs, keeping true to form, the Germans destroyed the air shaft of Bloc 2. At 1000hrs an assault team from 11th Company, III Battalion 83 IR moved on top of Bloc 2, preparing to cause additional damage to the turret and air shafts. Fifteen minutes later, Captain Pujade decided to surrender the fort. The Casemate de Crêvecoeur fell soon after, suffering the same fate as the rest: destroyed embrasures and blocked ventilation shaft.

The Ouvrage les Sarts held out through the morning of 23 May, along with Casemate de Héronfontaine. Both works had been under attack since 21 May by

Stukas and artillery that took aim at the embrasures and the turrets. The turrets of Sarts and Héronfontaine were knocked out. Lt Debret, commander of Bloc 2 of Sarts, was killed in the attack. On 22 May German pioneers moved on top of Héronfontaine but they were chased off by machine guns from Sarts. As soon as the surface was clear of Germans the shelling and bombardment started up again. At 2130hrs, after all weapons were destroyed, Lt Durif, commander of Héronfontaine, evacuated his men from the casemate. At 0530hrs on 23 May the bombardment of Sarts picked up again. At 0600hrs the mixed arms turret, which had been repaired overnight, opened fire again. An hour or so later the wall of the turret took a direct hit, locking it into a semi-raised position and it could no longer fire. At 1100hrs Captain Leduc surrendered the fort, effectively ending the defence of Maubeuge.

It is strange indeed to think about the causes of the fall of Maubeuge and there are many, both strategic and tactical, but the most incomprehensible of all and which would plague the works of SF Faulquemont and Rohrbach in the coming weeks, was the failure of the ventilation system and the concrete. It is almost unbelieveable that these major works of the Maginot Line held out for less time than the forts of Belgium and France in 1914 which were struck by much more powerful guns and that they surrendered because the crews were no longer able to breathe the air inside. They were equipped with powerful generators that operated when cut off from the electrical grid that drove a state-of-the-art ventilation system built to keep poisonous gas from getting into the fort. Yet the engineers left a way for the enemy to simply destroy or block the shafts and asphyxiate the men.

The Maubeuge position had other flaws. The ouvrages lacked any artillery that could have stopped or slowed the Germans as they approached the Sambre from the east and south. The mixed arms turrets fired on adjacent forts under attack but this was not possible when all were being attacked simultaneously and were therefore unable to put their own turrets in battery. Finally, even if there were flanking casemates they would have been oriented to repel an attack only from the north. The Germans attacked from the south and there was no provision for defending against an attack from the rear. This feature would also plague other sectors of the Line in the weeks to come.

Fortified Sector Escaut – 22 to 27 May

Before the fall of the forts of Maubeuge the Germans were on their way towards Valenciennes and the SF Escaut. The only Maginot Line 'fort' in that direction was the PO d'Eth, located on a farm south of the village of Eth. Commanded by Captain Dubos, it comprised two blocs. Bloc 1 was a simple casemate with JM/AC47 and JM flanking west and cloche AM and 2 GFM B. Bloc 2 housed a mixed arms turret and another flanking casemate for JM/AC47 and JM, plus a cloche GFM and LG.

The remaining defences were STG and CORF casemates and a couple of blocks built into the old Fort de Maulde. The fortifications of SF Escaut, including the Fort de Maulde, began to come under attack from German artillery on 20 May. The pace of the shelling picked up on the 21st. German infantry moving along the Flines-lès-Mortagne road were pinned down by 75mm shells from the Casemate Est de Maulde, despite the German shelling which lasted throughout the night of 21/22 May. The weak French artillery capability did not prevent the German's from surrounding the sector. On 22 May Fort de Maulde was hit by shells from a 305mm Skoda howitzer set up in the Forêt de Bonsecours near Condé-sur-Escaut. A dozen shells landed on top of the fort but didn't cause much damage to the casemates.

On 22 May, the PO d'Eth came under fire from 88mm Flak guns that fired on the embrasures from close range. The following morning the fort and the adjacent casemates of Jenlain and Talandier were surrounded. The 88s fired on Eth's mixed arms turret in Bloc 2 and the Jenlain casemate. Both were heavily damaged but remained a threat and the Germans could not launch an infantry assault. An 88 was brought up to within 800m of the mixed arms turret of Casemate de Jenlain. The casemate responded with machine-gun and 25mm anti-tank fire and the German gun crew scattered. Fort de Maulde was also shelled and in the evening 464 IR of 253 ID launched an unsuccessful attack on the fort. No infantry attacks

Casemate Talandier, SF Escaut, after its occupation by German troops. Note significant damage to the concrete, most likely from 100mm or 150mm guns. (Bundesarchiv)

were conducted on 24 May but the artillery shelling continued. On 25 May, an attack was attempted on Ouvrage d'Eth but this too failed. The 88 continued to fire on Bloc 2.

At 0345hrs on 26 May the Germans resumed shelling PO d'Eth. 88mm shells chipped away slowly at the concrete façade, piece by piece, like an ice pick, until finally a shell punched through the wall of Bloc 2 and exploded in the inner gun chamber. Bloc 1 was also put out of action. Around 0600hrs an assault team from Pioneer Battalion 28 and First Battalion of 7 IR headed for the fort and quickly surrounded it, gaining the top of the superstructure. Captain Dubos ordered the evacuation of the fort through the storm drain that, unbeknownst to the Germans, led to the adjacent casemate of Jenlain, about 600m to the west of Eth. Jeanlain was also in terrible condition and at 1020hrs its crew began to tumble out of one of the embrasures to surrender. The Germans did not know that Eth was connected to Jenlain and stared in surprise as 160 men climbed out of the casemate. Casemate Talandier surrendered shortly after.

Fort de Maulde was not yet completely surrounded and the Germans reduced the STG casemates that flanked the fort. In the afternoon of 26 May Captain Schwengler was ordered to evacuate the fort at night while the opportunity still existed. At 2300hrs, the 155mm gun of the casemate of Fort de Maulde fired its final shots and was sabotaged. The evacuation began at 0030hrs. The following morning the Germans found the fort abandoned. The French frontier and all of its fortifications from the North Sea to the village of Margut east of Villy-la-Ferté, were now in German hands.

Chapter 7

La Ferté – 16 to 19 May

It was not an easy decision to include this chapter. The main reason for considering its omission is that a few pages (in this case seven) do not do the story justice. We will never truly know what the men inside the fort experienced during the final hours. It was a horrible thing, that we do know. Similar to the strange fate of Captain Lévi Alvarès at Fort des Ayvelles in 1914, except in his situation it was a suicide. But no one will ever know what tortured thoughts led him to that end, just like no one will know what conversations were had in the tunnels of La Ferté when the lights went out and the men could see nothing but smoke until they suffocated. It was included for two reasons: it is a demonstration of perfect squad-level tactics to capture a fort – blind it, move in and destroy its offensive capabilities then smoke out the troops inside; and it shows how the French, by their omissions, allowed it to happen. French ineptitude and the collapse of communications with the fort's commander were a direct opposite to the perfection of the German operation. Here is how things unfolded.

SF Montmédy

S/S Tête de pont de Montmédy: 155 RIF (Lt-Col Culot). Thirteen *abris de tir* and *abris passif* (unarmed shelters) made up the defences of the village of Villy. These were added in 1939. The principal line of defence had two *abris de tir Barbeyrac*, one STG and one FCR blockhouse plus two STG artillery casemates with 75mm Model 1897/33 flanking west and east (My 1 Villy Ouest and My 2 Villy Est). Command setup was as follows:

- 3 CEO (Captain Aubert, also commander of Ouvrage Chesnois):
  - Ouvrage de La Ferté (Lt Bourgignon who, unfortunately for him, replaced Lt Guiard on 20 March 1940); CORF Casemates Margut, Moiry, Sainte-Marie and Sapogne; Ouvrage le Chesnois (Captain Aubert); CORF Casemate Christ, Thonne-le-Thil, Guerlette.
- 2 CEO (Captain de Gatellier, also commander of PO Thonnelle):
  - Casemate Avioth; Ouvrage de Thonnelle (Captain Gatellier); CORF Casemate Fresnois and Saint-Antoine and FCR Blockhouse My 12.
- 1 CEO (Captain Sachy, also commander of Ouvrage de Velosnes):
  - FCR blockhouse My 14 and CORF Casemates Ecouviez Ouest and Ecouviez Est; Ouvrage de Velosnes (Captain Sachy).

    ○ In the second line, eight FCR blockhouses and two STG casemates for 75mm 1897/33 (La Laiterie and Villecloye).

S/S de Marville, formerly *Secteur Défensif de Marville*, detached in March 1940 from SF Crusnes:

- 132 RIF (Lt-Col Blanchet); Line of the Chiers – four FCR and six STG blockhouses; principal line – one FCR, two STG and seven RFM type blockhouses, plus one RFM artillery casemate for 75mm 1897 (La Higny); CEZF defensive line Mangiennes to Pierpont had twelve STG blockhouses

La Ferté was the end of the Maginot Line in SF Montmédy. To the west were the weak defences along the Chiers. As of 13 May it stood alone east of Sedan. The 107 men of La Ferté believed they held a powerful position. The ouvrage consisted of two blocs connected by a tunnel 35m below ground. Weapons in Bloc 2 consisted of a refurbished 75R05 turret from Verdun converted to a mixed arms turret for JM and 25mm. Bloc 1 was equipped with a 47mm gun, but it was oriented to the east. The Germans would arrive from the west. La Ferté had no artillery pieces and the closest gun was Le Chesnois's 75mm turret, 8km away at the very limit of its range. Between La Ferté and Chesnois were the casemates of Margut, Moiry, Sainte-Marie and Sapogne. These were equipped with anti-tank guns and machine

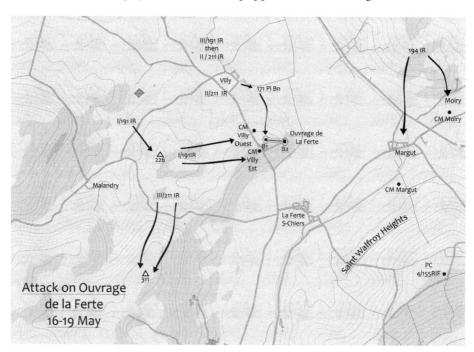

*The attack on the village of Villy and the Maginot Line ouvrage of La Ferté. This small infantry fort was the last fort on the left flank of SF Maubeuge. (*Deutsche Angriffe *…)*

guns. Two small casemates with 75mm guns – Villy-Est and Villy-Ouest – guarded the road behind Bloc 2.

On the night of 14/15 May the three regiments of General Weisenberger's 71 ID (assigned to Sixteenth Army with 104, 110, 115 IR and 69 Artillery Regiment (AR), 33 PJ Bn, 33 Recon Bn, 33 Pi Bn; 68 ID was directly under VII AK – Von Schobert with 169, 188, 196 IR, 168 AR, 168 PJ, Recon, Pi Bns) arrived north of the Chiers. General Eugen Ritter von Schobert ordered the division to attack the Chiers position at Blagny at dawn on 15 May. At 0500 the German guns opened fire. There was no French counterbattery response due to the fact that the gun crews had been withdrawn from the position during the night. General Huntziger feared that 3 DINA would be trapped by German forces moving in from Sedan to the west and he ordered the retreat, leaving the artillery pieces behind. General Braun's 68 ID also advanced towards Villy with 71 ID in the centre and 15 ID on the left. German infantry reached the Blanchampagne and Prêle Farm, about 300m from the Villy-Malandry Road where they came under fire of the machine guns of 23 *Régiment d'Infanterie Coloniale* (RIC – Colonial Infantry Regiment) (Colonel Cuzin). From the roof of the barn at Prêle farm the Germans could see the steel and concrete of the Ouvrage de La Ferté (known to the Germans as *Panzerwerk* 505).

At 1100hrs the 75mm gun of Villy Ouest opened fire and expended about 1,500 shells during the day. The village of Villy, called a '*Centre de resistance*', was defended by 1st Company II/23 RIC plus a machine-gun section from 155 RIF. The Germans meanwhile began moving troops towards the village with the objective to make contact with the defenders. Later that night the Germans opened fire with 210mm mortars, cutting the communications between the village and the regiment.

Von Schobert and Weisenberger discussed their plans. They decided that in order to capture the ridges along the Chiers it would be in their best interests to reduce the ouvrage, but not at all costs. Weisenberger was provided with the maximum firepower of VII Corps to accomplish the task. The corps artillery would open fire on the morning of 16 May: 0700hrs to 0730hrs – 210s and field guns to fire ranging shots; 0800hrs to 0830hrs – arrival of Stuka dive bombers; 0830hrs to 0900hrs – all guns to fire at maximum cadence. At 0900hrs the infantry would assault Bloc 2 with support of a Flak 88 battery to fire on the cloches. Prior to that attack the Germans needed to capture Côte 226 between Villy and Malandry and from there Côte 311.

German artillery opened fire around noon on 16 May. While the French kept their heads down, 194 IR launched a diversionary attack at Margut and Moiry. Meanwhile I/191 IR of Major Kranke attacked Côte 226, south-west of Villy. The hill, held by I/23 RIC, was captured in an hour of fighting. III/191 IR tested the defences of Villy, strongly defended by 1st Company of II/23 RIC with three 25mm guns, twelve MGs, 16 FMs and a 60mm mortar in the small blockhouses that made up the defences of the village. The Germans moved forward but were driven back by machine guns in the village, suffering heavy losses.

The artillery continued on both sides on the night of 16/17 May and General Weisenberger ordered IR 91 to take Côte 311 and Villy by the evening of 17 May. The village was pounded by four German batteries and a huge cloud of smoke rose into the air. Troops from III/191 IR of Major Zenker moved into the village but were hit by machine-gunners well hidden in the blockhouses inside the village and the attack was checked. At 1300hrs another bombardment on the village opened the way for Zenker's troops but the French fought just as hard as before. The Germans could not break through the ruins and were forced to retreat, this time for good. In the evening they were replaced by II/211 IR of Hauptmann Corduan.

III/211 IR moved against Côte 311. Departing from Côte 226 the battalion moved towards 311 but it was hit by the guns of a small blockhouse half way up the hill. Around nightfall the blockhouse was taken out by a flamethrower and the hill was finally captured. This was bad news for Ouvrage de La Ferté. The two casemates blocking the route behind the ouvrage, Villy Ouest and Est, were evacuated around 1630hrs on 17 May. Three men from 23 RIC had arrived at Casemate Villy Ouest to tell the commander, Lt Tyckozinski that the village of Villy had fallen. He had no way of confirming this but spoke with Lt Bourgignon at La Ferté who informed him the fort's mixed arms turret was blocked in the firing position and stuck pointing to the south and would be useless against an attack from the west. Villy Ouest was not equipped for approach defence and Tyckozinski made the decision to evacuate after sabotaging the gun. S/Lt Penalva of Villy Est also evacuated his crew. However, 9th Company of 23 RIC still held the village of Villy.

Throughout the evening of 17 May 210mm German mortars fired directly on La Ferté, opening up large gaps in the barbed-wire perimeter. Thirty shots per minute landed on top of the ouvrage. Bourgignon contacted Lt Labyt at Casemate Margut and requested he light up the top of the ouvrage since he had no means of keeping German pioneers from approaching the blocs. Margut flashed its powerful searchlight beam in short intervals towards Bloc 1 of La Ferté. At 2138hrs Bourgignon sent out a radio message stating he was under attack and requested support. Chesnois fired eighty shells from its 75/05 turret on La Ferté, but no attack was in fact taking place since the Germans were still attempting to get through Villy. At 0413hrs another request for support on La Ferté was answered by Chesnois but once again there were no German troops attacking.

This was to change on 18 May. Weisenberger was notified that both his Stuka and heavy gun support would be withdrawn later that day. He had no choice but to launch the final attack on Villy and La Ferté. At dawn, German 105s opened fire on Villy followed by an attack of two companies of II/211 IR. The defences, thought to be diminished by the incessant bombardment, were not so, but the pioneers located three machine-gun positions that were causing a great deal of difficulty and the Germans headed in that direction. Finally, at 1630hrs the exhausted French gave up and Villy was taken.

Weisenberger moved ahead with the attack on La Ferté. It would come from the direction of the newly captured village of Villy. The attack was carried out by

1st Company of 171 Pi Bn (Oberleutnant Germer). German guns opened fire at 1810hrs, all concentrating on La Ferté. This included three groups of three batteries of 210mm, one group of 150mm, three 100mm, six groups of 150mm howitzers, nine groups of 105mm howitzers and a Flak 88 battery. The guns opened fire for a short time. The 88s concentrated on the cloches with the intention of opening up holes in which to place explosives. The only worry the Germans had was if the 75mm guns of 3 RAC or Chesnois opened fire when the pioneers advanced. But the orders were given and the pioneer teams of 211 IR moved out from the south-east edge of Villy and 191 IR from Côte 226. While German shells exploded overhead and all around them, 191 IR joined up with Germer's 171 Pi Bn and Hauptmann Corduan's team from 211 IR and the pioneers moved in on La Ferté.

At 1815hrs the 88s opened fire on the cloches' embrasures and the turret. Sparks from metal striking metal showered the top of the ouvrage. Bloc 2 was equipped with a GFM and observation cloche. The embrasures were pointed in the direction from which the 88s were firing. A lucky shot flew right through the embrasure of the GFM, decapitating one man and killing two others. At this stage, with German 88s firing on the cloches and 100s suppressing French fire from Saint-Walfroy hill, there was nothing to slow the pioneer's advance towards the top of the ouvrage. Bourgignon was able to reach 3 DIC by telephone to pass on the news of the damage to the cloche but the French high command was so unaware of what was going on at the fort they seemed prepared to simply send out a repairman to fix the hole. General Falvy was completely unaware that Villy had fallen and German pioneers were on the rooftop of La Ferté.

A German group approached the cloche GFM of Bloc 2. Gefreiter Biermann attached an explosive to the north embrasure then ran for cover from the explosion. The next target was the mixed arms turret, jammed in the raised position. A 40kg charge was affixed to the top of the turret. The explosion lifted the turret cap. A smaller charge was placed on the side of the turret and this explosion lifted the cap out of its socket and dislodged it at an angle that left a small gap that opened to the inside of the turret housing. The pioneers tossed grenades and smoke pots and explosives through the opening. The crew inside didn't know what hit them and panicked. The cloche GFM was destroyed with three dead inside; the mixed arms turret was inoperable and probably irreparable; one of the 25mm guns and JM were broken off of their carriages; and the periscope in the observation cloche had been blown up and the floor of the cloche was collapsed. The interior of the bloc was full of smoke and seriously damaged from the shock of the explosions. The crew could think of nothing but to escape to the safety of the tunnels below. Only one man stayed behind in the engine room to try to keep the ventilator running but in their haste to run down the stairs the men had left the interior airlock doors at the top of the stairs open enabling the smoke to be sucked down the staircase.

Bourgignon spoke over the phone with the engineers of SF Montmédy and talked about blowing up the tunnel between the blocs. This led Aubert at Chesnois to surmise that Bourgignon thought he was under attack inside the ouvrage.

Aubert demanded that he send men back up to the top to defend the bloc from attack, as it was now completely undefended. Five volunteers led by Sergeant Boré grabbed grenades and headed up top, never to be seen alive again. Around that same time Bourgignon was informed by the 3 DIC chief of staff that a counter-attack by R35 tanks from 41 *Brigade de Char de Combat* (BCC – Tank Brigade) was under way. However, the attack failed and on the morning of 19 May there was no further news or signs of life from Ouvrage La Ferté.

Overnight, Germer's squad attacked Bloc 1. The 75mm guns of Chesnois, much to the dismay of the officers of the ouvrage, because they were at the limit of their range and would have little effect, were ordered to fire shrapnel rounds on top of Bloc 1. This occurred for a short time until the tank counter-attack began, during which time the pioneers were free to roam the surface with little danger of French artillery strikes. Instead, at 2210hrs, German batteries opened fire on La Ferté to button down the defenders. The French believed this was related to the counter-attack. The crew in the cloche of Bloc 1 did not think they were in danger – the pioneers would never attack under such conditions. This was not correct and the Germans moved from crater to crater, heading for the first cloche of Bloc 1.

The small team that included Gefreiter Grube of *Stosszug Grothaus*, later reported[1] he could hear the French crew talking inside the cloche. He placed explosives in the embrasure, ran to the back side of the cloche and waited for the explosion, which had the desired effect. His men moved on to the other cloches. It took fifteen minutes to silence three of them. The only one left was the GFM cloche which had its metal blinds closed. The explosives had no effect on the GFM so the Germans left it alone and proceeded to drop grenades, explosives and smoke pots into the other embrasures. The effects inside the bloc were similar to Bloc 2, causing tremendous damage. Smoke and flames filled the bloc and the ouvrage had no further defences.

During and after the attack Bourgignon was in contact with 3 DIC and indicated his intention to evacuate the ouvrage. General Burtaire of SF Montmedy could not understand how La Ferté had reached this stage. At 0330hrs Bourgignon spoke with General Falvy and told him that Bloc 1 only had use of one gun position, the 47mm flanking towards Margut. He suggested abandoning the ouvrage since most of the weapons were destroyed. Falvy ordered him to resist in place. Falvy was not opposed to evacuating the men but was not yet prepared to do so as long as they had one gun position remaining in Bloc 1. Bourgignon spoke with the PC of 155 RIF and told Colonel Henry that his men were starting to suffocate in their oxygen masks. Henry responded that Bourgignon knew his mission and his boss, Colonel Culot, had no authority to change it. Bourgignon responded that he knew and said, '*Adieu, mon colonel*'.[2] The final communication from La Ferté was around 0500hrs from Adjutant Sailly to Chesnois stating the fort could no longer hold out and they would attempt to reach the surface. That was it.

At dawn on 19 May the German pioneers placed a plank over the ditch of Bloc 2 and blew up the entry grill and the armoured door. They received no response from the FM. The inside of the bloc was filled with smoke. Germer's men did not proceed any further and returned to Villy. The FM of the undamaged cloche of Bloc 1 opened fire three times during the morning. The gun was silenced by a German shell in the afternoon. This was the last reaction of any kind from the fort.

Both sides simultaneously inflated and diminished the capabilities of the fallen fort. Weisenberger reported that *Panzerwerk* 505, one of the 'strongest ouvrages of the Maginot Line' in the Montmedy sector, had fallen. In early June French newspapers reported that Bourgignon and six of his men defended their *casemate* against the attackers. Hundreds of Germans were killed before capturing the *casemate*.

On 19 May French observers reported that the ouvrage no longer appeared to be occupied by the Germans. The following day a reconnaissance patrol was sent to find out the condition of the ouvrage. The Germans were concealed on Bloc 2 and the French patrol approached Bloc 1. The Germans fired a few rounds on the patrol and the French pulled out. On 25 May, another patrol returned and this time made it inside Bloc 1 through the grill and the entry door and encountered a terrible smell. The men approached the staircase and spotted a body on the stairs, then a second – both wearing gas masks. They could not breathe and left the Bloc. Two days later they returned with gas masks. Their goal was to descend the stairs but they came across a German guard outside and were chased off. That was the last French attempt to access the ouvrage.

Several days later the Germans went inside Bloc 2 but were unable to descend below because of the asphyxiating atmosphere. Finally, on 2 June men from 6th Company of 191 IR moved all the way to the bottom and found several bodies by the kitchen entrance. Further along they found the tunnel blocked by dead bodies. The German estimate was 150 to 200 bodies. This was incorrect because there were 107 men in the crew. They were later removed and buried in a common grave outside Villy. They were again exhumed and reburied by the inhabitants of La Ferté-sur-Chiers and Villy.

Chapter 8

Operations in late May and early June

While the Maginot Line fell in the north-west, minor actions continued in SF Haguenau. On 19 May, an overnight calm was broken around noon by German shelling on Rott, Geisberg, Steinseltz, Oberhoffen, Ingolsheim and Schoenenbourg. Bloc 7bis and the 120L sections responded on Château Saint-Paul, Schweigen and Rechtenbach. French counterbattery fire was being directed by Commandant Rodolphe from Hochwald's ditch casemate C6 from where all of the action could be observed. Observatory 07 reported German trucks moving between Mundat and Schleithal but they were out of range. The gun platforms of S4 were modified so the guns could reach this road.

At 1815hrs German troops occupied Wissembourg and Altenstadt unopposed and pushed patrols towards the lines in the Bois des Juifs. At 2000hrs, observers spotted red signal flares coming from French infantry requesting artillery fire on German patrols at Juifs. At 2045 additional support was requested from the vicinity of Rott and 81st *Bataillon de Chasseurs à Pied* (BCP – Light Infantry Battalion) who were holding the APs of Climbach and Rott. 135mm and 75mm turrets opened fire for one hour, striking the woods in front of the APs. Three hundred 75mm and 210 135mm shells were fired resulting in heavy German losses. Bodies were found by patrols the next day. The adjutant from 215 Artillery Regiment was captured. He served as the liaison with the infantry and confirmed to the French that an operation was taking place with the entire 215 ID, but this attack had been successfully stopped by French artillery fire. Rodolphe then ordered a strafing of all the forest roads that could be used by the Germans.

Seven hundred and sixty shots were fired on 19 May by the guns of SF Haguenau. The radio announced that the Germans were advancing towards Gise, Landrécies and north of Laon. The crews discovered things were going very badly in the north but they were reassured by the appointment of General Maxime Weygand as commander-in-chief of the French armies.

On 20 May German guns opened fire in the morning against Hochwald Est and the slopes to the south towards Bloc 7bis. At 0900hrs Maréchal de Logis Boesch was examining the filters in Casemate C9 when splinters from a 105mm shell struck him, seriously wounding him in the arm. He was evacuated to the rear and later lost his arm. He was the first casualty at Hochwald.

German shelling continued against Geisberg, Oberhoffen, Hochwald and the surrounding woods. Targets included Ingolsheim, south of Climbach, Cleeburg,

135mm turret of Bloc 6, Ouvrage du Hackenberg. (Dan McKenzie)

Steinseltz and Riedseltz. Around 1200hrs enemy infantry were spotted south of Wissembourg, west of the road near the Bois des Juifs. S1, S2 and S4 concentrated their fire on the location. From 1300hrs to 1330hrs there was renewed shelling near Climbach. Four-à-Chaux responded with Bloc 2's 75mm turret and pushed back a German company in front of the Ferme Boesch. S1, S2 and S4 concentrated on Schweigen and on the slopes south of Wissembourg.

On 21 May German artillery fired 100 shells on S/S Pechelbronn, the Geisberg, Hill 276 and to the south of Cleebourg. The French noted that a large number of German shells missed their target and many of them were duds. Shelling was heavier on S/S Hoffen, in particular Aschbach, Hoffen and Stundwiller. For the first time Obs 01, 02 and 03 spotted German movement north of S/S Hoffen in the territory abandoned by the French. At 2130hrs Schoenenbourg fired on Hill 276 where there was a strong presence of German patrols reconnoitring the Line. All in all, it was the calmest day in a week.

May 22nd was also a calm day. The Germans fired 400 shots on the line of surveillance and the villages of Rott, Steinseltz and the Geisberg. German air patrols were very active. At 0800hrs Bloc 7bis fired on a German aircraft flying over the region of Weiler. At 1400hrs S2 was ordered to fire on Böllenborn in Germany, north of Wissembourg. At 1550hrs Obs 07 reported trucks crossing the anti-tank obstacles of the Westwall. The 220mm guns of 156 RAP fired ten shots and all German movement ceased.

The men of 70 ID pulled out of SF Haguenau and were placed in reserve in the area of the town of Haguenau. Only two battalions of *chasseurs* (scouts) were left in the APs (81 BCP in front of Rott and 90 BCP on Geisberg) to reinforce the fortress troops. 22 RIF occupied the AP of Climbach and Col du Pigonnier. In the sub-sectors to the east, elements of 69 RIF and other regiments moved up to man the

APs. The radio reported a strong push by the Germans on Cambrai, Valenciennes, Arras. The front remained stable at Amiens, Laon, Rethel and Montmédy.

The next couple of days were relatively calm. Overnight the Germans fired on the entire surveillance line until 0410hrs. Five minutes later the SRO received several requests from French infantry for support in front of Climbach, Bois des Juifs and in advance of Col du Pigonnier, however no German infantry attacks took place. The next day 81 BCP sent out patrols north of Col du Pigonnier and found abandoned arms and munitions on the places occupied by the Germans during the abortive attack of 19 May. The radio reported violent fighting near Tournai, Cambrai, Arras, Bapaume and Amiens.

Similar action continued on 25 May. The following day the Germans fired 350 shots on Geisberg. Schoenenbourg was hit by thirty 150mm shells. One of the shells burst in front of the cloche of Bloc 5, shattering the lens of the episcope and sending shards of metal at the spotter, killing him instantly. He was the first victim at Schoenenbourg. The French episcopes were the weak spot of the observation posts. The engineers knew this and tests were conducted up to 1939 but no solutions were found to improve their design. In 1938, after some exercises that included attacks on the casemates, the sector commander wrote in his report: 'The casemates will perish by the cloche.' The accident at Schoenenbourg caused the engineers to try to reduce the risks. At Hochwald, 4cm steel plates were cut and placed in the portal of the episcope embrasure, which effectively condemned the post. In some locations periscopes were used instead. The Germans were well aware of this weakness and specifically targeted the episcope embrasures.

May 27th was also a very calm day. There was no major German shelling or patrols. A replenishment of munitions arrived at night via the 60cm railway from the depots. Hochwald received 6,600 75mm shells and Schoenenbourg 4,000. Over the next few nights Hochwald received 26,747 75mm and 3,552 135mm rounds, and Schoenenbourg 8,000 75mm. The crews worked very hard to offload the ammo and the magazines quickly filled up. Terrible news was announced on the radio: the Germans had reached the sea at Boulogne. The Allied armies were surrounded.

At 0130hrs on 28 May the French shelled the Bois des Juifs where German patrols were spotted probing the Line. At 0200hrs Bloc 7bis fired forty-five shots on the bridges at Wissembourg. The daylight hours were calm. At 1700hrs, from Obs 07, the group commander observed small groups of Germans between Moulin de Saint-Rémy and the forest. They were chased off by twenty shots from Schoenenbourg.

The Maginot Line crews received the news that Belgium had surrendered. For the first time they heard the news about La Ferté and the airborne attack on Eben-Emael. To protect against a similar attack on top of the forts, the following procedures were put into place: adjacent forts were directed to use shrapnel fire against enemy infantry attacking the surface of a neighbouring fort or casemate; active surveillance of the exterior was stepped up to be on the lookout for paratroops; Hochwald received five FT tanks from the army to sweep the surface in case of attack and three of the tanks were sheltered in the main gallery of Bloc 8; one battery of 25mm anti-aircraft guns was installed near Schoenenbourg, which also received three tanks. Each night, patrols looked to the sky for paratroops. The watch shift was reinforced and volunteers for the shift were numerous.

Attack on the Outposts of SF Sarre – 29 May

SF Sarre was organized as follows:

- S/S Lixing: 69 RMIF (Lt-Col Jobin), included ten STG blockhouses, two MOM artillery casemates for 75mm 1897 and the PAFs of Altviller and Holbach.
- S/S Altrippe (Leyviller): 82 RMIF (Lt-Col Matheu), with seven STG blockhouses, two MOM artillery casemates and PAFs Henriville and Marienthal.
- S/S Saint-Jean-les-Rohrbach: 174 RMIF (Lt-Col Duparant), with ten STG blockhouses, four CORF blockhouses built to defend the dykes and the PAFs of Loupershouse, Guebenhouse and Ernestviller.
- S/S Kappelkinger: 41 RMIC (Lt-Col Tristani), contained no STG or MOM structures, only field fortifications, plus the Avancée de Holving and PAF de Grundviller on Hill 252.
- S/S Sarralbe: 51 RMIC (Lt-Col de Mauny), also contained only field works, the Avancée de Knopp and PAFs Willerwald and Kisswald.
- S/S Kalhausen:[1] 133 RIF (Colonel Bertrand) under whose command was 1 CEC of SF Rohrbach (Lt Kersual):
  - CORF Casemates: Wittring, Grand-Bois.
  - Ouvrage du Haut-Poirier (Captain Gambotti).
  - CORF Casemates: Nord-Ouest d'Achen, Nord d'Achen, Nord-Est d'Achen.
  - 2nd Position – CEZF Line with STG casemates C1 to C22 (nine were not built).

On 29 May observers of SF Sarre reported an attack on Guebenhouse by armoured vehicles. In fact, these were motorcyclists and infantry in trucks that had surrounded the village. At 1715hrs a message was sent to 66 RAP to open fire on the southern edge of the towns where the Germans were positioned. The regiment fired 1,200 75mm, 100 105mm and 400 155mm shells. The Germans pulled back and the ruined village was re-occupied by III/174 RMIF.

On 2 June, a new attack was launched against the outposts. The target was Loupershouse, held by II/174 RMIF. Casemate Mc8E was attacked by anti-tank guns. The commander, Aspirant Andre Poncet was killed and three men wounded. Blockhouse M34 was attacked by a Pak 37. The bloc's FM held off the attack for a time but the defenders were driven out.

The Germans advanced in morning fog to surround the fortified strongpoints of Henriville and Marienthal, PAFs, north of the *Avancée de Barst-Cappel*, held by

82 RMIF. 15 GRCA and the *Corps Franc* of Lt Colombéro were ordered to retake the two villages. Henriville was cleared and the garrison of the PAF made it out of the encirclement. The troops of Marienthal also disengaged from the Germans and escaped the following night, but Colombéro was mortally wounded. 15 GRCA suffered heavy losses of sixty men; 82 RMIF lost ninety.

On 3 June, the Germans attacked and pushed 69 RMIF out of Holbach-les-Saint-Avold. Later that night Colonel Dagnan ordered the evacuation of AP Guebenhouse and Ernstviller. The evacuation was conducted quietly without the knowledge of the Germans who pounded the villages the next day, only to find them empty. Dagnan also pulled back troops of 15 RMIC to the PA south of Villerwald.

On the 41 RMIC front of Colonel Tristani, due to German pressure the advanced posts of Grundviller and Péri were evacuated and the Germans advanced into Grundviller and opened fire from a position south of the village. The battle around Grundviller lasted all day and French field artillery pounded the position in order to get the Germans to move back. House-to-house fighting took place in the village. At 2000hrs, German shock troops attacked one of the blockhouses of Sergeant Bontemps and tossed torches into the embrasures. The defenders ran out of the blockhouse. At 2100hrs the French were ordered to evacuate Grundviller and fired a flare into the air to signal retreat. The blockhouses of Grundviller defended the *Digue d'étang de Welschof*, east of the *Avancée de Puttelange*. The dam fell into German hands, thus giving them control of the water levels of the retaining dams situated downstream towards the French lines. Dagnan was furious the dam was given up without destroying the controls. He planned an operation to destroy the dam, fixed for 2200hrs on 5 June. Unfortunately, the Germans launched an attack instead.

In the afternoon of 5 June, the Germans bombarded the outskirts of Puttelange. The position was defended by 100 men in three PAs (PA 1, PA 2 and PA 3), two blockhouses (M24B and M30) and a large STG casemate that guarded the Sarreguemines road. The Germans advanced to the wire around the position and attempted to cut their way through. PA 2 was attacked around 2300hrs by German infantry. Heavy close combat followed and the French counter-attacked, but were forced to retreat to PA 3. The command post at Château Famin was evacuated. Isolated combat continued overnight. Contact with PA 1 was lost and there was no reserve to launch a counter-attack.

On the morning of 6 June PA 1 continued to hold out. The casemate, belonging to Sub-Lt Thomas, fired with all its weapons. A company of 88 BCP was ordered to counter-attack Puttelange. One column advanced towards Thomas's casemate and a second towards PA 1. French batteries provided supporting fire. A section of *chasseurs* commanded by Aspirant Bausson moved towards PA 1 but were blocked by the Germans in the cemetery. They were pinned down with several dead and wounded and called for reinforcements which arrived around 2000hrs and forced the Germans to retreat from PA 2. The *Avancée de Puttelange* was back in French hands. The dam of Welschof was still held by the Germans. Dagnan brought up a 47mm gun to hit the dam but the shots were ineffective.

On 29 May German troops reached the Yser in Belgium and later entered Calais. The following day the Armies of the North surrendered. On the last day of May combat opened up on the outskirts of Dunkirk. In SF Haguenau, 1 June was mostly calm, except for a 280mm howitzer firing on the entrances to Hochwald. At 1400hrs ten shots landed on the Auberge du Col du Pfaffenschlick[2] causing one dead and two wounded. Other shells struck Bloc 9, sending debris onto Bloc 8[3] where men were out sunning themselves. At 1600hrs S4 fired three shots on the steeple of Schleithal, site of a suspected German observatory. S4 then fired twenty-eight shots on Obere-Ringasse where the Germans had placed camouflage over the roads to mask their movements. At 1900hrs observers reported that the Germans had installed camouflage over a 'shiny' object south-west of Mundat, either a gun or a searchlight. Thirty-eight shots were fired from the turrets on the object and it was removed.

On 2 June German artillery concentrated on S/S Hoffen, shelling the villages of Siegen, Trimbarch and Buhl, causing fires to break out. The guns of Schoenenbourg and Hochwald fired in support of an operation by French *chasseurs* against the Villa Alfred. The German shelling of Schleithal started a huge fire, with flames shooting high into the air.

On 3 June, heavy fog prevented action on either side. June 4th began calmly but at 1500hrs Obs 092 was regulating fire against Schleithal from S4. The shelling began normally. The barrels were positioned below the camouflage netting and with each shot flames leaped out of the barrels. Suddenly, Commandant Rodolphe who was visiting Obs 092 saw that gun #2 had disappeared in a cloud of black smoke. He called to find out what had happened but there was no response from the gun battery. Schoenenbourg's command post came on the line to announce an accident with casualties. Rodolphe hopped in a car and sped off to Schoenenbourg. Guards at Bloc 7, the entrance to Hochwald Est, reported gravely wounded men being taken to the infirmary. There was still no word what had happened. Ambulances brought more wounded to the infirmary. Rodolphe started a preliminary investigation. The gun position was in terrible condition. A shell had exploded in the tube, breaking it in half, causing pieces of metal to go flying, hitting a neighbouring gun crew. One of the engineers on the scene, still in shock, believed it was a faulty fuse. Order at the battery was re-established and the working gun was set up and fired a few rounds. Specialists came in later to examine the damaged gun and to figure out what happened to prevent a reoccurrence in the other sections. The shells were taken away and replaced. The commander ordered the placement of shields between the gun positions to protect the gunners. The next day Commandant Rodolphe visited the wounded at the hospital of Haguenau. One gunner was evacuated to Saverne for an amputation. Otherwise there was complete calm in the sector. The radio announced the Germans were attacking along the Somme and in the region of Laon-Soissons.

June 6th was also a calm day. Bad news was delivered from Haguenau hospital. Derrendinger, one of the S4 gunners, had died of the wounds he had sustained during the gun explosion. His funeral was held at the cemetery of Haguenau. It was attended by Captain Cortasse and twenty gunners from Schoenenbourg. Rodolphe reported on the town of Haguenau – 'Evacuated and deserted, dismal, sad, like our hearts'.[4]

June 8th and 9th were also relatively calm. German workers were spotted 100m from the French outposts in the Bois des Juifs and in the Bois des Marronier. A new 120L section was installed near Bloc 7 of Schoenenbourg to face east where there was a growing menace from the Germans against S/S Hoffen. The new section was placed in battery and a horizontal platform added between the guns. The radio announcer passed on the news that German tanks were on the Bresle and fighting was taking place at Chemin-des-Dames and Rethel.

On 10 June German patrols attacked the bank of the Rhine at the casemate of Pont Seltz which was surrounded for several hours but later relieved. There was much more activity the next day. The Germans fired fifty shots on Hill 276 and Obs 04. At 0002hrs Commandant Rodolphe ordered harassing fire on Pont Sud de Wissembourg, to the south of Weiler, Villa Alfred, the south exit of Wissembourg, on Weiler and the slopes west of Weiler. These shots caused heavy losses and disruption to the Germans. The *Group Franc* of 77 RIF launched attacks on Hill 447 north of Col du Pigonnier to dislodge a German patrol. They were forced to pull back with several losses but one pioneer from 342 IR was captured. The radio reported that the Germans crossed the Seine between Rouen and Les Andelys. The Loire River was now France's only hope. The previous day France was officially at war with Italy. In the Maginot Line there was still no thought that the French line could be turned. The fighting was still far away.

In SF Crusnes, the crew of C24 was constantly alert for possible German incursions. They were on the lookout for a major infiltration from the north towards the Maginot Line. The observers reported that for a few days there was a suspicion that Hirps Farm near the Bois d'Ottange was occupied by German observers. Each time someone from C24 opened the door of the casemate a 77mm shell was fired at them and they had to dive for cover. The observers at C24 couldn't see anything specific. C28 (Casemate Réservoir) frequently spotted possible movement behind the green shutters of the large farm building, perhaps a small number of men – nothing that warranted calling in artillery.

On 2 June, Maréchal de Logis Vuillemard, through his periscope, spotted one of the farm's skylights open indicating it might be the location of a German observation post. The commandant of Bréhain decided to fire a few shells at the farm. Through the periscope the observer at C24, with telephone headset, waited for the sound of the command '*Coup parti … action commence*', and the observers giving out corrective coordinates; then repeating '*goniomètre-support* … *gisement 400* … *durée de trajet* …' The periscope turned in the direction of Hirps Farm. Nothing moved. From the other end of the phone line:

Service de Renseignments d'Artillerie (SRA): 'Hello O-12, are you ready?'
O-12:[5] 'Ready'
SRA: 'Shot has left'.

Three of Bréhain's blocs fired at once and unleashed a tremendous blast like rolling thunder, combined with the hissing sound of the release of the shells. The 75s encircled the farm with small gray puffs of smoke while the 135s threw geysers of smoke and clods of earth 10m into the air. The dovecoat was hit with the full force of the blasts, causing the roof to burst and fly into the air. The results were reported to the SRA by the observers:

'Explosions (bursts) – Explosions – bearing 1410 – Elevation 2 – Front 40 – Depth … Doubtful, about the objective, doubtful.'

Three minutes later a shot from the 135mm marked the end of the shelling, pieces of the farm's rabbit hutches falling in the nearby orchard. Hirps Farm burned.

The night of 4 June was dark and cloudy. There were flashes in the distance; artillery or lightning. The observer (Masson) was shaken by the shoulder by his mate, Daillet, who whispers: '550'. He points the periscope towards *gisement 550*. Nothing. A few moments later Daillet calls again and this time flashes are seen coming towards the Bois de Butte. The two men count silently… seventeen seconds from shot to explosion above the woods. Masson picks up the phone:

Bréhain SRA: 'I'm listening'.
O-12: 'Cannon flashes – *gisement* medium – 555 – distance probably 5500'
BSRA: 'Departures – 550 – 5500.'
O-12: 'Terminated.'

At Bréhain the SRA opens a chart on the table and looks for the location of the battery. Despite the uncertainty, Bréhain unleashes a volley of 100 shots and the German pieces are pulled out and moved elsewhere.

According to Masson, to be an observer, one must have a piercing gaze ('*regard perçant*') and a sure memory. He must know every inch of ground; to be able to say without hesitation which tract, on which site it is found and how many decigrades higher or lower than any other more important point. His partner Ricaud spots some bushes on the edge of the Bois d'Ottange that were different from the day before. It is incredible but true. It was a German 150mm emplacement that fired a few rounds on the barbed wire of C24. It was quickly dispatched by the guns of Bréhain. A few days later a large sign painted by the Germans is spotted at the ruins of Hirps Farm: 'Why continue this deadly combat?' The Germans know that the only response to their question will be an artillery shell.

On 11 June parts were delivered for the TSF which had been broken down for a few days. The men gathered around to hear the latest news. When they heard it, they wished the radio was still broken: Germans advancing on Paris. The French effort to stop them was hopeless. They have been shattered and cut off one from the other and are pulling back, vainly trying to stop the Germans and re-form a front. Each new phrase destroys the hopes of the crew. The question is asked of Lt Clerte: 'What will become of the Maginot Line? Along our front?' Clerte responds, 'What else would you expect her to do? Hold. Watch.'[6]

Part III

Abandonment and Breakthrough, 12 to 16 June 1940

Chronology 12 to 16 June 1940

12 June	The orders are given to evacuate and sabotage the Maginot Line beginning the night of 13/14 June.
14 June	The first fortress infantry divisions begin the retreat from the Line.
14 June	The Germans launch Operation Tiger to break through the Maginot Line between Sarreguemines and Saint-Avold. The breakthrough is completed the morning of 15 June.
14 to 15 June	Engineers begin the preparation to destroy the Maginot Line's offensive capabilities, including guns, munitions, lighting, motors and ventilation. The destruction is carried out in parts of certain sectors, in particular SF Montmédy.
14 June	German 162 and 161 ID plan an attack on SF Crusnes and SF Thionville.
15 June	A large convoy of 183 ID is hit by the guns of Ouvrage du Fermont while attempting to move through Longuyon.
15 June	95 ID moves through the Sarre Gap and to the rear of the Maginot Line.
15 June	262 ID attacks the forward outposts of SF Rohrbach.
15 June	264 ID attacks SF Haguenau's line of PAs. Fortress guns repel the attacks.
15 June	Thousands of French fortress troops of SF Thionville, Boulay and Faulquemont begin the exodus to the south.
15 June	German troops from 218 and 221 ID launch an offensive across the Rhine – Operation *Kleiner Bär* will result in the breakthrough of the weak Rhine defences, allowing the Germans to move towards the Vosges.

Chapter 9

The Maginot Line is Abandoned

While German Army Group A crushed the Allied forces in Belgium and swept into northern France, Army Group C kept watch on and continued to harass the troops in the Maginot Line. The Germans were in control of excellent observation positions overlooking the French lines. They didn't appear to be ready to launch a major attack at any point in the near future; simply to pin the French in place. General Prételat had other ideas and on 17 May contacted his commanders to pass on the following communications:

> We must maintain contact with the enemy but prevent losses in the forward positions in front of the Line.

- To Fourth Army – pull back towards the Maginot Line.
- To Third Army – above all, do not give battle forward of the fortress line. Do not hesitate to pull back the covering forces to shelter if necessary.

On 20 May Gamelin was replaced by Weygand. Gamelin had not shown the determination required of the moment. Weygand arrived on the scene on 19 May. He stopped off to see Gamelin and General Alphonse Georges[1] and later remarked to Prime Minister Reynaud[2] that all he felt from the two was a sense of hopelessness. Prételat received a call from his new chief on 20 May. Weygand exclaimed to Prételat that he understood the situation was difficult but nothing as of yet was a foregone conclusion. 'We must fight on to the end and find a way to stop the German tanks. We must give as well as take; to cause the enemy to worry.' He gave Prételat the authority to order Huntziger to take whatever means was necessary to do something.

In the north, the Panzers reached Abbeville and surrounded the two armies of General Billotte's[3] First Army Group[4] including eight British and twenty Belgian divisions – a total of forty-five divisions. Weygand flew into the midst of the surrounded troops to discuss the situation with Billotte and concluded the only course of action was to break out to the south and join up with General Aubert Frère's new Seventh Army on the Somme. Instead, the Allied divisions were driven further west – to Dunkirk. With this the French army lost its best fighting divisions. From 10 to 20 May the Allies lost sixty divisions.

Weygand had only two choices:

- Organize a front anchored against the west coast of France in order to maintain liaison with Britain and to guard Paris. In this case the Maginot Line would be abandoned.
- Cling to the Maginot Line and establish an entrenched camp in the east and abandon the coast and Paris.

Both options left no possibility for victory, only to hold out until the government could negotiate an armistice. After discussions with Georges, Weygand chose to fight on the Somme and Aisne but if the French army was unable to hold then the western flank would be lost.

On 26 May, Prételat and Weygand met in person for the first time. Together with Georges, the three discussed the Maginot Line. Prételat's position there was greatly weakened by the removal of units to the west over the past several days to build a line to stop the German advance. He wanted to know if it was still possible, and was Second Army Group still expected, to guard the front between the Rhine and the Meuse? From thirty divisions he started with on 10 May, he was down to ten, of which six were B divisions plus two Polish divisions. Prételat requested to move a part of the interval troops off the Maginot Line to create a reserve to manoeuvre and cover the flanks. He wanted to begin preparations to evacuate the Maginot Line.

Weygand replied that the fortress troops were static and had no means of transportation, therefore it was better to leave them where they were. Prételat remarked '*Qu'il est bon de prevoir le pire*' ('It is better to expect the worst') and that an evacuation of the fortified position must be considered. Weygand stated that French public opinion would not take an announcement that the Maginot Line was to be abandoned lightly. Besides, he had recently made the decision to hold on the Somme and Aisne and there must be no talk of retreat. There was also the aspect of a huge morale problem if the troops found out that the Maginot Line was to be abandoned. They would probably never understand how the French could abandon such an excellent position without a fight; arguably at the time, the strongest in France. Civilian morale would be equally affected. If the generals were concerned with civilian disorder the decision to abandon the Maginot Line without fighting, would cause chaos, in that France spent millions to develop defences they would never use. Morale would be destroyed by that.

Prételat pressed: 'And if we are broken on the Somme and Aisne?'

Weygand replied: 'Then we must request an armistice'.

In Weygand's mind, the Battle of France was lost and the army had to fire its last shots on the Somme and Aisne and after that it would be the end.

Prételat continued to push for the authorization to pull his forces back from the Maginot Line, claiming they could be better used in the days that were ahead if they were available for, perhaps, maintaining order among the civilian population. Weygand was adamant and the decision to keep the fortress troops in place remained for the time being, but, as it turned out, not for long.

George's orders the next day to Second Army Group confirmed Weygand's decision to hold fast on the Somme and Aisne with no thought of retreat to the Maginot Line or the Rhine. Huntziger was in step with Prételat. He also believed the best action to take if the Somme and Aisne were lost was to abandon the Maginot Line and retreat in good order to establish a centralized defence. It would also put France in a better position to negotiate an armistice.

Prételat and Huntziger prepared for one of the following foregone conclusions: if, to the left of Second Army, General Touchon's Sixth Army was broken, Huntziger could pull back but he must re-establish his defences on the Marne and try to head to the east of Verdun and Longuyon. If Huntziger was menaced to his left and contact was broken, he must pivot around Longuyon which, by consequence, would force the abandonment of the casemates and ouvrages of SF Montmédy. Condé did not immediately have to worry about abandoning the Line, however. The thought of abandonment and forcing the fortress troops to fight in the open was unimaginable but it was without a doubt exactly what would happen if Second Army pulled back first.

On 28 May Prételat met with Generals Victor Bourret of Fifth Army and Auguste Laure of IX Corps. If the Germans attacked on the axis Rethel–Châlons-sur-Marne, they could take the Maginot Line in the rear. He worried first and foremost about what might happen to Huntziger's army on the left. Bourret's and Laure's missions were to resist in place but to prepare for a rapid retreat if necessary. During the course of the meeting the three were notified that the Belgian Army had just surrendered.

Also on 28 May Fourth Army staff was pulled back from the Lorraine front to Troyes. General Hubert of XX Corps took command of Fourth Army effective 29 May. It was renamed the Sarre Group and included troops in SF Faulquemont (General de Girval), SF Sarre (Colonel Dagnan), 52 DI (General Échera), the First Polish Grenadier Division (General Duch) and two machine-gun battalions.

On 2 June Weygand, Georges, Prételat and Huntziger met at Châlons-sur-Marne to discuss the particulars of a retreat by Second and Third Armies if the Germans broke through from the west. The Germans were on the threshold of liquidating the Dunkirk pocket followed by the Somme/Aisne offensive – *Fall Rott*, to be launched on 5 June. At best, the French could hold out for three or four days. After that the front would collapse and the tanks would move into the breach to threaten the flank of Second Army.

The generals could not agree on what to do in that event and several issues were discussed, including what to do with the fortress troops if the army was forced to retreat. Huntziger suggested the fortress and casemate crews could be left behind to slow the German advance. In other words, the Maginot Line crews were to be sacrificed for the benefit of the field armies. Prételat wanted to avoid any troops being surrounded and preferred to abandon the Maginot Line. He viewed the crews as unable to defend themselves if left on their own.

The next day Weygand decided to create the Fourth Army Group (GA4) to the left of Second Army Group. Huntziger was placed in command. It comprised Fourth Army under General Réquin and Second Army under General Freydenberg. The Colonial Corps command passed to General Carles. Prételat was stupefied by the decision and communicated his disdain to Georges: 'You have put me in charge of the house but left the defence of the door to someone else.' Prételat's new mission was defence of the Maginot Line and the Rhine.

Phase two of the attack on France, *Fall Rott* (Case Red), was launched at dawn on 5 June. It consisted of an attack by Von Bock's Army Group on the Somme. Huntziger's new Fourth Army Group was scheduled to be operational on 6 June. German Army Group B penetrated deeply into the French line. The Maginot Line was not yet threatened but from 9 June the Germans entered the second phase of their operations. After Army Group B crossed the Lower Seine, the Germans conducted a second offensive by Army Group A on the Aisne.

On 7 June, the French began to pull back from the Somme. On 9 June, General Hoth's Panzers[5] broke out and headed to the Seine. On the same day, Von Rundstedt's Army Group A launched an offensive in the Argonne. This attack included a strike by Guderian's Panzer Group while German infantry bridged the Aisne River. Freydenberg's Second Army took the brunt of the attack but inflicted heavy losses on the Germans. Thousands of Germans were killed, wounded and captured.

The situation worsened as Army Group A advanced quickly towards the Plateau of Langres. On 10 June Huntziger pulled his troops back towards the south. He hoped to establish a line on the Marne at Virtry-le-Francois and to make contact with the Maginot Line in the vicinity of Longuyon-Mangiennes. This decision had an important consequence for the Maginot Line: The Montmédy bridgehead had to be evacuated by the interval troops on the evening of 9 June under cover of the guns of the Maginot Line. After this the forts were to be sabotaged and abandoned on the night of 12/13 June.

This was France's last gasp and it seemed that, despite some small victories, no one in the government or army held out any hopes of a change of fortune – a new 'Miracle on the Marne'. Weygand himself, while encouraging his men to fight on, but realizing it was only a matter of time, packed up his HQ at La Ferté-sous-Souarre and headed south to Briare. Paul Reynaud's government fled Paris for Tours and on 10 May Mussolini declared war on France. Weygand let it be known to Reynaud that the army could crack at any moment.

The front between the Meuse and the Aisne was holding on 10 June. However, 20 DI had pulled back so Prételat had no support on his left. Georges responded that he still had the fortress troops at his disposable. This statement in itself was an admission to Prételat that he had nothing to stop the Germans from caving in his left flank. Was it now possible to think about a retreat of Second Army Group and abandonment of the Maginot Line? The French retreated everywhere and

Georges admitted he had no plans. Prételat understood this to mean that Third and Fourth Army Groups were fighting their final battles.

On the afternoon of 10 June Prételat met with General Condé and in the midst of the conversation learned that Second Army was in the process of pulling back to a line 80km to the south, thus uncovering Third Army's flank. There was no possible way for Freydenberg's army to pivot on Montmédy or Longuyon.

Situation of Fortress Troops – 1 June 1940

Army	Infantry (MG Battalions)	Officers	Men
Second Army SF Montmédy	4 RIF (13)	Exact numbers unknown	Exact numbers unknown
Third Army XLII CAF SF Thionville SF Boulay	3 RIF (9) 4 RIF (11) 3 RIF (8)	610 755 565	18,000 22,600 16,800
XX Corps SF Faulquemont SF Sarre	4 RIF (12) 2 RIF (6) + 2 RMIC (6)	645 600	18,850 17,000
Fifth Army SF Rohrbach XLIII CAF SF Haguenau 103 DIF	3 RIF (9) 2 RIF (6) 5 RIF (12) 2 RIF (4)	575 525 670 485	16,850 15,250 22,000 15,500
Eighth Army 104 DIF 105 DIF XLIV CAF SF Altkirch SF Montbéliard SF Jura XLV CAF	2 RIF (4) + 1 RI (3) 1 RIF (3) 2 RIF (5) BCPyr (2) BCPyr (3)	300 135 165 235 85	10,000 4,500 3,300 7,390 2,750
Total	37 RIF / 2 RMIC (108)	6,350	191,090

On 11 June, figuring he was justified by the threat to his flank caused by the withdrawal of Freydenberg, Prételat took it upon himself to send out a preparatory order – IPS #10 – to the Second Army Group commanders. The message was desperate: Second Army Group could no longer wait on the Maginot Line to be surrounded by German forces. The Seine had been crossed, Paris surrounded and the Germans were on the way to the Marne Valley to outflank the French in Lorraine and Alsace. The retreat of interval troops must take place as quickly as possible. Prételat did not know it at that moment but Weygand was simultaneously

sending out the order for the general withdrawal. Finally, he and Prételat were in agreement.

The following day Weygand gave the order to the entire French Army to prepare for a rapid retreat to the south to re-establish a defensive position on the line of Loire–Doubs.

Preparatory order from General Weygand:

• GA4 – (Huntziger) – to fall back along the Line Châlons-sur-Marne – Troyes – Nevers
• GA2 – (Prételat) – Sarrebourg – Épinal – Dijon
  Instruction Personnelle et Secrète (IPS) # 1443/3 FT

On 12 June at 1300hrs the order was executed. At 1630hrs the order to abandon the Maginot Line was confirmed at GA2 by the Chief of Staff of the North-East. This was soon passed on to the local commanders, but the evacuation would not begin until the night of 13/14 June.

Prételat directed GA2 to move along the axis Sarrebourg-Épinal in five groups and converge on the Line of the Marne–Rhine Canal by 17 June and then move to the south as one. The plan called for the interval troops to begin to pull back from the main line on the evening of 13 June, the casemate crews on the night of 14/15 June and the crews of the infantry forts (POs) on 15/16 June and the artillery forts (GOs) on 16/17 June.

Prételat's IPS #10 order reached General Condé at 1330hrs. Talk of a retreat was nothing new for Third Army but no one had really expected it to happen. How could the army contemplate abandoning the fortifications and, worse, sabotaging them then having to fight in the open? Very heated discussions took place among the officers at Condé's headquarters at Fort Jeanne d'Arc. One of the officers remarked: 'Eight months of endless work, concrete poured day and night, trenches dug, shelters built, anti-tank ditches dug and all of this for nothing; to go fight somewhere else.' Another: 'We are betraying Lorraine; abandoning it after promising to defend it. If we leave without firing a shot and sabotage the blocs and casemates no one will understand. We will leave the people to become Prussians, like 1870.' Another: 'What will be the reaction of the crews of the ouvrages; to destroy their turrets, power stations, tunnels, after being told since the start of the war that we will stop the Germans on the Maginot Line? How will they accept to fight in retreat with a rifle?'

General Boell of 51 DI, upon learning of the evacuation and destruction of the Maginot Line, expressed his indignation and unbelief: 'I was staggered by the news. I had the impression that I had misunderstood. It is impossible to abandon the Maginot Line; this would be the sign of total defeat. [This was] impossible to accept.'[6] Lt. Col Rougier of 201 RI (51 DI): 'The regiment dug kilometres of trenches, thousands of gun emplacements. All of these efforts were done in vain. Tomorrow we must fight in the open field.'[7] General Boell: 'The Maginot Line was mystical for France. To abandon it [meant] total collapse.'[8]

The decision was hardest for those who had to tell their officers and men. General Loiseau of VI Corps called his division commanders at 1430hrs on 12 June. Loiseau believed this was the wrong decision and thought it best to fight on the Maginot Line. He refused to transmit the order in writing. Loiseau notified General Poisot of SF Thionville and General Besse of SF Boulay that they were to assemble two *Division de Marche* (DM – Marching Divisions) from their fortress troops and retreat to the Marne-Rhine Canal with 26 and 56 DI. Poisot, at his PC of Fort d'Illange, full of emotion, notified his command staff who were speechless upon hearing the news. General Besse did the same at his PC at Hayes. At the prescribed hour, 161 RIF, 160 RIF, 162 RIF, then the artillerymen of 153 RA and 23 RA were to be formed into a DM.

Marching Divisions Organized from Fortress Troops – June 1940:

- *Division Légere Burtaire* (DLB) – SF Montmédy: 132, 136, 147, 155 RIF; 99 RAMF; 1/169 RAP.
- DM Poisot – SF Thionville: 167, 168, 169 RIF; 70 RAMF; 151 RAP.
- DM Besse – SF Boulay: 160, 161, 162, 165 RIF; II/460 RP; 23 RAMF; 153 RAP; 30 BCC.
- DM Chastanet – SF Rohrbach: 166, 153, 37, XXI/153 RIF; CISF 207; 59 RARF.
- DM Senselme – XLIII CAF/SF Vosges: 154, 165 RIF; CIF 143; V/400 RP; 46 GRRF.
- DM Regard – SF Haguenau: I/22, II/23, XXI/23, 1 and II/68, II/70, II and III/79 RIF; 69 RAMF; 156 RAP.

Marching Groups – Groupements

- Groupement Gaillard: 57 RI, 5 RIC, 22 GRCA, 4 BCC.
- Groupement Dubuisson: 3 DIC, 1 DBILA, XXI/1 RTM, 444 RP, 482 RPC, 486 RPC, 65 RR.
- Groupement de Fleurian – XLII CAF/SF Crusnes: 128, I and II/139, XXI/149 RiF; CI 142; II/46 RAMF; 2/29, 1/5 BCC.
- Groupement de Girval – SF Faulquemont: 156, 146 RIF; 69, 82 RMIF; II and III/39 RAMF; I/163, I and III/166 RAP; I/142 RA; 15 GRCA.
- Groupement Dagnan – SF Sarre: 133, 174, XXI/174 RIF; 41, 51 RMIC; 49 RAMF; 166 RAP.

Further east the fortress troops of SF Rohrbach and SF Vosges were formed into a DM to retreat with 30 DI. Colonel Senselme was placed in command of the

DM in SF Vosges and he left Lt Col Renard of 165 RIF in charge of the troops left behind. However, unlike the Second and Third Army zones, the crews of the casemates and ouvrages were to remain behind. The crews of the ouvrages were notified of the retreat on 13 June. Rodolphe stated: 'Millions to build defences that will never be used. This decision is monstrous.' However, SF Haguenau had not received an order from Fifth Army to sabotage the ouvrages. At the time, it was only being held out as a possibility.

Commandant Exbrayat of Four-à-Chaux asked his staff: 'If we receive the order to sabotage the ouvrages, what attitude will we take [to such an order?]'. The unanimous response was to remain inside and fight.

Louis Chardonnet, commander of Bloc 2 described the conversation: 'On this day each one came to realize the overwhelming defeat of the army. Silence of mourning reigned in the tunnels'.

The reaction across the front was one of shock. Men stared at their commanders with blank faces. Lt. Morosolli, commander of Casemate la Verrerie, was notified by Lt Col Renard of 165 RIF that the regiment was to retreat but the crews of the casemates were to remain behind and hold out as long as possible. Renard told him to tell his men that a reserve division was to be moved to the intervals – this lie should help to keep up morale. The casemates were now alone in the forest.

SF Faulquemont – Téting – Lt Marchelli was notified at 2200hrs on 13 June that 146 RIF was leaving that night. Marchelli also commanded the three adjacent casemates and blockhouses.

Laudrefang – Chef de Bataillon Adolphe Denoix of I/156 RIF, placed in charge of the crews of SF Faulquemont, met with his men at Laudrefang to apprise them of the situation. The crews of the ouvrages and casemates were to remain in place and the rest of the troops were to be withdrawn.

Lt Vaillant, commander of Ouvrage d'Einseling, was hoping for the opportunity to make a stand against the Germans. When he announced the order to retreat to his men, many of them were in tears but the emotion was more one of anger and a continued willingness to participate in the general struggle.

At Kerfent, Captain Broché foresaw the upcoming tactical problem. A wooded area was located behind the ouvrages that would be difficult to defend, especially when it would soon be empty of friendly troops. 'Before us, between the fort and the frontier and behind it was an absolute void.' Broché felt an extreme sense of isolation and abandonment as there was no longer anyone to count on.

SF Boulay – Michelsberg was very active against the approaching Germans and with a full complement of munitions and supplies. The men took the news with great emotion. It had a terrible effect on morale, above all the lack of news. In the evening the 75mm turret fired about eighty shots on a German patrol at Chémery. Suddenly the power was cut off and the fort's diesel motors were cranked up. The next day the engineers discovered the local power station had been sabotaged and abandoned by French engineers according to army orders. The sense of isolation was now complete.

Anzeling – Capt Guillebot was trying to figure out how he would destroy 2km of tunnels. He would flood them, he concluded. Prior to that, the engineers would run the motors without lubricating oil, causing them to seize up. Then the guns would be sabotaged.

Some of the veterans of the 1914–18 war, like Lt Laurent of Métrich, still expected another 'Miracle of the Marne' and waited confidently for such an event. If they could hold for six months, then perhaps such a thing could happen. He expected another Vaux or Douaumont.

Immerhof – Captain Réquiston stated that the men's hearts were broken as they waited for the departure of 168 RIF. Many of the men said goodbye to close friends.

Bréhain – Commandant Vannier notified the men at 1730hrs. They remarked resolutely that Bréhain would do its duty.

At Molvange the officers realized no help was coming. All of the men would do their duty to the best of their ability.

Latiremont – 149 RIF was to be pulled out from this sector. German artillery activity was particularly heavy here, with the bombardment of Casemate C15 and C16 at 0755hrs, Jalaumont Ouest at 0800hrs, between Casemate Laix and Haute de la Vigne at 0815hrs, and Casemate Chenières Ouest and PO du Mauvais Bois at 0900hrs. Bloc 4 of Latiremont was hit at 0910hrs. At 1010hrs, Casemate Chenières Ouest was hit again, Doncourt at 1315hrs and the top of Latiremeont at 1440hrs. Latiremont's Commandant Pophillat told Klein, his adjutant, that if the message comes in to sabotage and evacuate, the response would be: 'We did not receive it. Do you understand what I'm saying?' Klein replied that he did.

Fermont – Captain Aubert had heard nothing yet of an abandonment of his ouvrage. His command included the territory from Longuyon to the Haute de l'Anguille. It included PO Ferme Chappy (now the westernmost fort of the Maginot Line), Ouvrage du Fermont, two casemates and two observatories (Puxieux and de l'Anguille).

The defenders of the Montmédy Bridgehead were the first units to evacuate the Maginot Line. They began their retreat on the night of 10/11 June. The bridgehead was a salient in relation to the rest of the position and the defenders first needed to pull back to align with the rest of the interval troops of SF Crusnes, then to engage in a coordinated withdrawal in line with those adjacent forces. The pull back of the two groups of interval troops began as scheduled on the night of 11/12 June. The fortress battalions were formed into a light division under orders of General Burtaire (*Division Légere Burtaire*).

Small groups of defenders were left behind in the forts to make noise so the Germans would not suspect anything was happening and afterward to begin the demolition of armament and equipment. The fall of La Ferté caused the earlier evacuation of the casemates nearby and those near Ouvrage du Chésnois and they had already been sabotaged. The motors were broken up, telephone lines cut and breeches removed from the 25mm guns. Food supplies were doused with diesel fuel and tossed into the ditch. The crews joined up at Ouvrage du Chésnois.

At the Ouvrages of Chésnois, Thonelle and Velosnes the crews punched holes in the diesel reservoirs and ran the motors until they seized up. They also wrecked the guns by removing the breeches and destroying the barrels. At Chésnois the 75mm turret guns were blown up by stuffing grenades inside the barrels. This was done as quietly as possibly so as not to alert the Germans. The Maginot Line needed to look as if it was still manned and operational. If the Germans knew the main forces had pulled out of the Line, they would move swiftly to cut off the French retreat. The crew of Chésnois left the fort at 0100hrs and headed for Verdun. The crews of the blockhouses on the Plateau de Marville left the night of 13/14 June, thus completing the evacuation of the defences west of Longuyon. Despite their attempts to conceal it, this activity did not go unnoticed by the Germans.

The German 169 ID bordered the bridgehead and found out very quickly what was going on. The commander, General Heinrich Kirchheim, sent patrols to observe the forts. From 0300hrs a patrol from 378 IR crept close to Velosnes and discovered it was abandoned. When this news reached the German command, the order was given to occupy the empty sector and move towards SF Crusnes which was also in the process of being evacuated.

Patrols from 379 IR found the Casemate de Moiry empty and from there the German troops moved out across the line of forts. At 1100hrs on 14 June the Germans were in control of Ouvrage du Chésnois and the neighbouring casemates. At 1415hrs 378 IR was in possession of Thonelle and Velosnes. At 2000hrs the lead elements of 169 ID passed the town of Montmédy and spread out along the line of Juvigny-sur-Loison – Iré-le-Sec – Bazeilles-sur-Othain, just 12km from the beginning of the position of Longuyon-Mangiennes.

In SF Crusnes General Renondeau, commander of XLII CAF, did not appoint a replacement to carry out the evacuation orders of General Prételat after the departure of the interval troops. This decision was left up to the commanders of the ouvrages. On the evening of 13 June, the interval troops pulled out on schedule under the protection of the guns of the large forts. Soon after, engineers began the work of destroying the roads, bridges and lines of communication in front of and behind the Maginot Line, cutting the links with the troops who stayed behind to wait out the final days.

For the crews of the casemates and forts, there was no hurry to pull out because the Germans were not yet making any threats against the position. XXXVI Army Corps[9] was beginning its move to the south. The interval troops abandoning the SF Crusnes and 169 ID were both moving south on a parallel course.

On 13 June plans were drawn up in the sectors to designate which troops would leave and when and to coordinate the demolition and destruction. At Third Army, General Condé gave the following orders indicating the timetable for sabotaging all of the functioning equipment of the forts and moving out to join up with the main army.

- J-Day – Measure A – reinforcements, interval troops, support troops to evacuate under cover the Maginot Line and casemate guns – 15 June at 0200hrs.
- J + 1 – Measure B – interval artillery and crews of the casemates to evacuate under protection of the ouvrages – 16 June at 0000hrs.
- J+2 and J+3 – Measure C – crews of the ouvrages to evacuate after destruction of the armaments and equipment, if the Germans gave them the time to do so – 17 June at 2200hrs.
- At 2200hrs on 17 June the ouvrages were to be destroyed, flooded or sabotaged prior to being abandoned. The men were to attempt to rejoin the army.

SF Thionville – Colonel O'Sullivan was appointed by General Poisot to oversee the evacuation. From his command post at the former German Fortified Group Illange, south of Thionville, O'Sullivan ordered the following dispositions:

- Measure A – evacuation included part of the fortress crews; a skeleton crew was to remain behind in the forts.
- Measure B – 17 June at 2200hrs – a larger group of fortress crews would depart under protection of a small covering force (*petite croute*) to give the impression the Line was still manned.
- Measure C – 18 June at 2200hrs – the covering force to depart from the forts as they saw fit.

SF Boulay – Colonel Cochinard was placed in command of the remaining forces in the sector. He developed a similar plan to the other sectors:

- 17 June – the majority of the crews to depart in the evening under protection of a covering force.
- 18 June – this covering force to remain behind to see to the destructions and at 0400hrs attempt to join the main group.

SF Faulquemont – the plan was to depart beginning on 17 June at 1700hrs, after destruction of the guns, munitions and equipment. The sector was placed under the command of Chef de Bataillon Adolphe Denoix who located his command post at PO du Laudrefang.

SF Rohrbach – Colonel Fuchs was left in charge by General Chastenet; Colonel Conrad was in charge of the artillery division.

SF Sarre – Colonel Dagnan was placed in command of the fortress troops that were left behind after the evacuation, plus two additional infantry divisions. The interval troops were scheduled to leave on the evening of 14 June under the protection of a light covering force which would depart twenty-four hours later. This would prevent a rapid advance of German troops from delaying the retreat of Third and Fifth Armies, which pulled back on the night of 13/14 June. The crews of Ouvrage du Haut Poirier and its five surrounding casemates – Wittring, Grand-Bois, Achen Nord-Ouest, Achen Nord and Achen Nord-Est – were scheduled to depart by the afternoon of 14 June. These crews were under the command of Commandant Jolivet who placed his command post at Haut Poirier. His plan was to then destroy the works by 2200hrs on 17 June.

General Ferdinand Lescanne, commander of XLIII CAF and in charge of SF Rohrbach and SF Vosges, saw the situation differently and perhaps realistically. In his estimation, the forts in the sector would have to hold out from the time the order was given to evacuate the interval troops. He gave no further orders regarding the abandonment and destruction of the Maginot Line.

SF Haguenau was placed under the command of Lt Col Schwartz. His command post was the Ouvrage du Hochwald. His orders were simple – stay in place but have the means available and ready to sabotage and abandon the Line when the order was given.

The Rhine defences were being guarded by General Laure's Eighth Army, part of GA2 under General Prételat. His troops were in the process of being reinforced when the order was given to retreat towards the Vosges. The only troops left to guard the line of casemates and blockhouses on the Rhine were part of an artillery group of 170 RAP.

On the evening of 14 June, the first fortress infantry divisions – 104 DIF (General Cousse) and 105 DIF (General Didio) began their retreat under cover of the casemate crews. The major retreat to the south by the Armies of the East had begun. The aim of the Germans was to disrupt that retreat. The task of Von Leeb's Army Group C during Phase 3 of Case Red was to attack the weakest sectors of the Maginot Line to hasten their surrender. He ordered his troops to attack the Sarre sector on 14 June and the Rhine on 15 June. The Germans ignored the fact that their manoeuvre took place right in the middle of the French retreat and it should have been a simple formality. In fact, the Germans experienced their first and only check during the Sarre campaign. They also found that the crews of the casemates and ouvrages, advanced posts and interval field works would not run after the first shots were fired but would defend their positions until they were destroyed or no longer had the capability to defend themselves. While the outcome of the fighting in the days to come seems to have been determined by the retreat of the main French forces, the fight itself was not going to be a walkover.

Chapter 10

German Breakthrough on the Sarre

Commandant Rodolphe commented in his notes of 13 June that it was the first of the darkest days – 'The Line is abandoned'. It was completely quiet in the sector but to the west the French army was falling back towards Alsace. At 1030hrs Rodolphe was informed SF Haguenau was left with one division to establish an anti-tank barrier between Nuits-sous-Ravière and Chaumont. All field artillery was to be pulled out and to prepare the forts for destruction upon receipt of orders to evacuate.

The command post was in utter chaos, with papers being burned. The infantry commanders left quickly to give the marching orders to their units, which would begin that night. The commander of the ALVF[1] ordered the trains to remove his two 320mm guns which had been in battery near Katzenhausen since September 1938. The guns never fired a shot.

The command at Hochwald was still dumfounded by the news. Millions of francs spent on the Maginot Line and it would be abandoned and destroyed without a fight while still in prime condition? The guns had performed magnificently. The Germans approached the Line but only with the greatest caution and in most cases were repelled by artillery fire. Nevertheless, orders had to be obeyed. Lt Col Miconnet met with Captain Brice, the engineer commander, to discuss how to execute the orders to destroy the monstrous fort's combat capability. The smaller pieces could be destroyed (guns, munitions, generators, etc.) but nothing could be done to put much of a dent in the concrete. Tons of explosives would be required for that. A team of sappers was chosen to discreetly put the plan into action.

At 1430hrs Schoenenbourg fired fifty shots north-east of Geisberg and in the vicinity of Schleithal where enemy movement had been spotted. S1 fired twenty shots at Robenthal; S4 fired 400 shots (its last) south of Schleithal. A German deserter was taken to 81 BCP at Col du Pigonnier where he was interrogated and provided information about German patrols, losses, etc. Entire companies were being brought up in trucks attempting to ambush the *Groups Francs*. Snipers hid in the woods and allowed French patrols to pass by, then opened fire.

The radio announcement for the day was bleak: Paris occupied – attack in direction of St. Dizier. The Somme front was broken and the Panzers were moving south-east. The departure of the interval troops to Chaumont opened the eyes of the fortress crews to the gravity of the situation. No one knew where a German attack would come from. Would it be a siege? Would it come from across the Rhine? On 13 June, all ground in front of the fort was empty, but the French knew the Germans were somewhere.

On the night of 13/14 June the Germans attacked blockhouse 31BC[2] (Aspirant Frère) located on the bank of the Rhine 1km south of Casemate Pont de Seltz (Chief Sergeant Aubertin). The blockhouse had a crew of eight men and two machine guns. A nine-man German patrol crossed over the Rhine at night and attacked the bloc. The first two attempts were thwarted. On the third the Germans cut through the wire and advanced towards the concrete. Five of the crew made a sortie out of the block with machine guns and counter-attacked. They forced the Germans to retreat and captured three of them. The Germans quickly got the message the Maginot Line was still occupied.

During the probing attack of the blockhouses on the French side of the Rhine, the evacuation of the Maginot Line began. Advanced posts, shelters and command posts received the order to move out. The long march south had begun.

On the left of Prételat's armies the Germans were pushing further south at the expense of Freydenberg's divisions. Second Army's front was being continually extended to a dangerous point. Freydenberg called Condé to ask for reinforcements. The Third Army commander was unable to provide any assistance and Freydenberg contacted Huntziger who, in turn, contacted Prételat's Chief of Staff, Bérard. Sixth Army was being menaced in Champagne, Fourth Army fleeing south of the Marne, while Second Army stretched its left from Saint-Dizier towards Vitry-le-François where the German vanguard was already moving. Huntziger's group was thus unable to block the Germans anywhere between the Marne and Aube. Prételat agreed to dispatch 56 DI to Second Army to plug up any holes in the lines. On the afternoon of 14 June, as if the situation wasn't bad enough for Prételat, the Germans launched a major offensive on SF Sarre.

Operation Tiger – The Sarre Offensive, 14–15 June

For a little over a month, Army Group C faced the Maginot Line from Luxembourg to Switzerland. During the current phase of Case Red, von Leeb's armies were now to go on the offensive and help bring about the capitulation of the French armies in Lorraine and Alsace.

Hitler's Directive Number 13 set out two objectives: along with the attack on the main French army in the triangle of Paris–Metz–Belfort in order to force the Maginot Line to surrender, a secondary operation was to take place with limited forces to pierce the Maginot Line at its weakest point, which was between Saint-Avold and Sarreguemines. Also, depending on the development of this situation, launch a stronger attack on the Rhine as long as it did not involve more than eight to ten divisions. As Guderian advanced from Langres to the Swiss frontier, the action in the Sarre and on the Rhine should pin down French forces in a pocket.

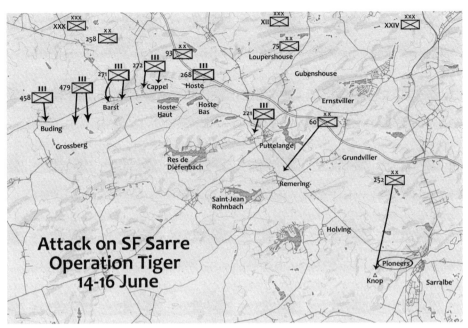

After the main French forces pulled out of the Maginot Line the Germans decided to attack the weakly-held SF Sarre. The battle turned out to be more difficult than anticipated. (OpenStreetMap)

Von Witzleben, commander of First Army, was tasked with the Sarre operation. The plan appeared to be limited in nature but the Germans were bringing a powerful force of three Army Corps supported by 1,000 guns and air support. The objective of Operation Tiger was to break through the Maginot Line.

In the Sarre sector the French had at their disposal the XX Corps of General Hubert under orders of Third Army. Hubert had two conventional divisions,

General Erwin Rommel, Northern France, May 1940. (John Calvin – wwii-photos-maps.com)

51 DI of General Échard and 1 DIP (*Division de Grenadier Polonais*) of General Duch to which was attached the fortress units – three regiments of *Mitrailleurs de Forteresse*, 69, 82 and 174 RMIF. These were positioned in the Sarre gap along with 133 RIF on the right.

On the morning of 13 June observers in the forward lines reported significant noise of enemy activity in the woods of Puttelange and Sarralbe: the rattling of tracked vehicles, motors and the neighing of horses. Thousands of German troops were moving into place. Worse, eighty German gun batteries had been spotted by reconnaissance aircraft – 300 guns located in front of the *Avancée de Puttelange*. Beginning on 12 June General Hubert began to pull his forces back from the advanced positions, except for the blockhouses of I/51 RMIC on the heights of Saaralbe, Bellevue, la Tuilerie and Knop. Hubert expected the troops of the First German Army to have panzers but they did not.

On 14 June at 0700hrs the Germans launched Operation Tiger – the offensive of First Army under General von Witzleben – between Sarreguemines and Saint-Avold. The German forces consisted of nine divisions, six in the first echelon:

- XXX Corps – 258 ID, 93 ID – Hartmann.
- XII Corps – 268 ID, 75 ID – Heinrici.
- XXIV Corps – 60 ID, 252 ID – Von Schweppenburg.

79, 198 and 168 ID were in the second echelon.

The offensive was scheduled to commence with a bombardment. German artillery forces included 259 batteries and approximately 1,000 guns, plus each regiment was supplied with Pak 37 and 88mm Flak guns and the support of squadrons of Stukas and Heinkel He-111s. When H-Hour arrived all of the guns would open fire. The follow-on advance was to be swift and complete.

The French troops of SF Sarre did not sit back and wait. Counterbattery fire against German assembly points had begun a few days earlier. Work on strengthening the position continued and there was no sign any French troops had been evacuated from the Line. The weather was not favourable to the Germans. The previous few days had been rainy and the ground and roads were muddy, making movement of vehicles and guns difficult.

The Germans did not expect the attack to be a walk in the park. The French bombardment and bad weather kept the soldiers awake at night. Oberst Hotzy of 472 IR wrote in the battalion journal that he expected German losses to be quite high in his particular sector of attack since the men would be attacking what many of them had held in awe for so long – the concrete bunkers of the Maginot Line.

Oberleutnant Gerd von Ketelhodt was selected to lead the first charge with two groups each of thirty *Stosstrupps* against the Knop heights. This was a spur about 252m in height defended by twenty-four men from II/51 RMIC, commanded by Adjutant Drianne. The main defences included five machine-gun blockhouses, trenches and barbed wire. Pioneers were to advance and cut through the wire surrounding the position while snipers zeroed in on the embrasures of the blocs. The attack was to be supported by a battery of 210mm mortars and Stukas. The aircraft were called away at the last minute but this did not affect the Germans' confidence in the success of the well-planned mission.

French observers continued to report the noise of German vehicles on the edge of the battlefield. At 0430hrs the artillery of II/174 RMIF opened fire on an assembly of troops at Elviller. At 0600hrs German artillery opened fire, signaling the commencement of the attack. German shells falling on the *Avancée de Puttelange* were coming from the Bois de Kalmerich. Within an hour German artillery was extending itself out across the Line and gaining in intensity minute by minute. The morning fog was thickened by the smoke of hundreds of shells that fell on the outposts of SF Sarre.

Because of French counterbattery and support fire, the attack on Knop did not start out well; several of the troops were killed and wounded, including those leading the pioneers. Kettelhodt wondered if the attack would be called off but it was not. At 0850hrs he gave the order to advance towards Knop. The bombardment of the 210s finally stopped at 0910hrs and the troops moved forward, cutting through the wire and slipping into the dead ground that could not be reached by the guns of the blockhouses. Pioneers tossed grenades and smoke pots into the embrasures and the French ran out, their hands in the air. Knop, defended by only twenty-four men, surrendered.

German shells continued to fall across the front. The shells struck villages, farms, blockhouses and depots behind the lines. Telephone wires were cut and radio antennas were knocked down. Two hundred and fifty men of I/51 RMIC guarded the heights of the left bank of the Sarre, the next position to be attacked. At 0800hrs Pak 37s were brought forward to fire on the embrasures of the blocs. The metal blinds of Blockhouse de l'Etang were closed up but a direct hit by a German shell struck one of them, punched through the metal and wounded two of the men inside. The rest of the men fled. The Advanced Post de la Tuilerie, located inside the Solvay factory, came under attack and the defenders fled toward the Canal de Houillières. At 0900hrs Commandant Dousset, commander of I/51 RMIC, gave the order to retreat.

After capturing Knop, the next attack was launched against an elevated advanced position defended by I/69 RMIF called Grossberg, near the village of Biding, situated in line with the MLR. It was a very weak position lacking in concrete structures but supported by three nearby casemates – the casemate of Lt Fraysse and 2nd *Compagnie de Mitrailleuses* (CM/2) on the left; Sub/Lt Duport's at the exit to Biding and the casemate of Lt Bellettre on the right at the junction with 82 RMIF. These were rustic to say the least – no lights, armour or visors in front of the embrasures. The Grossberg itself was defended by CM/3 (Capt Derrien) and CM/1 (Lt Capilaine), plus several small field fortifications called *abris en rondins*.[3]

At 0600hrs the Grossberg came under German fire, including from a Pak 37 that targeted the *abris de rondins* on the border of Forêt de Petite and Grande-Frêne. The Pak 37 took out most of the shelters and machine-gun positions. At 0900hrs the Germans appeared to the rear of 69 RIF's positions, skirting the northern PA of Grossberg which had been pulverized by German shells. German troops were also spotted climbing the hill's northern slope. 110 BCP was chosen to counter-attack. They moved up from Biding to the Grossberg and advanced on the Germans. The *chasseurs* were hit in the flank by automatic weapons fire, resulting in heavy casualties. Of the fifty-five men who started the attack, only eleven returned to Biding. Capt Derrien of CM/3 and several other officers of I/69 RMIF were killed. The Germans advanced and infiltrated to the rear of the French mortar positions. The remains of the French forces on Grossberg surrendered and the Germans moved on towards Biding.

The *Avancée de Barst-Cappel* encompassed two villages, Cappel, defended by CM/6 of II/82 RMIF Capt Doré) and Barst, defended by CM/7 (Capt Germain). It consisted of a large number of blockhouses and *abris de rondins*. Barst had four PAs and was more difficult to reduce:

- PA du Château (Adj Vignolles).
- PA de l'Eglise (Lt Schleiffen).
- PA du Verrou (S/Lt Weizorn) defended the flank of Barst.
- PA de l'Occident (Lt Maury) – covered the south-west.

When the German bombardment ceased III/272 IR (Major Löwrick) attacked Cappel. Twenty minutes later II/272 IR (Maj Wildermuth) attacked Barst. The PA of CM/6 was quickly reduced by the troops of III/272 IR. At 0930hrs the PA du Chemin-Creux near Barst came under attack. Despite a wire perimeter and machine guns the PA quickly fell. In less than two hours most of the Cappel position had fallen.

The Germans took advantage of the fog and smoke to move up two guns along the Marienthal road but they were spotted by observers of PA l'Eglise and chased off by grenades. Pak 37s fired on the shelters and blockhouses of Barst. Block C17's 25mm gun was taken out. The German attacks were ferocious. Individual squads launched attacks on the concrete which was pounded by artillery and Paks. The French fired magazine after magazine from their machine guns and emptied boxes of grenades. Barst was on fire and the Germans were in control of most of the village but they were held off by the PAs of l'Eglise and Occident. At noon, the Barst position continued to hold.

The village of Holving was located in the *Avancée de Moderbach* which ran along a crest protected by a dozen blockhouses including M118T-Holving Sud 1, an MOM infantry blockhouse with two tank turrets mounted on top. The bloc was surrounded by anti-tank rails and barbed wire sown with anti-personnel mines.

Casemate MC-24, SF Sarre. (NARA)

The fortified zone was defended by CM/9 of III/41 RMIC (Capt Courdavault). The blockhouses defended a glacis that rose gently to the crest towards the Bois de Wiederchen. The path to the top from the exit of the woods led up the slope. This was the path the Germans needed to take to capture the position and to do so they had to cross 800m of open space.

At 0630hrs the bombardment of the position began. All of the telephone lines were cut. At 0700hrs the bridge over the Moderbach between Holving and Hirbach was blown by the French. The Germans fired smoke shells and started their advance. Courdavault sensed correctly that German troops were advancing through the smoke and requested an artillery barrage along the glacis. By 0830hrs the Germans reached the anti-tank rails and attempted to work their way through the barrier. As they did so they were hit by machine-gun fire. To the south several Germans managed to break through and approach the blockhouses. French reserves launched a counter-attack. The Germans were pushed back and the French returned to their shelters. The shelling intensified and anti-tank guns took aim at the embrasures of the blocs. Blockhouse M12B-Holving Sud 6,[4] a shelter with two embrasures, was blown to pieces by a heavy shell. CM/9 took heavy casualties during the hour-long bombardment. The Germans moved out again in battalion strength along the glacis and reached the rails. The French couldn't believe their eyes. The Germans, obviously thinking the French positions were destroyed, advanced in thick formations towards the machine guns. The French waited until the Germans were within 500m and opened fire. The attackers panicked. Some of them turned around and headed to the woods for cover but they were 300m away and out in the open. Another group dove to the ground for cover. In as little as ten minutes the attack on Holving was broken up. To the north the Germans attacked II/41 RMIC at the Remering dyke, the only passage across the flooded ground. CM/7, commanded by Captain Raydelet, put up a strong fight and the Germans were blocked.

The Germans launched an attack north of the village of Puttelange, defended by CM/9 of III/174 RMIF. Blockhouse R4B for FM of Lt Tirbisch and two adjacent blocs guarded by a barbed wire belt and machine-gun blockhouses covered the Forbach road north of Puttelange and protected the *digue* [dyke] *de Loupershouse*, was attacked and damaged by Pak 37 shells coming from across the stream (*bief* [flood zone] *de Loupershouse*). The Germans did not press their attack and the bloc held off the German approach to the roadway.[5]

North-west of Puttelange the PA Confluent was defended by three blockhouses and an STG casemate. The Germans advanced in the smoke which blocked the view of the observers and the gunners in the blocs. The Germans set up a Pak 37 and fired on the embrasure of blockhouse C14, an infantry casemate guarding the road between Léning and Réning. As the smoke cleared the French in the PA fired machine guns at the Pak 37 and at a group of pioneers setting up a bridge to cross the Hostebach. Due to heavy losses to 222 IR the attack was called off. After the initial infantry attacks the Germans brought in air support and for several hours the Stukas attacked. The French had no anti-aircraft capability or air cover. Around 1800hrs the Germans launched another attack on Holving and heavy fighting took place until around 2030hrs. Once again the PA held.

The attack on Hoste-Bas was just as brutal. The objective was the *digue de Hoste-Bas*. The Germans attacked blockhouses C12B, R6B and MC8B.[6] Pak 37s caused heavy damage and the crews were forced to evacuate. Only M113N and C15N[7] on the *digue de Hoste-Bas* held out and the Germans moved on to attempt to cross the *Étang* [pond] *de Hoste-Bas* and *Hoste-Haut*. The passage between these two small lakes was blocked by barbed wire and mines and two blockhouses – R8B and M108N. The Germans set up anti-tank guns on the Cappel road to fire on the two blockhouses. Bloc R8B was heavily damaged and M108N, also called Calvaire 1, also took heavy damage.[8] Around 1030hrs a Stuka bomb hit R8B. German pioneers pushed towards the last obstacles. R8B continued to fight on but the crew was forced to surrender and the Germans moved on to the village of Hoste-Haut. Despite heavy pressure, the Germans were unable to break through SF Sarre until the morning of 15 June, reducing the holdout blocs one by one.

S/S Kalhausen was located on the right of SF Sarre and was under the command of 133 RIF. It included the Ouvrage du Haut-Poirier commanded by Captain Gambotti. He received a call from 133 RIF on 14 June at 1000hrs and learned the French had pulled back from the intervals. He was ordered to stay at his position and protect the movement of interval troops involved in the retreat and, most importantly, to hold the position to the limit of his means. Gambotti's men were pleased to learn they would not be forced to abandon Haut-Poirier. Morale was still good since they had a mission other than running away from the Germans. They were under no misconception how things would end. Haut-Poirier had no artillery support from any of its neighbours. The field artillery was gone. The fort was left with anti-tank guns and machine guns. However, events changed rapidly and so did the orders. On 15 June at 0330hrs Gambotti received a message from 133 RIF notifying him that on 17 June at 2200hrs he was to cease resistance of Haut-Poirier and the five adjacent casemates, at which time the crews were to rejoin 133 RIF at Sarre Union.

Based on the current situation with the fall of SF Sarre, it was most likely that this order could not be executed since the Germans were even now moving to the rear of the Maginot Line. Gambotti's escape route was cut. Would the Germans be content to wait for an armistice or launch an attack and suffer needless casualties since the war was, for all intents and purposes, over for the French? Sadly, the German generals chose the latter and lives were needlessly lost. This also gave the Maginot Line one last opportunity to demonstrate its capabilities.

The Maginot Line was now completely abandoned and in the process of being surrounded by German troops. Three-quarters of the personnel in place in early June were gone. Those left behind could only imagine their fate and what would happen in the coming days. Would it end quickly like the forts of Maubeuge or in agony like La Ferté? Would the forts be abandoned and sabotaged like SF Montmédy? Or would it be an 'obstinate struggle of long duration' that went on for weeks or months? The answer would be revealed in the days to come.

Chapter 11

The Remaining Sectors, 14 and 15 June 1940 – *Notre univers, c'est le béton*

In Ouvrage du Hochwald, Dr. Adrian described Commandant Rodolphe: 'He was cold and distant; sunken; pale; tears in his eyes. I was informed that our men were to form a marching division a few days from now after destroying our fortifications. Rodolphe stated that this decision was "demented".'[1] Lt Col Schwartz, the commander of SF Hagenau, remarked that he was 'hoping to play a less humiliating role at the end of his career'.[2]

On 14 June SF Haguenau received orders to resist in place until receipt of new orders. It was the strongest sector because it still had a large contingent of infantry. Each RIF left behind a battalion and 70 DI left troops from 81 BCP. Some 12,000 men remained, plus the three large artillery forts and forty casemates. The infantry remaining behind spread out in the evacuated zone to cover the approaches.

No enemy artillery fire took place on 14 June but a large group of aircraft passed from east to west, returning ninety minutes later. Around midnight the Luftwaffe was flying reconnaissance behind the SF Haguenau, observing troop movements at Haguenau and Walbourg.

The most forward line of the sector's *Points d'appui* (PA) and APs followed a line west to east:

- Ferme de Boesch to north of Climbach.
- Route de Climbach to Col du Pigonnier.
- Forest house of Scherhol.
- Hill 276.
- Crest of Geisberg, hamlet of Geitershof.
- Blockhouses of Oberseebach, crests west of the village, blockhouse of Trimbach, then north of Hill 194 and village of Eberbach to the Seltz and Rhine.
- The right bank of the Rhine was held by the casemates on the banks and several strongpoints to their junction with SF Bas Rhin.

The Germans had not yet made contact with the sector APs. German patrols knew the Line very well by now but their movement was kept hidden from French observers in the Forêt de Mundat and the north-south ravines between Schleithal and Lauterbourg.

On 14 June at Casemate C24 in SF Crusnes, the armoured door of the casemate banging shut, sounded like a gong. The men wondered when it would open again. When would they see the outside except through the tiny opening of the embrasure or through the lens of a periscope or episcope? When would they again breathe fresh air? The isolation of the casemate was now complete. Behind there was nothing moving in the line of trenches and dozens of blockhouses that could now be used by the enemy. There was fifteen days of food remaining that had to be made to last for forty-five.

A group of Germans was spotted: 'Alert, alert … 1201 – Group of enemy infantry – *Gisement* 402… Site-4, Front 30 – Depth 3 – K2 *plus haut* 2.' A few seconds later: '1202 – Group of German infantry – *Gisement* 719 – Site-9 – Front 20 – Depth 0.4 – Edge of B.I'.[3]

In the casemate's gun chamber the 47mm gun was retracted and replaced by JM#2. Guéran, with his eye on the JM's scope, swept the terrain. Reinal, on the other set of twin guns (JM#1), nicknamed '*Lucienne*' and '*Nicole*', waited. Deloor and the Renaud brothers readied the replacement magazines. Chef Sartel was sitting at a small table in the chamber examining the fire plan. Masson climbed into the cloche VP and spotted the targets. 'What is Bréhain waiting for?' he thought to himself. A group of about 100 enemy troops was only 800m from C24. A second group was 1,500m away, leaving the Bois de Butte near C26 (Casemate Nouveau-Crusnes Ouest). The reason for the hesitation was that C26 was hidden from view and no one knew for sure what was going on over the hill.[4]

The turrets of Bréhain were heard firing in another direction. The periscope was replaced with a Type 'N'.[5] Masson spotted a helmeted German in shirtsleeves on the top of K2, looking through binoculars in the direction of C24. A machine gun

Casemate de Route d'Ottange in SF Crusnes. The casemate bears a small sign on the right identifying this as Panzerwerk 388. The Germans assigned their own system of identification numbers to the Maginot Line works. (Marc Romanych)

was heard and the man dropped the binoculars and disappeared, or fell, behind the slope, condition unknown. The machine gun belonged to C25 (Casemate Crusnes Est). Sartel was ordered to the cloche GFM to man the 50mm mortar. When the first group reached H2, he was to open fire while C25 fired its JM.

Vuillemard phoned the SRA of Bréhain: '1203 – second group is stopped – *gisement* 734 – site-8 – front 10 – depth 0.5 – on R.17.

A minute passed and the turrets open fire. The enemy appeared on hill K2. C24 could only see their helmets. SRA: 'Bloc 4 for 1203 – length of trajectory – 11 seconds – *coup parti*!' The Germans were pinned down by Bloc 4, the mortar of C24 and the JM of C25. The 75mm turret covered R17. The MG and mortar covered K2 and K3. The two groups of Germans then headed for the cover of the woods.

The orders to the *Ensemble de Bitche* were the same as SF Haguenau – head south but wait for orders after destruction of arms and munitions. 'Do not execute but prepare to do so' (Lescanne – LVIII Corps). At Ouvrage du Welschoff Capt Lhuisset did not take the evacuation order seriously. It couldn't possibly be authentic, but it was. The idea of sabotage was unbelievable. Lhuisset read the order to his staff. Lt Haite did not want to share it with the staff for morale purposes but felt it should be discussed with the staff over at Haut-Poirier. The neighbouring ouvrage was under separate jurisdiction. If Haut-Poirier's evacuation timing was different, it might very well put Welschoff in danger of having no flanking support.[6]

Lt Caraman, chief engineer of Welschoff, was sent to Haut-Poirier to confer with Captain Gambotti and Commandant Jolivet. The latter revealed that they were ordered to sabotage the ouvrage and casemates by 17 June at 2200hrs and then head to the south. Caraman was shown the order from Condé. It read: 'The mission of the crews of Haut-Poirier and the five casemates of the sub-sector ceases 17 June at 2200hrs. At this date, the crews will join the regiment on the axis Sarre-Union – Fénétrange.' (Colonel Bertrand, Commander 133 RIF). Thus, it was confirmed that Welschoff would have no flanking protection after 17 June.

The imminent fall of SF Sarre would leave a 30km gap between the ouvrages of Haut-Poirier and Téting, a gap through which the Germans were advancing in force. By the time Gambotti's crew destroyed the fort and marched away on 17 June they would most likely be cut off. Commandant Jolivet had shown up on the doorstep of Haut-Poirier in the afternoon of 14 June with orders in hand announcing he was in charge of the '*Groupement Haut-Poirier*', that included the ouvrage itself and five adjacent casemates: Wittring, Grand-Bois, Achen Nord-Ouest, Achen Nord and Achen Nord-Est. Just exactly why Jolivet was placed in charge was a mystery to the men. He had no technical knowledge of the workings of the ouvrages.[7] The officers, speaking discreetly amongst themselves, agreed to follow his orders, but if he put the crew in danger they would go behind his back.

On 15 June engineers began working on the destruction of the casemates and ouvrages of *Groupement Haut-Poirier*. The plan was to link the explosives by wire to an electrical detonator and blow up all the blocs and tunnels at once. The engineers would booby-trap the main armoured door to go off upon arrival of the Germans.

Interval troops left SF Faulquemont on the night of 13/14 June. As of the 14th no orders had arrived for the crews of the ouvrages adjacent to SF Sarre who assumed they would be following the same action as the other sectors. They hoped to be able to remain where they were, simply because they were trained to fight from the fortress, not in the open field. (*Notre univers, c'est le béton*).

Commandant Denoix was placed in charge of SF Faulquemont. He was responsible for forming the marching divisions and supervising the destruction and abandonment of the Maginot Line. Denoix set up his PC at Laudrefang.

Around 15 June the ouvrages of SF Faulquemont received specific instructions regarding the destruction of equipment:

- JM – remove the latch (*système de fermeture*) and the gas cylinder and then break the gun into pieces including the viewing scope.
- 47mm – Remove the breech, break the gas tube and destroy the pointing system.
- Upon abandonment, destroy the equipment inside the cloches and the turrets.
- Break up the turret controls and break the counterweight loose so it falls into the ditch. Finally, sabotage the lift by cutting the cable.
- Before leaving the ouvrage, sabotage the doors and firewall, block them open and set fire to the diesel fuel.

In the evening of 15 June SF Faulquemont lost its *Voltigeurs* (skirmish units), as well as the crews of the casemates, who were not under the command of the sector. This included Casemates Bambiderstoff Nord and Sud, Quatre-Vents Sud and Nord and Laudrefang. This was the only sector set up in this manner. The officers of Laudrefang made their objections known to Denoix, arguing that the casemates were an extension of their defences. After some discussion Denoix allowed a small force to occupy the casemate of Quatre-Vents Sud to cover the Saint-Avold–Faulquemont road. Unfortunately, the previous occupants had been given the order to sabotage the casemates. Everything inside the casemate was broken up and soaked with diesel fuel. The food supplies were brought out, broken open and dumped into the ditch where they were doused with diesel. Dossiers and plans were burned. However, Bambi Nord was the only place where the fuel was set on fire, lighting up the night sky for miles around.

On the evening of 15 June twenty-two men left Laudrefang to occupy Quatre-Vents Sud. Except for this casemate the destruction continued. Weapons were sabotaged, ammunition tossed into the well, breeches removed, lunettes cracked. At night, the crews headed south to join the rest of the army.

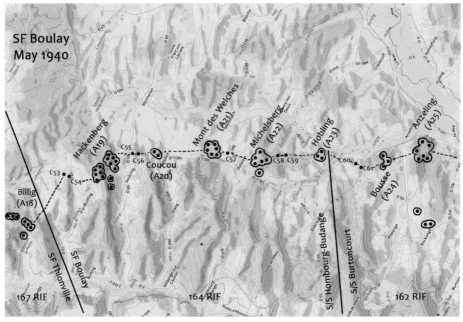

SF Boulay, one of the most powerful sectors of the Maginot Line. (OpenStreetMap)

SF Boulay was the most powerful sector of the Line. It included the following:

(A – Ouvrage; C – Casemate; O – Observatory; X – Shelter)
S/S Hombourg Budange: 164 RIF (Commandant Orgebin as of June 1940):

- X20 – Hummersberg; C53 – Hummersberg Nord; C54 – Hummersberg Sud.
- A19 – Hackenberg (Chef d'Escadron Ébrard then Chef de Bataillon Ismeur as of 13 June 1940).
- C55 – Veckring Nord; C56 – Veckring Sud; X21 – Veckring.
- A20 – Ouvrage du Coucou (Captain Roques).
- X22 – Coucou; O4 – Chênes-Brûlés; X23 – Chênes-Brûlés; X24 – Klang; X25 – Mont des Welches.
- A21 – Mont des Welches (Chef de Bataillon Tari).
- C57 – Menskirch; Bb44 – STG Blockhouse.
- A22 – Ouvrage du Michelsberg (Commandant Pelletier).
- Bb43 – STG Blockhouse; X26 – Bilmette; C58 – Huberbusch Nord; C59 – Huberbusch Sud; X28 – Ising.
- A23 – Ouvrage du Hobling (Captain Boileau).

S/S Burtoncourt: 162 RIF (Lt-Col Sohier):

- C60 – Edling Nord; C61 – Edling Sud; X29 – Hestroff; O10 – Hestroff; X30 – Rotherberg.

- A24 – Ouvrage de Bousse (Captain Ramaud).
- A25 – Ouvrage d'Anzeling (Commandant Guillebot).
- A26 – Ouvrage de Bérenbach (Captain Ramaud).
- X31 – Bockange; X32 – Gomelange; X33 – Colming.

S/S Tromborn: 161 RIF (Lt-Col Viret):

- C62 – Éblange.
- A27 – Ouvrage du Bovenberg (Lt Lambret).
- BCa2 – RFM Casemate Bovenberg; C63 – Langhep Nord; C64 – Langhep Sud; BCa1 – RFB Casemate Ottonville.
- A28 – Ouvrage du Denting (Captain Coste).
- A29 – Ouvrage du Village de Coume (Lt Lussus).
- A30 – Ouvrage Annexe Nord de Coume (Sub-Lt Dillenschneider as of 9 June 1940).

S/S Narbéfontaine: 160 RIF (Lt-Col Bouet):

- A31 – Ouvrage du Coume (Lt Soubrier).
- A32 – Ouvrage Annexe Sud de Coume (Captain Faucoulanche).
- C65 – Bisterberg Nord I; C66 – Bisterberg Nord II; C67 – Bisterberg Sud III; C68 – Bisterberg Sud IV.
- A33 – Ouvrage du Mottenberg (Captain Cloarec).
- C69 – Sud du Mottenberg.

German troops inspect Bloc 24 of Ouvrage du Hackenberg. Bloc 25 and the anti-tank ditch can be seen in the background. (Bundesarchiv)

The sector's disposition was assigned to Colonel Raoul Cochinard. His orders included three steps similar to the other sectors:

- Measure A – *Voltigeurs* and crews in the small interval blockhouses to evacuate Saturday, 15 June 2200hrs. Casemate crews to remain in place.
- Measure B – Positional artillery – withdraw in two steps – 120mm battalions (50 men), S/S Hombourg-Budange to depart 15 June at 2200hrs with 250 infantrymen commanded by Lt Olive. The following day 400 artillerymen of the nine positional batteries (five batteries of 155mm (II/153 RAF), one 240mm (I/153) and three batteries of 155mm (III/153)) to sabotage their equipment and form up under Capt Delpartive of II/153 RAF.
- Measure C – Fortress crews to depart Monday, 17 June at 2200hrs, leaving behind a small element to slow the Germans and another small group to complete the sabotage. They were scheduled to leave 18 June at 0400.

The crews of the Maginot Line in SF Boulay were also to be organized, or transformed, into DM. The DM Order of Hackenberg was set up as follows:

- Out of forty-three officers, 122 NCOs and 854 men – two infantry companies under Lt Barbelin and Lt Chauvay; two artillery companies under Capt Graïset and Lt Dupont; one company of sappers under Capt Voyen.
- The men to bring a three-day supply of food, 50,000 rounds of ammunition, two FM per company.
- The delaying force was placed under Captain Julien Combemord. Comprised of a small force of men – crews from the cloches and turrets – to destroy the munitions. A group of sappers of Capt Leviche to place explosive charges.

There was a major problem when troops attempted to move to the rear. On the night of 14/15 June, French engineers (sappers) blew up the munitions and fuel depots to the rear, drawing German attention. Plus, all of the bridges over the rivers (Canner, Nied Allemand, Nied Français) had been destroyed.

Meanwhile, the Germans remained active. On 15 June at 2200hrs, German patrols, possibly alerted by the detonations at the depots, were spotted by observers at Michelsberg attempting to approach the ouvrage entrances. The 75mm turrets chased them off. Captain de Saint-Sauveur, artillery commander of Michelsberg, called to discuss reciprocal support fire with Captain Gaston Salomon, his counterpart at Anzeling. Salomon surprisingly replied that they were in the process of burning their munitions and target plotting documents, so reciprocal support would be rather difficult. This event showed that the sector was in a state of complete confusion, disarray and misunderstood orders. Saint-Sauveur had to be wondering if Measure C was underway early and perhaps he had missed something. He contacted Chef d'Escadron Ébrand at Hackenberg to try to find out what was going on. He was told Measure C was still on schedule for 17 June at 2200hrs.

At PO Hobling, Captain Boileau received an order from Commandant Pelletier of Michelsberg to prepare to depart and for sabotage. Boileau, surprised by the order, contacted Chef de Bataillon Tari, commander of Ouvrage du Mont des Welches, to see if he had received the same order from Pelletier. Tari couldn't believe what he was hearing and confided to Boileau that nothing had changed and Measure C was still scheduled for Monday. Boileau informed his adjutant, Lt Blangille, to tell the men that they were now not leaving – it was a false alert and to put the ouvrage back in a state of defence. Word arrived too late at PO Bois de Bousse. The commander, Captain Ramaud, gave the order to the crew to depart. The equipment was broken up and the breeches dropped into the latrines. Bousse ceased to function as a weapon of war. Meanwhile, Pelletier contacted Ébrand at Hackenberg and finally understood that the departure order was only intended for the *Voltigeurs*. The crews were not to leave until Monday. Pelletier passed this news on to Saint-Sauveur, just in time – in fifteen minutes the turrets were to be destroyed.

Throughout the ouvrages, men went to work to fix the damage, removing charges and salvaging documents. The crew of Bousse marched off to the rear, their destination Château d'Orville. On 18 June, they were captured by the Germans 40km behind the Maginot Line.

SF Thionville

SF Thionville was the most powerful sector of the Maginot Line, with 6,000 men and eleven ouvrages, seven of which were equipped with artillery. It included the following:

(A – Ouvrage; C – Casemate; O – Observatory; X – Shelter)
S/S Angevillers: 169 RIF (Chef de Bataillon Toussaint):

- A8 – Ouvrage de Rochonvillers (Chef d'Escadron Guillemain).
- C36 – Grand Lot; X2 – Grand Lot; C37 – Escherange Ouest; C38 – Escherange Est; C39 – Petersberg Ouest; C40 – Petersberg Est; X3 – Bois d'Escherange; X4 – Petersberg.
- A9 – Ouvrage de Molvange (Commandant Justamon).
- C41 – Entrange; X5 – Bois de Kanfen; C42 – Bois de Kanfen Ouest; C43 – Bois de Kanfen Est; X6 – Zeiterholz.

S/S Hettange-Grande: 168 RIF (Lt-Col Ferroni):

- X7 – Stressling.
- A10 – Immerhof (Captain Requiston).

- X8 – Hettange; O9 – Hettange; X9 – Route du Luxembourg; O10 – Route du Luxembourg; X10 – Helmerich.
- A11 – Ouvrage de Soetrich (Commandant Henger).
- O13 – Boust; C44 – Boust; X11 – Barrunshof.
- A12 – Ouvrage de Bois-Karre.
- X12 – Bois-Karre; C45 – Basse-Parthe Ouest; C46 – Basse-Parthe Est; X13 – Rippert; X14 – Bois-de-Cattenom.
- A13 – Ouvrage du Kobenbusch (Commandant Charnal).
- A14 – Ouvrage d'Oberheide (Lt Pobeau).
- O20 – Cattenom; C47 – Sonnenberg.
- A15 – Galgenberg (Captain de la Teysnonnière).
- A6 – Ouvrage de Sentzich (Lt Langrand).
- Cb8 – Sentzich; C8 – Koenigsmacker Nord; C9 – Koenigsmacker Sud; C50 Métrich Nord; C41 – Métrich Sud; X15 – Krekelbusch.
- A17 – Ouvrage du Métrich (Chef de Bataillon Lauga).
- X16 – Sud de Métrich; X17 – Nonnenberg; X18 – Nord du Bichel; C52 – Bois de Koenigsmacker; X19 – Sud du Bichel.
- A18 – Ouvrage du Billig (Commandant Roy).

Colonel Jean-Patrice O'Sullivan, an infantryman, was left in charge of the evacuation of SF Thionville. His command post was at Fort d'Illange in Thionville, a former German fort built in the early 1900s. Two-thirds of the sector's casemate crews were ordered to remain in place, the remainder to be evacuated. Measure B called for evacuation of the positional artillery and Measure C the crews of the ouvrages. There was far too much ammunition to destroy without drawing the attention of the Germans. Therefore, modifications had been made to Measure C. It would be split into two parts:

1. 17 June, 2200hrs – departure of the Gros Ouvrages. A small contingent to be left back until 18 June at 2200hrs to cover the departing troops.
2. 18 June at 2200hrs – after destroying the armaments and if possible the munitions, the stragglers could move at liberty

SF Crusnes

In SF Crusnes the casemates of S/S Marville and Montmédy had been sabotaged a few days earlier. General Renondeau left no one in charge of the men like in the other sectors. As a result, there was no plan for evacuation and instead there was confusion as to who was in charge. Commandant Pophillat of Latiremont was the ranking officer and he took charge of the S/S of the 149 RIF while Commandant Vanier of Bréhain took that of 128 and 139 RIF. The only orders the commanders had received so far were to defend in place. 128 RIF's orders were to hold until munitions and supplies ran out. Pophillat's orders to his men were to bar the road to a German advance.

Captain Daniel Aubert of Fermont had the same understanding. Fermont and its neighbours were to defend until supplies and munitions were exhausted and hold out as long as possible. Lt Thibeau of PO Chappy ordered his engineers to prepare a destruction plan, just in case. However, the order to evacuate never arrived.

Meanwhile the Germans were considering what to do with the Maginot Line. As of 12 June, they were in a wait-and-see posture. They knew about the French withdrawal south of the Meuse and the withdrawal of Freydenberg's Second Army on 11 June. But what about the Maginot Line? They had discovered on 11 June that the Montmédy sector fortifications had been vacated. The Germans suspected similar action would follow along the entire Line. They planned two operations accordingly, the selection of which depended on what action was taken by the fortress troops:

- Operation Steinschlag – If the troops of the Maginot Line pulled out and left a weak force in place the Germans would attack and break through the Line.
- Operation Lawine (Avalanche) – If the Maginot Line was completely evacuated the Germans would pursue fleeing French forces.

Either operation would take place on 14 June with 24-hour warning and consist of a two-pronged attack:

- 162 ID (General Franke) to send one regiment between PO Mauvais Bois and PO Bois-du-Four, while 329 IR (Oberst Hühner) attacked Ouvrage du Bréhain.
- 161 ID (General Wilck) with one regiment to attack the Bois de Kanfen in the direction of Hettange-Grande – the passage between Molvange and Soetrich.

Neither operation was supported by heavy artillery or aircraft, revealing a gross underestimation of the defensive capabilities of the fortresses. In all likelihood, the Germans would suffer heavy casualties from the Maginot Line's guns.

Early on 14 June General Kaupisch[8] (Höheres Kommando XXXI[9]) was informed by Oberleutnant von Hammerstein of 162 ID that it appeared the French were abandoning the Maginot Line. Patrols from 183 ID confirmed this in their own report of the movement of trucks behind the Line followed by explosions. General Kaupisch agreed with these assessments that an evacuation was taking place. These reports were not a surprise. To the west the Marville and Montmédy sectors were completely empty of French troops and the ouvrages and casemates were destroyed and abandoned. 183 ID sent a patrol out of Longwy towards Longuyon which encountered no resistance. This caused General Kaupisch to change his plans and order an encirclement of the Line from the west. However, the reports were inaccurate. In reality the ouvrages were still occupied and automatic weapons and artillery fire was still being heard. This part of the story did not reach Kaupisch. On 14 June 183 ID moved out along the RN18 towards the Maginot Line.

On 15 June at 0400hrs the seemingly endless 183 ID convoy was spotted by an observer in the Casemate de l'Ermitage.[10] Lt Riotte, commander of the casemate, looked for himself and could see a line of motorcycles, cavalry, trucks and artillery pieces, headed for Longuyon. Other observers in SF Crusnes reported the convoy and the 75mm turret at Fermont's Bloc 1 prepared to fire. From Lt Émile Delhaye's Bloc 3 it was possible to see the top of the Ossuary of Douaumont 40km away and some features of Longwy 15km to the north. But his periscope was at that moment fixed on the Germans. The location of the target was plotted and quickly passed to Bloc 1's Maréchal de Logis Chef Bogaert. The two 75mm barrels opened fire with high-explosive rounds at maximum cadence. The inside of the turret became hot as a furnace as the shells were loaded non-stop into each gun as fast as they could be brought up the hoist from below. Target after target on the RN18 was hit. The turret was retracted to cool the guns and to check the calibrations, giving the Germans time to regroup the convoy. The turret was raised again and the guns opened fire. By the end of the day the Germans had given up their plans to travel on the RN18 and sought alternate routes on the back roads, out of the range of Bloc 1.

Around 1500hrs a group of heavier horse-drawn artillery was spotted travelling along the Plateau de Noërs, south-west of Longuyon by observers at Casemate de Puxieux. The French guns once again zeroed in, hitting several vehicles, and the convoy dispersed.

Further east, 162 ID was ordered to march on a north-south axis that would take it between Latiremont and Bréhain. This decision was made in the belief

The gun chamber of a 75mm Model 1933 turret. The two guns are right and left, the directional controls in the centre underneath the arched gun carriage. (Hans Vermeulen)

that the westernmost position of the Maginot Line was being silenced by 183 ID. But it was quickly evident that the Maginot Line was active and powerful. The movement to outflank the Line via Longuyon had turned into a disaster.

On 16 June at 1530hrs General Franke sent an emissary to the burned-out Hirps Farm north of PO Aumetz. Commandant Vanier of Bréhain was notified and sent a few men to meet with the Germans. A message was handed to Lt Dars, commander of Casemate du Réservoir, which he took to Commandant Vanier. The memo outlined the strategic and tactical situation and suggested the ouvrages be evacuated. Vanier was given three hours to respond. That same evening General Wilck's 161 ID was marching around 183 ID to move up behind SF Crusnes.

SF Boulay – 15 June

In SF Boulay, General Sixt von Arnim, commander of 95 ID, and General Vogl of 167 ID sent patrols towards the Maginot Line to see how they would react. At 0700hrs on 15 June the Germans occupied Lemestroff between Billig and Hackenberg. The two forts had enough firepower to turn the village into a crater but the task was left to Billig. The crews fired 75mm and 135mm guns to clear out the German camp. At 1030hrs a column of motorized artillery was spotted at Bouzonville by observers at Michelsberg, heading towards Freistroff. Bloc 5's 75mm turret guns pounded the road. Afterwards the Germans took no chances and the roads in the sector were deserted.

A German patrol approached the PO Annexe Sud de Coume. The crew of the fort had worked over the winter to clear the nearby woods but the Germans managed to move up to where they were only 100m away. They took cover in the trees and as they approached Bloc 1 they were chased off by FM fire. The crews at Hobling and Kerfent also exchanged fire with German patrols.

SF Faulquemont – 15 June

95 ID passed through the Sarre Gap and moved up behind SF Faulquemont. On 16 June Captain Denoix at Laudrefang was informed that elements of 95 ID were at Mainvillers, 10km to the rear. A bit later a report came in that German cavalry were moving along the Redlach-Tritteling road, 4km behind the ouvrage. It appeared, at least for the men of SF Faulquemont, that the sabotage and withdrawal from the Line was now, by force of circumstance, cancelled.

Across the Sarre gap, Captain Gambotti was worried about being cut off. He sent out a few small patrols which encountered the Germans at Diemeringen, 15km away. Gambotti asked Jolivet: if the Germans were 15km away now, where will they be on the night of 17 June at 2200hrs? It was clear to him as well that there would be no evacuation.

SF Rohrbach – 15 June

SF Rohrbach was a powerful sector that included the following defences:

S/S Bining: 166 RIF (Lt-Col Subervie), with troops of 2 CEC (Captain Jouhanet), included the following:

- CORF casemates: Ouest de Singling, Nord-Ouest de Singling Gauche, Nord-Ouest de Singling Droite.
- 240 – Ouvrage du Welschof (Captain Lhuisset).
- CORF casemate Bining.
- 250 – Ouvrage de Rohrbach (Captain de Saint-Ferjeux).
- CORF casemates: Station de Rohrbach, Rohrbach.

S/S de Légeret: 153 RIF (Lt-Col Mauvin), with troops of 3 CEC of SF Rohrbach (Capt Stern):

- CORF casemates: Sinnerberg Ouest, Sinnerberg Est, Petit-Réderching Ouest, Petit-Réderching Est, Petit-Réderching, Seelberg Ouest, Seelberg Est, Judenhoff, Fröhmüle, Holbach.
- 300 – Ouvrage du Simserhof (Lt-Col Bonlarron).
- Casemate Légeret, Abri Légeret, Observatoire Freudenberg, Abri Freudenberg, Casemate Freudenberg, Abri Reyersviller.
- Advance Posts of Bettviller, Hoelling, Welschof/Kappellenhoff, Bitcherberg.
- MF Schweyen.

S/S Bitche: 37 RIF (Lt-Col Combet), with 1 CEC of SF Vosges:

- 350 – Ouvrage du Schiesseck (Chef de Bataillon Stoquer).
- Casemate Ramstein Ouest, Casemate Ramstein Est, Observatoire de la Citadelle.
- 400 – Ouvrage d'Otterbiel (Captain Le Glaunec).
- Casemates Champ d'Aviation Ouest, Champ d'Aviation Est, Abri Kindelberg, Casemates Rochat Ouest, Rochat Est, Petit-Hohékirkel, Grand-Hohékirkel Ouest, Grand-Hohékirkel Est, Abri Le Camp.

On the afternoon of 15 June Captain de Saint-Ferjeux of PO Rohrbach was ordered to make contact with the APs of Guising and Olferdingerhof. Two patrols were sent out to them. The patrol to Guising returned two hours later but the men sent to Olferdingerhof were overdue. While observers in Bloc 1 searched for the men they heard rifle fire. Fifteen minutes later two of the men from the patrol returned. They had been ambushed by the Germans. Two men were dead, one wounded and one captured. To make matters worse, the Germans came into possession of the evacuation order for the APs to take place on the evening of 15 June. This information was passed on to 262 ID. That same evening the APs came under heavy attack, perhaps because the Germans knew the troops were pulling back and the men were trapped. The APs were saved by the heavy guns of Simserhof and Schiesseck and the crews made a successful getaway. The Germans attacked the APs at Gros-Rederching in front of PO Welschoff. During the night, the men of the APs there broke out in small groups and headed south to join up with 166 RIF.

SF Haguenau

Lt Col Schwartz, commander of SF Haguenau, realized on 15 June that there would be no retreat or sabotage in his sector. He received a message from Fifth Army headquarters – General Bourret – warning of a possible attack from the rear. The new mission of SF Haguenau was to hold in place and to pin down German forces as long as possible and to cover the rear of the main army. No troops or materials currently in the fortified position were to be moved. Schwartz was thus tasked with fixing as many German units as possible in the north-east: 12,000 men against 60,000 and fortifications too numerous to fully occupy. A proposal to abandon and destroy the blockhouses and shorten the defensive line was made impossible by a German dawn attack by 264 ID (General Eric Danëcke) on the Line of advanced posts held by 79 RIF and 23 RIF.

AP 7, commanded by Sub/Lt Paul Mayer, was attacked at 0230hrs on 15 June. Mayer fired green and red signal flares to alert the Oberroedern sector of the attack. AP 7 was the closest to the line of casemates and was defended by two Hotchkiss machine guns. Mayer called AP 8 and 9, located along the Seebach Valley, but there was no response. Suddenly German infantry appeared, heading towards AP 7 from the direction of AP 8. Mayer's two machine guns opened fire. The guns fired so many rounds they overheated and had to be cooled down. Mayer called for reinforcements but it was apparent the entire line was under attack. He then called the observer at Casemate Bois d'Hoffen to give him the location of the Germans. A moment later the 75mm turret gun of Schoenenbourg's Bloc 3 opened fire on AP 8 and the Germans fell back.

Further east at Ebenbach, the blockhouses of 23 RIF came under heavy fire and the French were forced to pull back or be killed. The blockhouses to the north of Oberseebach were hit by Pak 37s. In response, Hochwald's Block 7bis, commanded by Lt Henri Anglès, fired forty shots and the assault was stopped. By 0700hrs the shelling in the vicinity of Geitershof was fierce. German wounded lay all around in front of the barbed wire. Meanwhile the Germans reappeared at Aschbach to the rear of Mayer's PA and he requested another round of artillery support in the direction of PA 8. This time the three 75mm casemate guns in Hochwald's Bloc 6 opened fire.

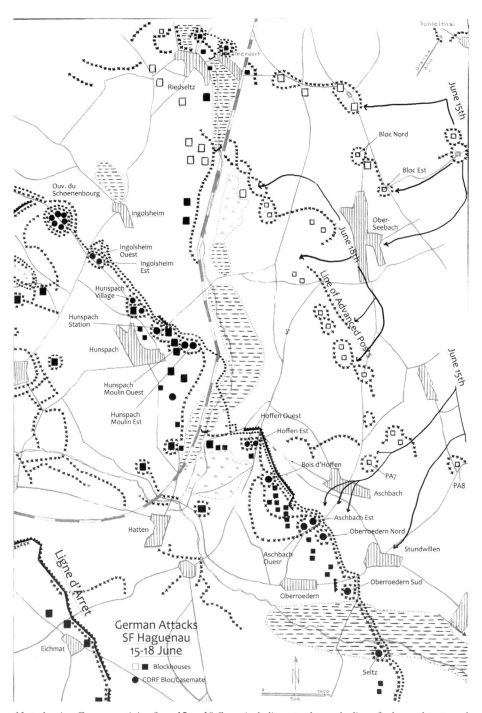

Map showing German activity from 15 to 18 June, including attacks on the line of advanced posts and the casemates in the Hoffen–Aschbach–Oberroedern sectors. (Deutsche Angriffe Gegen Staendige und Verstaerkte Feldmaessige Befestigungsanlagen in Zweiten Weltkrieg)

Near Trimbach, AP 10, 11 and 11bis were attacked from three sides. Lt Jung, chief of AP 11 and also chief of the group of APs under the command of 79 RIF, telephoned Captain Quinet at 4 CEC headquarters to say he could not hold much longer. His guns were running out of ammunition and he was in danger of being surrounded. He asked Quinet to fire a white flare at 1700hrs if Quinet believed that Jung should evacuate with his men. After 1700hrs he estimated they would run out of ammunition. Commandant Henry of I/79 RIF ordered the men to resist and the flare was never launched. The men of AP 10 and 11 held until 1830hrs then surrendered. Lt Schaal's men escaped from PA11bis. Near PA 7, 246 ID's advance was halted. Hochwald and Schoenenbourg together fired 5,200 rounds on the Seebach Valley.

German attacks continued the following day. The guns of the ouvrages, in particular of Lt Anglès's Bloc 7bis and the 135mm turret of Sub-Lt Coquard in Bloc 1, fired in salvoes of six to ten shots. Schoenenbourg's two 75mm turrets in Blocs 3 and 4 also contributed. German attacks were heavy against Oberseebach but so were their casualties.

Here is an account of the 15 June action from Rodolphe's viewpoint:

A series of bombardments were executed between 0300hrs and 0400hrs: Schoenenbourg fired forty shots on the north-east exits of Wissembourg and forty shots on the passage above Altenstadt. From 0250hrs support fire was provided for AP Geisberg.

German artillery opened fire at 0300hrs, concentrating on S/S Hoffen, causing many fires in the villages, especially Aschbach. After the bombardment, the Germans attacked the advanced posts where a small number of men occupied positions meant for a company and that were very difficult to protect. AP 8 and AP 9 were attacked from all sides and the French were pushed out. The Germans poured through the

The Artillery Command Post of Ouvrage du Hackenberg, sometime in 1939. (Jean-Yves Mary)

breach and moved out to surround the neighbouring APs. At 0448hrs Schoenenbourg poured supporting fire on AP 7. Eighty shots from Bloc 3 caused the Germans to halt their attack, but it continued along the Line from Riedseltz to the Rhine.

At 0500hrs Blockhouse Obserseebach called for artillery support. Fifteen minutes later, one hundred shots were fired to the north and north-east of Geitershof in relief. One by one the defenders called for help. The Germans now moved through the breach between AP 8 and 9 to the east of Aschbach towards Stundwiller. The main German effort was the attack on AP 7. Around 0830hrs the Germans entered within range of Hochwald's Bloc 6. At 0838hrs the infantry in the blocs at Trimbach (including AP 10) were holding their position and Germans were being cut down in front of the barbed wire. At 0840hrs S/S Hoffen reported an attack on blockhouse Obserseebach Est and fifty shots from Bloc 7bis chased off the Germans. At 0845hrs Geitershof was occupied by the enemy and support was requested. Bloc 7bis fired eighty shots and the Germans were chased out with several casualties. Around the same time Schoenenbourg fired on AP 8 and 9 where Obs 03 spotted Germans moving for an attack on AP 7.

At 0858hrs Obs 07 spotted German shelling coming from Ferme Fronackerhof. It is from here that attacks were being launched on Obserseebach. The farm was within enemy lines. Hochwald's Bloc 6 fired one hundred shots south of Obserseebach where the Germans were looking for a path to the north to surround Blockhouse Obserseebach Est. At 0930hrs the Germans attacked the blockhouse with a Pak 37, firing at the embrasure and killing Adjutant Chef Dagrenat. The French evacuated the bloc and fell back on AP 2 south-west of the village. This news was related to the Group Commander by the PC of S/S Hoffen, who decided to counter-attack.

East of Trimbach, the crew of PA 11bis, which assured liaison with the APs of 23 IR, were forced to retreat as their flanks were exposed by the pulling back of neighbouring units. The Germans captured the village of Eberbach and reached Hill 194, which serves as a magnificent observatory across the French lines. Only S5 could reach the area and fired 140 shots, causing the Germans to go for cover. To bolster artillery support, the group commander ordered one of S1's guns turned east in order to be able to hit Obserseebach.

For the next couple of hours, the ouvrages and 120L sections fired on Blockhouse Obserseebach Est, which is still occupied by the Germans. The counter-attack to recapture the blockhouse got underway. Schoenenbourg supported it along with Hochwald's Bloc 7bis. At 1318hrs three turrets fired eighty shots each and the bloc was recaptured by a Sergeant and six men. The Germans pulled back to the east and dug trenches.

From Anspach, now occupied by the Germans, an attempt was made to surround AP 7 from the south. A German machine gun was set up in the bell tower of Anspach to support the attack but Schoenenbourg fired fifty shots and knocked it out. The Germans reinforced Obserseebach. PC 141b requested support against the German infantry closing in on Aschbach from the Seebach valley. Two turrets from Schoenenbourg fired one hundred shrapnel rounds. At 1830hrs an attack was launched on AP 7 from the north-east along a sunken road, followed by an attack from the south where reinforcements were still pouring into Anspach. 150 rounds of 75mm and 120mm held the Germans back. At 1800hrs AP 10 and 11 of Trimbach ceased combat – they ran out of ammunition. They held out all day long against continuous attacks, causing heavy German losses and delaying their movement to the south. All night long Schoenenbourg's turrets fired in support of AP 7. A total of 5,200 shots were fired on 15 June

The main German objective was the salient that made up the Line at Oberroedern where French artillery support was difficult. They launched very strong attacks against a weak defence but only made minor gains with heavy losses. No night attacks were launched and they took the time to regroup.

The French put up a very vigorous resistance. The effort of the gunners was excellent, especially at Schoenenbourg. The guns provided precise, rapid fire and excellent support to French troops under a withering German attack. The gunners worked shirtless in the stifling furnace of the gun chambers, with a hot sun beating down on the metal. Morale was excellent. The garrison sensed that a decisive battle had begun and no help was coming from the outside.

15 June – SF Crusnes – C24

The departure of the interval troops made the observers' task more difficult. Now they not only had to keep watch in advance of the Line but also to the rear. Night was the worst. It could hide the descent of paratroops or pioneers moving towards the rails and possible capture from behind. The observers in the cloche were always in pairs, moving between the view port and the periscope and always listening. Meals were now rationed and consisted of two-thirds of a tin of corned beef (*boite de singe*), a tin and a half of tuna, or two-thirds of a tin of sardines, fourteen biscuits and a spoonful of jam. The evening meal was a thick soup made from concentrated tablets. To drink: a quarter-litre of wine or demi-quart of Eau-de-Vie or a litre of filtered water.

Exodus from the Line – 15 June

On the evening of 15 June, 3,500 men marched away from the Maginot Line in SF Thionville, SF Boulay and SF Faulquemont:

- Immerhof – seventy men and two officers left at 2300hrs and marched through a desolate Hettange-Grande while the guns of the Maginot Line fired to the rear (at their backs), lighting up the night sky. The next day they reached Metz.
- Oberheid – twenty-four men and two officers marched to Metz where they were captured.

- Molvange – sixty men in three squads; two squads were captured at Metz. The third, led by Lt Mathieu, reached Charmes on 17 June.
- Galgenberg – 121 men led by Lt Albert Brenn.
- Métrich – 279 men and eleven officers reached Nomeny in requisitioned vehicles but had to abandon them at the blown bridge across the Seille.
- Billig – 150 men and Lt George Michel reached Saint-Julien-les-Metz on the morning of 16 June. At dawn on 17 June they reached Nomeny then moved on to Nancy.
- Rochonvillers – unknown number captured near Manoncourt-en-Woëvre on 25 June, where they were notified the armistice was in effect.

The exodus from the Maginot Line continued for the next couple of days and is a story in itself.

Chapter 12

The Rhine Offensive – 15 June

The Rhine defences were weak and lacked depth but they certainly did not lack in number. The river banks were part of three Fortified Sectors, the SF Bas-Rhin, which extended 60km from south of Drusenheim to Diebolsheim; the SF Colmar, 50km to Blodesheim and SF Mulhouse about 25km to just below Kembs.

SF Bas-Rhin included (the numbers after were a designation exclusive to some Rhine blocs; the number after the slash (/) indicates the defensive line – 1st, 2nd, or 3rd):

S/S Strasbourg: 172 RIF (Lt-Col Le Mouel), with CEC 3 of SF Bas-Rhin and CEC 4 of SF Bas Rhin:

- The zone of CEC 3 encompassed the 1st Line (Casemates of the Banks of the Rhine) with seven CORF casemates and one STG blockhouse guarding the Pont de Kehl; Casemates Kintzig Nord, Kintzig Sud, Bassin-aux-Pétroles, Sporeninsel, Bassin-de-l'Industrie, Blockhouse Ponts de Kehl, Casemate Champ de Courses and Petit Rhin.
- CEC 4 guarded Casemates Musau, Ruchau, Hackmessergrund, Rohrschollen, Paysans, L'Auberge, Christian and the 3rd Line Casemates Stall 18/3 and Cosaques 19/3.

S/S Erstein: 34 RIF (Lt-Col Brocard) with CEC 5 and 6 of SF Bas Rhin:

- CEC 5: 1st Line: Casemate Gerstheim Nord, Gerstheim Centre, Gerstheim Sud; 2nd Line (Line of shelters): Abri Langkopf 10/2, Abri Langgrund 10bis/2; 3rd Line (line of villages): Casemate Plobsheim 20/3, Tuilerie d'En Haut 21/3, Gerstheim 22/3.
- CEC 6: 1st Line: Casemates Rhinau Nord, Rhinau Centre, Rhinau Sud; 3rd Line: Casemates Moulin d'Obenheim 23/3, Ziegelhof 24/3, Neuergraben 25/3, Friesenheim 27/3, Oberweidt 27bis/3.

SF Colmar included:

S/S d'Elsenheim: 42 RIF (Colonel Fonlupt) with 1st and 2nd CEO of SF Colmar:

- 1st Line: Abri Léopold 53/1, Schoenau Nord 52/1, Schoenau Centre 51/1, Casemate Schoenau Sud 50/1, Limbourg Nord 49/1, Abri Limbourg Pont 46a/1, Casemate Limbourg Sud 46/1, Sponeck Nord 45/1, Eiswasserkopf 40/1.

- 2nd Line: Abri Schoenau Petit-Rhin 15/2, Limbourg-Ferme 16/2, Sponeck Auberge 18/2.
- 3rd Line: Casemates Ried 28/3, Esperienwald Nord 29/3, Espereinwald Sud 30/3, Nachweidt 30 bis/3, Saasenheim 31/3, Richtolsheim 32/3, Marckolsheim Nord 34/3, Markholsheim Sud 35/3, Artzenheim Nord 36/3, Artzenheim Sud 37/3, Baltzenheim 38/3.

S/S Dessenheim: 28 RIF (Lt-Col Roman) with 3rd and 4th CEO of SF Colmar:

- 1st Line: Casemate Fort Mortier 32/1, Pont de Bateaux de Neuf-Brisach 31/1, Abri Pont Rail de Neuf-Brisach 30b/1, Casemate Pont Rail de Neuf-Brisach Nord 30/11, Pont Rail de Neuf-Brisach Sud 29/1, Ochsenkopf Nord 27/1, Ochsenkopf Sud 24/1, Geiwasser Nord 23/1, Geiwasser Sud 22/1, Mangsheim Rhin 21/1, Steinhubel 17/1, Grossgrun 16/1.
- 2nd Line: Abri Cimetière des Juifs 21/2, La Sirène 23/2, Casemate Vogelgrün 24/2, Abri Geiwasser-Village 25/2, Nambsheim Digue 26/2.
- 3rd Line: Casemate Kunheim Nord 39/3, Kunheim Sud 40/3, Biesheim Nord 41/3, Biesheim Sud 42/3, Algolsheim Nord 44/3, Algolsheim Sud (Est) 45/3, Nambsheim Nord 47/3, Balgau Sud 49/3, Fessenheim Nord 50/3, Fessenheim Sud 51/3, Chapelle Ste-Colombe 52/3, Blodelsheim Nord 53/3, Blodelsheim Centre 54/3, Blodelsheim Sud 55/3.

SF Mulhouse included:

S/S Schliebach: 10 RIF plus the CEO of 10 RIF and 5th CEO of 104 DIF:

- 1st Line: Casemate Chalampé-le-Bas 14/1, Ameisengründ 13b/1, Chalampé Berge Nord (NE) 11/1, Abri Pont de Bateaux de Chalampé 8b/1, Pont Rail de Chalampé Nord 8/1, Pont Rail de Chalampé Sud 7/1, Casemate Chalampé Berge Sud 6/1.
- 2nd Line: Casemate Chalampé Nord-Ouest 34/2, Chalampé Sud-Ouest 35/2.
- 3rd Line: Casemate Rumersheim Nord 56/3, Rumersheim Sud 57/3, Bantzenheim Nord 58/3, Bantzenheim Sud 59/3, Ottmarsheim Nord 60/3, Ottmarsheim Sud 61/3, Hombourg Nord 62/3, Hombourg Sud 63/3, STG Blockhouse Hardt Sud 66 and Sauruntz 77.

The troops guarding the Rhine had been alone since the general withdrawal of GA2 on 13 June. Only a light covering force was left behind to mask the retreat of the main army. The Rhine defences were manned by seven battalions with eighteen pieces of artillery. The weapons in the casemates were only capable of firing at short range while the German guns could fire several hundred metres. The German Seventh Army of General Dollman with seven divisions supported by 300 artillery pieces faced the French. Seven hundred assault

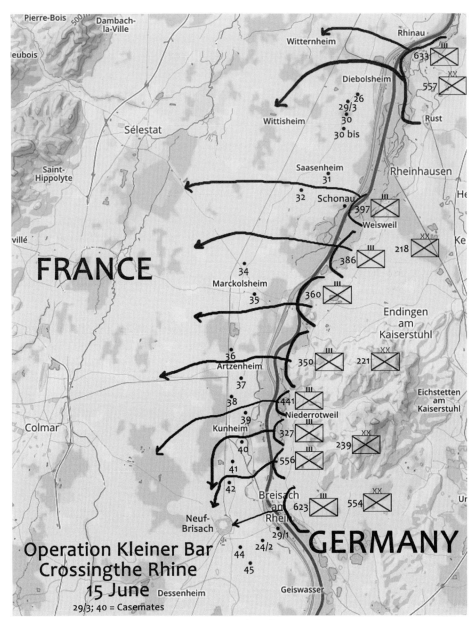

Operation Kleiner Bär, *the attack across the Rhine.* (OpenStreetMap)

boats were available to carry the Germans quickly across the river to establish bridgeheads and build temporary pontoon bridges to bring the main army and vehicles across.

Main effort XXXVII Corps (General Alfred Wäger) with two divisions: 218 ID (General Grote) and 221 ID (Gen Pflugbeil). From north to south:

- 218 ID – a battalion of 397 IR (Oberst von Busse) to cross from the western side of Weisweil to the south of Schoenau. Two battalions of 386 IR (Oberst Manitius) from west of Whylen across to Mackenheim.
- 221 ID – two battalions of 360 IR (Oberst Klockenbring) to cross at Limburg and, together with 386 IR, to attack I/42 RIF (Commandant Culomb). Two battalions of 350 IR (Oberst Koch) to attack the sector on the road to Artzenheim, defended by II/42 RIF (Commandant Gagneux).
- Höheres Kommando z.b. V XXXIII (General Georg Brandt) with 239 ID (General Neuling) to cover the southern flank of the attack. Two battalions of 441 IR (Oberst Hacker), with two battalions of engineers to take a bridgehead between Artzenheim and Baltzenheim in the sector of II/42 RIF. Two battalions of 327 IR (Oberst Drebber) and a pioneer battalion to attack Kunheim in the area held by 9 *Bataillon de Chasseurs Pyrénéens* (BCPyr) (Commandant Ninous).
- 623 IR (Oberst Veterrodt) of 554 ID of XXXIII Corps to attack Vieux-Brisach where they would construct a bridge for 556 ID to move to Neuf-Brisach which was defended by I/28 IF (Commandant Chappey).

557 ID of General Karl Ritter von Prager's XXV Corps was to make two diversionary attacks at Strasbourg, the first also attacking north of Wantzenau and the second near Rhinau. 555 ID was also to feint north of Strasbourg while attacking in the south. 633 IR of Oberstleutnant Wordt was to attack Rhinau with III/633 IR of Hauptman Glattenberg in the lead, followed by II/633 IR of Oberstleutnant Kissel and I/633 IR of Major Hoffmeister.

Operation *Kleiner Bär* (Little Bear), as the offensive was called, was executed in two phases. On the night of 14/15 June assault troops moved into place along the German bank of the river. The bombardment along a 30km front from Schonau

German troops crossing a river. (Bundesarchiv)

to Neuf Brisach began at 0900hrs. Flak 88s and Pak 37 anti-tank guns fired point-blank on the French casemates of the bank of the Rhine, which at the time were still capable of returning fire. The German gunners directed their guns on the cloches and embrasures which were quickly neutralized and all observation capability lost. The Garchery blockhouses suffered the same fate, punched full of holes by the high-velocity rounds. The bombardment lasted only ten minutes and the casemates were quickly reduced.

At 0920hrs, German assault troops moved out across the river concealed by a heavy fog. French resistance was stiff, especially from Casemate Schoenau Sud, causing the attack to be suspended. The guns were then aimed at the blockhouses south of Schoenau and the Germans moved in this direction to establish a bridgehead.

Captain Pohl, commander of I/360 IR of 221 ID, watched the destruction of Casemate Dichschädel in awe. An 88mm shell struck the front of the casemate dead centre. Three subsequent rounds struck the exact same spot and ricocheted away. The fourth shot struck the same spot, creating a small opening in the concrete. The following shots enlarged the opening and the casemate filled with smoke. The seventh shell disappeared inside the casemate and the eighth shell exploded inside. It was a sight to behold.

On the left, in the vicinity of Marckolsheim, 221 ID was tasked with capturing the position of 42 RIF. The Germans pulverized the blockhouses in this sector:

- G10 – eight killed.
- G11 – captured.
- G12 – evacuated.
- G14 – four dead prior to being evacuated.
- Pont-de-Bateaux (CM 31/1) – Sub-Lt Grosperrin – full of holes, the entire cloche exposed through the concrete.
- Casemate 231 of Geiswasser Nord – same as PDB – with the cloche suspended in mid-air and the surrounding concrete destroyed.

The Germans mopped up the remaining casemates along the bank that continued to resist.

- Limbourg Nord (49/1) – three dead.
- Abri Limbourg Pont (46/a1) – two dead including its commander Lt Grunewald.
- Sponeck Nord (45/1) – one dead.
- Sponeck Sud (41/1) – two dead but the casemate held out for a longer time.

The Germans then spread out into the Forêt du Rhin towards the principal line of resistance, the casemates of Artzenheim and Baltzenheim. Less than one hour after landing on the French side the Germans began to construct a pontoon bridge across from Limbourg.

Blockhouse Pont de Rhinau Nord after Operation Kleiner Bär *in June 1940.* (Denkschrift – Marc Romanych – digitalhistoryarchive. com)

Further south at Neuf-Brisach in SF Colmar, 239 ID faced the 9th BCPyr,[1] 623 IR from 554 ID faced 28 RIF and 556 ID faced 10th BCPyr. 623 IR attempted to cross to the right bank but faced difficulty from blockhouses that had not yet been reduced, plus the French had field artillery batteries in this sector. The Germans were pinned down along the bank and suffered mounting casualties. General Brandt called a halt to the operation.

Phase 2 of *Kleiner Bär* began at 1300hrs along the front of 103 DIF. It was carried out by 633 IR of 557 ID of XXV Corps. The Germans quickly crossed over the Rhine and just as quickly neutralized the French blockhouses on the banks as well as Casemate Rhinau Nord. Rhinau Sud continued to hold out but could not stop the German advance to the villages behind the banks of the Rhine. At 1700hrs the Germans captured Casemate Ziegelhof. In the evening the Germans had achieved their goal of crossing the Rhine and establishing a very strong presence in French territory, but they had not reached their main objective – the Rhine-Rhone canal. The most successful operation of the day was the second phase that included 633 IR's advance to the line of villages.

On the morning of 16 June *Kleiner Bär* continued. The Germans headed in force towards the line of villages. Stukas joined in the attack and reduced the casemates that still held out along the banks of the river. The pilots dropped 500kg bombs in front of the embrasures in order to block them with debris. The explosion of the bombs shook the casemates and severely affected the morale of the defenders. The incessant bombardment had the desired effect, damaging or blocking the embrasures and making their continued occupation impossible. Soon thereafter, Casemates Rhinau Sud, Schoenau Sud and Pont-Raid Sud were captured while Schoenau Nord and Centre and Pont-de-Bateaux were evacuated. Biesheim Sud and Artzenheim Nord were also evacuated. Lt Senter, the commander at

Battzenheim, was killed when a bomb exploded in front of the embrasure, sending the machine gun flying back into the gun chamber. The crew gave up soon after.

Casemate 34/3 – Marckolsheim Nord – was a double CORF casemate, type M2F. It was commanded by Adjutant Guilbot and twenty-one men of 2 CEO of 42 RIF. The casemate was hit by German artillery, air and attacked by pioneers with explosive charges. This attack cost the lives of nine French soldiers. The casemate was destroyed, with large pieces of concrete broken off; the interior burned up, the munitions having exploded inside. Some accounts mention that a flamethrower was used by the pioneers but neither the French or German reports mention the use of one.

Casemate 35/3 – Marckolsheim Sud – was a CORF casemate with two embrasures for JM/AC47 and two JM; three embrasures for FM, one cloche JM, one cloche GFM A (FM/50mm mortar). The casemate had a crew of thirty, commanded by Lt Marois. On 16 June, the casemate was attacked from the air. On 17 June 221 ID attacked in the direction of Marckolsheim, held by I/42 RIF of Commandant Coulomb. 34/3 and 35/3 held up the progress of 360 IR but the Germans brought up a Flak 88. The piece was directed at the cloche of 35/3. This, plus the large craters left by the bombing, hid the approach of German pioneers to the casemate. Upon their arrival, they tossed explosives through the cloche embrasures and smoke started to pour out of the casemate. Sergeant Heintke, carrying a 25kg explosive charge, moved stealthily along the façade of the bloc towards the gun embrasures. He reached the central embrasure which was spitting

Casemate Pont de Bateau. The concrete was completely eaten away by German shells, exposing the structure of the cloche GFM. (Author's collection)

out machine-gun bullets towards the attackers. Heintke tossed the explosive through the opening and hit the detonator, causing an enormous explosion followed by a jet of flames that shook the foundation of the casemate. The crew, with one dead, was unable to breathe and Marois surrendered at 1800hrs.

On the evening of the 16th the line of resistance was forced at Marckolsheim but the villages, organized as strongpoints, held out. The German advance was suspended until the next day. Later in the evening 104 DIF received the order to retreat to the Vosges behind defences set up by 54 DI. This was carried out at 0700hrs on 17 June. With that the Germans headed towards Colmar.

On the night of 17/18 June, as a consequence of the breakthrough on the Rhine and the German push towards Strasbourg, the city was evacuated and all possible destructions were made along the river – railway and road bridges. The evacuation of Strasbourg was followed by the evacuation of the Rhine casemates of SF Bas Rhin which were sabotaged and abandoned. This in turn exposed the entire right flank of SF Haguenau, commanded by Lt Col Schwartz. To avoid being surrounded Schwartz decided to withdraw the units of 70 RIF from S/S Herrlisheim to the Forêt d'Haguenau after sabotaging the sector's casemates.

Conclusion – Operations from 14 to 16 June

It is difficult to make a judgement on the value of the defences during the Rhine and Sarre operations since by the time of the German attack the positions had been so degraded by the retreat of the main armies. In SF Sarre the defences that required a large number of men to man them, were seriously weakened. The French stopped the Germans for a short time but they were eventually ordered to retreat. The troops manning the Rhine defences had no artillery support to oppose the German crossings and the gap between the bank of the Rhine and the Line of casemates was too wide, allowing the Germans to move quickly across, consolidate their position and move on. The Rhine position had never been reinforced with flanking casemates. Flanking 75mm guns would not have stopped the crossing but could have slowed down the subsequent advance. The key to the defeat was once again the loss of the interval troops.

Having broken through the Rhine and Sarre defences, the Germans could now not only move out to the south to chase the retreating French, but could move in behind and attack the Maginot Line from the rear. 95 ID began to deploy behind the Line at SF Faulquemont and headed towards the rear of SF Boulay. 262 ID headed east to come around behind SF Rohrbach. Several of the smaller ouvrages would be severely tested in the days ahead.

Further west the Germans exploited the abandonment of the Plateau de Marville to surround SF Crusnes and move on towards Thionville. The Germans explored the possibility of a strong punch through the Line between PO Bois du Four and PO Mauvais Bois, but instead sent ID 183, to the rear of the forts via the

Plateau of Noërs, now devoid of any French troops. This manoeuvre began on 14 June and ended plans for the retreat of troops in SF Crusnes. They were now cut off and would have to fight in place.

On the other hand, in SF Thionville, Boulay and Faulquemont, Measure B was undertaken as planned. The artillerymen, the section of covering troops and the men inside the forts who were not deemed critical to its function evacuated their positions the evening of 14 June. The positional artillery crews had no means of moving their guns (horse or motor vehicle) and were forced to spike them and leave them behind. The infantry was not much better off and many soldiers became trapped within the enclosing German ring.

Due to the confusion of the evacuation, troops in SF Boulay misinterpreted orders, causing further confusion. Captain Guillebot, commander of the Ouvrage d'Anzeling, ordered his men and those of other works in his command to begin sabotaging the equipment. This was to be carried out according to Measure C and Guillebot was two days early. The technicians at Hobling, Bois de Bousse, Anzeling and Berenbach got to work and began the sabotage of the armament. Fortunately, a counter-order was given to stop the sabotage but it came too late for Bois de Bousse where Captain Ramaud's men had already begun, in particular in the telephone exchange. The fort was abandoned during the night. Two nights later the crew was captured east of Metz.

The following day, 15 June, Colonel Cochinard moved his command post from Hayes to Anzeling. He gave new instructions: Measure B (departure of artillerymen) was executed the same day at 2000hrs but Measure C was suspended until receipt of new orders. The orders for the crews to stay in the ouvrages and resist in place came from General Condé of Third Army.

In SF Faulquemont the crews of eight interval casemates (Bambiderstroff Nord and Sud, Einseling Nord and Sud, Quatre Vents Nord and Sud and Bois de Laudrefang Nord and Sud) abandoned their positions after conducting the planned destructions. The only measure taken to put a halt to what was taking place was the reoccupation of Quatre Vents Sud by several men from Laudrefang so as to be able to cover the Saint-Avold road. Lt Vaillant, commander of Laudrefang, also sent men to occupy the casemates of Einseling. On the afternoon of 16 June, the Germans were firmly in place behind the line of ouvrages. General Girval gave the order to evacuate the ouvrages the next day but by then the situation had worsened. Commandant Denoix took the initiative to cancel the order and to resist in place.

In SF Sarre the attempt to retreat was made impossible by the German advance. Some French troops still had a chance to get away – those of Ouvrage du Haut Poirier and its five surrounding casemates. Commandant Jolivet, discovering that Ouvrage du Welschoff had been given the order to resist in place, wasn't sure what action he should take. Finally, after making contact with Lt Col Bonlarron of Simserhof and hearing on the radio that Pétain had requested an armistice, Jolivet cancelled the evacuation order and chose to resist in place.

Along the Fifth Army front, in SFs Bitche, Vosges and Haguenau, an evacuation was still possible because the Germans who were moving towards the east were still some distance from the position. The consequences of the breakthrough on the Sarre and Rhine would, however, lead General Bourret to order the fortress troops to resist in place. This would create a so-called rampart against German troops to the rear of the retreating French.

In SF Haguenau, Lt Col Schwartz already knew that the Germans did not intend to wait passively since the retreat of the main French army left them with a free path in which to move.

The Maginot Line Prepares for the Final Battles

It soon became evident that the remaining ouvrages of the Maginot Line were not going to be sabotaged and abandoned; instead the crews were going to fight to the end – exactly what that 'end' would be was unknown: siege, capture, escape, or possibly death inside the tunnels in the manner of the men of La Ferté.

The ouvrages were prepared and well-equipped against frontal attacks. German troops were under surveillance in the zone of each individual observatory and of each fort. Every route leading to the main line of resistance, every tree, body of water, road, or building was plotted on a map and could be shelled within minutes. The 75mm casemate blocs provided flanking fire to cover the intervals and the casemates were equipped with artillery and machine guns. Dead ground was covered by 50mm, 81mm and 135mm mortars. The front was well covered. The same could not be said of the defences to the rear, which barely existed and from which the attack would come. In nearly all cases, the commanders had failed to prepare for such an event.

Commandant Fabre of Ouvrage du Grand-Hohékirkel of the Bitche Ensemble, was one of those who had taken precautions to prepare for a siege from all directions. The Ensemble included the casemates of 154 RIF, under protection of Grand- Hohékirkel's 75mm turret in Bloc 4. The rear defences included regular patrols to the rear

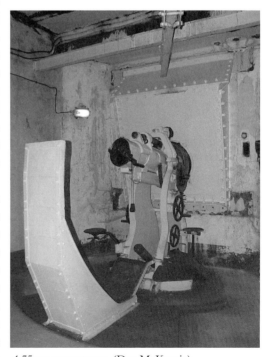

A 75mm casemate gun. (Dan McKenzie)

and in the direction of the Camp de Bitche. Fabre was anticipating the direction from which the Germans were coming and hoped to slow them down with his patrols. Lt Bollack, head of one of the detachments of sappers, cut access to the ouvrage by blowing large craters in the roads with explosives. The railway bridge was destroyed. Supplies left at the railway station of Bannstein were burned. Nothing was to be left for the Germans – material, munitions, or food.

A group of engineers was sent into the Bois de Wolfschaden to cut, burn and blow up as many trees as possible that were blocking the view of observers. The light barracks were booby-trapped with petrol cans and grenades that would go off if the Germans approached. Patrols scoured the abandoned blockhouses and brought back several machine guns, FMs and rifles, plus thousands of rounds of ammunition and hundreds of grenades. Barbed-wire belts were tripled in width in front of the entrances to the ouvrage. A triple row of anti-tank rails was placed in front of the EM. At the EH the communications trench was half-filled with dirt and a mine was placed in the trench that could be set off electronically. Finally, sandbags were placed in front of the armoured door to absorb the shock of bombardment. A 47mm naval gun was placed in the corridor, aimed at the grill of the EM.

Unfortunately, other commanders did not take the same steps as Fabre. The failure to clear the heavily-wooded areas behind Ouvrage du Bambesch and Kerfent would, in the days to come, significantly contribute to the rapid fall of those forts.

Chapter 13

The End of the Armies of the East

Beginning on 13 June, four French armies (Second, Third, Fifth and Eighth), with eleven corps, attempted to escape to and establish a new defensive line further south. On the left, in the sector of Third Army, the retreat was pressured by the Germans who quickly figured out what was happening and sent motorized troops to the rear of the French. Meanwhile, the right wing of GA4 attempted to establish a line of defence at Vitry-le-François–Sainte-Menehould to prevent the envelopment of the Maginot Line. In the centre the retreat was executed under the protection of the forts and as a result the French units retreated without any German pressure.

On 14 June, the situation took a dramatic turn. 1st Panzer Division seized Saint-Dizier, cutting the thin cordon that connected GA4 to GA2. This breach gave the Germans new ideas on how to conduct the battle. They decided to send Guderian's Panzers towards the Swiss frontier, while Kleist's Group moved in the direction of Dijon and Lyon. The panzers swiftly moved unopposed towards their objectives while the French moved only on foot.

On the left, XXI Corps absorbed the Marching Group Dubuisson (3 DLC, Light Division Burtaire). The corps fought in front of Verdun and dramatic combat took place on Côte 304 and the Mort-Homme. On 15 June Verdun fell into German hands. The French situation worsened. Guderian's Panzer Group crossed the Saône and threatened to close off the only passage still open along the Swiss border. The breakthrough at the Sarre and Rhine also forced the French into a fighting retreat while the Germans bit at the heels of the rearguard.

The retreating fortress troops hoped to reach the Marne-Rhine Canal and form a new defensive line from Pagny-sur-Moselle to Lutzelbourg and take control of the Toul-Nancy bridgehead. On 17 June, the fortress troops of DM Fleurian set up on the Marne-Rhine Canal and the Moselle between Foug and Liverdun while 51 DI deployed to the west on the Meuse and 58 DI to the east. The latter two units had recently detached themselves from the Verdun region with the help of XLII CAF, covered on the right by VI Corps, including two marching divisions – DM Poisot from Thionville and DM Besse from Boulay. On the morning of 15 June, these two DMs arrived at the Line of Thiaucourt–Pont-a-Mousson–Delme. On 17 June DM Poisot was positioned south-west of Nancy, while DM Besse reorganized between Flavigny-sur-Meuse and Saint-Nicolas-du-Port.

XX Corps was in the centre of the French armies that included DM Girud (SF Faulquemont) and DM Dagnan (SF Sarre). Group Girud retreated via Delme – Château-Salins where they set up on the evening of 15 June. Group Dagnan headed towards Altviller to set up between Hellocourt and Gondrexange beginning the evening of 16 June. Further east XLIII CAF consisted of two marching groups that retreated on the evening of 16 June on the axis Drulinger-Sarrebourg (DM Chastenet) and La-Petite-Pierre – Phalsbourg (DM Senselme). XLIII CAF set up on the canal while DM Chastenet set up from the Étang de Gondrexange to Hesse and DM Senselme from Hesse to Artzwiller.

On 17 June Marshal Pétain, to everyone's shock and dismay, addressed the troops on the radio: 'It's with a broken heart that I tell you we must cease combat.' This announcement took all of the wind out of the French sails. To make matters worse – as if they could get worse – elements of Guderian's group closed the door on the Armies of the East. At 0800hrs on 17 June, a reconnaissance detachment of 29 ID (motorized) reached the Swiss frontier near Pontarlier and at 0900hrs the vanguard of the division reached the town. The Germans continued their push south and found themselves to the rear of the Larmont defences of SF Jura (*Supérieure* – Upper Fort and *Inférieure* – Lower Fort) and the Fort du Joux, which were occupied by 23rd *Bataillon d'Infanterie Légère d'Afrique* (BILA – African Light Infantry Battalion) and 170 RAP. Fort Larmont Supérieure was shelled and surrendered around 2000hrs. Fort du Joux held out until 24 June. To escape this disastrous situation, General Condé devised a plan to block the German advance beyond the canal. XX Corps and XLIII CAF were chosen to sacrifice themselves in this effort.

The German attack on the Marne-Rhine canal was launched on the morning of 18 June. The canal was covered in a thick fog. The main attack was in the front of XLIII CAF. It started with a violent bombardment, followed by an infantry attack. The aim of the Germans was to cross the canal at Hemin and Xouaxange in the sector defended by 37 RIF, which was forced to pull back to the line Lorquin–Landange.

On the left 133 RIF also pulled back to the Port du Col des Français, but launched a counter-attack that halted the German advance. 133 RIF pulled back further in the evening. Before the open breach, General Lescanne decided to modify his position and in the evening DM Chastenet pivoted towards the front of the Vosges in order to bar access from the west.

Heavy fighting took place to the north in front of VI Corps at Maixe (7 DI) which fell into German hands and at Aingeray where the Germans crossed the Moselle before capturing Nancy in the early afternoon. At the end of the afternoon VI Corps was being pressed from the east and units still capable of fighting established a line on the Meurthe at Saint-Nicolas-du-Port. In the morning of 19 June DM Poisot was on the Moselle at Pont-Saint-Vincent and DM Besse on the Meurthe at Saint-Nicolas-du-Port. The attack allowed the Germans to open a breach in the French line at the heights of Rosières-aux-Salines. The rest of DM Poisot joined up with DM Besse and pulled back towards Haroué and Bayon.

XLIII CAF was in equally bad shape. Pressed by the Germans, DM Senselme pulled back towards Harzwiller and Hazelbourg and by the end of the day was dispersed in the area of Abreschwiller. DM Chastenet engaged in a fighting retreat towards Badonvillers–Raon L'Étape and on 20 June did an about turn to face the Germans coming from Bertrambois, Saint-Quirin and Rupt-des-Dames. On 20 June, the men of DM Besse were captured near Germonvillers.

On the evening of 21 June, organized resistance came to an end except for a series of encircled pockets that would also be reduced throughout the day. At Nancy, General Dubuisson, who took command of the surrounded troops between Nancy and Toul, still had 68,000 men from eight different divisions, but the morale of the troops was very low and their will to fight was equally low. On the evening of 21 June, Dubuisson ordered his Chief of Staff, Colonel Plaicard, to make contact with the Germans to negotiate a cease fire. Plaicard met with General Endres, commander of 212 ID, who accepted a parley to take place the following morning. Dubuisson also dispatched Colonel Cuzon, commander of the divisionary infantry of 3 DLC, to contact General Feige, commander of the German troops of XXXVI Corps. Feige was not as agreeable as his subordinate and demanded surrender without conditions which Cuzin accepted without negotiation. The surrender document was signed at 1530hrs on 22 June.

General Lescanne, commander of XLIII CAF, with 30,000 men, was positioned atop the Col de Donon where he hoped to hold out until the armistice. Early on 23 June a French officer who was a prisoner of the Germans was sent to Lescanne to inform him the armistice was signed[1] and that the Germans were ready to call a cease fire. After further negotiations, Lescanne agreed to surrender his troops on 24 June at 1130hrs. The surrender order contained a clause stipulating that all surrendered arms would be left intact.

More and more small groups held on in the region of Saint-Dié. At Bourgonne, the elements of DM Girval and 54 DI (General Coradin) awaited the next move. General Condé's command post was now at the Forest House of Pimpierre, not far from the Col du Haut-Jacques. Condé's forces numbered about 50,000, mostly from XX Corps. On 22 June German emissaries presented themselves at 0700hrs at one of the barricades and were taken to meet with Generals Girval, Hubert and Condé. The latter believed the situation grave enough to surrender his troops, which he did at 1230hrs.

XIII Corps was at Gérardmer. In the morning of 22 June, German advance elements penetrated the village's outer defences and worked their way to the centre. At 1015hrs General Misserey, XIII Corps commander, ordered a cease fire.

General Laure of Eighth Army, in his PC at La Bresse, was joined by Generals Tencé and Mena of XLIV CAF and General Cousse of 104 DIF. The Germans made contact with the French on the evening of 21 June. At dawn on 22 June the last defences fell and the Germans approached General Laure's command post. Laure ordered a cease fire of troops at La Bresse.

Few of the remaining troops waited for the armistice to surrender. Among them were 2,500 men of 105 DIF of General Didio at Rouge-Gazon, not far from the Ballon d'Alsace. In the morning of 25 June, Didio was glad to see the day of the armistice arrive, hoping to be sent to the Free Zone with his men since he had not been taken prisoner. Unfortunately, this situation did not allow him to escape the fate common to the defenders of 105 DIF, who also fell into captivity.

For the French armies, the debacle that started on 10 June with the surprise seizure by German commandos of key roads on the border, ended in the passes of the Vosges Mountains. From that very first day the armies moved backwards toward their ignominious end. The armies of the east that surrendered included troops that fought in Luxembourg during those first critical hours, like 3 DLC and the marching units that pulled back from the Maginot Line beginning on 14 June. In the midst of all of this sadness, though, a light still flickered. During the ten days when hundreds of thousands of men fled to the south a small remnant remained inside the concrete of the Maginot Line, abandoned by the main armies, and continued to fight on under terrible circumstances.

After the German breakthrough on the Sarre and Rhine, the Germans moved in behind the Maginot Line works, with a view towards reducing them and bringing about their surrender as quickly as possible. The attacks were more often of a limited nature rather than coordinated, general attacks. They consisted of the infiltration of small patrols and artillery harassment. Nevertheless, some of the action was heavy, resulting in German casualties as well as the significant destruction of several blocs by German artillery, especially the 88mm Flak gun. On the French side, most of the reciprocal action was carried out by the crews in the casemates and turrets, as well as defenders guarding the entrance blocs.

Inside the ouvrages, morale was a rollercoaster of highs and lows. The main armies were already miles away and no relief of any kind was planned or attempted. The crews were completely isolated except for scattered bits of news from the outside via radio or telephone. The only thing the Maginot Line crews had to fight for now was what remained of French soil, whatever lay behind the barbed wire obstacles. Their situation was otherwise hopeless. The only positive thing they had to hold on to was being permitted to go to the Free Zone after the armistice rather than becoming prisoners of war. The alternative was to go down with the ship and take as many Germans with them as possible. The brightest gleam was that they still had their honour to defend.

After the French armies headed south all the Germans needed to do was drink coffee and smoke and write letters and wait until the armistice was signed. On the contrary, for what can only be considered reasons of boasting or personal ego or adding a rare reference to a CV that they captured a Maginot Line fortress, some German commanders chose to attack and capture an element of the Maginot Line, despite the casualties it might cost their men. Granted, the armistice talks could have collapsed but it would seem more prudent to sit and wait for a few days than to sacrifice more men. The French fortress troops, however, had nothing to lose and would gladly continue to fire their guns until they ran out of ammunition, which was several weeks away. They were being given a final chance to preserve their honour and perhaps finish the chapter in such a way that they could hold up their heads for the rest of the lives, despite what happened in the days to come.

Commandant Roy of Billig spoke of holding out for three months and Rodolphe wished to 'finish in beauty'.

Part IV

The Alps – French Victory, 10–25 June 1940

Chronology 10 to 25 June 1940

10 June	Mussolini declares war on France.
17 June	Eight 149mm turret guns from the Italian Chaberton battery fire on the Briançonnais Sector of SF Dauphiné, covering an Italian advance into the French valleys.
21 to 25 June	Italian Alpine Corps launch Operation Bernardo against SF Savoie. Crews of the French outposts and blockhouses prevent the Italians from breaking through the passes.
21 to 25 June	Four Italian divisions attempt to break through the Col du Mont Cenis but are stopped by French crews in the small infantry border posts.
21 to 24 June	Italian troops attack towards Modane, location of the strongest forts of the Maginot Line in the Alps. The guns of the ouvrages bar the Italian advance.
22 June	The guns of Chaberton, fired on for several days by heavy French 280mm guns, are finally silenced.
17 to 24 June	Ouvrage Roche-la-Croix fires thousands of shells, thwarting numerous enemy attacks in the Vallée de l'Ubaye.
20 to 24 June	Italian advances in S/S Sospel of SF Alpes-Maritimes are stopped by the guns of Ouvrage Monte-Grosso and Agaisen.
14 to 17 June	The guns of Sainte-Agnès, Mont-Agel and Cap Martin fire continuously against Italian incursions in the Corniches sub-sector.
20 June	A large Italian force launches an attack on Menton in an effort to break through to the coastal road to Nice. The small outpost of Pont-Saint-Louis blocks all movement along the coastal road. Nine men hold off the Italians for six days.
22 June	A major attack along the entire Sub-Sector front is stopped by the guns of the Maginot Line. The Italians attempt to outflank Pont-Saint-Louis and penetrate Menton but are driven back.
24 June	Italian forces attacking from the outskirts of Menton reach the Mediterranean coast but are stopped by the guns of Cap Martin and Mont-Agel. This is the high-water mark of the Italian Alpine offensive of 1940.

Chapter 14

Mussolini's Attack on the Southern Maginot Line

While the troops of the Maginot Line in the north waited for the the Germans' next move, events were unfolding along the French-Italian border to the south where a new threat, the Italian army, was getting ready to test the fortress line. Mention of the combat that took place in the southeast is rare. Most of the attention is paid to events in the north. The Maginot Line sectors in the French Alps were very much detached from those of the north. There was never any reason for coordination between the two regions. In some of the best books written about the Maginot Line there is hardly any mention of the forts in the south, even though they were as capable, if not more so, of stopping an invasion as the northern forts. The fact is that the fighting that took place in the Alps is very well documented and the results were very interesting. Except for the occupation of a few streets in the town of Menton, the Italians were driven back along the entire front. For the French, it was a complete victory until the armistice took it away.

The troops of the Maginot Line in the south, the 'Army of the Alps', commanded by General René Olry, were placed on alert on 22 August 1939 and took up position in the forts a few days later. The Army of the Alps was made up of XIV Corps, commanded by General Etienne Beynet, and XV Corps, commanded by General Alfred Montagne. Their mission was strictly defensive.[1] Since there was no major threat in the south and a growing one in the north, beginning in September about two-thirds of alpine troops were sent to the north-east, leaving behind a number of Fortress Demi-Brigades (DBAF) and *chasseur* battalions. *Section d'Éclaireurs Skieurs* (SES)[2] troops guarded the advance posts, backed up by positional artillery from the ouvrages and interval batteries.

The Alpine region of the Maginot Line consisted of the following fortified sectors:

SF Savoie: This extended from le Beaufortain and the vallon de Séloges to the north to the Camp des Rochilles near the Col du Galibier to the south. To the right was SF Dauphiné and to the left the *Secteur Défensif du Rhône*. The primary mission of the sector was to cover the passes from Italy, in particular the Col du Mont-Cenis in Maurienne and the Col du Petit-Saint-Bernard in Tarentaise. The secondary passes, the Val d'Arly, Col de Seigne and the Petit Mont-Cenis were also under its protection.

The CORF gave priority to the defences in Maurienne because of the long common frontier with Italy in that area. During this time, all of the zone of the Plateau of Mont-Cenis as well as the narrow Vallee Étroite belonged to Italy. The passages to France were thus more numerous than those facing Tarentaise. For this reason, the latter suffered greater cuts than Maurienne. Finally, in 1937 some small ouvrages were begun but incomplete in 1940.

The sector was unequal in terms of the strength of its fortifications. The south was much stronger than the north, although the employment of several Séré de Rivières forts helped to alleviate the imbalance. In 1939/40 the MOM added a second line of defences to the rear of the sector in all of the main valleys (Maurienne, Doron, Tarentaise, Val d'Arly).

The SF Savoie was defended by fortress troops and reinforcements. In June 1940, the sector was commanded by Colonel Michel de la Baume and included the following units:

Fortress Units

- 16 DBAF (Lt-Col Vergezac) with 70 *Bataillon Alpin de Forteresse* (BAF) and 80 BAF and 6 *Bataillon de Chasseurs Mitrailleurs* (BCM).
- 30 DBAF (Lt-Col LaFlaquiere) with 71, 81 and 91 BAF and 164 RAP.

Vallée de la Tarentaise: Commander Colonel Michel de la Baume:

S/S Beaufortin: Lt Col Vergezac (16 DBAF), consisted of the following:

- AP Séloges, Blockhouse Bellegarde.

S/S Tarentaise: Lt Col de Branges (215 RI):

- Abri AP Le Combottier, Barrage Petit-Saint-Bernard, La Redoute-Ruinée, AP Le Planay, Abri AP La Tête du Plane, Abri AP Les Savonnes.
- Position de barrage du Bourg-Saint-Maurice: Barrage de route Versoyen, Ouvrage le Chatelard, Ouvrage Cave-à-Canon.
- Séré de Rivières forfs: Fort Vulmix(s), Fort le Truc, Blockhouse La Platte, Batterie Courbaton.

S/S Palet-Vanoise: Commandant Carenco (70 BAF):

- AP La Vanoise.
- Second position: Vallée de l'Arly, Vallée du Doron de Beaufort, Vallée de la Tarentaise, Vallée du Doron de Bozel.

Vallée de la Maurienne: Commander General Boucher (66 DI):

S/S Haute-Maurienne: Lt Col Roussel (281 RI):

- Quartier du Mont-Cenis: Abri Ouillon, Blockhouse Le Mollard A, B and Abri Le Mollard, Blockhouse Les Arcellins.
- AP Revêts, Barrage Les Revêts, Fort de La Turra.
- Quartier du Val d'Ambin: Blockhouse Mont-Froid, Abri Mont-Froid, Abri La Beccia, Abri Ouest de la Tuile, Abri Crois de Colleret, Abri Casse Blanche.

S/S Moyenne-Maurienne: Lt Col Laflaquière (30 DBAF):

- Quartier d'Amodon: Abri L'Orgère, Abri Amodon, Obs Amodon.
- Quartier de l'Arc: Ouvrage Sapey, Fort Sapey, Fort Replaton, Ouvrage Saint-Gobain, Ouvrage Saint-Antoine.
- Quartier des Cols Sud: Sous-quartier Arplan – Obs Granges et Turra d'Arplane; Ouvrage Le Lavoir, Ouvrage Pas-du-Roc, AP Le Fréjus, AP La Roue, AP Col de la Vallée Étroite, Ouvrage Arrondaz.

S/S Basse-Maurienne: Lt Col Dussaud (343 RI):

- Quartier de Valmeinier: Casemate Côte 2415, Casemate NE de la Baisse de la Pissine.
- Quartier de Valloire: Ouvrage Les Rochilles.
- Second Position: Barrage de Basse-Maurienne – Position du Pas-de-la-Porte, Position du Pas-du-Roc, Fort Le Télégraphe, Bloc Col des Trois-Croix.

SF Dauphiné: This was located between SF Savoie in the north and SF Alpes-Maritimes in the south. It stretched from Casernement de Rochilles to Casernement des Fourches. SF Dauphiné guarded two major routes that were the axis formed by the valleys of the Haute Durance (Briançon) and Ubaye (Barcelonnette). Other small border passes were nothing more than mule trails, not favourable to the movement of large bodies of troops, even in good weather.

Originally named SF Hautes-Alpes in 1924 (a designation it kept until 1933), the area was replete with Vauban and Séré de Rivières fortifications. The CORF planned a very ambitious programme that was later postponed or abandoned to the benefit of SF Alpes-Maritimes. In the end, only a few artillery works from those originally planned were built by the CORF. Construction of remaining works of this sector was done by the MOM.

The Ubaye valley contained the artillery works of Roche-la-Croix, St Ours and Haute-Restefond. The Ouvrage de Janus was built in the Valleé de Haute Durance. It was complemented by the refurbishment by the MOM of some of the old forts, infantry works or outposts. Despite these restrictions, SF Dauphiné was very strong and resisted the Italian invasion well.

Ouvrage du Janus, SF Dauphiné. (Pascal Lambert, wikimaginot.eu)

SF Dauphiné was divided into three areas, geographically corresponding to the valleys of Briançon, Queyras and Ubaye. These areas were divided into sub-sectors, themselves divided into districts.

Commander: General Cyvoct with the following units:

- 75 DBAF (LtCol Bonnet) with 72, 82, 92, 102 BAF.
- 157 DBAF (Lt Col Soyer) with 73 and 83 BAF.
- Artillery (Colonel Marie) with 154 and 162 RAP.

Briançonnais: commanded by General Cyvoct:

- S/S Haute-Clarée:
  - Guisane: Ouvrage Col-de-Granon, Fort L'Olive, Blockhouse Les Acles (La Cleyda), AP Plampinet, PA Rocher des Dix Heures.
- S/S Haute-Durance:
  - Cerveyrette – Ouvrage La Vachette, Barrage Pont de la Vachette, Obs Croix de Toulouse, Barrage Montgenevre, Ouvrage Janus, AP Chenaillet, Ouvrage Gondran E, Ouvrage Les Aittes.

Vallée du Queyras: commanded by Lt Col Bonnet (75 DBAF):

- S/S Guil:
  - Infantry positions and machine-gun blockhouses.

Vallée de l'Ubaye: commanded by Colonel Dessaux:

- S/S Ubaye:
  - Ouvrage Plate-Lombard, AP Larche, Fort (Battery) Viraysse, Ouvrage Saint-Ours Haut, Abri Nord-Est de Saint-Ours, Abri Nord-Ouest de Fontvive, Ouvrage Saint-Ours Bas, Obs Serre-la-Platte, Ouvrage Roche-la-Croix, Abri Ancien Camp, Batterie Roche-la-Croix Supérieur, Obs La Duyère, Obs Les Challanches, Fort Tournoux, Fort Grouchy, Batterie XII.
- S/S Jausiers:
  - Abri Col de Restefond, Ouvrage Restefond, Ouvrage Granges-Communes, AP Les Fourches, Ouvrage La Moutière, Abri La Moutière, AP Le Pra, 36 Blocs on the Col de la Braisse, PA de Maurin, PA du Castelet (Châtelet), Blocs Fouillouze, Blocs Trois-Mélèzes (cote 2018), Blocs Les Sagnes.

The *Secteur Fortifié des Alpes-Maritimes* (SFAM) covered a zone from Haute-Tinée to the Mediterranean coast. The SFAM was the largest fortified sector in the Alps. Construction began in 1924 in response to threats from Italy. The fortress troops covered the southern part of the SFAM where the fortifications were the strongest and most numerous. The northern region was under protection of alpine reinforcement troops, in particular the 65 DI.

SF Alpes–Maritimes: commanded by General Magnien with the following units:

- 40 DBAF (Lt Col Sauvajon) with 75, 85, 95 BAF.
- 58 DBAF (Lt Col Mercier de Saint-Croix) with 76, 86, 96 BAF.
- 61 DBAF (Lt Col Marquilly) with 74, 84, 94 BAF.
- Artillery: 157, 158, 167 RAP.

65 DI's sector:

S/S Mounier: (Colonel Astolfi):

- AP Saint-Dalmas-le-Selvage, Ouvrage Col de Crous, Abris A and B of Col de Crous, AP Isola, Ouvrage Col de la Valette.

S/S Tinée–Vésubie: (Lt Col Marquilly):

- AP Valabres Nord, AP Valabres Sud (Annexe), Ouvrage Fressinéa, Casemate STG Abelièra, Ouvrage Rimplas, Ouvrage Valdeblore, Ouvrage La Séréna, Casemate STG La Petite Tétière, Casemate STG La Bollinette, Ouvrage Caire-Gros, AP Conchetas, Casemate STG Venanson, Ovrage Col du-Fort, AP Castel-Vieil, Casemate STG Roquebillière, Ouvrage Gordolon, Casemates CORF Bas de Gordolon, Casemate (Type 1bis) Chapelle Saint-Sauveur, AP Le Planet, Ouvrage Flaut, Casemate STG La Bollène Est and Ouest.

SFAM sector:

S/S Authion: (Lt Col Brun):

- AP Col de Raus, Ouvrage Baisse de Saint Véran, Blockhouse Pointe des Trois Communes, Abri La Forca, Abri Mille-Fourches, Ouvrage Plan-Caval, Ouvrage La Béole, Ouvrage La Déa, Abri Col d'Agnon, Casemate CORF Arboin.

S/S Sospel: (Lt Col Sauvajon):

- AP La Croix de Cougoule, Ouvrage Col de Brouis, Ouvrage Monte-Grosso, Casemate MOM Nieya Nord, Ouvrage Agaisen, Abri Champ de Tir de l'Agaisen, Abri La Tourraque, Casemate STG Golf de Sospel, Casemates MOM Place Gianotti, Bévéra, Oréglia, AP Castes-Ruines, Casemates MOM Saint-Christophe Nord and Sud, Ouvrage Saint-Roch, Casemate MOM Campaost, Ouvrage Barbonnet (Fort Suchet), Casemates MOM Barbonnet Sud.

S/S Corniches: (Lt Col Mercier de Sainte-Croix):

- Five MOM casemates, AP Baisse de Scuvion, AP Pierre-Pointue, Ouvrage Castillon, Obs Pic de Garuche, Abri Col des Banquettes, AP La Péna, AP La Colletta, PA Fascia Fonda, Casemate MOM Madone de Gorbio Nord and Sud, Ouvrage Sainte-Agnes, PA Castellar, Casemate MOM Gorbio Nord and Sud, Ouvrage Col de Garde, Ouvrage Mont-Agel, Obs Est de Mont-Agel (CORF), AP Collet du Pilon, Obs Mont-Gros de Roquebrune, Ouvrage Roquebrune, Abri Croupe-du-Réservoir, Abri du Carrefour des Corniches, Casemates MOM Vesqui Nord and Sud, Cap-Martin Tunnel, Barrière Pont-Elisabeth, Ouvrage Cap Martin, Barrage Pont-Saint-Louis.

SD Rhone, SF Savoie and SF Dauphiné were part of XIV Corps; SF Alpes-Maritime XV Corps.

The 'Alps' run in an arc from Hungary through Austria and Switzerland, then make a sweep to the south below Geneva to the Mediterranean. What is commonly known as the French Alps are part of the Western Alps. This chain includes the following (highest point in parentheses):

- Chablais Alps – Lake Geneva to Col des Montets.
- Graian Alps – Col du Mont Cenis to Col du Petit Saint Bernard (Gran Paradios – 4,061m).
- Dauphine Alps – Col du Montgenevre to Col du du Mont Cenis (Barre des Ecrins 4,102m).
- Cottian Alps – Colle de la Maddalena to Col du Montgenevre.
- Maritime Alps – Colle di Tenda to Colle della Maddalena.

The main passes guarded by the Army of the Alps were:

- Colle di Tenda (Col de Tende) – 1,908m.
- Colle della Maddalena (Col du Larche) – 1,994m.
- Col de Montgenèvre – 1,854m.
- Col de Fréjus – 2,537m.
- Col du Mont Cenis – 2,084m.
- Col du Petit Saint-Bernard – 2,157m.

As such, the nature of the frontier did not leave much room for manoeuvre and was extremely favourable to the defender.

Italian Order of Battle

The Italian forces included the 'Alpini' divisions. These were originally established in 1872 to defend Italy's northern borders. The soldiers were from the northern regions and familiar with the territories in which they would fight. Soldiers of the Alpini wore the Green Flame collar patch and a *Capello Alpino* (alpine hat) with a black feather, thus coining the nickname the '*Penne Nere*', or Black Feathers. The Alpini battalions were deactivated after the First World War. In 1935 Mussolini reformed six divisions: 1st Alpini Division 'Taurinense', 2nd 'Tridentia', 3rd 'Julia', 4th Cuneense, 5th Pusteria and 6th Alpi Graie.

Fourth Army, commanded by General Alfredo Guzzoni faced SF Savoie and included the following units:

Alpine Corps (General Luigi Negri), Operation B (Bernardo):

- 2nd Tridentina Alpini Division (General Ugo Santovito).[3]
- 1st Taurinense Alpini Division (General Paolo Micheletti).
- 101 Trieste Motorized Division (General Vito Ferroni) – from the Armoured Corps (General Fidenzio Dall'Ora).
- Raggruppamento Levanna (organization unknown).

Facing SF Dauphiné: I Corps (General Carlo Vecchiarelli):

- 11 Brennero Division (General Arnaldo Forgiero).
- 59 Cagliari Division (General Antonio Scuero).
- 1 Superga Division (General Curio Barbasetti di Prun).
- 24 Pinerolo Division (General Giuseppe De Stefanis).

IV Corps (General Camillo Mercalli):

- 1 Sforzesca Division (General Alfonso Ollearo).
- 58 Legagno Division (General Edorado Scala).
- 26 Assietta Division (General Emanuele Girlando).
- 3 Raggrumento Alpini (organization unknown).

Facing SF Alpes-Maritimes: First Army (General Pietro Pintor):

II Corps – (General Francesco Bertini), Operation M (Maddalena):

- 16 Pistoia Division (General Mario Priore).
- Varaita Po Raggruppamento (organization unknown).
- 36 Forli Division (General Giulio Perugi).
- Cuneense Alpini Division (General Alberto Ferrero).
- 33 Acqui Division (General Francesco Sartoris).
- 4 Livorno Division (General Benenuto Gioda).

III Corp (General Mario Arisio):

- 6 Cuneo Division (General Carlo Melotti).
- Gessi Alpini Raggruppamento (organization unknown).
- 3 Ravenna Division (General Edoardo Nebbia).

XV Corps (General Gambara Gastone) – Operation R (Riviera):

- 22 Cacciatori delle Alpi (General Dante Lorenzelli).
- 37 Modena Division (General Allessandro Gloria).
- 5 Cosseria Division (General Alberto Vassarri).
- 44 Cremona Division (General Umberto Mondino).
- 5 Pusteria Alpini Division (General Amedo De Cia).

On 10 June Mussolini declared war on France and Great Britain. His goal was to capture enough French territory prior to the armistice to earn a say in the negotiations and to seize the former Italian provinces of Nice and Savoie. Based on an almost 5:1 advantage of Italian to French troops, it would seem that the rapid fall of the south was a foregone conclusion, especially now that German troops were moving to the rear of French forces near the Swiss border.[4] This development was troublesome for Italy. If Germany advanced far enough prior to the armistice or captured the alpine sectors, Italy would be left with none of the spoils. As if that were not bad enough, the winter of 1940 was severe and it was not yet over in mid-June. This made an offensive in the Alps nearly impossible. All of the Italian lines of communication were covered by the guns of the forts. It didn't matter how many troops the Italians had; there were only so many passes into France, all narrow and easily defensible. Nevertheless, the Italians underestimated the value of the French defences and decided to launch an attack.

For the first ten days, Italian operations consisted only of minor skirmishes that only demonstrated the advance posts were solidly defended. The Italians needed to bring forward a much stronger force if they wanted to break through the Line.

Operations in SF Savoie – Vallée de la Tarentaise

On 21 June the Italian Army Corps Alpino opened a two-pronged attack called Operation B – Bernardo, the Italian name for the Petit-Saint-Bernard pass. Italian

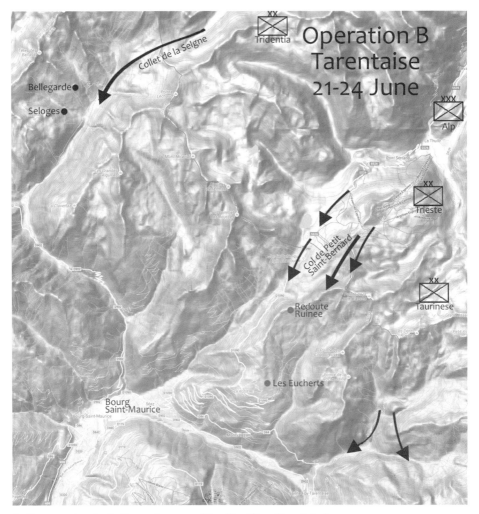

Italian operations in the Tarentaise sector of the Alps. (OpenStreetMap)

infantry moved out in the snow in the direction of Bourg-Saint-Maurice and Beaufortin. One group took the RN 90 which crossed the Petit-Saint-Bernard pass and descended into the Rosière Valley. The other group moved towards the Col de la Seigne which descended into the Valley of Les Chapieux.

The 1 Taurinese Division was tasked with clearing a path for the 101 Trieste Motorized Division and the 133 Littorio Armoured Division (Armoured Corps). The small AP of Redoute-Ruinée blocked their path. The redoubt was manned by thirty-six men of 70 BAF equipped with one machine gun installed in a casemate and two 81mm mortars placed out in the open, plus seven FMs. The crew was commanded by Sub-Lt Desserteaux. The mission of Redoute-Ruinée was to watch the road from the Petit-Saint-Bernard and to notify the sector artillery commander if the enemy was spotted. A secondary mission was to interdict the passage through the Traversette and Petit-Saint-Bernard passes.

The 2 Tridentina Division moved towards the Col de la Seigne to force the French position, guarded by the SES of 7 *Bataillon des Chasseurs Alpin* (BCA) of 80 BAF, commanded by Lt Bulle. The 80th was in contact with and supported by elements of 199 *Bataillon de Chasseurs de Haute Montagne* (BCHM) at Mont Tondu. The route to the valley of the Isère below the pass was blocked below the Col de l'Enclave in S/S Beaufortin by the Blockhouse Bellegarde, commanded by Lt de Caslex and the length of the glacier by the Advanced Post (Ouvrage) of Séloges,[5] manned by forty men of the CEO 70 BAF commanded by Lt Drevon. French heavy artillery support was provided by 150mm Model 1919 guns of III Battery, 9 *Régiment d'Artillerie Divisionnaire* (RAD – Divisional Artillery Regiment) at Condamines.

At 0800hrs, Italian artillery, most likely from 21 Motorized Artillery Regiment,[6] launched a brief bombardment of AP Redoute-Ruinée supported by aircraft. This was followed up by an infantry attack. The conduct of the attack suggested that the Italians most likely no longer considered Redoute-Ruinée to be a threat. They were wrong. As they approached the position the French opened up with a deadly fire, supported by artillery, and drove the Italians back to their starting position.

At 1100hrs the Italians began a second bombardment. They attempted to advance along the RN 90 but it was blocked by French demolitions carried out earlier on the small Pont de la Marquise. The Italian vehicles were unable to move through the blockage so they tried instead to send a group of motorcyclists via an alternate route. French machine-gun and artillery fire put a stop to this action. At the Col de la Seigne the Italians were under constant fire from French positional artillery and the guns of the Ouvrage de Séloges.

The Vallée de Beaufort to the west was undefended, opening up the possibility of an Italian breakthrough at the Col de l'Enclave. 179 BAF (Bataillon de la Valserne) previously defended the valley, but had been relocated to guard against the threat of German troops moving down the Rhone Valley. 9 RA also pulled out and could no longer support the Bourg-Saint-Maurice position. The SES of 80 BAF moved up to guard the Col de l'Enclave.

On 22 June fighting continued at Petit-Saint-Bernard in the vicinity of PA Les Eucherts[7] to the rear of Redoute-Ruinée which was held by 3rd Company of 215 RI (Sgt Boyer). Around 1100, Italian shells damaged the Eucherts-Redoute Ruinée cable car leading up to Redoute-Ruinée, thereby isolating the small garrison. The French defenders fought back with small arms and supporting artillery but in the evening the decision was made to pull the troops back from the advanced posts. Redoute-Ruinée was now isolated.

At Col de la Seigne, 22 June began with a strong attack on the Blockhouse de Bellegarde. Ouvrage du Séloges had been neutralized by Italian artillery and was unable to prevent the Italians from capturing Bellegarde. Lt de Caslex was killed during the attack. French artillery succeeded in preventing the Italians from also capturing Séloges. In the afternoon, a heavy, two-pronged attack was launched against the Col de l'Enclave. It was stopped by the small group of defenders led by Lt Baille who set up an excellent machine-gun position overlooking the road to the pass.

On the morning of 23 June, the defenders of Redoute-Ruinée waited for an Italian assault but nothing happened. There were no more attacks against the AP. Italian engineers repaired the Pont de la Marquise at the Col de Petit-Saint-Bernard and at 0700hrs seventeen Italian motorized units[8] moved forward. This was observed at Redoute-Ruinée but there was no longer any telephone contact with the main forts. The commander sent a carrier pigeon to alert the artillery commander Colonel Montvernay. Meanwhile the lead vehicle in the column drove over a mine and blocked the convoy. French shells began to rain down on the stalled convoy, causing a large number of casualties.

During the day, an Italian patrol approached the Blockhouse[9] de Versoyen[10] and attempted to move up along the anti-tank ditch. The crew from Ouvrage le Chatelard, south-west of Versoyen,[11] fired machine guns on the patrol. The battle also raged at Séloges but Italian casualties mounted and enthusiasm for continuing the attacks waned. An Italian battery opened fire on Séloges but 164 RAP countered with a 150mm barrage and the shelling ceased. All Italian activity ceased soon after.

No attacks took place on 24 June against S/S Tarentaise. In the evening the Italians moved back to their points of departure. On 25 June, after the cease fire went into effect, an Italian patrol approached Versoyen. Adjutant Bernard warned the Italians to leave, prompting them to open fire. At 1400hrs, a second attempt was made to approach Versoyen but this time the French fired into the air. The Italians moved to within 300m of the bloc but they were hit by a machine-gun burst, wounding three of the Italians. After this they stayed away.

On 2 July, the Redoute-Ruinée was evacuated with honours.

SF Savoie – Vallée de la Maurienne (S/S Haute-Maurienne)

In the S/S Haute-Maurienne, First Italian Army Group, commanded by General Vecchiarelli, launched a three-pronged attack:

- Right wing – Susa Division to attack Bessans.
- Centre – Principal axis of attack by two divisions: 59 Cagliari Division to force a passage in the direction of l'Esseillon and 11 Brennero Division to force the Col du Mont Cenis in the direction of Haute-Maurienne.
- Left wing – 1 Superga Division to move on Galibier and Saint-Jean-de Maurienne.

The frontier in the sub-sector passed over the summit of the Col du Mont Cenis, a wide plateau that ascended up from Moncenisio. On the French side the approach was less simple and was defended by several fortified positions. The powerful Ouvrage de la Turra[12] was an excellent observation point and defended the plateau with two casemates, each with two 75mm guns, plus four 81mm mortars mounted in the open, two machine guns and three FMs. The defenders were a mix from 4th Battery of 164 RAP, commanded by Sub-Lt Chandresis and an infantry company of 71 BAF[13] commanded by S/Lt Prudhon, also the ouvrage commander. The AP of Revêts, armed with two machine-gun and one observation casemate, an entry with FM and an outside mortar battery, had a crew of twenty men commanded by Aspirant Cavin. The crew included twenty-three men from 11th Company of

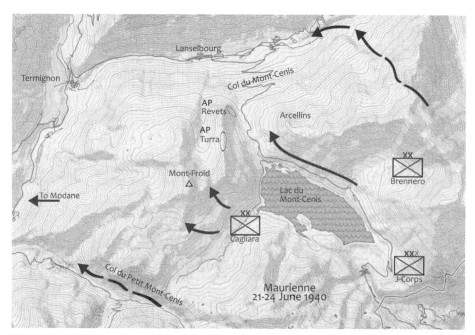

The Italian Alpine Corps attacked the Col du Mont Cenis. (OpenStreetMap)

I/281 RI.[14] The small unfinished Blockhouse des Arcellins (A2)[15] guarded the road leading to Lanslebourg-Mont-Cenis on the opposite side of the valley.

At 0900hrs on 21 June the Italians appeared at the Col de la Tomba, prompting a response by the SES of 99 RIA which was forced to pull back despite support from the 75mm guns of la Turra. The ouvrage fired 100 shells during the day and had some success, hitting an Italian column of snow tractors stuck in a minefield. The day was calm until around 1200hrs when Italian artillery, notably the 149mm turret guns of Batteria della Paradiso,[16] opened fire, a prelude to an attack on AP Revêts. The men of la Turra sheltered in underground tunnels. Revêts did not have the same degree of protection and the post shook with each shell and the telephone lines were cut.

At 0300hrs on 22 June Italian artillery opened fire. The bombardment continued until dawn when the Italian infantry, supported by light armoured vehicles, moved ahead against AP Revêts. At 1400hrs a heavy fog descended across the front and the Italians attempted an attack on Poste de la Turra but the French were ready and repelled the attack. At 1500hrs two assault groups attacked the Blockhouse des Arcellins on the heights of Ouillon and captured the crew and the position. This was the only concrete structure captured by the Italians during the campaign.

At 2100hrs a new attack was launched on the Pas de la Beccia but the French saw it coming and the attackers were chased off by a 75mm gun. By the evening of 22 June, the Italians occupied Haute-Maurienne but the French still held Mont Cenis, despite the capture of Blockhouse des Arcellins.

At 0530hrs on 23 June action continued at La Turra but was again stopped by the fort's 75s. Revêts held off an attack from the direction of Arcellins. A violent bombardment followed and continued into the early hours of 24 June. Another attempt at La Turra and Revêts was stopped that day. At 1600hrs heavy fog and snow rolled in and fighting stopped six hours before the armistice.

SF Savoie – S/S Moyenne-Maurienne

This sector was the strongest in the Maurienne region. The town of Modane was surrounded by a group of artillery forts, old and new. The Italians had the advantage of the terrain as they were in possession of a large, heavily-fortified salient that ran along the border between Maurienne and Briançon. It provided them with an excellent base of departure.

Italian troops headed down the Vallée de l'Arc via Le Planey and La Thuile and came in range of the guns of the Ouvrage du Sapey's Casemate de Maurienne,[17] equipped with two 75mm Model 1933 howitzers. On 22 June at 1515hrs the guns fired on and stopped a column of Italian muleteers near Bramans. The next day an Italian threat came from the region of Hortière and Aissois. Casemate Maurienne fired thirty-three shots on advancing troops in the region of Planey.

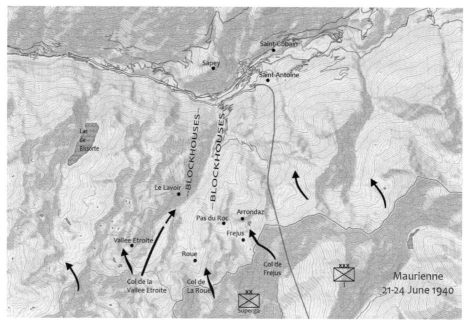

Attacks in the Maurienne sector. (OpenStreetMap)

On 24 June, Italian infantry were spotted near the Chalets Soliet. The artillery command post of Ouvrage de Saint-Antoine called in the coordinates to Casemate Maurienne. From 0650hrs to 1045hrs the guns fired 143 rounds on the Italians. That afternoon it fired on a column of muleteers moving towards Notre-Dame-de-Déliverance. In the evening, with the cease fire looming, the guns were ordered to fire until all of their ammunition was expended.

In the Bissorte Valley heavy fog and French guns held off an Italian advance. The results were not the same in the Vallée de Charmaix. At 0500hrs on 20 June a small Italian detachment moved across the border and attacked the AP de la Roue.[18] The commander, Adjutant Lissner, called for supporting fire from Ouvrage Le Lavoir,[19] commanded by Captain Deyris, and Ouvrage du Sapey.[20] The enemy troops were driven off by the guns of the forts.

On 21 June, a major artillery duel took place in the south. The Italians targeted the ouvrages throughout the day. The French responded in kind. The Ouvrage du Pas de Roc,[21] commanded by Captain Chanson,[22] was a prime target. The *téléferique* (cable car) cable leading up to the fort was cut and the GFM of Bloc 1 was pounded by the Italian guns. In the afternoon, all infiltrations towards the Vallée Étroite were stopped by the guns of Lavoir.

Since the morning, an Italian machine-gun crew had been firing at the AP of Fréjus.[23] The crew was just about ready to abandon the bloc when, around 1400hrs, Pas du Roc fired its 81mm mortars and dispersed the Italian gunners. Around 1600hrs the observer at Fréjus spotted an Italian mortar crew setting up in a nearby field. This threat was quickly eliminated by the mortars of Bloc 4 of Pas du Roc. A new attack was launched at 1730hrs by I Battalion, 91 Infantry Regiment[24] which attempted to bypass the Col de la Rousse and attack the AP de la Roue. The attackers were stopped by the AP's machine guns. At 1745hrs they were joined by the mortars of Lavoir and the Italians fled. At 1830hrs Ouvrage du Sapey fired on an Italian gun crew at the Col de la Vallée Étroite. At 2000hrs Sapey fired on and dispersed a column headed towards the Col de la Roue. At 2020hrs the fort fired seventy-two shots, driving off a small unit assembling at Col de la Vallée Étroite.

On 22 June, a renewed enemy effort threatened the APs of Fréjus, La Roue and Col de la Vallée Étroite.[25] Italian troops approached AP Fréjus but were hit by flanking fire from Ouvrage d'Arrondaz's[26] machine guns and mortars. At the AP de la Roue and Col de la Vallée Étroite, the Italians tried a new approach. They moved a battery of mountain guns within range and fired directly into the embrasures of the APs. The response came from Lavoir and after a few shots the Italian guns were destroyed. This was followed by an assault against La Roue. Around 1800hrs, helped by the fog, a large force moved to within 50m of the post, cut through the barbed wire and attacked the AP. With no way to alert Lavoir to the need for support and the phone line having been cut, the crew attempted a sortie and attacked the Italians with grenades. As night fell the Italians fell back.

A heavy fog lay over the battlefield on 23 June. The Italians did not attempt any attacks during the day but during the night of 23/24 June, infantry from 91 IR went on the attack. The weather was still very bad and caused serious problems for the Italians. It also made it difficult for the French to spot them. They believed the Italians had moved on top of the Ouvrage d'Arrondaz and Pas du Roc. The crews heard machine guns firing at the blocs. Arrondaz, Pas du Roc and the AP of Fréjus and Lavoir fired mutually supporting barrages at each other to pin down the attackers. Bloc 4 of Pas du Roc fired on top of Arrondaz while Bloc 1 of Lavoir joined in. Pas du Roc's mortars in Block 4 fired on Bloc 1 and the observatory of Pas du Roc. A French sortie discovered that the Italians were gone, or had never been there in the first place. The lack of dead or wounded made it appear as though the latter may have been the more accurate explanation. The crews were firing at shadows. But the support fire continued. From 0420hrs to 0530hrs the blocks of Fréjus and Sapey fired on top of Arrondaz. Around 0945hrs the front was again quiet.

June 24th was a quiet day but action picked up again around 2000hrs, just a few hours before the cease fire was to come into effect. Italian troops near Pas du Roc were hit by the guns of Lavoir. Pas du Roc fired on Arrondaz and AP Fréjus and also on the frontier area to the limit of the range of the guns. Sapey fired 144 shots at the AP de Fréjus[27] and 246 at Arrondaz. The guns finally stopped firing at 0010hrs on 25 June. The final occurrence was the explosion of the barrel of the 81mm mortar of Lavoir, which wounded two of the crew.

SF Savoie – S/S Basse-Maurienne

The Vallée de la Clarée was guarded by the Ouvrage Les Rochilles[28] and AP de l'Aiguille-Noire, a small bloc with four FMs. The fifty-four men of 91 BAF at Les Rochilles were supported by interval troops and six 155mm Model 1877 guns at Fort Télégraphe. On 21 June, the Italians closed in on Rochilles. A patrol dispatched from the ouvrage found the Col de Nérache and Col des Murandes occupied by the enemy. The Italians seemed ready for an attack but it was not in the direction of the ouvrage as expected. Rather, they passed out of the range of the guns and attempted to sneak past at Saint-Michel-de-Maurienne. On the night of 21/22 June, having gone through the Cols de Valmeinier and de Nérache, they occupied the Cirque de Valmeinier. This was defended by a company from 91 BAF supported by the guns of Fort Télégraphe. Once the shells started to fall the Italians were forced to take cover. By 1000hrs the threat to the sector had been removed. A flanking counter-attack by French troops from Rochilles succeeded in pushing the enemy back completely. The Italians made no other attempt at an attack in the sector.

SF Dauphiné

Briançonnais (S/S Haute-Clarée and S/S Haute-Durance)

In June 1940 Briançon was a very strong position with a mix of old and new fortifications. It was held by 75 DBAF and gunners from 154 RAP. Italian operations in Briançon centered on the powerful Italian battery of Chaberton that dominated the area with eight 149mm guns. The battery had been built by Italian Army engineers from 1888 to 1908 in response to a possible French threat at the Colle de Monginevro. The battery was built at 3,130m to dominate the French forts. Eight towers topped with 149mm guns served as the main long-range weapons. The battery was manned by 150 men of the 515th Battery.

On 17 June at 1735hrs Chaberton opened fire, eight shots at a time over regular intervals. The first target was Fort de l'Olive as well as several interval batteries. The damage was minimal. On 18 June, Italian activity increased, the main pressure coming against the Acles salient.

Italian motorized units were spotted on the Route de Clairières by observers at the Ouvrage du Janus.[29] In June 1940, the shooting angle of the embrasures had been expanded by chipping away at the concrete in order to provide a defence towards the Col de Montgenèvre. The information was passed on to the command but no action was taken at the time. The French did not fire as long as the Italians remained in a defensive posture and they did not fire towards the border. On 18 June, Italian guns fired on Ouvrage du Janus, cutting the power cable. The generator inside the fort was activated.

On 20 June, the enemy infiltrated the village of Montgenèvre and the nearby woods, the Bois de Suffin and Bois de Sestrières, in an attempt to establish a point of departure for a subsequent attack. Italian infantry moved out of the Bois de Sestrières, heading towards Gondrans and the Point d'Appui de Rocher de Dix Heures,[30] held by 91 BCA. Their objective was to outflank the fortifications of the Col du Montgenèvre.

On the same day Chaberton opened fire with all eight guns in support of the Italian attack. Three hundred shells landed on top of Janus and on les Aittes,[31] the observatory of l'Infernet and Gondrans. Because of the damage being done the French command gave the order to neutralize Chaberton. A battery of four 280mm Model 1914 heavy mortars belonging to 6th Battery of 154 RAP (Lt Miguet) were brought in to do the job. Two guns were place at Poët-Morand on the south-west slopes of Gondran, the other two at l'Eyette below Infernet. Around 0900hrs, additional enemy columns crossed the Cols de Gimont, Bousson and Chabaud, heading towards la Cerveyrette. At 1100hrs, they were spotted by the observers at Aittes who fired machine guns in that direction. This was enough to stop the enemy advance.

On 21 June from 0700hrs to 1600hrs Chaberton, enveloped in a heavy fog bank, fired all eight guns at the Redoute de Lenlon,[32] and Ouvrages de Gondran[33] and Janus. A total of 900 149mm shells and fifteen 210mm landed on top of Janus. The ouvrage consisted of a mix of old and new structures of the former Fort de Janus. The fort's masonry blockhouse suffered significant damage and the 95mm battery was also damaged, a ventilator shaft was demolished and shells fell inside the battery through holes made by previous shots. Finally, the vaulting in the access tunnel to the blockhouse cracked. The modern section of the ouvrage remained undamaged, however. Italian shells even missed the artillery observers' periscope in Block 4 that had been left in its raised position throughout the bombardment.

Lt Miguet's guns were in place and he was given the go-ahead by Colonel Vallet, sector artillery commander, to open fire on Chaberton. The fog finally lifted at 1000hrs and the gunners were given a clear view of the fort. Regulation of the firing was controlled by the observers at Janus and the shots began to land on the summit of Chaberton. After only three shots the fog rolled back in. Miguet had to wait until 1530hrs for the air to clear again and the four 280mm guns pounded Fort de Chaberton to pieces. The Italians kept firing even as French shells hit, aiming for the old Fort de Briançon from which they suspected the French guns were firing. One by one the guns were put out of action.

On 22 June, thick fog blinded the observers. Enemy infantry, after failing to capture the passes, proceeded against the heights in between. In the Bois de Suffin the Italians moved against AP Rocher-de-Dix-Heures to Fort de Janus. Because of the advance against Rocher-de-Dix-Heures, the gunners at Janus decided to modify the 75mm mortar embrasure in order to be able to fire at a greater range without hitting the concrete surrounding the embrasure. This involved chipping away at the embrasure's concrete to widen the firing angle. At dawn on 23 June Captain Weise executed shots from the 75 outside the angular range of the fort. The shots fell 60m in front of Rocher-de-Dix-Heures.

At 1200hrs, the garrison requested urgent support from Janus. Despite the fog 216 shells landed near the outpost. Taking advantage of the fog, the Italians moved towards le Charvin and from there to the AP of Chenaillet[34] which had been under heavy fire since 0500hrs. At 1400hrs Janus spotted about 100 men east of Chenaillet but they were in dead ground and the fort could not intervene. The telephone line had been cut by the bombardment so there was no way to alert the AP. Ninety minutes later, when the fog lifted, the French could see the Italians had captured the AP and were installing mortars on top. However, Janus's artillery opened fire and the Italian effort proved a failure in the end. In the evening the Italians made another attempt on Rocher-de-Dix-Heures but were stopped again by the mortars of Janus and with that they retreated. In the morning of 21 June Janus continued to fire on several targets – a column of thirty trucks heading towards Clarières, the cable car of Mont-Fort-du-Boeuf and the route de Césanne.

Chaberton still had some life left in three of its turrets but despite the fog the French 280mm battery also kept up the pressure. The 280s fired twenty-four shots on Chaberton which was saved from complete destruction only by the armistice. Miguet's battery fired a total of 101 shots and destroyed six of the eight guns.

As the armistice approached it seemed that every gun was firing and the French guns continued until midnight. The last boom echoed off the sides of the mountains, then silence. In Briançon, as at Maurienne, the Italians had failed to reach the main line of resistance and ironically, their strongest fort had been destroyed.

Vallée du Queyras (S/S de Guil)
There were no permanent fortifications here due to the nature of the terrain. It was organized around a series of infantry positions at the heights of Abriés and a ligne d'Arrêt of Sommet-Bucher to Chateau-Queyras. The defenders were from 75 DBAF, commanded by Lt Col Bonnet, 45 DBCA and five SES, supported by twenty-eight artillery pieces.

The attack on Queyras began 21 June by 3rd Alpine Division against the frontier outposts. The defenders staged a fighting retreat and rallied at Abriés. In mid-afternoon, the Italians were pressing hard but the French put up a vigorous defence and accurate fire from their artillery forced the Italians to retreat. On 24 June, the Italians attacked again in several places but these were lackluster and the offensive in Queyras ended as each side waited for the coming armistice.

Vallée de l'Ubaye (S/S Ubaye, S/S Jausiers)
At 0500hrs on 22 June, observers at PO de Plate-Lombard[35] could not believe their eyes: the path leading down from the Col de la Stoppia (2850m) was entirely black; an entire enemy battalion. Supporting artillery was immediately notified and 105mm guns of 3rd Battery of 162 RAP responded and stopped the attack. Machine-gunners from surrounding forts cleared up the remaining pockets.

Ouvrage du Roche-la-Croix's[36] 75mm mortars in Bloc 5 fired from the flanks at the exit of Col de la Stoppia. A second attack at 1700hrs was also stopped. On 23 June, the Italians attempted to penetrate via the Col de Gypiere above Fouillouze Haut to outflank the PO de Plate-Lombard. Some isolated Italian units made it to the Vallée de l'Ubaye where they surrendered to the French.

On 17 June, Italian patrols penetrated into French territory in this vicinity. An SES patrol spotted the Italians and pursued them to the Cabane du Lauzanier. At 1510hrs Roche-la-Croix's turret opened fire. The Battery of Viraysse[37] reported a direct hit and twenty minutes later the Italians fled back over the border. On 20 June, Italian artillery shelled Viraysse with a 280mm or a 305mm. In other action, Bloc 6 of Roche-la-Croix spotted Italian observation posts on the Tête-des-Partes and fired a few rounds that landed on them.

On 21 June, a large mass of Italian troops of 44 Infantry Division descended via the Col de Sautron and another group from 43 Infantry Division via the Col des Morges. The objective was Battery Viraysse. The Italians made a feint towards the Col de Larche. A column of 300 muleteers with a hundred mules climbed from the Lac de la Madeleine towards the Tête-des-Partes and were spotted by the Viraysse observatory. At 1050hrs, the muleteers were dispersed by fire from 13th Battery of 293 *Régiment d'Artillerie Lourde Divisionnaire* (RALD – Heavy Divisional Artillery Regiment) with 155mm CS Model 1917 guns. Ten minutes later the 75mm turret of Roche-la-Croix completed the job.

On 22 June, from 0800hrs to 1125hrs the Italians, despite powerful French counterbattery fire, notably from the 75mm turret of Roche-la-Croix, concentrated their fire on the AP de Larche and the Viraysse observatory which was hit by 240mm shells. At 0900hrs, telephone communication with the observatory was cut and the observers switched to radio. Several battalions appeared in the passes between the Col de Larche and the Col le Brec de Chambeyron. At 0805hrs Roche-la-Croix's Bloc 6 and Roche-la-Croix Supérieure directed fired on the two battalions descending from the Col des Morges in the direction of the Rouchcouze Ravine. From 1030hrs to 1600hrs the guns continued to pound the enemy, firing 320 rounds. Roche-la-Croix's 75mm casemate guns intervened on the exits from the frontier passes as well as assisting the defenders of Plate-Lombard.

The Italians continued to attempt to capture Viraysse throughout the day. The defenders in the direction of the peak of Tête-Dure were forced to retreat to AP Larche around 1600hrs, leaving Viraysse isolated and surrounded. They returned to their position during the night and at dawn attempted to make contact with the defenders of Viraysse. Snow fell on 23 June and no action was taken against Viraysse. In the valley, Maison Méane had been threatened since the beginning of the day and the crew was forced to evacuate at 1000hrs. Bloc 6 of Roche-la-Croix fired against Italian troops at the village of Larde, then at 1400hrs and 1520hrs it dispersed two columns of muleteers moving down from the Col de Larche. At 1700hrs, the Italian columns moved back across the border via the Col des Morges.

The Italians were well aware of the role being played by Viraysse in observing their every movement. Around midnight on 23 June they launched a new assault on the position. The defenders, reinforced by SES, pushed the enemy back with grenades as they approached the perimeter.

On 24 June, despite bad weather that included snow, the Italians pressed their attacks. Roche-la-Croix's casemate and turret intervened. From 0420hrs, 100 rounds were fired to disperse about 250 Italians descending from la Tête-Dure. Ten minutes later, a hundred men crossed the border at the Col de Larche. The first salvos fired by the fort stopped the lead elements of the column. Most of the men in the column fled. This action lasted until 0800hrs, when a new column of muleteers was spotted at the foot of Col de Larche and were chased off by several French rounds. Fog covered the battlefield until 1330hrs. When it lifted, an impressive spectacle was revealed: a large number of Italians had been killed and wounded at Col Rémi and Tête-Dure, pounded by French artillery and machine guns. An additional 335 men threw down their arms and surrendered.

Around 1535hrs a long column of muleteers was spotted at Vallon du Lauzaner headed for the frontier. One shot from Roche-la-Croix's Bloc 6 created disorder in the column and men and mules fled. At 1600hrs a patrol of twenty men was spotted near the village of Larche. The turret fired thirty rounds causing heavy casualties. Only a few Italian soldiers escaped. The final shots from Bloc 6's turret were fired between 2030hrs and 2040hrs on a mountain battery coming down the Col des Morges. The clouds moved in after twenty-four shots, blocking the view of the gunners. During the day, the mortars of Bloc 2[38] of Ouvrage du Saint-Ours Haut had their first action against enemy activity on the slopes of Tête-de-Siguret. These were most likely to give the crew something to do and the empty out their magazines. At the end of the day the situation was completely reestablished on the French side. The position of Larche remained in French hands.

On 16 June, the Italians had moved towards the border at Col du Fer, pushing the SES troops back to AP Le Pra.[39] At 1800hrs the next day they crossed the border. The 75/32 howitzers of Bloc 6 of Ouvrage du Restefond[40] fired twenty rounds towards the forest house of Tortissa and Lac de Vens. The Italians did not press their attack. On 21 June at 0845hrs, two enemy companies passed further north at Col du Pourriac. They were spotted by the observatory of Fourches which called in the target to Restefond. The fort's 75/32 and 75/31 mortars fired 180 shots to block the line of Pas de la Caval – Lac d'Agnel.

On 23 June from 0245hrs to 0815hrs there was a heavy bombardment of the AP Les Fourches.[41] At 0400hrs, the 75/32 of Restefond conducted interdictory fire on the region of Pourriac, Trois-Évêches and Lac d'Agnel, key routes used by the attackers. At 0800hrs, the smoke from the shelling lifted and AP Fourches spotted a group of Italians at Pourriac and another group descending via the Pas de la Caval. The AP's machine guns opened fire and the Italians dived for cover. At 1100hrs, caught between the machine guns at Fourches and the artillery fire from Restefond, the Italians could not advance and retreated under cover of a snow squall. In the afternoon, they took advantage of the fog and snow to attempt another attack via the Col des Quartiers d'Août and the *bosse* (knob) du Lauzanier in the direction of Sagnes. Observers at Sagnes guided the targeting of the 75/31 mortar of Restefond, stalling the new attack.

French guns opened fire again on 24 June on positions occupied by the enemy in the Col des Quartiers d'Août. From 2030hrs to 0035hrs all of the guns of the sector and Restefond fired in the direction of the border. At dawn on 25 June all of the French forts were still flying the French flag. A total of 13,000 shells were fired in Ubaye-Restefond from 17 to 24 June, 30 per cent of them by the Ouvrages of Roche-la-Croix, Saint-Ours Haut and Restefond.

SF Alpes-Maritime

SF Alpes-Maritime was the strongest sector of the alpine Maginot Line defences, especially between the sea and Authion where there was an artillery ouvrage, nine mixed ouvrages, three small ouvrages, two observatories and six APs along a 35km front. Beyond Authion the concentration was not as dense – one unfinished mixed fort, two mixed forts in the Vallée de la Vésubie and four ouvrages (one mixed) in the Vallée de la Tinée in which there were also four unfinished roadblocks.

The main Italian effort in this sector – Operation R (Riviera) – was directed between Sospel and the Mediterranean Sea. There were two reasons: this was the shortest distance from the border to Nice and Marseilles; and because the snow was less deep closer to the coast. The attack was carried out by the XV Corps of General Gambarra with five divisions, two in the forward echelon (5 Cosseria Division facing Mention and 37 Modena Division facing Mont-Ours). The

From Bloc 6 of Ouvrage d'Agaisen, SF Alpes-Maritimes, S/S Sospel, looking across the town of Sospel towards Fort Barbonnet. (Dan McKenzie)

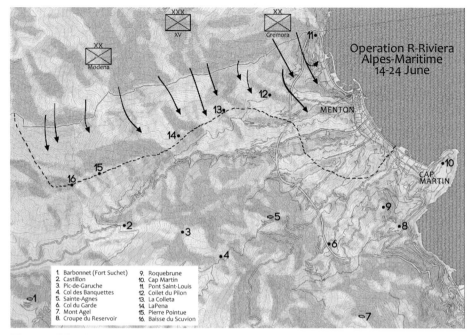

Operation R-Riviera
Alpes-Maritime
14-24 June

MENTON

CAP MARTIN

1. Barbonnet (Fort Suchet)
2. Castillon
3. Pic-de-Garuche
4. Col des Banquettes
5. Sainte-Agnes
6. Col du Garde
7. Mont Agel
8. Croupe du Reservoir
9. Roquebrune
10. Cap Martin
11. Pont Saint-Louis
12. Coilet du Pilon
13. La Colleta
14. LaPena
15. Pierre Pointue
16. Baisse du Scuvion

The powerful Italian attacks of Operation R were repulsed all along the front by the guns of the Maginot Line. Italian troops captured a few streets in Menton but were unable to move forward en masse. (OpenStreetMap)

III Corps of General Arisio with the 3 Ravenna Division faced Saorge and included the *Gessi Raggruppamento Alpini.*

Secteur de la 65 ID (S/S Mounier and S/S Tinée-Vésubie)

There was not much action here. On the afternoon of 20 June, a demonstration was carried out from the Col du Lombarde. Italian forces descended into the Vallée de Castillon only to find themselves in the field of fire of the automatic weapons of the AP of Isola.[42] The Italians were blocked in the valley, 3km from Tinée. The following day they appeared in the vicinity of Mont-Giraud, 6km north of Rimplas, out of the range of the ouvrages. Patrols then crossed the border north of Saint-Martin-Vésubie. At 0950hrs, Bloc 5 (Block Valdeblore) of the Ouvrage de Rimplas[43] opened fire on the farm of Villar.

On 22 June, the unfinished Ouvrage du Col de la Valette was shelled. The visibility was poor but it did not stop the Italians from attacking Tinée in the region of Bourguet (S/S Mounier). In the afternoon, the French opened fire and the Italian attack was stopped. At 2000hrs Bloc 4 (also called Block Tinée) of Rimplas joined in. To the east the Italians used the Vallon de Cabane-Vieille to approach la Bolline. The movement was spotted by the APs which requested support from Rimplas. The time was 1133hrs. Further east the Italians infiltrated via the Vallée du Boréon, de la Madone-de-Fenestre and de la Gordolasque, which led from the border to La Vésubie. It was the turn of the Ouvrage du Gordolon[44] to fire its first shots.

On 24 June, the Italians continued to advance via the Gordolasque. This was observed by the periscope of the Ouvrage de Flaut, which fired 81mm mortars from Bloc 4, joining the 75/33 mortars of Gordolon and forcing the Italians to turn back.

Secteur du SFAM (S/S Sospel)

On 15 June at 1000hrs, Italian mortars near the Col de l'Arpette fired on the SES of 85 BAF who fell back to Mont-Ainé. Fifteen minutes later the 75mm turret of Ouvrage du Monte-Grosso[45] replied, scoring a direct hit on the mortars which went flying into the air, sending their crews running. Additional 149mm and 210mm Italian artillery returned fire on the top of Monte-Grosso, wounding a sentry in the observation cloche. Monte-Grosso's guns fired throughout the following day (16 June) on a group of Italians crossing the frontier near Col de l'Arpette, then on the 17 June against an enemy battery north of l'Abeillon. The fort continued to fire up until the armistice.

It remained mostly calm until 20 June when the Italians took advantage of an early morning fog to send 300 soldiers past the Col de l'Arpette to threaten the village of Breil. Directed by observers and infantry, Monte-Grosso's 75mm turret and Ouvrage d'Agaisen's 75[46] fired about 500 shots, forcing the Italians to retreat.

In the evening the 155mm Mougin turret of Fort de Barbonnet fired twenty shots into Italy on the Pont de Libri that crossed the Roya and over which Italian reinforcements were headed for Breil.

On 21 June, the SES of 85 BAF returned to its post of Mont-Ainé. The Italian battery of Mont-Alto was hit by counterbattery fire from the 75mm turrets of Monte-Grosso and Agaisen. The Italians took advantage of a thick fog to disengage the attackers that surrounded AP Pierre-Pointue.[47]

On 23 June, the fog cleared and the Italians moved a column towards the Vallée de la Roya. They were immediately hit and dispersed by the shells of Monte-Grosso. Similar action occurred on 24 June against troops heading from Cuore toward

Bloc 2 of Ouvrage d'Agaisen. The lower level contained two 81mm mortars, the upper level two 75/31 guns. (Dan McKenzie)

la Bévera and in the Libri region. An Italian patrol heading towards the AP of
Castes-Ruines[48] was hit by machine-gun fire from Bloc 2 of Agaisen. The 75mm
turrets of Agaisen and Monte-Grosso fired about 3,500 rounds and were hit by
149mm, 210mm and possibly 380mm guns in return, 2,000 on Agaisen and 3,000
on Monte-Grosso, the most bombarded of all in the Alps. One shell struck and
dented the cap of Monte-Grosso's 75/33 turret but that was the full extent of
the damage. At Agaisen, a bomb from an aircraft fell between the observatory and
Bloc 3, creating a huge crater but causing no further damage to the fort.

S/S Corniches

The first Italian operations were carried out on 14 June with surprise attacks in
the direction of Castellar. From 0320hrs to 0600hrs the SES pulled back under the
pressure. At Plan-du-Lion, the men of 25 BCA were overwhelmed by the Italians
who seemed to be coming from every direction. They fell back and fired green
flares, signalling a request for support. The observatory of Ouvrage de Sainte-
Agnès[49] saw the flares, but because Sainte-Agnès's guns were not oriented toward
the frontier they alerted the artillery of the casemate of Barbonnet which faced the
advanced posts of S/S Corniches.

At 0507hrs the Bloc du Barrage of Ouvrage du Cap Martin[50] fired eight shots
towards the forward post of Pont-Saint-Lous. At 0517hrs the 155mm battery at
Sainte-Agnès (2nd Battery) and at 0530hrs the two 75/33 turrets of Ouvrage du
Mont-Agel[51] opened fire. All of the passages across the frontier came under heavy
harassing fire and the Italians were forced to turn back. At 1900hrs the SES moved
back to their original positions. The Italians knew that any future attacks would be
spotted and the troops hit by the guns of the forts.

On 17 June at 0217hrs two bombs were dropped from an aircraft on the Col
de Banquettes. Mont-Agel's two turrets responded by shelling the border at
Bricco Treitore. At 1715hrs a large group of Italian infantry was spotted on
the road from La Mortola. The gunners needed the permission of the artillery
commander, Lt Col Charmasson, to fire across the border and it was given at
1736hrs. Mont Agel again fired its turret guns, expending about 3,000 shells
during the day.

The attack on the town of Menton began on 20 June, in conjunction with the
attack on Breil. The Italians attempted to break through at Pont-Saint-Louis with
a frontal attack combined with a flanking attack from the mountain above Menton.
The only route for tanks was along the coast road. To move ahead, they needed
to neutralize the Advanced Post (Barrage) of Pont-Saint-Louis[52] and remove the
barricade blocking the road (*barrière rapide*). At 0815hrs, a company attempted to
attack and destroy the crew of the AP, who alerted Cap Martin. The crew used
up fifteen magazines for the machine guns against the Italians who were tossing
grenades at the entry door loophole. A minute later, shells from Cap Martin rained
down, wounding many. At 1000hrs, all of the ouvrages of S/S Sospel in range of

Menton opened fire on the coastal road, including two batteries of 155mm guns at Fontbonne, the 155mm battery of Saint-Agnès and Bloc 6 of Mont-Agel.

The Italian flanking attack through the hills above Menton was carried out and Granges Saint-Paul (1.5km north of Menton) was surrounded. Italian troops headed in the direction of the Boulevard de Garavan, east of Menton but the PA de La Colle, manned by 96 BAF, put up a strong resistance. Cap Martin and Ouvrage du Barbonnet provided support and at 1100hrs the attack was checked. Meanwhile, around 1500hrs, a reckless attack against the barricade at Pont-Saint-Louis was driven off by three 37mm rounds fired from the AP.

At the same time (around 0930hrs) Cap Martin was hit by about a hundred 75mm and 149mm shells. The observers were unable to locate the guns' positions. In the afternoon, the clouds over the mountain lifted and the observatory of Roquebrune spotted the location of what they suspected was a railway battery. The other observers now zeroed in on the track and tunnels east of Menton. The Italian railway battery opened fire again at 2030hrs. Smoke from the barrels was spotted by observers at Mont-Agel who confirmed it was a battery on railway platforms moving along the coastal line.

On 21 June attacks were limited to the bombardment of APs in the region of Castellar and PA Collet du Pilon and Cap Martin. Italian vehicles on the Bordighéra-Vintimille road gave warning of another offensive. Approaches to Pont-Saint-Louis were easily chased off by Cap Martin. News of the railway battery reached the command post of the Sous-Secteur des Corniches of Lt Col Mercier de Sainte-Croix (58 DBAF) at La Turbie.

On 22 June at 0700hrs the Italians launched a major attack along the entire front. The Cosseria Division moved towards Menton in two columns from Plan-du-Lion, forcing the SES to retreat. Fog helped two Italian regiments to take the Granges Saint-Paul road above Menton. They headed for the l'Hôpital Barriquan[53] and then to Boulevard de Garavan, which led down into Menton. The fortifications in this sector, from Cap Martin to Barbonnet, were attacked by air and artillery. All of the French guns executed arresting fire and harassing fire but the Italians succeeded in reaching the Quartier Saint-Vincent in front of Menton.

Further north the Modena Division attacked in the direction of Castillon along the routes leading from the frontier passes (Col de Cuore, Col de Treitore, Castel del Lupo). At 0800hrs, after a brief artillery preparation, enemy columns moved out en masse in fog that helped them to easily get forward. They attempted to push back the SES troops but were confronted by the APs of Baisse-de-Scuvion and Pierre-Pointue. The command posts of the sub-sector received calls for support. PA de Fascia Fonda – Côte 965[54] was captured but the attackers were hit by the guns of AP de La Péna. At 1000hrs, the advance was blocked 400m from AP Collet du Pilon. At this time Mont Agel's turrets opened fire.[55]

Ouvrage du Barbonnet (Fort Suchet)[56] fired a few 75mm rounds between the Cima de Crese and the sea. At 1035hrs, however, the barrel of Bloc 2's 75mm

The Mougin turret of Fort Barbonnet, looking across Castillon to the Mediterranean. (Dan McKenzie)

gun #2 exploded. The lights blew out and the ventilator stopped, making the air unbreatheable. Two of the crewmen were killed and six others wounded, including the Maréchal de Logis and the Chef de Pièce. The accident was the result of a shell exploding inside the barrel. Action inside the casemate was finished for all intents and purposes, even with the other two guns operational. The old guns of the Mougin turret then took over. They had so far only fired one shot. The gunners fired several test rounds then at 1400hrs fired seven more rounds towards the frontier at Granges-Saint-Paul, Mont-Gramondo and Mont Razet.

By the end of the morning the Italians were advancing via the Col de Cuore. An attack on Mont Razet was imminent but Obs 013 of Saint-Agnès could not see the troops because of the fog. The machine gun in the GFM cloche of Castillon fired non-stop on the surface of Pierre-Pointue to stop the attackers from reaching the entry doors. At 1329hrs, Bloc 3 of Saint-Agnès opened fire on Col du Razet. The 75/31 mortars fired forty rounds and most hit their targets. AP Pierre-Pointue was relieved but only temporarily. The 81mm mortars of Bloc 6 of Castillon took their turn towards Chapelle Saint-Bernard and AP La Péna.

At the end of the afternoon the SES and troops from some of the field outposts pulled back, thus putting the APs in the main line of attack. Throughout the night Saint-Agnès fired ten rounds per hour on Razet while the Italians continued to threaten Pierre-Pointue and Baisse-de-Scuvion. Around 2100hrs a fresh attack was attempted on Pierre-Pointue. The attackers tossed grenades at the embrasures of the casemates. The crews moved back from the embrasures and switched their points of defence to the door and corridor. Around midnight Adjutant-Chef Lanteri alerted Ouvrage du Castillon[57] by radio of the imminent danger of the attack and the shells of Mont Agel's turrets began to fall on top of the AP. All night long the APs maintained interdictory fire but by morning the situation was unclear. Baisse de Scuvion attempted to thwart an attack on Razet and Pierre

Pointue was still in contact with the rear. La Péna fired its mortar on Italian troops infiltrating between the posts. La Colleta and Collet du Pilon also found themselves surrounded.

Observers were still searching for the location of the railway battery but were hampered by fog. Cap Martin was shelled at 0830hrs. Twenty minutes later two locomotives were spotted and the train's guns were seen in battery in front of the tunnel of La Mortola. Due to the angle, the Block de Barrage of Cap Martin could not get a good shot. At 0930hrs a 155mm positional battery found the target. Its shots landed short, giving the train time to pull back into the shelter of the tunnel. Most of Mont Agel's guns now fired towards the tunnel causing serious damage to the train. The shells finally immobilized the locomotives and the 155mm batteries of Saint-Agnès and Fontbonne finished the job. The AP Pont-Saint-Louis had now been silent for twenty hours – the telephone line was cut and the short-wave radio was not functioning. At this point it was considered to have been lost.

At 0425hrs on 23 June enemy activity was spotted on the Massif du Razet which was solidly blocked by the APs of Baisse de Scuvion and Pierre Pointue. Bloc 2 of Saint-Agnès and the turrets of Ouvrage du Barbonnet countered all enemy infiltrations. Monte-Grosso's and Agaisen's 75mm turrets also provided support. At 0730hrs troops from Pierre Pointue launch a sortie and captured several Italian prisoners. At 0825hrs, the remaining guns in the damaged 75mm casemate at Barbonnet were back in action. At 1535hrs Barbonnet's turrets swept the Massif de Razet and the vicinity of Baisse de Scuvion. After the twelfth shot Captain Finidori, commander of Ouvrage du Castillon ordered a cease fire as the AP was now clear of enemy troops. Further south, AP Pilon was hit by an Italian 65mm gun. At 2250hrs Mont Agel's turrets opened fire around the AP then extended their target zone towards the border.

At 1030hrs the occupants of AP Pont-Saint-Louis, still alive, heard noise coming from the direction of Menton. Taking advantage of a light fog the Italians were moving up to the rear of the AP with a ladder. They came to within 3m of the post. The FM fired non-stop and the crew threw grenades at the attackers. In twenty minutes the assault was repulsed and everything was under control. The Italians made no further attempt at an assault.

Italian aircraft were in control of the skies. Throughout the morning twenty-five aircraft bombed the main line of resistance between Roquebrunne and Cap Martin a well as the Fort de Tête de Chien and PO Croupe du Reservoir[58] in an attempt to open up a path for another attack. The entire region was enveloped in heavy smoke, blocking the view of the observers. At 1540hrs the smoke cleared and observers spotted Italians moving in the town of Menton. A general attack was in progress towards the plateau of Vesqui on the RN7. At 1542hrs, the 81mm mortars of Cap Martin and the 135mm howitzer of Saint-Agnès fired on a large Italian column. Despite the destruction of the railway battery, Cap Martin was shelled by a 305mm gun. At 1600hrs a shell landed in front of the 75mm embrasure of Cap

Martin's Bloc 2. The gun chamber filled with smoke but there was no damage and the gun continued to fire on the coastal plain.

At 1750hrs the casemate guns of Cap Martin, Roquebrune and Saint-Agnès (except for the 81mm mortar) and Bloc 6 of Mont Agel executed arresting fire on Menton. At 1800hrs, observers signaled that the Italians had infiltrated below Cap Martin (Usine à Gaz) and were headed towards the Ouvrage de Roquebrune via La Vallonet. The machine guns of Cap Martin and Roquebrune opened fire. This combined action, along with the positional artillery's participation, broke up the attack. However, it appears the attack had never been as serious as first realized, perhaps because of the fog, or perhaps they were seeing ghosts. Due to the earlier artillery barrage, the Italians had no intention of approaching the ouvrage.

On the morning of 24 June, the weather was terrible. Heavy rain fell across the coastal range. Cap Martin continued to fire its 75mm guns at the Port of Menton. Italian troops around Cap Martin's Usine à Gaz were hit by 81mm mortars which also destroyed several houses. The Italians halted any further moves. At 0910hrs Cap Martin reported the presence of tanks on the Place d'Armes of Menton setting up to open fire. Since Pont-Saint-Louis was not responding, this seemed plausible. In reality, Pont-Saint-Louis still held out and the barrier blocking the road was still in place, blocking all passage on the coastal road. The sentries of Cap Martin, undergoing heavy bombardment since 20 June, were also seeing hallucinations since no tanks were present. The only actual Italian operation conducted was in the afternoon between Ouvrage du Roquebrune and Col de Garde, where a company of 90th Infantry Division, taking advantage of fog and smoke, attempted to cross the Gorbio and head towards the main line of resistance. On their way, they came across a patrol from 4 RTS and could move no further.

Things were calm in front of the five surrounded APs. At 1700hrs a convoy was spotted at the train station of Ventimiglia. A gun from 1st Battery, 157 RAP at Mont Agel fired eleven rounds. Several vehicles in the convoy exploded indicating a probable supply of ammunition. The fire burned all night long and into the next morning. At 1800hrs Pont-Saint-Louis was hit by 210mm howitzers, a prelude to an attack that never materialized. At 2300hrs the shelling stopped.

The final attempt to capture AP du Pilon took place at 2115hrs. The Italians surrounded the AP but their movement was spotted by AP de La Coletta and Mont Agel and after a few shells landed the enemy retired. At 2143hrs, Bloc 5 of Mont Agel fired on Plan du Lion (between La Coletta and Pilon) where a red flare was seen. This was the last shot of any ouvrage of the SF Alpes-Maritime. At 2146hrs the order was received to cease fire unless attacked by infantry.

Overnight, French patrols reoccupied Vesqui and moved to the slopes of Est du Vallonet. On 25 June the Italians had reached only as far as the Pont Elisabeth, 1,300m from Cap Martin. All of the APs held out. Pont-Saint-Louis's crew was relieved that night. None of the ouvrages had fallen.

Cease Fire and Armistice – 25 June

Stipulations of the armistice:

- Article 1 – not detailed here.
- Article 2– Italians to hold in place.
- Article 3 – From this line to 50km in as the crow flies will be demilitarized. [The DMZ – the first line starts from the edge of land conquered by the Italians to a second line 50km in.]
- Article 4 – DMZ will be evacuated by French troops in ten days following cessation of hostilities with the exception of personnel strictly necessary for guarding and maintaining the ouvrages, casernes, magazines and military buildings.
- Article 5 – Mixed arms of the ouvrages and munitions must be rendered non-usable.

The forts need not be disarmed but made non-operational. The French had ten days to pull out with their weapons (5 July). Everything still in place after that date belonged to the Italians.

On 27 June, the APs were evacuated and the doors locked. Several days later the ouvrages were evacuated and everything that could be moved was taken except for the heavy material and certain artillery pieces.

Mussolini visited the Col du Mont Cenis on 29 June and could not help but spot the French flag still flying over AP la Turra. The crews of Turra and Revêts did not leave until 1 July after sabotaging their 75mm guns. Redoute-Ruinée's crew evacuated the day after that.

Mussolini chose not to join the Germans in their initial attack on France. Therefore, he was left to fight only in the Alps. He believed that, since the Germans were now to the rear of the French, all he had to do was mop up and take possession of Nice and Savoie. To accomplish this objective, he had to join the fight quickly. The Germans asked him to delay his attack after the 10 June declaration of war. At the time, he believed the French army was already defeated due to bad morale and that they would be unable or unwilling to oppose an attack. Plus, many French troops had been moved to the north-east, weakening the position.

On the contrary, the French line was still solidly defended and weather conditions were remarkably favourable to the French with a late snowfall that closed off several routes. Mussolini did not launch a major attack until 20 June. The attack had to be rapid and violent in order to capture as much ground as possible in as short a time as possible. The first attempts were met by furious resistance. Each attack was checked and the Italians did not have the capability to capture the position. The fortress troops and the infantry units fulfilled their roles and preserved this territory.

Order No. 31
Officers, NCOs, Brigadiers and Cannoniers:

The armistice came upon us in full battle while we accomplished our Supreme duty for the homeland.

I know you well. I know that during the hour of combat I could count on you. I read in your eyes your impatience to participate in a gigantic struggle in which the country is engaged.

You have brought dedication and magnificent bravery. You have shown that you are among the best Sons of France and you have added to the glory of the flag of the regiment.

I am proud to have been your chief during the duration of hostilities and I thank you with all my heart for all you have so generously done.

The tasks ahead are less glorious but I'm sure you will do them with the same discipline and with the same military spirit.

When peace sends you wherever it does, hold your head high. By your work, in unison with all of France, become a moral force that nothing can ever break.

Stay faithful in your remembrance of the Regiment and guard from the bottom of your heart a thought for the Chef de Corps to whom you have given immense satisfaction to have been listened to, understood and obeyed with satisfaction and without reserve.

Vive le 157e RAP

Vive la France

P.C. – 25 Juin 1940
Le Lieutenant Colonel Charmasson
Commandant le 157e RAP

Part V

The Final Battles, 17 to 25 June 1940

Chronology 17 to 25 June

17 June	The German encirclement of the Maginot Line results in the cancellation of the final evacuation and destruction orders. Fortress troops are ordered to hold in place as long as possible.
17 June	Pétain announces the need for a cease fire and armistice, severely damaging troop morale.
18 June	German attacks resume against the PA line in SF Haguenau.
19 June	Two task forces from 215 ID launch an attack on the blockhouses and casemates of SF Vosges, punching a hole through the defences.
20 June	Heavy attacks are launched against the casemates of Aschbach and Oberroedern. After heavy, close-quarters fighting the Germans are pushed back and the Line holds.
20 June	339 IR attacks SF Faulquemont from the rear. Ouvrage du Bambesch is pounded by 88mm guns and surrenders.
21 June	Ouvrage du Kerfent is next in line to be attacked and surrenders on the same day.
21 June	The three holdouts on the right flank of SF Faulquemont – Einseling, Laudrefang and Teting – are pounded by German artillery and Einseling thwarts an assault. The forts hold out until the armistice.
21 June	German 305mm guns are among the vast artillery train used against Ouvrage du Fermont in an attempt by 161 ID to capture the fort. Despite the pounding all the fort's guns are operational and the attack is unsuccessful.
21 June	Ouvrage du Haut-Poirier is attacked by artillery and infantry. Devoid of supporting artillery, the fort surrenders on 22 June.
22 to 23 June	Ouvrage du Welschof is next in line for attack. The fort is pounded and surrenders on 23 June.
21 June	Troops of 257 ID attack the Ensemble of Biesenberg near Bitche but are stopped by the guns of Ouvrage du Grand-Hohekirkel.
22 June	Ouvrage du Michelsberg in SF Boulay is attacked by troops from 95 ID. The guns of the surrounding forts in the sector are too powerful and the German attack fails.
24 to 25 June	Some of the heaviest combat takes place in the final hours. At 0035hrs on 25 June the fighting comes to an end.

Chapter 15

German Attacks on the Maginot Line – 17 and 18 June

In the afternoon of 16 June, Cochinard had a conversation by telephone with Lt Col O'Sullivan, who informed him that the Germans were moving swiftly past Longuyon and into the rear of the Maginot Line. O'Sullivan figured SF Thionville would be directly threatened on either 16 or 17 June. He asked Cochinard if he still intended to execute Measure C and Cochinard replied that he was of a mind to suspend it that evening. Cochinard, believing his command post at Hayes to be imminently threatened, moved it to Ouvrage d'Anzeling. Around 1930hrs he sent out orders to his subsectors to move up Measure B from 2200hrs to 2000hrs and that Measure C was suspended pending further orders. O'Sullivan relocated his command post from Fort d'Illange to Ouvrage du Metrich.

On 17 June O'Sullivan made it official and sent a message to all of the ouvrages under his command: 'Measure C is cancelled. Resist in place until all munitions and supplies are exhausted.' General Condé also sent out a message to Jolivet, Denoix, Cochinard and O'Sullivan from his command post at Gerardmer that the crews of the ouvrages must not pull back on 17 June but hold until receipt of new orders. Condé knew that the crews had little to no chance of escaping to the south and would better serve the army by containing as many German units as possible in front of and behind the Maginot Line.

Ouvrage de Bréhain was operating in a siege atmosphere. The fort was placed on alert due to a possible attack by the Germans. The hours of darkness were particularly ominous. Observers were jumping at shadows and seeing hallucinations of Germans approaching the fort. On the night of 14/15 June the machine-gun turrets of Blocs 1 and 2 fired thousands of rounds and the 75mm turret fired shrapnel on top of the fort. The night of 16 June was particularly troubling. Germans were spotted on top of Casemate de Laix and tanks were reported heading towards the entries to Bréhain. However, the Germans had no tanks in the vicinity. Once again, it was nothing but phantoms.

On 17 June Pétain delivered what could have been the death blow to the morale of the Maginot Line crews, only five days after the announcement of the abandonment of the Line. At Four-à-Chaux Commandant Exbrayat confiscated all of the TSF transmitters lest the men hear false news and rumours. Captain Saint-Ferjeux of PO Rohrbach kept the news hidden from his men and energetically announced the ouvrage would fight to the very end. The reaction of other commanders was varied. Captain Lhuisset of Welschoff wanted to give the order to cease fire but was persuaded to delay it for the time being. Lt Col Bonlarron of Simserhof was cautious and ordered the guns to fire only against direct acts of hostility. Cochinard ordered his commanders not to engage with enemy emissaries.

At Grand-Hohékirkel Commandant Fabre wept at Pétain's awful announcement. After regaining his composure, he brought his officers together and announced that mention of an armistice had no effect on his orders to resist in place to the end. He would accept no demand for surrender. He passed on to the commanders of the casemates that any crew that abandoned its post would be treated as traitors and fired on by the guns of Grand-Hohékirkel.

The Germans took Pétain's announcement as an opportunity to intimidate the ouvrages into giving up. A emissary from 183 ID delivered an ultimatum to the men of Rochonvillers to lay down their arms and surrender. Commandant Guillemain chose not to respond. Further attempts to approach the fort were met with threats to keep away.

In SF Faulquemont on 18 June, three emissaries were sent from 278 IR of 95 ID to Laudrefang. After being blindfolded and taken to Bloc 4, they threatened to bombard the fort with heavy artillery and aircraft if the crew didn't surrender. After refusing the ultimatum and releasing them, Captain Cattiaux ordered the crew of Bloc 3 to fire on any Germans spotted on the road to Brantstuden, from which the emissaries had come.[1] The following day another group approached with a flag of truce, this time from 167 ID. They were chased off by machine-gun fire aimed either side of them. From this point on the Germans got the message. Additional attempts were made in other sectors to pressure the commanders to surrender. Kerfent, Einseling, Village du Coume, Rohrbach, Hackenberg, Sentzich and Galgenberg received German visitors but none surrendered.

June 16th arrived in SF Haguenau. It was a calm night but it would not remain so for long. The majority of the action of the day centered on the line of advance posts and the support provided there by the fortress artillery units. During the night, several German patrols approached PA 7 but were forced back by shelling from Schoenenbourg and Hochwald. At 0500hrs the blockhouses of Oberseebach were attacked, in particular the north bloc, but the artillery support was strong and the Germans were pushed back. At 0600hrs S1 fired north of Oberseebach where the Germans attempted to turn the French flank. The attack quickly ran out of steam. At 0930hrs there was an attack from the north of Aschbach against PA 7. Obs 03 spotted the attack and Schoenenbourg fired eighty rounds at the attackers who rapidly dispersed. The shelling continued all morning from Aschbach to Oberseebach on Germans infiltrating the two villages.

At 1015hrs a new attack on Aschbach was stopped by fire from Schoenenbourg and Bloc 6 of Hochwald. A couple of hours later the Germans mounted a strong effort to take PA 7, firing 200 77mm rounds on the PA followed up by an infantry attack. Schoenenbourg fired on PA 8 and 9, the German jump-off point. Several units were stopped but one unit infiltrating from the north-east got to within grenade range. They were forced back by fire from PA 7 and artillery from Bloc 6. Additional attempts were made during the day to capture PA7 but by nightfall the Germans were unable to make progress and rested on what they had captured that day.

Later that night Rodolphe ordered the shelling of German positions. For three hours, Niederseebach, Oberseebach, Aschbach, Trimbach and Siegen were targeted. Twenty shots per objective and per hour were fired to conserve Model 17 shells which were running short, especially at Schoenenbourg. A total of 1,712 rounds were fired during the day.

Ammunition supplies were also getting critical for the casemates of SF Crusnes. Plenty of ammunition remained for the 50mm mortars and the 47mm guns, but only 100,000 rounds for the machine guns, enough for an hour of serious fighting. Fortunately, the casemates crossed fire with their neighbours and could be regulated to conserve ammunition.

Ouvrage du Haut-Poirier – 17 June

On 17 June at 0715hrs, Jolivet, waiting for orders from LVIII Corps that would tell him what to do next, was notified by Lt Col Bonlarron that his men should, in his opinion, remain in place, but the order was not a firm one. Jolivet was also concerned about being left behind by Bonlarron so he gave the order to prepare to depart at 2200hrs according to the original order. The crew of Haut-Poirier very regretfully accepted their fate. The Germans, knowing that an evacuation was soon to be under way, launched a bombardment of the ouvrage. The officers were listening to the radio and heard Pétain's armistice announcement and that German tanks were approaching the Swiss border. Gambotti and the officers now believed that a retreat would be too dangerous and a useless sacrifice. Around 1300hrs Jolivet made up his mind to cancel the orders to retreat.

Ouvrage du Fermont – 17 June

Around 0430hrs the cloches of Blocs 1 and 2 were suddenly peppered by machine-gun fire from the west. Observers discovered that the shots originated from a small abandoned blockhouse located within the anti-tank rails that masked the blockhouse's embrasures from Bloc 1's 75mm turret. Lt Boury, commander of Bloc 1, ordered the blockhouse to be reduced. He directed the gunners to use *obus de rupture*[2] to cut the rails and expose the embrasure. Six shots later the embrasure was in full view. The gunners then switched to high-explosive rounds. During this short interval, the Germans occupying the blockhouse fled and did not return.

Bloc 4 of Fermont was a flanking casemate equipped with three 75mm guns arranged *en echelon*. At 0500hrs the bloc, commanded by Sub-Lt Bouley-Emy, came under fire from a German Flak 88 gun. Every three minutes a shell struck the façade. The armoured embrasure blinds were closed and the gunners sat back and waited, trusting that the 1.5m thick concrete would protect them.

Around 0700hrs, two engineers who worked in Fermont's power station were sent in to do something about rising temperatures in the room's expansion chamber caused by a modification to the construction. They decided to cut an opening in the ventilation shaft. While using a welding torch, a piece of molten metal fell into a gutter that contained a small amount of diesel, causing a fire. Close by 193,000 litres of diesel was stored and if it exploded the fort was finished. The fire alarm was sounded and the firefighters used sand to surround the flames. There were fire extinguishers inside the engine room but it was too hot to enter. The men finally contained the fire but it was a very close call. Several men were affected by smoke and needed oxygen.

In the afternoon Captain Aubert received a call from Bloc 4 notifying him that the wall of the block was on the verge of being pierced by the continual fire of the 88. Throughout the morning the high-velocity gun chipped away at the concrete and reinforced steel bars, deepening the crater being formed in the wall. The 88 was firing from the vicinity of Arrancy-sur-Crusnes but the observers were unable to pinpoint the gun's location. As the shells were just about to break through the wall, the German gunners ceased firing, the reason unknown. The final shell broke off a chunk of concrete that fell into the casemate, causing some minor damage. It was an incredible stroke of luck for the fort, combined with the success in putting out the fire in the engine room. The time was 1615hrs. The engineers went outside to repair the damage with an armour plate, while inside the bloc the hole was sealed up with concrete.

SF Haguenau – 17 June

June 17th was a much calmer day for SF Haguenau and there were no moves towards the APs of S/S Hoffen and PA 7 in particular. However, at 1210hrs the field command post of 79 RIF reported an attack on Oberseebach. Schoenenbourg and Hochwald Est fired 200 rounds, Bloc 7bis laying down a barrage on the centre of the village. Twenty minutes later Obs 03 spotted Germans preparing for an attack in the direction of PA 3. Schoenenbourg fired eighty shots, dispersing the attackers.

The Casemates of Oberroedern Sud and Seltz telephoned that Stundwiller and Buhl were now occupied by the Germans. They were setting up observatories and light machine-gun positions in the church bell towers. The Bellevue Farm was also occupied but the Germans were driven out by the 37mm gun of Casemate Seltz.

German artillery fire began to intensify in S/S Hoffen. Batteries of 150mm guns were moved up and fired on the casemates in the vicinity of Hunspach. At 1630hrs the APs of Geisberg reported hearing what they suspected to be armoured vehicle engines from the direction of Wissembourg and Altenstadt. The commander of S/S Pechelbronn, Chef de Bataillon Fabre, requested artillery support on the exits south of Wissembourg and Altenstadt and 240 shots were fired on each objective. An additional 370 shots were fired by the three 75mm turrets on the indicated targets. At 1815hrs Bloc 13 of Hochwald Ouest (135mm casemate) fired nine rounds north of Lembach, where isolated German units had ben spotted. Thirty minutes later Hochwald Est fired fifty-two shells on the railway line east of Wissembourg. S5 fired thirty shots on Hill 194. All in all, 1,820 shells were fired on 17 June.

The situation was critical in the south-west. At the end of the day, the Germans were moving on Eschbach, south of Woerth. Nothing significant was reported on the Rhine or in the Haguenau Forest. The news that Pétain was requesting an armistice caused great concern among the troops. They knew their situation was precarious but they still expected that the French armies would recover. The fortress troops were now alone and no orders were forthcoming. Still, the Maginot Line troops did not lose courage. They had food supplies for two months and enough munitions for three. They would hold out until the end. The crews remained calm and the guns continued to function superbly.

SF Crusnes

Every night in SF Crusnes the Germans attempted a surprise attack on a casemate. One night it was C29, the next PO Aumetz. They were always driven off but, with crew fatigue setting in, it was just a matter of time before their vigilance slipped.

SF Haguenau – 18 June

On 18 June German infantry resumed attacks on the APs of SF Haguenau. The first attack took place at 0350hrs, after a preliminary bombardment, against the position of 79 RIF. The PC of S/S Hoffen in Abri du Buchholzerberg (PC 845) reported that PA 3bis west of Oberseebach was under attack. Hochwald's Bloc 7bis fired forty direct-fire shots (*tirs direct*) and forty harassing shots (*en harcelement*) in support but the German 246 ID[3] attacked PA 4, which held out despite the strong attack. Bloc 6 also fired forty shots in support. The crew of PA 4 requested the aim shifted 200m to the right and the attackers were chased off. However, at 0604hrs, PA 4 fired a flare requesting additional support and then retreated from the position, leaving behind several prisoners. One hundred and fifty shots from Bloc 6 and Bloc 4 forced the Germans to take shelter inside the now-vacant PA. The troops in PA 5, without flanking support, also pulled back, abandoning the post. At 0700hrs Captain Potevin, in command of this section of S/S Hoffen, ordered a counter-attack to retake PA 5. The attack by thirty men was supported by Bloc 6. The PA was retaken but had to be evacuated due to German artillery fire.

The attack on the PA line ended but heavy German artillery fire continued along the ridge to the west and on the adjacent woods. German artillery was set up north-west of Trimbach. Obs 02 and 03 plotted the location and 200 shots were fired, forcing the guns to pull back. At 1000hrs and 1115hrs 7bis fired on the battery at Trimbach.

In the early afternoon, the main German effort was shifting to the west where they began to penetrate towards Lembach. Bloc 12 and Bloc 13 of Ouvrage Hochwald Ouest fired shrapnel rounds on the Gendarmerie of Lembach. At 1600hrs Bloc 14 (135mm) shelled the forest house which caught fire and German troops evacuated it.

German artillery opened up again on PA 4 at 1700hrs. At 1707hrs German infantry prepared to retake PA 5, captured earlier in the morning but later evacuated. Schoenenbourg and Hochwald Est's guns broke up the attack. From 2300hrs to 0130hrs they poured harassing fire on German troop movement near Oberseebach, Niederseebach, Trimbach, Buhl and Stundwiller. At 1600hrs the blocs of Kuhnenmuhl were captured after several direct shots by German guns, possibly 88s. During the night of 18/19 June the APs of S/S Hoffen were abandoned. The defence was too weak (100 men per kilometre of front) to be sustained and the troops were needed on the MLR, now under attack from the south.

Lt Col Schwartz was notified that troops of Sub-Sector Bas Rhin had begun to pull out during the night. A battalion of 70 RIF and 2 CEC were still south of Strasbourg and in danger of being outflanked. The fall of Strasbourg was imminent – it would be evacuated and declared an open city.

Action in SF Thionville in late June

This sector was relatively unscathed during the war, seeing only minor action, perhaps due to the fact it was the strongest sector of the Line. The forts and casemates received sporadic shelling from 105mm and 150mm guns. Ouvrage Kobenbusch was hit by several 280mm shells but they did little damage. Bloc 5 of Ouvrage du Rochonvillers,[4] a flanking 75mm artillery casemate, was very visible in the surrounding landscape and was struck from the rear. The façade of the bloc was hit by shot after shot and damaged quite heavily. Typically, the embrasures for the guns were closed off with steel blinds but one of them was not closed properly and at 2100hrs on 22 June a well-aimed shell flew through the embrasure opening and exploded inside the gun chamber. One crewman was wounded and the 135mm howitzer damaged. The observers of Rochonvillers hunted for the German battery, but could not locate it.

Minor skirmishes took place in other areas. On 18 June, in the sector between Rochonvillers and Molvange, a German detachment moved out of the woods and approached Blockhouse Cb14 bis[5] near Angevillers. The machine guns of the Casemate du Grand Lot (C36)[6] and the 135mm turrets in Blocs 6 and 7 of Rochonvillers easily located the Germans and drove them back into the woods. On 21 June at 0430hrs a German anti-tank gun, probably a Pak 37, opened fire on Bloc 9 of Rochonvillers. The bloc's machine-gun turret responded and the German anti-tank gun was silenced. Typically, when under fire the turrets were retracted for protection but in this case the MG turret stayed in battery and was hit by several German anti-tank rounds, although it survived. One of the 75mm guns at Bloc 5, while using high-explosive shells, blew up, killing one gunner and wounding the other.

PO Oberheide (A14),[7] on the extreme edge of the Cattenom salient, was exposed to heavy German artillery fire and attempted infiltrations by German patrols. Ouvrage du Kobenbusch (A13)[8] and Galgenberg (A15)[9] provided protective fire during these instances, but the 75mm turret of Kobenbusch was under constant German observation and was hit every time it rose up to fire.

The wooded area between Ouvrage du Billig (A18)[10] and the casemates of Hummersberg (C53 Nord and C54 Sud) was another danger area. The Germans made several attempts to infiltrate through the woods and rained tons of shells on the defences. On 15 June, an attempt to approach the Casemate de Hummersberg was repulsed by Billig and Hackenberg. The 81mm turrets revealed their weaknesses during this ordeal. A fire broke out inside Ouvrage d'Immerhof's 81 on 14 June. One of the barrels at Galgenberg burst and it took three days to make repairs. On 15 June, a shell exploded inside the turret at Billig.

Things were much worse at night for the defenders because observers in the isolated casemates sounded the alert for anything that moved. Shadows and sounds were often mistaken for German pioneers. But in the case of SF Thionville, the action was taking place elsewhere.

Chapter 16

Breakthrough in the Vosges

Attack on SF Vosges – 19 June

The CORF took for granted that in itself the geography of SF Vosges – wooded, with hills running along the border – would constitute a formidable barrier. Some casemates and blockhouses were built on the slope of each hill and large tracts of forest were cleared. What the sector needed most was manpower. After the interval troops pulled out on 13 June the sector was very poorly manned. About 2,000 men were left behind, along with about twenty casemates and blockhouses. 6 CEC had seventy-one men and six blockhouses per kilometre. Their orders were to hold out as long as possible.

The sector was organized as follows:

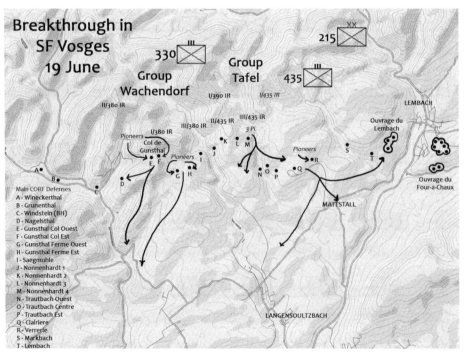

The Vosges was another weaker sector attacked by the Germans in late June. They easily broke through the thin line of blockhouses and casemates. (OpenStreetMap)

S/S Philippsbourg: 154 RIF (Lt-Col Lambert), with 2nd, 3rd and 4th *Unités d'Équipages de Casemate* (UEC – Casemate Team). It included:

- Ouvrage du Grand-Hohékirkel (Commandant Fabre) with Abris Dépôt and Wolfschachen (CORF).
- 2 UEC: Casemates Main-du-Prince Ouest, Main-du-Prince Est, MOM/RFL Casemate Biesenberg, Casemates Biesenberg I, II, III and IV, Casemate Biesenberg, Casemate Biesenberg V, VI, VII,[1] Casemate Glasbronn.
- 3 UEC: Casemates Altzinsel, Rothenburg, Nonnenkopf, Grafenweiher Nord-Est, Grafenweiher Centre.
- 4 UEC: Casemate Grafenweiher Est, Dambach Nord (a.k.a. Neunhoffen), Dambach Sud, Wineckerthal Ouest, APs Erlenmüss and Neuweiher.

S/S Langensoultzbach: 165 RIF (Commandant Renard), with 5 and 6 UEC:

- 5 UEC: Casemate Wineckerthal Est, Grünenthal, Windstein, RFL Casemate Windstein, CORF Blockhouses Nagelsthal, Col-du-Gunsthal Ouest, Col-du-Gunsthal Est.
- 6 UEC: CORF Blockhouses Gunsthal Ferme Ouest, Gunsthal Ferme Est, Saegemühle, Nonnenhardt 1, 2, 3, 4, 5, Trautbach Ouest, Trautbach Centre, Trautbach Est, CORF Casemate La Verrerie, CORF Blockhouse La Clairière, La Verrerie, Marbach, Lembach.
- Ouvrage du Lembach (Captain Drouin).
- Ouvrage du Four-à-Chaux (Commandant Exbrayat) and Casemate Schmelzbach Ouest.

After 18 June, the method for conveying support requests to Four-à-Chaux (FAC), the closest ouvrage to S/S Langensoultzbach, was changed to allow the casemate crews to contact the artillery command post directly. However, the system was dependent on the maintenance of telephone contact. If the lines were cut the crews could fire flares – green signalling FAC to fire on the casemate – but the observers could only see, at most, 1,000m and therefore would not be able to tell precisely from which casemate the signal originated. The 75mm turret of FAC could only reach Windstein, leaving Grunenthal and Wineckerthal Est and Ouest uncovered. Hochwald Ouest's 135mm turret in Bloc 14 could only reach as far as PO Lembach.

On 11 June, General Baptist Kniess, commander of 215 ID[2] was ordered to attack SF Vosges. On 15 June, the order was simplified to concentrate on the weakly defended wooded area between Bitche and Lembach, the S/S Langensoultzbach. Kniess sent out patrols to locate the weakest points to attack. On 16 June, the line of advance posts was evacuated and the front line now being probed by the Germans was the line of casemates – Wineckerthal Est, Windstein and Col de Gunsthal.

The Germans planned a two-pronged attack using two regiments of 215 ID. 435 IR led by Oberstleutnant Theodore Tafel, attacking Casemate La Verrerie and Blockhouse Trautbach. 380 IR, commanded by Oberstleutnant Freiherr von Ow auf Wachendorf, attacked with three battalions, objective Froeschwiller. A battalion of 435 IR, attached to Wachendorf's group, attacked Nehwiller to the west of Woerth. 215 ID was provided with a heavy artillery contingent, including elements from 246[3] and 262 ID.[4] Four 88s accompanied the force plus heavy guns from *Artillerie Abteilung* (AA) 800 with 355mm guns plus two 420mm guns.[5] Kneiss was also provided with the support of a squadron of Stukas. The attack was scheduled to kick off on 19 June at 0600hrs, but the bulk of the heavy artillery was still on the way to the front, fighting its own battle with muddy ground. Nevertheless, Kniess gave the order on 18 June to attack the following day.

The artillery bombardment of 19 June centered on Casemate La Verrerie. It included 100mm and 150mm guns. Smoke quickly covered the hills and ravines, blocking the view of the observers. The French believed an attack was imminent. Nagelsthal, Gunsthal Ferme, Windstein and two blockhouses on the Col de Gunsthal were also being shelled. The gunners of Four-à-Chaux and Hochwald were alerted and waiting for targets. This included Four-à-Chaux's 135mm turret in Bloc 1, Bloc 2's 75/32 turret and Hochwald Ouest's Bloc 12 (flanking artillery casemate with two 75mm/29 guns), Bloc 13 (mixed flanking casemate with 135mm) and Bloc 14 (135mm turret).

Wachendorf's artillery hit Casemate Nagelsthal and the two blockhouses of Col de Gunsthal (Ouest and Est). The primary purpose of the shelling was to open up a passage through the barbed wire and keep the crews away from the embrasures. Tafel's attack passed between the blockhouse of Trautbach and Casemate Marbach. The shelling continued for two hours. At 0900hrs it ceased

Casemate La Verrerie, SF Vosges. US Army photo taken in December 1944. (Marc Romanych)

and the casemate crews readied their guns for an assault. However, instead of an infantry attack, the crews were greeted with the sound of Stukas. The aerial bombardment lasted for thirty minutes, then German pioneers poured out of the woods with Pak 37s and explosive charges. A company from III/380 IR was sent towards Blockhouse Gunsthal Ferme. The attackers quickly found out that the shells had not cut a path through the wire and that the crews, despite the shelling, were firing at them with machine guns. The 75mm turret of Four-à-Chaux opened fire and added to the German losses. One of the companies, led by Leutnant Schweiger, cut through the wire and set up a Pak 37 close to Gunsthal-Est. The 37mm shells concentrated on the embrasure of the blockhouse. While the gunners ducked for cover the Germans moved forward. The battle there was over very quickly. Gunsthal Ouest and Nagelsthal suffered the same fate. At Nagesthal a German explosive charge blew up beneath the embrasure, filling the bloc with smoke. Gunsthal Ouest's crew also gave up and the Col de Gunsthal was in German hands.

Tafel's group and 215 ID were surprised by the determined resistance of the casemates. Several were finally forced to surrender only by moving pioneers close enough to toss explosive charges or smoke grenades through the embrasures. Although it didn't seem as if any support was coming from Hochwald or Four-à-Chaux, the forts were firing with maximum effort on German targets in the casemate zone. The 75mm turret of Lt Chardonnet and the two 75mm casemate guns of Hochwald's Bloc 12, fondly nicknamed '*Liliane*' and '*Christine*', responded as quickly as possible to every request for support. Around 1000hrs a German 75mm gun battery was set up north of Lembach and opened fire on Four-à-Chaux's Bloc 5 while the machine-gun turret was raised. The battery was spotted and the gunners were driven away. At 1130hrs they returned but the 135mm turret drove them off again.

By the end of the morning, patrols from Tafel's group passed through the Line of casemates where mop up operations continued. Around 1030hrs a patrol approached PC 1360, the command post for sub-sector Langensoultzbach and for 6 UEC. Captain Genin, commander of 6 UEC, was forced to destroy the telephone equipment and abandon the position. The remaining casemates were now cut off. Casemate La Verrerie, commanded by Lt Morosolli, could still communicate by radio but Tafel's group was fast approaching. The Germans opened fire on the cloche with a Pak 37, destroying the scopes and FM. The Germans were now around and on top of the casemate and tossed smoke bombs and grenades through openings in the cloche. A box of 50mm ammunition exploded. Lt Morosolli used the radio to contact the artillery PC of Four-à-Chaux to request the casemate be shelled. Within moments the fort's 75mm shells landed on top of the casemate. The firing ceased but the Germans pressed the attack. They tossed burning branches into the embrasures where the only remaining FM was located and then lowered an explosive charge from above, dangling it in front of the opening, finally destroying the last gun. The crew used the final moments to sabotage the motor and then stepped out of the door, arms raised.

Wachendorf's group continued to exploit the breach at the Col de Gunsthal, but the surviving casemates and blockhouses continued to inflict casualties. On the east flank, German artillery pounded Blockhouse Gunsthal Ferme and Saegemuhle and pioneers advanced with Pak 37s. Gunsthal Ferme was silenced but the crew held out. A large hole was created in the embrasure by the 37mm. The machine-gun platform was broken and all of the crew were wounded to varying degrees. Around 1630hrs the crew surrendered. The crew of Saegmuhle escaped at around 2000hrs.

On the west flank Windstein and Wineckerethal received the wrath of the Luftwaffe. A 500kg bomb forced the crew of Windstein Ouest to evacuate the bloc. Wineckerthal Est and Grünenthal were hit by a group of Stukas, destroying all of the equipment and weapons. Both crews attempted to make their way back to friendly lines but they were captured. In the early morning hours of 20 June the remaining casemates and blocs gave up: Nonnenhardt III, Wineckerthal Ouest, Dambach, Neunhoffen and Graffenweiher Est.

Now that the line of casemates in the Vosges had fallen, 215 ID made its way south. At 1600hrs 380 IR arrived at Froeschwiller and headed to Woerth to meet up with Tafel's group. In the evening 380 IR marched into Haguenau. The regiment met up with the vanguard of 257 ID of General von Viebahn.[6] 215 ID continued towards Mutzig.

On 19 June, while SF Vosges was under attack, there was considerable German activity against SF Haguenau. The Germans began the day with an attack against PA 2, 3 and 4 which were evacuated by the French. The Germans pounded the crest of Mittel and Unterwald where they suspected the presence of a French force. At 0630hrs the bridges over the railway at Hunspach station were blown up and all French forces pulled back to the west of the railway.

At 0910hrs, in conjunction with their attack on SF Vosges, German aircraft bombed French positions west of Four-à-Chaux. Twenty-seven aircraft attacked Ouvrage du Lembach. The bombing cut the telephone lines to the SF Vosges. Observers switched to radio but the signals were very weak. Hochwald Ouest was shelled by 105s and several shells landed on Casemates 4 and 5 of the ditch and on the Redoubt.

The command of SF Haguenau believed the attack against SF Vosges was only a diversion and prepared for an attack on the sector. Inside Hochwald it was very difficult for the command. They were completely out of touch with what was going on outside. The only news about the combat came from observers via telephone and that avenue was now cut off. They heard nothing of the sound of battle. All of the observatories were blind and they had no idea what was going on except for bits and pieces from the fortress artillery and the infantry commanders.

In the afternoon, the worst assault against the forts to date took place from the air. From 1215hrs to 1235hrs Four-à-Chaux was bombed by eighteen aircraft.

A Stuka. (Bundesarchiv)

Hochwald fired its 75s in DCA[7] mode but they only reached a height of 1,500–1,800m. The German aircraft flew safely above this altitude and freely struck their targets. At 1510hrs and 1700hrs Hochwald Ouest was struck by about forty German bombs that landed on Blocs 12 and 13 and Casemate 1. At 1630hrs aircraft bombed the entries of Schoenenbourg. Stuka attacks continued into the evening against Hochwald.

At sunset, several engineering teams went outside to examine the damage caused by the Stukas. They also cleared away debris and rocks lying near the turrets. Tons of earth and rock had been thrown up by the bombs, but the engineers were pleased to report that the damage to the concrete was insignificant. Only the vents of Blocs 6, 12 and 13 had been demolished. At Hochwald-Est two bombs destroyed the counterscarp wall and created a breach that would allow access to the ditch.

Lt Col Schwartz reviewed the day's events. In the afternoon, the Germans had broken through the lines of SF Vosges after taking out the casemates defending the access roads. After the fall of Casemate La Verrerie they pushed towards Mattstall and on to Langensoultzbach and Woerth. 215 ID attacked with a 20:1 advantage followed by elements of 246 ID whose mission it was to manoeuvre into the French rear via Soultz and Rittershoffen and surround the Maginot Line. Troops from 246 ID were spotted earlier crossing the Mundat forest. In the evening, it was reported that a German battalion now occupied Morsbronn and Gunstett. Woerth was captured. The Germans held the western flank of the Haguenau Forest and captured the town of Haguenau itself at 2000hrs. In response Schwartz pulled all the remaining troops out of the APs in S/S Pechelbronn to defend the southern front.

Another important event took place in the evening. 70 RIF reported that S/S Bas-Rhin had been evacuated during the day. The regiment was now in danger of being turned from the south and received the order to retreat and destroy all material useful to the Germans. 70 RIF executed the evacuation order and at night were facing south-west in the vicinity of Schirrheim-Schirrhoffheim. 1st

Company of 81 BCP was ordered to turn to face south-east along the anti-tank ditch between Hermerswiller and Kuhlendorf, a front of 6km. The ground here was very broken and liaison between the units very difficult.

In the forts, the men worked all night to restore order. The bombardment caused distress but confidence was regained when the men saw how well the concrete had stood up against the bombs. Schwartz knew that a massive attack was coming. The wounded were treated in Hochwald's infirmary, now the only medical facility available after the fall of Haguenau.

Aschbach and Oberroedern – 20 June

Now that the Germans had broken through the line of advance posts, their next objective was to cut through the centre of SF Haguenau. The operation was carried out by General Erich Denecke's 246 ID and directed at the casemates in the vicinity of Aschbach. Denecke was being pressured by his superiors to move ahead quickly. The attack was scheduled for 20 June. It was to be a cautious advance. Denecke was first ordered to send small patrols towards the casemates and hopefully talk the crews into surrendering. This was a very difficult location to attack, blocked by the powerful casemates of Hoffen, Aschbach and Oberroedern,[8] supported by the guns of Hochwald and Schoenenbourg. The terrain was hilly and unfavorable to the placement of Flak 88s and self-propelled 88s were brought forward.

On the morning of 20 June German heavy artillery, including AA 800's 355mm gun, was in range and opened fire on the casemates of Hoffen, Aschbach and Oberroedern. 313 IR and 352 IR were tasked with punching a hole through the line. The German plan was as follows: at 1530hrs, German artillery would fire smoke shells to mask the arrival of the infantry while 88s and Pak 37s zeroed in on the casemate embrasures and visors. Meanwhile, from 1600hrs to 1700hrs, aircraft from Kampfgruppe 28 would launch an attack on the casemates.[9]

Casemate d'Oberroedern Sud. (Pascal Lambert, wikimaginot.eu)

The artillery attack on Casemate Oberroedern Sud, commanded by Lt Marcel Reiffel, began in the afternoon. Throughout the night the crew heard German trucks to the east at Stundviller. Reiffel's crew fired 50mm mortar rounds into the village, while Schoenenbourg's and Hochwald's turrets struck German batteries spotted by the casemate observers. Finally, the 88s opened fire on the cloches, signaling the arrival of the attackers.

Aschbach Est was hit by pinpoint strikes from 88s and Pak 37s. One shell broke off the periscope of the observation post and also destroyed a replacement a few minutes later. With that, armoured shields were installed in the embrasures and the cloche was evacuated. The shelling continued and as they struck the cloche, it sounded to the crew like a gong. Each Pak 37 shell made a 3–5cm dent in the metal. The 88, even at 1,500m range, made a 15–18cm hole in the moulded steel. A German company approached Aschbach Ouest and the casemate's gunners opened fire with the twin machine guns.

Around 1600hrs Reiffel, still present in the observation post, spotted a hole in the roof of a café at Stundviller and suspected the Germans were using the building as an observation post. As he was leaving the cloche to call Schoenenbourg, he was replaced in the cloche by Sergeant Delsart. Suddenly an 88 shell scored a direct hit on the cloche. Reiffel screamed at Delsart to come down but another shell exploded inside the cloche. In less than a minute, Delsart was dead. A moment later a squadron of Stukas came on the scene and the bombs started to fall. The results were terrible for the crews of the casemates. Lt Didier of Hoffen Est remarked that the shaking was so violent that he felt like he was on a boat at sea. The 500kg bombs opened up craters 8–10m in diameter. Earth was thrown up into the air, covering the machine gun cloche of Aschbach Ouest. Bombs exploded all around and ricocheted off the steel and concrete. The telephone lines were cut and the casemates were cut off from the artillery command posts which were, at the time, undergoing their own pounding from the air. A bomb fell inside the ditch of Abri d'Hoffen, dislocating the bloc and cutting off power. The crew was evacuated.

A Stuka dropped a bomb in the ditch of Casemate Oberroedern Nord, rocking the casemates on its foundations.[10] After releasing the bomb, the Stuka pulled out, rose up, turned around and headed straight for the casemate's northern firing chamber. The bombs hit, knocking the men to the ground and damaging the electrical generator. The steel blinds were down and the casemate filled with smoke. Lt Vialle, also the engineer, got the generator going and the air cleared. He then rallied his petrified crew and made preparations for the infantry attack to come. Now that the telephone communications were cut off, Vialle launched a green flare to signal to the ouvrages to fire on top of the casemate. German troops assembled in front of the barbed wire and *Stosstrupps* approached the casemate. Their objective was to place charges against the entry door. The Reibel machine guns opened fire. The 47mm anti-tank gun crew had a view of the Germans outside the embrasure and opened fire with the gun, blowing every man in the path of the shells to pieces. Vialle, observing from above, spotted a Pak 37 being set up 300m away. He placed the 50mm mortar in battery and fired away, but he now became the main target. German bullets rang off the cloche and broke the mortar in two pieces. An 88 joined in with the 37mm and shook the cloche. Vialle moved down to the main level. One of the crew fired his FM through the porthole of the entry door at an approaching German while others were struck by the casemate's machine guns. With this the Germans were done and the assault was over.

A similar attack took place at Aschbach Est but was repelled by machine guns and the mortar. The casemate had no communications with the artillery PC but finally a connection was made with Bloc 4 of Schoenenbourg. The situation was passed on to Captain Cortasse in the PCA and within a few minutes, shells from Schoenenbourg and the 135mm turret of Hochwald started to fall, bringing the attack by 246 ID to an end.

June 20th was the worst day since the start of the war for SF Haguenau. In S/S Pechelbronn the French tried to slow the German advance. Roads were cut and blocked by huge craters. The bridges at Rott and Riedseltz were blow. In S/S Hoffen the Germans opened up a preparatory bombardment at dawn on all of the casemates and blockhouses between the Bois d'Hoffen and the Seltz. German Pak 37s and 88s trained their sights on the embrasures and the armoured cloches. The shelling continued all day long despite French counterbattery fire. The German gun crews were replaced as fast as they were taken out. German guns took a heavy

Bloc 1 of Ouvrage d'Hochwald, showing damage to the terrain from aerial bombardment. (Denkschrift – Marc Romanych – digitalhistoryarchive.com)

toll on the periscopes and embrasures, forcing the crews inside to abandon their posts. This combined with fog, made observation very difficult.

At 1600hrs the Stukas returned to attack Schoenenbourg and Hochwald (Bloc 6 and the casemates). Another group bombed Abri Hoffen. The 135mm turret of Hochwald Est fired anti–aircraft shells. Bloc 4 of Schoenenbourg succeeded in driving the Stukas to a higher altitude. At 1515hrs the Stukas attacked Hochwald Est and Schoenenbourg fired AA rounds at an altitude of 200m. The Stukas dropped bombs on Bloc 1 and 7bis but due to the DCA fire they were less accurate. At 2000hrs twenty-seven aircraft attacked Schoenenbourg, Hochwald Est and Casemate Hoffen. Eighteen aircraft converged on Schoenenbourg and the fort disappeared from view under a huge cloud of smoke and dust.

The Germans were hoping for a swift advance like the previous day in SF Vosges but the French response from the forts was too strong. The advance to Soultz was stopped. For the first time the 75mm guns in the counterscarp casemates of Hochwald were used. The guns, with a range of 9,500m, were tasked with defending about 300m of the ditch against tank or infantry attack. Beginning in December 1939 the Group commander developed alternate firing plans so these guns could be used against distant targets attacking from the south.

German attacks were stepped up throughout the day between Kutzenhausen, Surbourg, Soultz and Hatten, on the road west of Soultz and between Kutzenhausen and Pechelbronn. Hochwald Est and Schoenenbourg fired on all these locations. Numerous German units were spotted north-east of Stundwiller and 1km north-east of Buhl. At the same time the Germans were moving north-west of Soultz and the town was threatened from several directions. The German attack was halted by fire from Schoenenbourg. The Germans were also advancing in the south. The PC of 22 RIF reported German troops at the Engineer's Depot 800m south-east of Lobsbann. The 75mm of Bloc 16 and the 135mm of Bloc 14 each fired twenty rounds and drove the Germans off. The radio transmitted the appeal of Marshal Pétain to the French and confirmation of an armistice discussion taking shape, but for the Maginot Line troops, the battle continued.

The attacks on SF Haguenau were now coming from both the north and south and the Germans had set up a large number of artillery pieces to fire directly at the forts and casemates; in particular, the embrasures and cloches. At 1030hrs concerted attacks on the south were repulsed by infantry and artillery but renewed at 1330hrs after preliminary shelling from 77mm and Pak 37 guns, and again at 1900hrs. German units infiltrated west of the village of Soultz and, beginning at 2000hrs, threatened the northern exit where French units were retreating towards Schoenenbourg. The Germans approached Lobsbann from Pechelbronn and Lampertsloch but were repelled by mortar and artillery. The 135mm turrets stopped all German activity with accurate and powerful strikes. Stuka attacks continued through the evening against the ouvrages and casemates in the zone of attack to clear the path for the infantry. Little damage was done but nerves were sorely tested.

Chapter 17

Attacks in the West – SF Faulquemont and SF Crusnes

SF Faulquemont

The SF Faulquemont was organized in two sub-sectors:

S/S de Steinbesch (also referred to as S/S Zimming): 156 RIF (Lt-Col Milon):

- A34 – Ouvrage du Kerfent (Captain Broché).
- A35 – Ouvrage du Bambesch (Captain Pastre), Aca3 – RFM casemate Bambesch (artillery 75mm 1897); C70 – Bambiderstroff Nord; C71 – Bambiderstroff Sud.
- C72 – Einseling Nord, A36 – Ouvrage d'Einseling (Lt Vaillant), C73 – Einseling Sud; C74 – Quatre Vents Nord; C75 – Quatre Vents Sud; Aca2 RFM casemate Stocken (artillery 75mm 1897).
- A37 – Ouvrage de Laudrefang (Captan Cattiaux).

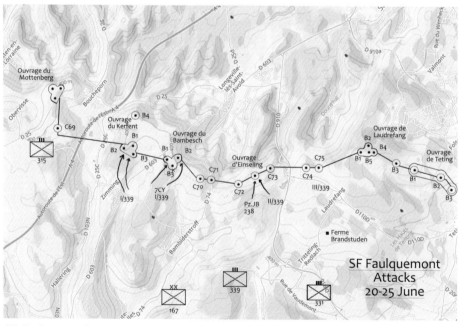

SF Faulquemont, location of attacks by 167 ID. Ouvrage du Kerfent and Bambesch surrendered after intense shelling but Einseling, Laudrefang and Têting held out until the armistice. (OpenStreetMap)

S/S Bois des Chênes: 146 RIF (Lt-Col Prat) included:

- C76 – Bois de Laudrefang Nord, C77 – Bois de Laudrefang Sud.
- A38 – Ouvrage de Téting (Lt Marchelli), Aca1 – RFM casemate Téting (artillery two 75mm 1897), plus thirty-three blockhouses for machine gun and anti-tank; four Pamart casemates; field fortifications for seven 65mm guns, thirty-four dismountable turrets and eight 25mm anti-tank guns; eight observatories.

After von Witzleben's troops (First Army of Army Group C) broke through SF Sarre he moved his divisions behind the Maginot Line, intending to wait until the forts surrendered. No attacks were planned at the time. 167 ID,[1] commanded by General Oskar Vogl, passed through the Sarre Gap behind General Sixt von Arnim's 95 ID[2] and moved in behind SF Faulquemont. On 19 June 331 IR of Oberst Heinrich Lechner, a motorized unit, moved around to the rear of the Ouvrage du Téting and Laudrefang. Lechner sent emissaries towards Bloc 3 of Laudrefang and the men were shot at from the fort. This caused von Witzleben to have a change of mind and to authorize an attack on the forts from the rear. He allowed some 'circumstantial' operations to be carried out, as long as they were low risk. Not only was the go-ahead given, but the attacking regiment would be equipped with two 88 groups, two batteries of 20mm guns and IV/195 AR's heavy guns from 95 ID. Lechner wanted to attack right away but 20 June was chosen as the date.

Additional German units arrived during the night of 19/20 June. 339 IR and 315 IR marched in behind the Line. 315 IR's objective extended from PO Denting to PO Mottenberg while 339 IR attacked from Téting to Kerfent. Oberstleutnant Franz Haas of 167 ID was ordered to begin the attack in the afternoon. There was some accompanying good news. Vogl was informed that patrols discovered that the woods south-west of Bambesch[3] had not been cleared, ran all the way to the edge of the fort and were empty of French troops. A company of assault troops could be moved through the woods to attack from close range. Dead ground was also discovered where an 88 could be placed very close to the fort. Vogl ordered 339 IR to commence the attack.

Ouvrage du Bambesch consisted of three blocs –

German 88mm Flak gun on display at Ouvrage du Fermont. (Dan McKenzie)

Bloc 1, also called Bloc North, was equipped with a mixed arms turret; Bloc 2 (Centre) was an entrance with a flanking casemate facing south for JM/AC47; Bloc 3 (South) was also an entrance with a flanking casemate facing north. Bambesch was supported from the north by its neighbour, PO Kerfent. The two Bambiderstroff casemates (Nord and Sud) to the south were sabotaged and evacuated on 15 June. Bambesch's mission as of 17 June was to hold and fight in place. The commander was Lt André Pastre.

The fort had major problems. First of all, it had no artillery of its own, no artillery support from adjacent forts and no flanking fire from the casemates. The tree line was much too close to the fort and could easily be infiltrated by an attacker. This was a grievous error that should have been addressed earlier. The woods should have been cut down, burned or booby-trapped, or barbed wire strung between the trees; anything to slow down an attack. Plus, Pastre had lots of time to do something about it.

On 20 June Pastre was in telephone contact with the commanders of the adjacent works – Lt Vaillant at Einseling, Cattiaux at Laudrefang and Marchelli at Téting. The Germans were already in action against Bloc 3 of Laudrefang, a prime target because the bloc's 81mm mortars covered Téting. Around noon a German gun opened fire on Bloc South from the direction of the Albach Valley. Ten minutes later the sentries spotted an 88 plus several anti-tank guns firing on the south bloc.

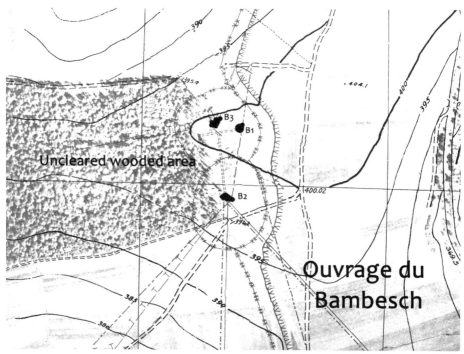

This map shows how close the woods were to the rear of the fort. (NARA)

Each shot chipped away at a small chunk of concrete on the bloc's façade. Pastre requested support from Einseling but its machine-gun turret was too far away. He also sought support from Kerfent and the 81mm mortars of Laudrefang but again, the distance between the forts was too great.

The 88 continued to fire at the south bloc. The concrete was being eaten away, exposing the steel reinforcing rods embedded in it. These in turn were being cut to pieces and the shells bit deeper and deeper into the wall. The bloc's defences were completely neutralized and the breach in the wall grew larger. Pastre decided to evacuate the bloc. Around 1630hrs the 88mm gun ceased firing.

Carbon monoxide levels inside the fort began to rise and the centre bloc filled with smoke fumes. Something was wrong with the ventilation system. Perhaps one or more of the shafts was blocked. At that moment Pastre was informed that the machine-gun turret in Bloc 1 was not working. The fort was now in extreme danger. When the south bloc was evacuated the staircase to the lower tunnels was left undefended. If the Germans broke into the south bloc there was nothing to stop them from reaching the main tunnel. The death of the entire crew of La Ferté was on the mind of the men of the officers' council as they met to discuss the fate of the fort. They did not want to see a repeat of that tragedy. The engineers were asked about the fort's defences and survivability. It was determined that the ventilation system could not be repaired. The subject of surrender was raised. The south bloc had been abandoned, the MG turret was inoperable, the Germans were attacking the north bloc and assembling in the woods for a major attack. After further discussion the decision to surrender was affirmed. It was a needless sacrifice to fight on, especially when an armistice was just a few days away.

Bloc 3 of Ouvrage du Bambesch. (Bundesarchiv)

Hauptmann Ackerman's 7th Company of 339 IR was situated in the Bois du Bambesch. They were surprised to find the woods clear of any obstacles. Nevertheless, they had no intention of attacking the fort. A *Panzerjäger* detachment was now at the north bloc, having cut through the wire. They tossed grenades at the entry doors and into the ditch. Around 1900hrs a French officer came to the door and signalled their desire to surrender. The men followed him out of the ouvrage. The men of 339 IR were shocked that the fort had fallen into their hands so easily, intact except for the damage described earlier. The news reached General Vogl's headquarters at Mainvillers around 2000hrs. The rapid fall of Bambesch with only minor casualties convinced Vogl to rethink his plans and order a general attack at dawn on 21 June.

Vogl's plan up until the fall of Bambesch had been to attack Téting and then move north to attack Einseling and Laudrefang. He now had new options and decided to enlarge the breach in the centre of the Line. The new attack was directed at Kerfent and Einseling, to the north and south of Bambesch, to be followed by Laudrefang and Téting. Major Gollé, commander of IR 339, proposed that the plan of attack on Kerfent would begin with a bombardment by 105mm and 150mm guns of IV/195 AR, then extend to Einseling. Two 88s were placed on Bloc North of Bambesch to fire on Kerfent's Bloc 3. Three 20mm and sixteen Pak 37s plus machine guns were placed in the woods of Kerfent to neutralize Mottenberg's flanking capabilities and to hit the main target, Bloc 2, the entrance

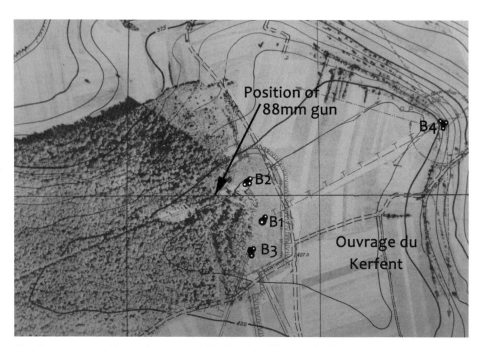

The Germans were able to advance to within less than 50m via the forest road from Zimming. The commander of Kerfent took no measures to improve defences to the rear. (NARA)

to Kerfent. The assault was carried out by two *Stosstrupp* companies, a machine-gun company, two groups of pioneers and a squad carrying cans of fuel to toss into the embrasures.

At 0200hrs on 21 June, 3rd Company of IR 339, commanded by Oberleutnant Schmidt, advanced into the Bois de Kerfent. Their goal was to reach and cut through the wire surrounding Bloc 2. Once again the commander of Kerfent, Captain Broché, had not taken precautions to prepare the woods against infiltration. At 0330hrs, two 20mm and four Pak 37s and heavy machine gun crews reached the north edge of the woods in sight of the Casemate Sud de Mottenberg and the PO Mottenberg on a crest at the opposite side of a valley. The bombardment was scheduled to begin at 0600hrs. At 0545hrs the assault forces were in place. At 0555hrs the 88 opened fire from Bambesch and the troops and Paks moved up to the eastern edge of the woods. The most dangerous part was that the Germans had to cross in front of the entrance bloc in plain view of the occupants. The entry was defended by a JM, two GFM cloches and a cloche LG. Hopefully the German guns would first take out the French defences. If this proved to be insufficient, Gollé would bring an 88 down the forest road leading to the ouvrage.

The bombardment began at 0600hrs. Captain Cloarec of Mottenberg responded with Bloc 3's machine-gun turret and Casemate Sud de Mottenberg with their JMs. The French had multiple targets to choose from and one lucky shot struck Oberst von Lichtenstein of IR 339 in the head, a wound he died of later that evening. Gollé ordered Schmidt to move 3rd Company forward. The Germans advanced to within 80m of the entrance to Kerfent. At the same time the 88s opened fire from Bambesch on Bloc 3, commanded by Chief Sergeant Joseph Bara. The shells tore away at the façade of the bloc. Huge pieces fell into the ditch. Chief Sergeant Chary suggested the men move below. Around 1900hrs the JM was hit and flew across the gun chamber, destroying the telephones and electrical cables and the platform for the second Reibel. Another shell passed through the hole in the embrasure created by the missing gun and struck a box of 47mm shells which caught fire. The fire was extinguished and a team moved the shells out of the chamber to safety. Bara moved the 47mm gun into the embrasure in place of the missing JM. The firing continued into the dark of the night and IR 339 waited in the woods.

A battery of 88s was set up overnight within 1,200m of Bloc 3 and opened fire, blasting away at the concrete and steel reinforcing bars and punching holes in the 25cm thick steel of the cloche. Bara now considered evacuating the bloc. How long would it take for the 88mm shells to break through the concrete? Finally, the decision was made and Bara ordered the troops to head below. The munitions were moved out, the airtight doors closed and a three-man guard volunteered to stay behind in the event the Germans broke in. One of the men entered the gun chamber and peaked through the hole created by the 88 and spotted a German patrol advancing towards the bloc along a communications trench leading from the woods. Pak 37s fired on the bloc to cover the movement of the patrol. The pace of the shelling slowed since it now appeared the bloc was abandoned. The two other men of the volunteer guard climbed up into the western cloche, location of the 50mm mortar. Also spotting the patrol, they started firing at the Germans. A moment later a shell struck the cloche and the men climbed back down the ladder, joined their comrade and headed for the staircase.

Due to a miscommunication, Captain Broché was under the impression that, when Bloc 3 was abandoned earlier by Bara and his men, it was because the Germans had broken into the bloc and fighting was taking place in the stairwell. Reports show that, even after the war was over, this was still being reported as an actual event: that the munitions had exploded in the block and because of this the bloc was evacuated, that the Germans entered the bloc and pursued the crew down the stairs and were finally held off by the FM of the armoured door at the base of the stairs. The German reports do not mention any such occurrence.

When it came time for the *Stosstrupps* to advance against Bloc 2, the sun shone brightly on the parade ground in front of the entrance. The Germans would be required to cross 60m of open ground in bright sunlight and Gollé did not want to risk heavy losses. He phoned the Flak troops at Bambesch and ordered them to bring one of the 88s over and set it up on the forest road. This would bring the powerful gun to within 150m of the left flank of the bloc. The 88 was in place by 0730hrs. Its target was the north cloche. It took the Germans twenty minutes to punch through the metal and to chew up the embrasure. The gun was moved up 50m more and took aim on the FM embrasure. Fifteen minutes later, the gun was moved forward another 20m. Kerfent had no way to stop the gun and it did its brutal work on the face of the bloc. Inside Bloc 2, conditions were better than expected and the FMs were still capable of repelling an assault on the entry door. Broché's report was much bleaker, practically pronouncing the bloc dead. On the contrary, what Gollé feared the most was about to happen.

The German assault team advanced on Bloc 2, firing machine guns at the embrasures on either side of the door. At that point the machine-gun turret of Chief Sergeant Haussy was elevated and fired on the woods. Mottenberg's machine-gun turret also joined in and fired on the soldiers crossing the parade ground. Some of the Germans fled for the woods, others backed up against the concrete of the bloc for cover. The critical moment had arrived. Gollé could withdraw, giving the victory to Broché. If Gollé resumed the attack it was probably over for Kerfent.

A German 105mm battery provided a kind of rolling barrage in front of the German troops, crashing into the cloches and turrets. Gollé ordered the Flaks and Paks to open fire again. He was informed that two heavy machine-gun sections were on their way and at that moment he decided to launch the attack. Several of Lt Mehnert's infantry crossed over the parade ground and were in reach of the entry. However, his men did not have any explosives and the benzene troops could not get close enough without coming under fire of the FMs. Mehnert knew he had to do something and, shouting at his men to move and the French to surrender, tossed everything he had – grenades, smoke, bullets – at the bloc. He heard a shout and a cheer coming from behind and, looking up, spotted a white flag being pushed out through the embrasure of the cloche. Gollé's courageous decision had worked. Kerfent was finished.

Broché was convinced that Bloc 2 must be evacuated, thus, as far as he knew, both Blocs 2 and 3 were abandoned. However, this was not the case. The Germans were not yet inside Bloc 3 and had not reached the door of Bloc 2. Broché called together his council. The officers concluded that they could not continue without great risk to their men. They felt the men had fought honourably and had held out to the end. Broché later remarked that he wanted to avoid the deaths of his men in the galleries, as had happened at La Ferté. Broché hesitantly notified Commandant Denoix at Laudrefang of the surrender. Broché later indicated that Denoix understood but Denoix never mentioned the conversation having taken place. II/IR 339 now moved on to attack Einseling while III/IR 339 looked south to Téting.

The bombardment of Laudrefang began on the morning of 21 June. One man was killed in the *cloche de guet* of Bloc 2 when a shell hit the embrasure directly and struck Chief Corporal Jean Gauer in the head. Lt Choné of Bloc 3 reported to the adjutant, Lt Vincent, that his turret had maintained fire throughout the night to keep the Germans from approaching the wire. He also reported that seven German batteries had been spotted between the Ferme de Branstuden and Côte 400. One of his machine guns was damaged and the shells continued to chip away at the concrete façade. Vincent ordered Choné to retract the turret and wait until things calmed down. Vincent then called Lt Keller at the Casemate de Quatre-Vents Sud who reported German activity behind Einseling. It looked like the Germans were planning something there.

Einseling was the new objective of IR 339. The fort was a 'Monobloc' design, originally planned to be connected by tunnel to the two adjacent blocs, now designated Casemates Einseling Nord and Sud, but there had been insufficient funds to complete the construction. The two casemates were evacuated on 15 June but Vaillant's engineers installed a telephone line to each one and at night a small patrol with an FM manned each casemate, firing the gun to give the Germans the impression the casemate was permanently occupied. Vaillant later wrote that it was an incredible show of bravery that these volunteers occupied what was, for all intents and purposes, a dead casemate – no light, ventilation, weapons (except what they brought with them), or even doors – especially in the dead of night. But the ruse worked. The Germans were convinced up to the armistice that the casemates were operational and they wasted dozens of 88 shells on them. Einseling was in an excellent location on the front slope of the ridge, out of site from the rear. The Germans had no direct shot at the bloc from the rear, but the ouvrage also could not see to the rear unless the turret was raised, which put it in danger of being hit by an 88. Lt Albéric Vaillant, commander of Einseling, counted on observers at Casemate Quatre-Vents Sud and Laudrcfang to keep watch on the glacis that sloped away from the rear of the fort.

Around 0730hrs II/IR 339 attacked. Infantry moved forward behind a rolling barrage from 105 and 150mm batteries, moving up the glacis in full view of the observers at Laudrefang and Casemate de Quatre-Vents Sud. The *Stosstrupps* moved ahead quickly but were slowed down when they reached the wire

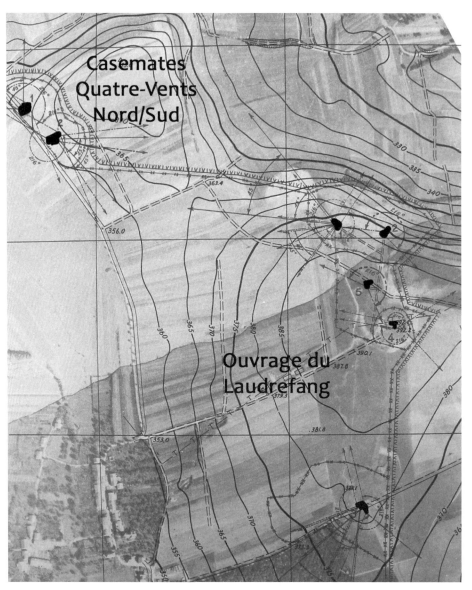

The vicinity of Ouvrage du Laudrefang. (NARA)

surrounding the fort. At Laudrefang the 81mm mortars in Bloc 1 opened fire. Einseling's turret was placed in battery and opened fire and the glacis was covered in exploding shells. The JM in the cloche opened fire. The mortars did devastating work on the pioneers and the Pak 37 guns. The Germans of II/IR 339 took their wounded and headed to the rear.

German artillery responded by pounding Bloc 1 of Laudrefang. Around 1000hrs a German armour-piercing shell passed directly through the FM embrasure of Bloc 1 and exploded, rupturing the water tank, ventilation pipes and diesel motor. The façade of the bloc was chipped to pieces. Despite the damage the gunners took every opportunity to fire back with the 47mm anti-tank gun and 81mm mortars.

Ouvrage du Téting was commanded by Lt Xavier Marchelli. The ouvrage was composed of three combat blocs. Bloc 1, not connected to the rest of the fort, was a small-arms casemate; Bloc 2 was equipped with a machine-gun turret modified to the mixed arms version; Bloc 3 served as the entry with a 47mm gun. The bloc was pounded for two days by German artillery. The concrete was pitted and the steel reinforcing rods were sliced through. Bloc 2's machine-gun turret could fire in all directions but the amount of time it could be kept in battery was limited. Bloc 1 was 30m from the edge of the woods. Its only connection to the other parts of the fort was by telephone.

On 19 June, a shell hit the embrasure of the firing chamber of Bloc 3 and exploded, wounding one of the gunners. Another shell cracked the episcope of the southern cloche. A breach in the concrete was blocked up with sandbags. On 20 June at 0900hrs, after a calm night, a Pak 37 began firing at the entry door. An 88 opened fire and the projector mounting pole snapped; the radio antenna mounts were pulled out of the concrete.

Meanwhile the cloche machine gun opened fire and a moment later shells from the 81mm mortars of Lt Choné's Bloc 3 at Laudrefang crept towards the edge of the

Casemate Hoffen Ouest, similar in design to Laudrefang. Note the 81mm mortar embrasures in the lower level. (Pascal Lambert, wikimaginot.eu)

woods, hitting two 105mm pieces. The Germans holding the woods were pinned down and remained there until the armistice. Because of this check General Vogl decided not to launch an attack towards the north in the direction of Mottenberg. He was surprised that four mortars and a machine-gun turret could stop two battalions.

SF Crusnes

This was a powerful sector consisting of mostly CORF construction. It included the following:

S/S Arrancy: 149 RIF (Lt-Col Beaupuis):

(A = Ouvrage; O = Observatory; C = Casemate; X Surface Shelter – all structures are CORF)

- A1 – Ouvrage de Ferme-Chappy (Lt Thibeau).
- O2 – Puxieux and C1 – Puxieux.
- A2 – Ouvrage du Fermont (Captain Aubert).
- C2 – Bois-Beuville; O4 – Haut-de-l'Anguille; C3 – Haut-de-l'Anguille Ouest; C4 – Haut-de-l'Anguille Est; C5 – Bois de Tappe Ouest; C6 – Bois de Tappe Est; C7 – Ermitage Saint-Quentin; C8 – Praucourt.
- A3 – Ouvrage de Latiremont (Commandant Pophillat).
- C9 – Jalaumont Ouest.

S/S Morfontaine: 139 RIF (Colonel Ritter):

- C10 – Jalaumont Est; O7 – Haut-de-la-Vigne; C11 – Chénières Ouest; C12 – Chénières Est; C13 – Laix.
- A4 – Ouvrage du Mauvais-Bois (Captain Colonna).
- C14 – Morfontaine; C15 – Villers-la-Montagne Ouest; C16 – Villers-la-Montagne Centre; C17 – Villers-la-Montagne Est.
- A5 – Ouvrage du Bois-du-Four (Lt de Mecquenem).
- C18 – Verbusch Ouest; C19 – Verbusch Est; O-10 – Ferme du Bois-du-Four; C20 – Ferme Thiéry; C21 – Bourène Ouest; C22 – Bourène Est.

S/S Aumetz: 128 RIF (Colonel Roulin):

- C2B – Ouest de Bréhain.[4]
- A6 – Ouvrage de Bréhain (Commandant Vanier).
- C23 – Ravin de Crusnes; C24 – Crusnes Ouest; C25 – Crusnes Est; C26 – Nouveau Crusnes Ouest; C27 – Nouveau Crusnes Est; O1 – Réservoir; C28 – Réservoir; C29 – Route d'Ottange Ouest; C30 – Route d'Ottange Centre; C31 Route d'Ottange Est.

- A7 – Ouvrage d'Aumetz (Lt Braun).
- C32 – Tressange; C33 – Bure; C34 – Fond d'Havange; C35 – Gros Bois; X1 – Gros-Bois.

The guns of Ouvrage du Fermont were a thorn in the side of German troops marching past Longuyon, in particular the 75/33 turret with its range of 11,900m. Because of this the Germans decided to reduce Fermont and Latiremont. The attack would be carried out by General Hermann Wilck's 161 ID. It was scheduled to begin on 21 June with a heavy artillery bombardment that included the 305mm mortars of *Schwere Artillerie Abteilung* (SAA) 641. Three batteries of 210mm mortars, six 105mm, two 88 and several Pak 37s made up the artillery contingent. The assault troops were from 371 IR (Oberst Newiger), *Panzerjäger Abteilung* 241 (Hauptmann Ewert)[5] of 161 ID and pioneers led by Major Lau. Their mission was to attack the turrets and cloches with explosive charges, and 37mm and 47mm guns were moved up from the Bois de Beuville to the edge of the anti-tank rails behind Fermont's entrance bloc.

Lt Rousseau, artillery commander of Latiremont, was in contact with Lt Braye, Fermont's artillery commander. Latiremont's Bloc 6, commanded by Lt Belhoste, was equipped with three 75mm casemate guns that flanked to the west. Lt Belhoste's bloc was placed on alert to support Fermont in case of a German attack.

On 21 June, the observer in Bloc 2 of Latiremont's VDP cloche reported columns of smoke rising 50m into the air above Fermont, the result of 305mm shells falling

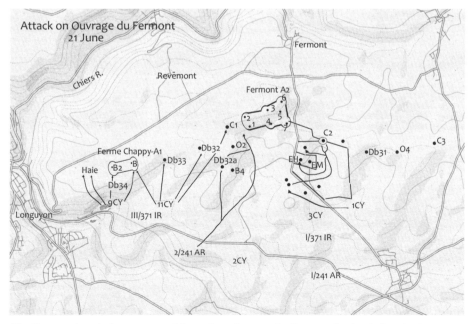

The Germans launched an unsuccessful attack on Ouvrage du Fermont, despite shelling by heavy guns including a Skoda 305mm howitzer. (OpenStreetMap)

on Bloc 1. Shells exploded on the concrete but didn't cause any damage. The gunners inside the bloc were ordered to move away from the turret. The turret was safe, even from direct hits, but a shell hit the GFM cloche, cracking the steel. The crack had to be soldered immediately to maintain an airtight seal in case the fort was placed under suppression against a poison-gas attack or to clear out smoke. The large shells continued to strike the turret cap but caused no damage.

Three kilometres away to the west, PO Chappy was hit by 105mm and anti-tank shells from Pak 37 guns set up in or near abandoned blockhouses[6] near the small fort. Around 0630hrs a 37mm shell hit the AC47 gun of Bloc 1 flanking west, denting the embrasure. Flames penetrated through the frame of the gun site. The crack was quickly repaired by the engineers. Specialist Le Brun, gunner in Bloc 2's JM cloche, was hit and killed when a shell burst against the lens of the scope. Denis Guissard, the machine-gunner in Bloc 5's GFM, was ordered to fire on a group of German soldiers advancing under cover of a thick cloud of smoke between Bloc 5 and the EH. As soon as Guissard opened fire his machine gun was hit by a shell. He climbed down to get a new weapon and when he returned to the platform the cloche was hit again and he was badly wounded.

The cloches of the entry blocs were also being hit by Pak 37s firing from the route de Beuville, supporting the movement of German infantry towards the anti-tank rails. From his position in Bloc 3's observatory, it appeared to Lt Delhaye that the Germans were advancing almost lackadaisically, as if they expected to simply walk up and into the fort. This is exactly what General Wilck was expecting after a long and brutal bombardment, that the 305mm and 210mm guns had destroyed the fort's combat capabilities and demoralized the crew. But the actual damage to Fermont was minor. Equipment losses consisted of two JMs, four 50mm mortars and two FMs, plus the human casualties, light but still sad. The Germans were shocked to see the two machine-gun turrets, plus the 81mm and the 75mm rise up to, as Lt Delhaye remarked, 'begin the great carnage'.

Hautpman Ewert's assault troops moved towards the wire. Bad weather limited visibility so his men felt confident they could approach safely. They set up 47mm anti-tank guns that were immediately spotted and hit by the 75mm. The gunners packed up and moved to another location. From there, 47mm shells struck the cloche of the EH, ricocheting off the thick metal and shaking the bloc. French observers, looking through the viewing port of their own 47mm gun in the firing chamber, could see nothing of the enemy. The episcope in the cloche was hit by a shell that exploded and instantly killed the observer, Florian Piton.

The guns' tracer rounds were finally pinpointed and the FM fired in that direction. The coordinates were then passed on to Lt Bourbon's Bloc 5. In less than a minute the 81mm turret was raised, turned and fired twenty shots at the German gun. The shells fell short and while the range was being adjusted the German crew headed for cover in a blockhouse adjacent to the Bois de Beuville. A few quiet minutes passed and the Germans returned to the gun. The 81mm turret crew was waiting and a barrage of mortar shells fell on top of the surprised German crew. A large cache of shells exploded and the battery was destroyed.

Meanwhile the 75mm casemate guns of Latiremont's Bloc 6 fired on the edge of the Bois de Beuville. The French shells unfortunately did the work for the Germans, opening up gaps in the wire. A small squad of Germans moved forward. Their luck didn't last long and they were hit by Bloc 5's mortar firing at maximum cadence. Bloc 1's 75mm turret also opened fire, pinning the Germans down in the Bois de Beuville. All of Fermont's blocs now opened fire; a classic example of the Maginot Line's close-range capabilities. A group of pioneers approached the Observatory of Puxieux which was in range of Bourbon's mortars and could move no further. An attack was attempted against PO Chappy that was countered by Casemate Puxieux's JM/AC47 that flanked to the west. One by one the German 47mm guns ceased firing. Around 1100hrs the German assault teams were retreating towards the woods south of Fermont. In the early afternoon, a group of Germans approached with white flags, requesting to collect their dead and wounded. Aubert ordered a cease fire to allow them to carry out their gruesome task. The German attack was over and further action against Fermont was forbidden.

All the other forts and casemates of SF Crusnes were under attack at one time or another, in some form or another and in varying degrees of intensity, most notably in the S/S Aumetz. On 19 June, the Germans placed a Pak 37 battery on the crest of Anciens Puits and opened fire on the façade of PO Aumetz's Bloc 3.[7] The impacts were numerous but the damage caused was minor. The Pak was destroyed by the guns of Bréhain. Later, two German patrols moving along the Metz-Longwy railway line were struck and sent running by Aumetz's machine-gun turret in Bloc 2 (S/Lt Curien) and the guns of Ouvrage du Rochonvillers. On 20 June, the Germans launched an attack on the forward blocs of Ouvrage du Bréhain from the Ferme Hirps. They were immediately spotted by observers and fired upon by the guns of Bréhain.

Chapter 18

Attacks on Haut-Poirier and Welschoff, 19 to 23 June

Geneal Edgar Theissen was commander of the Austrian 262 ID.[1] He left IR 462 to the north of the Maginot Line east of the Sarre to cover a 35km front, while 482 and 486 IR crossed the Sarre on 20 June and moved through the gap to the south. The regiments were slowed by bottlenecks and destroyed bridges left in the wake of the French retreat. Theissen chose Haut-Poirier as his first target. When it fell, the casemates would follow suit and then he would attack Welschoff. When the two regiments crossed behind the Maginot Line Theissen had only a battery of 150mm and no Flak 88 guns.

On 20 June German reconnaissance patrols scouted the zone to the rear of the forts. Between Kalhausen and Rahling a patrol found several blockhouses only a few hundred metres behind Haut-Poirier and a large quantity of abandoned munitions. Theissen moved Pak 37 crews into the blockhouses. On 21 June patrols

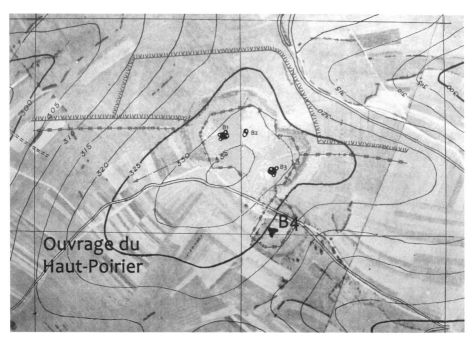

The vicinity of Ouvrage du Haut-Poirier. By mid-June, with the fall of SF Sarre, the fort was completely without artillery support and the Germans easily moved around its flank to the rear. (NARA)

confirmed that neither Haut-Poirier nor Welschoff had any field or fortress artillery support. Welschoff was at the very limit of Simserhof's 75mm turret range. The attack was ordered to commence at 1300hrs.

262 AR set up 15cm guns north of Kalhausen to target Haut-Poirier. Around 1500hrs the guns opened fire on Bloc 3 (Lt Bonhomme). Because of the configuration of the fort, the mixed arms turret was useless against targets to the rear. The block could only fire in that direction with its twin machine gun. The crew of the turret was unable to respond. The crew of Haut-Poirier watched helplessly as thousands of German troops moved unmolested along their left flank and occupied the villages behind the Line. They had no way to stop them.

The infantry attack began with a bombardment and shelling by the 150s, Pak 37s and small arms. Smoke was dropped and the teams moved into the blockhouses closest to the wire perimeter. At 0815hrs Lt Bonhomme reported the blockhouses behind the fort were now occupied by Germans. At 1500hrs the 150mm fired anti-concrete shells and the 105mm fired armour-piercing. On the north flank, IR 462 of Oberst Eisenstück created a diversion by advancing *Stosstrupps* towards the fortress line while, to the south, IR 482 of Oberst von Schrocten assembled behind Welschoff and IR 486 of Oberst Wolfsberger behind Haut-Poirier. Theissen forbade any attacks by the infantry until Haut-Poirier was a smoking ruin.

German shells struck the surface of the blocs. In early afternoon Captain Gambotti was notified of the presence of thick smoke outside Bloc 1. The air was tested for poison gas but the results were negative. It was determined to be a smokescreen to mask the advance of infantry. Around the same time a battery of 150mm guns of 262 ID was positioned between Schmittviller and Oermingen to the rear of Haut-Poirier. Bonhomme's Bloc 3 was the main target and the 150s were joined by Pak 37s firing from the former French blockhouses. German[2] troops were waiting behind the blockhouses, moving along the French trenches towards the fort. The only thing that could counter their advance was the casemate of Nord Ouest d'Achen (S/Lt Will)[3] and a jury-rigged mortar in Bloc 1.

The bombardment increased in intensity. A shell struck the rear façade every five to six seconds. There was a sort of screeching sound corresponding to the penetration of the shell in the concrete, then afterwards the explosion and a trembling of the bloc. A loud metal bang signalled the cutting of the searchlight mounting pole by a 150mm shell. Shells slowly ate away at the concrete and cut through the metal reinforcing rods.

Gambotti discussed the situation with Jolivet. The fort was being torn to pieces. Smoke and dust surrounded and covered the fort. The only defence was the training machine gun in Bloc 3. Bloc 1's mortar was dislodged by a Pak 37. Achen Nord-Ouest was also being hit hard by German shells and was filled with smoke. Gambotti and Jolivet realized there was nothing they could do. The blocs would be eaten up until they were destroyed, then the infantry would move forward.

PO Welschoff went on alert on 19 June after the appearance of German troops moving around to the rear of the Line. Trucks were seen heading towards the village of Singling, 1,500m behind the ouvrage. Lt Haite climbed the stairs to Bloc 1 and looked through the periscope towards Singling. He could clearly see German troops entering the small village. At 1530hrs Haite watched as the Germans set up a 150mm gun on the south edge of Singling, 1,300m from Welschoff. He ordered the entry door closed, expecting the gun to fire at any moment. The grill was closed but the armoured door left open to allow air into the fort. Unfortunately, the first German round flew through the portal and cut through the bars of the grill.

Welschoff, like Haut-Poirier, had no artillery of its own. All the interval artillery was gone or had been sabotaged. Bloc 5 of Simserhof provided the only support. The bloc's 75mm guns could reach Welschoff, but only if the wind was blowing in the right direction. Haite quickly called for help from Simserhof. Capt Urbero, Commandant of Artillery at Simserhof, answered the call and was informed about the gun firing on Welschoff from the village of Singling. He was given the coordinates.

The second shot from the German gun landed in the ditch that was full of petrol dumped there in anticipation of the sabotage and evacuation of the fort. The fuel caught fire and sent a column of smoke high into the air. Captain Gambotti called from Haut-Poirier to find out what was going on and S/Lt Fritz of Welschoff's

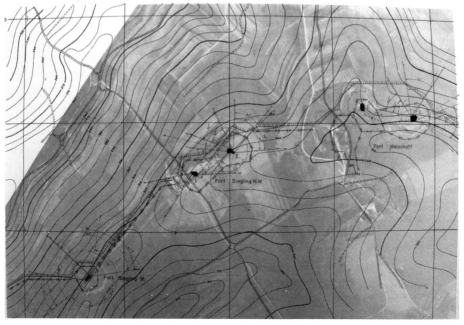

Ouvrage du Welschoff was attacked from the rear. Its only artillery support came from Ouvrage du Simserhof. (NARA)

Bloc 1 assured him it was the fuel that was burning. The fifth shot of the 150mm struck the fort at the same time as Urbero notified Haite that Simserhof's first barrage was underway. Haite waited but nothing: then suddenly a succession of explosions enveloped the German gun. Simserhof fired twenty-five shots that landed a few seconds apart and the German crew fled. They returned a few minutes later and opened fire again but Simserhof responded just as quickly with a salvo of thirty shots. Haite let Simserhof know that the gunners were retrieving the gun and pulling out.

Bad news arrived. At 2200hrs Welschoff was informed that Haut-Poirier was surrendering. Throughout the afternoon Haut-Poirier's Bloc 3 was hit by 150mm and 105mm shells that bit ever deeper into the concrete. Shells struck every six seconds. The last strands of the metal reinforcing rods gave way and a shell broke through the inner wall. Around 1830hrs the shelling stopped. Some of the men from the bloc were sent down to the lower level for a rest while several men stayed behind in the upper level. Suddenly there was a terrible explosion. The lights went out. The platform of the cloche collapsed. The inside of the firing chamber was a horror. A 150mm shell had breached the wall below the JM. It passed through the outer chamber and exploded in the inner chamber, the location of 300 47mm anti-tank shells and 500 50mm mortar shells. Everything went up. Three men were killed instantly. Bonhomme wandered through the bloc in shock, trying to make sense of what had just happened, but failing to do so. Gambotti called Lt Kersual at Casemate Nord d' Achen to let him know that Haut-Poirier had no more means of defence to the rear. Lt Will of Casemate Nord-Ouest d'Achen fired his casemate's JM towards Bloc 3. Around 1930hrs, however, the gun broke down.

In Bloc 1, a 50mm mortar was attached to a ball mounting in the cloche embrasure specially rigged by engineers a few days earlier. Due to the nature of the setup and the fact that there was no viewing scope, the operator did not have a line of sight to targets, so they were called in from the other cloche. However, there was no observer in the other cloche so, in fact, the mortar was worthless.

Gambotti looked for a way to seal off Bloc 3 from the rest of the fort. There were two options: blow up the stairs or block the access tunnel at the foot of the stairs with concrete poured between steel rails. The latter would also seal off the kitchen and the power station and if the enemy gained access they could shut down power to the rest of the fort. The result: no light or ventilation.

The council of officers met at 2000hrs. Jolivet was not a fortress man and therefore he was not looked up to by the men. Yet he was the senior officer and he would be the one making the final decision. He pointed out that the original, limited mission of Haut-Poirier was to hold out until 17 June, when the fort would be sabotaged and abandoned, an order he himself had rescinded. The truth was, he added, the Germans had conquered most of the country and were moving south. The Armies of the East were surrounded and Pétain had requested an armistice. Haut-Poirier faced an assault that might proceed into the tunnels of the fort at any moment because Bloc 3 was now undefended. The fort had no artillery support from anywhere. He repeated Pétain's awful words, '*Il faut cesser le combat!*' The officers agreed that surrender was indeed the only option. A continuation of the battle was a needless sacrifice of the men, one that could very well result in the death of the entire crew. There were some arguments but in the end, they all realized the decision was correct.

Gambotti gave the command to raise the white flag. The task went to Lt Isnard of Bloc 1 who burst into tears at the thought of having to raise a white flag over his bloc. Nevertheless, he returned to the bloc to do the task and affixed a white towel to the cloche. Ten minutes later two Austrian officers approached and were let inside to discuss terms. After a call from Jolivet the five casemates around Haut-Poirier also surrendered. The crew slept in the fort overnight and on Saturday morning, 22 June, they marched into captivity.

The most serious consequence of the fall of Haut-Poirier and the surrounding casemates was that the Germans could approach Welschoff without any opposition – its flank was now completely unprotected. The surrender also shortened the German line by 6km and freed up two battalions. 262 ID now moved in that direction. The attack for 22 June was delayed until Sunday to put all of the elements in place. The heavy guns were positioned in battery west of Singling, out of the range of Simserhof and patrols looked for abandoned blockhouses in which to place Pak 37s. Late in the morning of Saturday, 22 June, Sub-Lt Hirsch, commander of Casemate Ouest de Singling, spotted three anti-tank guns being set up at Casemate Nord-Est d'Achen. The Germans were surprised when Hirsch's AC47 opened fire on the battery. A 150mm gun responded by firing at Hirsch's casemate.

That evening news spread that the armistice had been signed. German soldiers in the vicinity of Welschoff celebrated, firing flares and ringing church bells in the French villages. The guns of Simserhof and Schiesseck continued to fire, signaling that the Maginot Line was still in operation. At this moment one wonders why the Germans continued to carry out attacks until the actual cease fire was declared. They could have pulled back out of range and simply waited for it to be officially over.

At dawn on 23 June 262 ID's artillery pounded Welschoff. A 105mm targeted the JM of Singling Nord-Ouest, wounding one gunner and killing the other. Singling Ouest was also targeted. The Singling casemates were no match for German artillery. To fight on meant death for the crews. At 0830hrs the white flag was raised over the casemates.

Simserhof's gunners attempted to support Welschoff by firing on a 150mm battery west of Achen Nord but the shells fell short. The 150s, only 1,000 metres away, fired three shots per minute on Sub-Lt Fritz's Bloc 1. The AC47 in Bloc 1 was destroyed and the bloc enveloped in smoke. The 47mm shells were moved out of the bloc to prevent an explosion inside the chamber. Welschoff had nothing with which to counter a Pak 37 that fired on Bloc 3 of Lt Jaques. French casualties mounted. The men prepared for an infantry attack on the entry door of Bloc 1. Shelling from the 150s continued into the early evening. A hole appeared next to the gun embrasure of Bloc 1 and with each new shot the chamber filled with smoke. The men moved to the lower floor for shelter.

A heated discussion took place between the officers, along the same lines as at Haut-Poirier. Captain Lhuisset agreed to delay surrendering until the following day to see if there was any more news about the armistice, perhaps avoiding the need to surrender. In the meantime, he ordered a white flag to be placed at the top of the staircase inside Bloc 1 to prevent a massacre in the event the Germans broke into the bloc. The order was passed to Bloc 1 by telephone and the flag was put in place. Nerves were frayed and the presence of the white flag was devastating to morale. The night was, however, calm.

At 0430hrs the Germans opened fire on Casemate Bining's western firing chamber. Lt Pierre, commander of the casemate, ordered the men to move the munitions to the lower level of the casemate. The cache included 47mm, 50mm shells and grenades. As they were forming a chain to start the move a German shell flew through the entry door which was torn to pieces and the shell exploded inside the casemate. The crew had to get out fast in case a second shell followed. The breeches of the AC47s were pulled out and the men fled the casemate. At 0515hrs a white flag was raised over Casemate Bining.

At 0730hrs Captain Lhuisset asked for news of the armistice. He was told it was 'imminent'. Everything seemed calm until the Chief of Engineering was notified that the Germans were dropping tear gas down the kitchen exhaust shafts. The vents were closed and the ventilation system activated. At 0915hrs Bloc 1 reported that Germans had been inside the bloc during the night but had probably been chased off. The crew had opened up some firing loopholes in the cracked concrete the previous night and in the morning, they noticed the holes were blocked up. They also spotted fresh boot prints in the dust. With this news Lhuisset gave the order to abandon the bloc and put up the white flag on the outside. The same order was passed to Blocs 2 and 3. Lhuisset headed for the emergency exit of Bloc 3. He was done and with that the fort fell into German hands.

SF Haguenau

On 21 June, the Germans tightened the knot around SF Haguenau. Around midnight the sounds of heavy machine-gun fire and exploding artillery shells were heard by Obs 092 and 088, coming from the area of the casemates of Bremmelbach. Also, overnight, requests came in from observers at Casemate 6, Casemate 9 and the casemates of Drachenbronn claiming the fort was under attack. Sentries were reporting the sighting of assault groups between Blocs 1 and 4. Schoenenbourg and Hochwald fired close to 900 canister rounds at shadows. Miconnet sent

Captain Zyromski, *Directeur de Tir* for Hochwald Est to one of the sentry posts to confirm the presence of the enemy. He personally saw nothing at Obs 06 or Bloc 2, but the sentries assured him they saw movement, silhouettes jumping into shell craters firing at them.

The consensus of the officers at the PC was that these were perhaps small patrols sent to test the local defences. No one at Hochwald Est wanted to admit this was an actual attack of any kind and that the enemy could possibly have come that close to Blocs 1 and 6. The simultaneous attacks on Casemates 9, 6 and the Drachenbronn casemates led them to the conclusion that it was a test of the defences but they would wait until daybreak to go out and look for bodies. A patrol sent out in the afternoon found no evidence that any Germans had set foot near the fort.

Perhaps the explanation was as follows: At 2347hrs Hochwald Est fired protection rounds on Abri Valkmuhl, believing the Germans were attempting to approach the entrances of Hochwald. A sentry – nervous – tired perhaps after the Stuka bombardment, nerves frayed – thought he saw shadows moving towards the fort and opened fire with his FM. The other sentries saw the tracers of these rounds and, thinking they were being fired on, fired back, hitting their neighbour's cloche. Bullets then began to ricochet off the metal of the adjoining casemates. A sentry at Casemate 6 also reported the use of a flamethrower. This was later debunked and found to have been a fire set off accidentally in a pile of nearby brush.

In hindsight, it's easy to view these events with skepticism, but at such a tragic time as late June 1940, completely surrounded by the enemy, it was more than logical to suspect a classic attack on the fort. The details of what the men thought they saw was pushed up the chain of command and, based on events at Eben-Emael and La Ferté, no one laughed them off. Although they may seem fantastic, they were at the time taken very seriously and investigated thoroughly. The same episodes were reported at Lembach and FAC, which had also undergone heavy aerial bombardment and where the sentries were naturally shocked and nervous.

At 0820hrs the Stukas returned to bomb Schoenenbourg, followed by a violent artillery bombardment and air attack on the casemates east of Hoffen. It appeared to be preparatory to an attack. It was also apparent that, contrary to reports received the previous day, the Line had not been breached except at Oberroederen Nord. The casemate had been surrounded for a few hours but the Germans had since pulled back.

At noon, German troops occupying Seltz headed north and were forced back by French machine guns placed at the cemetery of Retschwiller, held by the *Group Franc* of 22 RIF. Most of the action took place in the south, from Lampertsloch to Lobsann. A heavy attack on Lobsann was repulsed by thirty minutes' worth of fortress artillery fire. At Hunspach, a German company heading towards the railway was dispersed by Bloc 6 of Hochwald Est. In the late afternoon, the Germans infiltrated Hoffen and Leitersweiler from Soultz. The French lines were too extended and they were unable to stop the capture of the two villages.

*Command Post
of Ouvrage du
Schoenenbourg.*
(Dan McKenzie)

Reilershoffen was later occupied without combat. Other minor incursions too place in the north but there were no major breakthroughs.

At 1900hrs Schoenenbourg's PC reported the ouvrage had been hit by a very heavy calibre gun. For ninety minutes, fourteen shots from a German 420mm howitzer were aimed at the fort. The shells tore up the surface of the fort but most of them overshot. One shell struck the north-west angle of Bloc 4, blowing out a chunk of concrete. Just 1.5m further and the shell would have hit the visor plate of the cloche and exploded inside, possibly setting off the 1,200 rounds of ammunition stored near the turret.

The fortress artillery remained intact and in good order. Not a single barrel was lost and the crews were still in relatively good spirits. Obs 02 had been put out of commission, however, its two periscopes and cloche embrasures pulverized by anti-tank guns and 88s. The JM in Obs 03's GFM was destroyed but the periscope was operational. The telephone lines of the two observatories were cut and they had to rely on TSF to communicate with Schoenenbourg. Due to the fall of the central part of SF Vosges, Four-à-Chaux and PO Lembach and the remaining casemates were placed under the command of SF Haguenau.

Chapter 19

Michelsberg, Bitche, Haguenau, 21 to 23 June

Fortified Ensemble of Bitche – 21 June

257 ID[1] was commanded by General Max von Viebahn whose desire was to capture one or more Maginot Line forts. His sphere of command included the heavy works of Simserhof, Schiesseck and Grand-Hohékirkel. Oberst Karl Fusik, commander of three battalions of 457 IR of 257 ID, was also anxious to attack an 'ouvrage'. His troops moved out on two axes. One objective was the Abri-caverne de Kindelberg, in S/S Bitche, located on the rear slope of the Kindelberg, south of Camp de Bitche. It was not an ouvrage, rather it was a cavern shelter with light small-arms defences. Another target was PO Rohrbach, commanded by Captain Saint-Ferjeux, located on the Plateau of Rohrbach north of the village of Rohrbach-lès-Bitche. Why did Fusik select Rohrbach? According to some locals and deserters, the fort contained a large contingent of Alsatians Fusik believed were more likely to surrender to the Germans. On the morning of 21 June Fusik sent emissaries towards the fort. Much to his surprise they were fired on before they could get close. Fusik had received his answer regarding a quick surrender.

On 21 June *Stosstrupps* from 457 IR approached Abri Kindelberg and were hit by 75mm shells from Grand-Hohékirkel. Another group approached Rohrbach

Bloc 5, Ouvrage du Simserhof. US Army photo taken in December 1944. (NARA)

supported by three Pak 37s. The attack, directed on the entry of Bloc 2, was broken up but a Pak fired on the embrasures of the bloc, damaging an FM and injuring the gunner. A call was placed to Captain Urbéro at Simserhof and a moment later the 75mm turret guns of Bloc 5 fired in support of Bloc 2, driving back the attackers.

Casemate Biesenberg was located within the protective umbrella of Grand-Hohékirkel's 75mm turret, although it was officially part of SF Vosges. It was an MOM/RFL type artillery casemate for two 75mm Model 33 guns that covered the Schwarzbach valley to the east. The '*Ensemble*' of Biesenberg included four blockhouses located west of the casemate and three to the east, identified as Biesenberg 1 to 7, equipped with FM. The ensemble included machine guns and 50mm mortars. The blocs were of a weaker construction, hardly a match for an 88. Lt Foll was commander of 2 CEC and the ensemble of Biesenberg. He felt fairly confident in the protection of Grand-Hohékirkel's 75, but what if the casemate and blockhouses were attacked all at once? How would the gun cover the entire area successfully? The same situation had arisen on 19 June when Four-à-Chaux was called upon to simultaneously defend the casemates at Aschbach.

On 21 June Adjutant Thiébault of Infantry Casemate Glasbronn (Ca 482) to the south called Foll to tell him two Germans were at the door with a white flag saying the war was over. Foll told Thiébault to tell the Germans to get lost. He then called Captain Constant Bayron, PCA of Grand-Hohékirkel and requested a few shots towards Glasbronn. A moment later the turret of Bloc 4 of Lt Andriot dropped a couple of rounds near the casemate and the Germans fled.

That same day the Germans attacked Biesenberg. At 1330hrs, as was their habit, the Germans sent an emissary who was promptly chased off. After the gesture was rebuffed the attack was quickly underway and the crew ran to their posts. The FM was ordered to fire short bursts towards the edge of the woods to the south. Foll, located in Casemate Biesenberg, yelled out to warn the Germans not to approach the casemate. A German machine gun opened fire. Foll responded with the 50mm mortar on the location of the trenches in the woods. Sergeant Robert in Blockhouse Biesenberg 4 also fired his 50mm mortar into the woods where the Germans were located. The Germans moved up two Pak 37s and fired several shells, hitting the episcope of the south cloche and destroying the bloc's FM. Foll telephoned Grand-Hohékirkel and the fort's 75mm turret opened fire, silencing the 37s and machine guns. With that the woods fell silent except for the sound of insects. The Germans pulled back, having underestimated the power of the small casemate. They suffered heavy casualties during the foray and no further attacks were attempted by 257 ID.

The attack on Michelsberg – 22 June

General Sixt von Arnim's 95 ID was operating north of Vogl's 167 ID. Its objectives were Mont des Welches, commanded by Captain Tari, and Michelsberg,

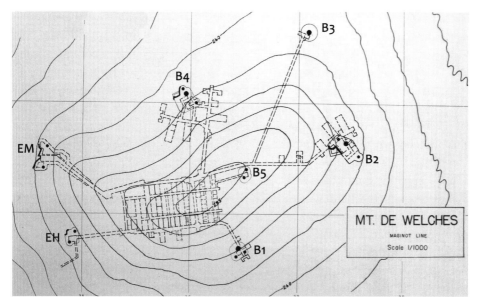

Target of attacks by 95 ID, Mont des Welches and Michelsberg held out with strong support from adjacent forts of the most powerful sector of the Maginot Line. (NARA)

commanded by Commandant Pelletier. The two ouvrages were flanked by the giant fortress of Hackenberg to the north and Anzeling to the south. Von Arnim's force was not equipped with Stukas or heavy artillery. Why here? Who knows?

The attack on the two forts was scheduled for 22 June. The German artillery was commanded by Oberst Beisswanger of 195 Artillery Regiment – 95 ID. Its mission was to neutralize the artillery of the ouvrages. 195 AR was comprised of:

- I/193 AR – Flak 88 battery (Hauptmann Model).
- 4/371 – 20mm.
- 195 *Panzerjäger* Battalion (Major Gutzeil) .
- 14/278 IR Pak 37 and 13/ 278 IR infantry guns to cover the advance of III/ 278 IR.

Stosstrupps were scheduled to attack Michelsberg while the guns of Mont des Welches and its observers were pinned down by 88s and the two AR 195 groups. After the preliminary bombardment, emissaries were to be dispatched to the forts to attempt a parley. If that failed, all artillery was to target Michelsberg.

German reconnaissance patrols were sent out on the afternoon of 21 June to test French resistance. Michelsberg's tripwire was Blockhouse 9 and 9bis[2] on the route d'Ising along the edge of the Jungwald 300m behind the entry bloc. Any troops approaching Michelsberg would come under the fire of the blockhouses. This is precisely what happened on the 21st. Sergeant Pinard, chief of the two blockhouses, spotted the Germans moving in his direction. He stepped outside the casemate with an FM to drive off the Germans. As he was about to do so, Michelsberg's Bloc 3 of Sub-Lt Grenier, equipped with an 81mm turret, dropped three salvoes of fifty-four shells into the trees of the Jungwald. The 135mm turret of Bloc 6 fired eight shots. Several Germans were wounded or killed.

At 0730hrs, Adjutant Chef Meric of Observatory 09 which was located in Bloc 2,[3] phoned Michelsberg's artillery commander, Captain de Saint Sauveur, to inform him of German movement in the village of Dalstein, north of the ouvrage. At 0700hrs, General von Arnim, afraid his artillery batteries would be spotted and targeted before they could all be set up, began the attack. Captain de Saint-Sauveur telephoned Sub-Lt Kaas, commander of Bloc 5 and Lt Deschamps of Bloc 6. Kaas put his 75mm turret in battery and fired one shot. The 135mm in Bloc 6 was better suited to hit the targets

Lt Deschamps standing in front of the 135mm turret in Bloc 6 of Ouvrage du Michelsberg. (Pascal Lambert, wikimaginot .eu)

at Dalstein. Saint Sauveur also alerted Capt Agostini, artillery commander at Welches, Captain Gasset, *Directeur de Tir* of Hackenberg and Captain Salomon of Anzeling to the attack. Hackenberg's 75mm casemate guns in Bloc 5 and 75mm turret in Bloc 2 prepared to give support.

Another call from Meric in Obs 09 reported that anti-tank guns were being set up on the route de Hombourg and infantry was spotted in the trench near l'Usine de Houve. Activity also was increasing in the village of Dalstein. The intensity of counter-action from the Maginot Line also increased. With perhaps hours left before a cease fire the forts had no worries about running out of ammunition. Mont des Welches' guns concentrated on the Bois de Klang to the west. Anzeling's 75mm turret in Bloc 4 scoured the road near Volmerange and went after German infantry near Dalstein. Michelsberg's guns pounded the rear of the ouvrage, severely hampering the German concentration.

Around 1600hrs, German 88s were in place and fired at random on Blocs 2 and 3 of Michelsberg, located on the northern edge of the woods overlooking Dalstein. This time the shelling was sporadic. Instead of concentrating on one spot the

Intermediate level of the 75mm Model 1933 gun turret of Bloc 5, Ouvrage du Michelsberg. (Hans Vermeulen)

guns swept the façade of the blocs, causing damage but nothing on a par with the destruction unleashed on SF Faulquemont and Rohrbach.

At 1630hrs three German officers approached under a flag of truce. Von Arnim believed morale at Michelsberg was so bad that the French would be happy to give up. The Germans were blindfolded and brought to Pelletier in the entrance bloc. They praised him and his men for their brave resistance but assured him that very few forts were left. Pelletier knew this was false. He coldly told the Germans that he had his orders and they would be carried out. The men were escorted back outside by Saint Sauveur, this time with no blindfold. They were told they had fifteen minutes to get away and after that the French would open fire again. Captain de Saint-Sauveur had in fact left their blindfolds off for a reason – so the Germans could see how little damage the 88s had caused. This was reported to 95 ID who realized that if 260 shots from an 88 had caused no damage then heavy guns were needed, for example, the 420s, but this was not in the plan.

The Germans fired another 500 shells on Mont des Welches and 160 on Michelsberg. The Maginot Line guns were too powerful and responded to every threat almost instantaneously. In light of the day's events, von Arnim called off the attacks on the two forts. Their artillery was too powerful and their range would not allow the Germans to concentrate their forces for a successful attack. It was also impossible to set up an 88 battery within 1,000m where it would do the most damage. At 1830hrs the 95 ID was ordered to march south to Châlons-sur-Marne.

That evening an order was sent out to the divisions of Army Group C forbidding any further attacks against the forts of the Maginot Line.

SF Haguenau, 22 to 23 June

June 22nd began as a calm night and a much calmer day in SF Haguenau. There were no German attacks in S/S Hoffen, just small patrols spotted throughout the sector. Schoenenbourg and Hochwald fired on enemy movements or potential threats. At 1600hrs the *Groupe Franc* of 22 RIF was ordered to retake Retschwiller. The 135mm turret of Hochwald Est fired forty shots on the west side of the village. Ten minutes later, after hearing machine-gun fire, Obs 088 spotted about thirty men running from Meisenthal towards Memelshoffen. This was the *Groupe Franc* retreating.

At 1615hrs a 420mm began to fire on Schoenenbourg. The shots were being directed by a balloon over the region of Dierbach. There were approximately seven minutes between shots. Several of the shells did not explode and dust and smoke marked the spot where the shells hit. The turrets were retracted to prevent any possible damage.

At 1912hrs Obs 088 spotted a German battery setting up near the railway south of Katzenhausen. Bloc 7bis fired twenty shots on top of the battery. The crew ran off and a huge plume of black smoke rose from the site. Forty more shots finished off the four pieces left behind. Ten shots were fired on a German column of vehicles in the woods north of Hoeschloch and the column was dispersed.

At 2100hrs all the observatories reported seeing numerous multicoloured flares rising up from the German lines north of S/S Pechelbronn and SS/Hoffen. This was undoubtedly a signal of the signing of the French-German armistice. Around 2145hrs a German officer and soldier from 404 IR (246 ID) were captured riding bicycles near Soultz and taken to Hochwald. They spoke of the 'angry' artillery fire from the fortresses that harassed them non-stop. They confirmed the precision of the shots, stating that 'these artillerymen could kill a hare in a race'.[4]

It appeared the Germans were staying out of range of Schoenenbourg which had hampered their progress from the east. At the end of the day the northern part of the Line was very calm, with isolated activity in S/S Hoffen and further east. In S/S Pechelbronn German detachments were seen near Schafbusch and several patrols near the Grossenwald. In the south the Germans continued to push towards Mattenmuhl. They made no move towards Lobsann which had been abandoned by the French. At 1000hrs the commander of S/S Pechelbronn sent defenders to the edge of the woods north of Lobsann to recover some supplies left behind after the retreat.

South of Schoenenbourg the Germans pushed forward to the ridge facing the village but they were forced back by infantry and artillery fire. In the Haguenau Forest the Germans launched a surprise attacks on the forest house and village of

Schirrheim where they captured a company of 70 ID. Sporadic German harassing fire continued on the casemates of S/S Hoffen and on French positions to the south, in the region of Niederbetschdorf. The Germans held the areas east and south of the village, but were pinned down by French artillery. The French lines in S/S Hoffen were very thin and it was possible the Germans were looking to break through and cut the French forces in two in the region of Hatten. However, near Lobsann the two 135mm of Hochwald and the 75mm plus the casemate guns held them off. Bloc 16 of Hochwald Ouest's northern section fired 270 shots at targets south of Lobsann.

Schoenenbourg's Bloc 3 fired shrapnel rounds north of Ingolsheim and was hit in the turret by a 105mm shell. The fragment impeded the full lowering of the turret and overnight it was removed with a chisel. The Group commander ordered the turrets to be very selective with their targets and not to expose themselves to damage for a non-urgent request.

On 23 June, the Germans attempted to push towards the north at Mattenmuhl, but they were blocked by the fortress guns. An attack at Rittershoffen was also repulsed. Otherwise, it was mostly calm. Mostly the Germans hid in the woods. The front lines were empty of troops however, larger units penetrated south of the sector. At 0800hrs German vehicles entered Rott and were fired on by the 135mm turret of Hochwald Est. The shells fell and a huge column of black smoke rose into the air.

Heavy artillery of SAA 800 concentrated on Schoenenbourg – medium and heavy calibre – 105mm, 150mm and 420mm. At 0752hrs the 420mm fired fourteen shots – one every seven minutes. During this bombardment, the men moved down into the lower galleries where it was much quieter. They cringed around the sixth minute, waiting for the next shell to fall and shake the earth. Bloc 3's turret was hit by a shell on the advanced armour but the damage was minor – a few small cracks. One 420mm shot knocked off the vent stack (*champignon* – 'mushroom') of Block 6 and flung it 50m in the air. Another shell fell within 2m of the turret of Bloc 3 and broke off a small chunk of concrete. The steel wedges of the armoured collar were left intact. Other shells shook the ground between Blocs 4, 5 and 6. At 1000hrs German horse-drawn artillery was spotted in the south-east corner of Grosswald. Bloc 7bis fired fifty shots. Men and horses fled in panic and several horses were killed.

The night of 23/24 June was calm. The only sounds came from the French guns firing on German infantry formations spotted observatories at Steinseltz, Rott, Oberhoffen. There was no movement behind the German lines. They were positioned north and south of the Maginot Line, waiting for orders. There were no large German columns, only sporadic sightings – a vehicle here, a motorcycle there. At 1500hrs German 105s fired on the village of Schoenenbourg from the south. At 1630hrs Schoennebourg was shelled heavily by 105s, aiming at the turrets. It was suspected that German observers were watching from the woods of Ober-, Mittel-

and Unterwald, so Bloc 6 of Hochwald Est laid down a barrage of sixty shots. The German shelling continued into late evening and the church in Schoenenbourg village caught fire. At 2010hrs there was a renewed concentration of 105mm and 150mm on Schoenenbourg and the woods behind the fort. Hochwald was not hit. Around 2320hrs sporadic machine-gun fire was heard in Schoenenbourg village where the church continued to burn.

In the Haguenau Forest and to the south the Germans mounted strong attacks from Sessenheim. 1st Company 68 RIF, defending the village of Statmatten, repulsed general attacks at 1730hrs and 2000hrs. They received the support of 81mm mortars from the direction of Fort-Louis which fired on the woods south of Sessenheim until 0130hrs on 25 June – Armistice Day.

Chapter 20

The Final Shots

June 23rd to 24th were the most violent days leading up to the armistice in terms of artillery action. The Germans were happy to sit back and wait. Patrols kept their distance and the turrets kept firing to keep things that way. On the evening of 24 June, Italy signed the armistice and a cease fire would go into effect throughout France on 25 June at 0035hrs. Several ouvrages continued to fire until the last minute. Some fired a few rounds afterwards.

The unofficial announcement over the radio created a dilemma for the fortress commanders. Some, like Fabre of Grand-Hohékirkel, insisted on waiting for official cease-fire orders through the chain of command and he would continue to fight the war until the war was officially declared over by French army authorities. For Fabre, any approach by the enemy, whether accompanied by a white flag or not, would be treated as hostile. He would not recognize the authority of any French prisoner brought to the fort by the Germans. The crew of Grand-Hohékirkel was ordered to stay at their posts and be ready to repel any attacks.

Around midnight the Germans rang the church bells of Haspelscheidt. Grand-Hohékirkel responded by firing all of its guns in all directions. It is likely that Fabre was simply expending as much ammunition as possible before time was called so as to leave nothing behind for the Germans.

To the west, Rohrbach was the target of German artillery beginning on the morning of 24 June. The German guns were in range of Simserhof's 75s, forcing them to be placed at a distance of 2,000m from Rohrbach. Lt Paul Hacquard directed the aim of Simserhof's gun from the periscope of Rohrbach's cloche in Bloc 1.[1] The Germans responded with 105s and 150s but caused little damage.

Captain Saint-Ferjeux, commander of Rohrbach, was fully expecting a German attack. Rohrbach was now on the left flank of the Line and the blocs were ready for any attack. The embrasures were reinforced with sandbags to cushion the blasts and the men in the lower level were prepared to fight off an attack in the underground if it came to that. Ammunition was moved out of the upper level of the firing chamber to prevent an explosion if a German shell penetrated the block or came through an embrasure. The morale of the men was excellent and the word surrender 'was not part of our vocabulary'.[2] However, the German attack never came. General Theissen was content to shell the fort into surrender but Saint-Ferjeux had the last word. When the order to cease fire was received he declared, 'We are still holding. They did not get us'.[3]

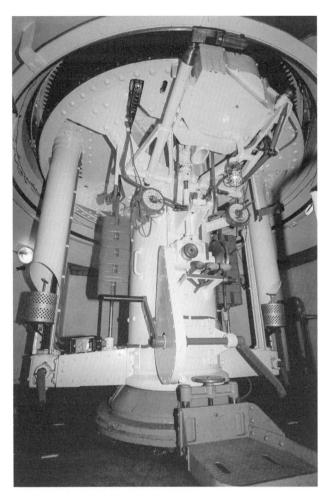

The mixed arms turret in Bloc 1 of Ouvrage du Rohrbach. (Hans Vermeulen)

In SF Faulquemont a heavy bombardment continued on 23 to 24 June against Einseling, Laudrefang and Téting. Since 21 June 167 ID had shelled the three forts incessantly, concentrating especially on Laudrefang. The 81mm guns of Lt Cointet's Bloc 1 were the main point of resistance for the trio and covered Einseling. The 81mm mortars of Lt Choné's Bloc 3 covered Téting. Commandant Denoix: 'At 40m underground, [all] 24 hours [of the day] were identical; [there was] neither day nor night. The noise indicated that the earth above was being hammered, but we could only see through the eyes of the telephone operators in the blocs who gave the location of where the shells landed and the damages [they caused].'

The shelling caused serious damage to Lt Keller's Casemate de Quatre-Vents Sud. An 88mm shell snapped the mast of the searchlight and it fell into the ditch. On the evening of 23 June, the armoured door was bent and sagging and shells struck the rear inner wall of the casemate. Electricity and lighting was cut off and the ventilator stopped. Thick smoke filled the gun chamber and the men started to think about asphyxiation and catastrophe. The casemate became a death trap. Then a call came in from Lt Vincent that crystallized the situation – they were about to unleash a general barrage. All arms in the sector opened fire. Sergeant Geneste – 'To work, guys. Your friends have need of you!'[4]

Lt Vincent knew that time was running out for Laudrefang. Bloc 1's concrete façade was getting thinner and thinner. At 1800hrs on 23 June the JM was put out of commission and the firing chamber evacuated. A shell hit the JM, knocking it back into the chamber and blowing away the embrasure support, leaving a huge hole. Each subsequent shell enlarged the breach. At night, the hole was covered over by a steel plate.

Bloc 3 was in equally bad shape, except for the two mortars in the lower level. At 1300hrs on 24 June, anti-tank shells aimed at the entry door broke the grill to pieces. The periscope was hit and could not be repaired. Around 1825hrs Vincent was informed the cease fire was just a few hours away. The end was coming one way or the other but Laudrefang held on for that which was more honourable. The atmosphere inside Bloc 3 was stifling. German shells screeched when they struck the concrete before they exploded. They made a monstrous sound like a gong each time they struck the cloche. At 2100hrs the turret was hit and could not be retracted.

At Téting, Marchelli asked himself the same questions going through Choné's mind at Bloc 3. Could they withstand the bombardment much longer? The firing chamber of Bloc 3 was uninhabitable. All of the embrasures were twisted, a JM was broken, the 47mm gun was out of commission and the FM of the cloche was

JM/AC 47 combination in Ouvrage du Schoenenbourg. (Dan McKenzie)

smashed to pieces. More than sixty rounds came through the breach in the wall into the chamber. Marchelli moved the ammunition and the men to the lower level until the engineers could restore ventilation to the bloc. The bombardment on 24 June was not as bad as the previous day but it intensified in the afternoon. Marchelli felt the need to hit back at the Germans and ordered Choné to fire at the officer's barracks on the route of Laudrefang-Téting. This had no effect on the German rate of fire and Marchelli ordered the machine-gun turret to fire on the village of Téting. Around 2330hrs Marchelli received a message from Denoix stating that the armistice was probably signed but to be vigilant and await further orders. This was confirmed by a supplemental message stating the armistice had been signed at 1835hrs on 24 June and hostilities were to cease six hours later at 0035hrs on 25 June.

The German bombardment of Téting continued until the final moments. Marchelli was furious and ordered the mortars of Bloc 3 to continue to fire on the outskirts of Téting. A mortar barrage struck an unlucky Pak 37 crew. Marchelli wanted to have the last word. But, at 0035hrs the guns stopped firing one after the other, then silence, except for the humming of the ventilation system.

In SF Boulay, the guns of Hackenberg, Michelsberg and Mont des Welches maintained a 10km firing radius the German patrols avoided. Anzeling continued to fire and the Germans responded in kind against Bloc 9. The best way for the gunners of Anzeling's 135mm and 75mm turrets to forget that France was beaten was to continue to fire the guns, which they did right up to the end. The 75mm turret of Bloc 7 of Anzeling fired its final two shots at 0030hrs. After this Sub-Lt Cézard removed the wedges of the cradle locks of his pieces. After firing the guns, the barrels, now free from their recoil brakes, flew out of their cradles and were hurled violently against the wall of the turret.

At 2315hrs on 24 June Colonel Cochinard sent a message to the crews of SF Boulay stating that French radio had announced that a cease fire was taking place overnight. All the ouvrages will cease fire at 0035. Destruction of arms and munitions was forbidden. Troops were instructed to remain calm and dignified. Until new orders were received it was forbidden to leave the ouvrages.

SF Thionville remained calm until the end. The Germans did not attempt any further attacks, only small patrols here and there. O'Sullivan passed on the details of the armistice and the cease-fire order. All German emissaries were to be directed to A17 (Métrich). 'Keep the doors locked and the crews below. More than ever, show dignity and discipline' (O'Sullivan).

A few hours prior to the cease fire, the cloches of Hackenberg were attacked by German guns. Commandant Ebrand ordered Billig to fire on the surface of Hackenberg Ouest and the EM (2,030 shots). He also ordered Mont des Welches to provide support. The last action in SF Thionville was carried out by Billig's Bloc 5. From 2200hrs until midnight on 24 June the turret fired 2,030 shots on top of Hackenberg to counter German infiltration. Calm returned to the sector after midnight.

The Germans ceased attacks in SF Crusnes after the debacle at Fermont. On the evening of 24 June a few shots were fired by Fermont and Latiremont. Bréhain fired several 75mm and 135mm rounds on Villerupt and the Camp de Morfontaine. At 0010hrs the 135mm turret in Bloc 5 of Lt Graveel harassed the outskirts of Villerupt and Audun-le-Tiche, then ceased firing at 0030hrs. The remaining munitions were moved down to magazine M2.

At PO Aumetz, contrary to orders, Lt Jean Braun decided to sabotage the guns. The fort was completely cut off because a telephone coupling chamber had been discovered and sabotaged by the Germans. The radio was functional but it could only connect with Bréhain. There were no attacks on the ouvrage. On Sunday, 23 June a small German patrol approached the barbed wire of Bloc 3. A German soldier was shot down and killed by the FM of the bloc. On 24 June, the machine-gun turret fired towards the village of Aumetz on buildings occupied by the Germans. Despite the stipulations of the armistice not to sabotage any of the weapons, Braun ignored the order. He could not let them fall into German hands. He wanted to continue firing after 0035hrs and to pull his troops out in small groups and escape but he realized this would cause needless deaths. He called his officers together and they were of one accord. They had no time to waste. Their plan was to burn the official documents and archives and the weapons would be destroyed after 0035hrs. The machine-gun turret would be broken so it could not be raised; the JMs destroyed and the breeches pulled out and dumped into wells. The optical equipment, motors and mechanics to raise the turret would be broken up. The electrical system was to be left, along with ventilation and transmissions in case they were needed. Munitions were unsafe to destroy.

At Latiremont, Pophillat considered blowing up the fort. A huge supply of munitions remained – 1,600,000 machine-gun rounds, and 45,000 75mm and 81mm shells. Pophillat discussed this with his officers and they concluded it would take days to place munitions and explosives throughout the fort to cause the kind of damage they were looking for. The idea was abandoned.

In the small casemates, unlike the ouvrages, men had been sealed up for several weeks. They literally lived on top of each other in cramped quarters with nowhere to go to get away. The crews suffered false hope, slept poorly and alerts at night were too frequent. Hygiene was poor, too little water to get clean – only enough for emergency purposes. The rations were poor and no longer satisfied. There was a constant noise of ventilation, gunfire, comings and goings in the narrow corridors, poor lighting, bare, damp concrete walls. Throughout the night of 24 June, the the JM of Casemate Tappe Ouest fired until the barrels were red-hot. At Casemate de l'Anguille the sentries pulled out of the cloches at 0030hrs. At l'Ermitage they waited, each man wanting to be left alone to think. At Casemate Praucourt, Sub-Lt Moitry gave the order, upon cease fire, to pull the guns out of the embrasures, clean the barrels and grease the breeches. Capt Aubert called Lt Hamelin at Puxieux to tell him it would be over at 0035hrs.

At 2330hrs, Adjutant-Chef Brégon of Observatoire de Puxieux requested fire support from Fermont against a nearby patrol. It was hard to believe this was happening at this late hour, but Lt Boury, commander of Bloc 1's 75mm turret, was happy to oblige. The bloc fired a total of 1,300 rounds between 2030hrs and 0030hrs.

At 0035hrs Fermont ceased fire but the JM of Casemate Beuville was still firing. Renardin, chief of the casemate, when called by Braye to see what was going on, stated that he wanted to stop but a German machine gun set up in Blockhouse 318 kept firing at him and the sentry spotted shadows in the wire. The matter was discussed in the PCA. The French did not want to restart hostilities – it was probably a small squad who had not received the cease-fire orders. Braye ordered Lt Bourbon to fire a few 81mm rounds on Casemate Beuville's wire and the surrounding area. The rounds landed in front of Blockhouse 318 but the firefight continued for another hour past the armistice. At 0140hrs the last shell of its short history was fired by the Maginot Line and all was calm. The most powerful fortress ever built was silent.

Message from QG of SF Haguenau – 25 June – 0015

1. Notice from National French radio sent at 2330hrs to announce that all fire must cease at 0035hrs night of 25 June.
2. Nothing will change until 0035hrs regarding defence.
3. All elements of SFH must stay in their positions currently without giving up any terrain.
4. Make no contact with any enemy envoy.
5. Make contact only with an envoy of French command after verifying their identification by the sector commander, the only one qualified to review their documents.
6. Refuse any receipt prior to 0035.

Signed – Schwartz, Lt Col CC of SFH

At 0026hrs Obs 088 and 092 reported machine-gun fire coming from Schoenenbourg village. The Germans were attempting a surprise attack on the southern edge of the Bois d'Hoffen and were repulsed by French infantry fire. At 0035hrs the commander of S/S Pechelbronn gave the cease-fire order. At 0040hrs Commandant Rodolphe ordered 'A1, A2, A3, cease fire!' It was finished. A tremendous sadness was felt by the troops who were unable to understand how the nation had fallen so quickly. SF Haugenau had fought well and continued to be able to resist.

At 0700hrs a German envoy arrived at Hochwald Est. He was received by Captain Barrier, artillery commander of Hochwald Est and Lt Weisé, chief of Obs

06. They told the envoy they were awaiting the orders of their chiefs and it would be best for him to leave, which he did.

In the early morning of 25 June General Denecke of 246 ID sent an envoy to Hochwald Est with a letter requesting a rendezvous at Rott. It was addressed to the commander of the 'Ouvrage Haute-Forêt', indicating that he must be ready to surrender the fort. Lt Col Miconnet replied verbally to the envoy that he had no intention of surrendering the fort; that he was waiting for orders from his commander. The men were now ordered to start cleaning up inside the forts, disposing of trash, etc. The Germans were for the most part, unseen. At Casemate C24: 'Waiting, waiting and it's finally over.'[5]

Chapter 21

The Bitter End

The forts that surrendered after the armistice did so as follows: German generals were very successful in convincing the French to give up the ouvrages of SF Crusnes, which they began to do on the morning of 27 June. Commandant Vanier of Bréhain met with General Wilck, commander of 161 ID, at Rennes. He moved on from there to Metz to meet with General Kampisch, commander of XXXI Corps. Vanier agreed to surrender PO Mauvais-Bois, PO Bois-du-Four, GO Bréhain and PO Aumetz on the morning of 27 June. On the same day, after contacting Vanier, Commandant Pophillat, commander of Latiremont, also went to Rennes to meet with Wilck. After a brief meeting, he negotiated the surrender of the forts under his command – PO Chappy, GO Fermont and GO Latiremont – to take place on the morning of 27 June.

On 27 June, the crews of SF Crusnes assembled outside the entrances of their respective forts and marched off to the casernes of Doncourt, Morfontaine and Errouville. The forts were left behind intact except for PO Aumetz. An inquiry was conducted by the Germans to determine if Braun had violated the terms of the armistice but nothing came of it and he went into captivity with the rest of the men.

SF Thionville was placed under the authority of Commandant Charnal of Ouvrage du Kobenbusch. On 26 June, he contacted General Dippold, commander of 183 ID, to negotiate surrender. Charnal signed an agreement with Dippold without the knowledge and concurrence of Lt Col O'Sullivan. The agreement stipulated that the forts would surrender at the beginning of July. Dippold did not want to wait that long and the forts were in German hands on 30 June.

It was more difficult for the Germans to obtain surrenders on the other side of the Moselle. There, the commanders refused to do so. In their minds, they only heard via radio that the armistice was signed but had not received any official communications from the French high command, something they had every right to expect. This refusal was reported to the Armistice Commission who agreed to send a French delegation to the commanders to hasten their surrender and to explain that the forts west of the Moselle were already in German hands. The commission dispatched Colonel Marion, Lt Col De Souzy and Lt Col Simon. De Souzy went to Alsace to meet with Lt Col Schwartz near Lobsbann to ask him to hand over the ouvrages of Alsace. The surrender was signed at Hochwald to come into effect on 1 July.

Lt Col Simon's mission was to the Bitche sector, accompanied by General von Witzleben. They were permitted to enter Grand-Hohékirkel to meet with its commander, Fabre, and Bonlarron of Simserhof. The forts were immediately surrendered.

Colonal Marion travelled to Anzeling to meet with Colonel Cochinard. He was taken to Landonviller, command post of XXXXV Corps and met there with Lt Col O'Sullivan and Denoix. The following day Marion met with the commanders of Kobenbusch, Galgenberg, Bréhain and Latiremont, which were already being handed over to the Germans. The ouvrages at SF Boulay also surrendered and were evacuated on 2 July. Several specialists stayed behind to assure maintenance continued. They left several weeks later. The forts would not see friendly faces again until late 1944.

The Final Days at Hochwald

26 June: The guns are cleaned, spent shells are removed, barracks and living quarters cleaned up. Inspections are performed. The Sector commander asks the commander of the German infantry division to put him in contact with the French commander so as to receive instructions. He is under the impression that his men will go to the free zone since they were not captured prior to the armistice.

Fortified Sector of Haguenau
Order No. 46

Officers, NCOs, Corporals, Brigadiers and Soldiers of the Fortified Sector of Haguenau:

Despite the forceful methods put forth by the adversary, you did not allow the fortified line to be breached.

Thanks to your tenacity and your capacity to manoeuvre you have maintained your cohesion
THE ENEMY DID NOT PASS.
You are surrounded by an imperishable glory and you have gained the admiration of your adversary.

I have asked the command for each of the men present in SF Haguenau from 14 to 25 June, to receive a collective citation for the Croix de Guerre for exceptional duty. In the days of testing ahead that await you, through discipline and confidence in the destiny of our beloved Brotherhood, you will remain a living example of unconquered resolve.

Vive la France!

Lieutenant-Colonel Schwartz
Commandant le S.F.H.

27 June: Cleanup continues. Documents outlining the firing reports are prepared for transport to the archives. Group commander visits Hochwald Ouest to view the damage.

At 1800hrs the Germans ask for a head count to determine which location the men will be sent to. The hope that the men will be sent to the free zone is confirmed.

28 June: No orders yet. The men are getting nervous. There are rumours of a visit from the French General Headquarters, but no one shows up.

29 June: Still no word. In the afternoon, an envoy arrives from 246 ID, Captain Von der Heide. He is an Austrian from an old French family and speaks the local dialect well. He gives an account of the final fighting. He was at the head of an assault on PA 4. His men were continuously menaced by the turrets of Schoenenbourg and jumped into the trenches to escape the effects. He was quite shocked to see how little damage the Stukas caused on Hochwald Ouest and how the guns were able to continue to fire.

30 June (Sunday): Announcement of the arrival of the envoy from *Grand Quartier Général* (GQG – General Headquarters). At 1100hrs Mass is celebrated in the main gallery near M1. '*Sauvez, sauvez la France*' is sung and there are many with tears in their eyes. At 1500hrs the GQG officer passes through Woerth. Lt Col Schwartz and his staff assemble to meet him 200m from Bloc 8. At 1530hrs a large vehicle arrived, carrying Lt Col de Souzy of Weygand's staff, accompanied by the Chief of Staff of 246 ID. The men presented arms then each was introduced to De Souzy. They went inside the fort to the PC. Lt Col Schwartz takes Miconnet aside and informs him that the men are prisoners of war. This is a shock to the small group as it was totally unexpected.

'*Ce lent cortege muet dans la demi-obscurite des galleries reassemble a l'enterrement de la France …*'[1] At the PC, Schwartz pointed out on a map the location of the men on 25 June at the time of the armistice. He strongly protested that the fate of the men was being announced now, five days later. De Souzy and the German remarked that they understood how they must feel, how this decision is wrong, but all they could do is pass on the message. He continued by saying that the fortress troops are considered to be surrounded and need to lay down their arms. De Souzy requested an account of the attack against the forts. Rodolphe accompanies him to Schoenenbourg where he was informed that, despite the intensity of the attack, the fort is intact. At 1800hrs De Souzy prepared to leave. Rodolphe once again asked for him to intervene on their behalf. The government must know their situation. De Souzy promised to do so but the chances were slim. As a final shot that could perhaps be taken as a threat, Rodolphe explained that the forts still had the capability of holding out for a long time. The German envoy requested that the men be ready to leave their position the following morning and that they will be interned at Haguenau. Orders are sent out to the men at 2300hrs.

On 1 July at 0700hrs the men assembled in front of Bloc 8 of Hochwald Est. The flag was lowered and the columns marched off towards Lobsbann. Technicians stayed behind to keep the fort operating until the Germans took control. This was done according to an agreement between Lt Col Schwartz and General Denecke.

At 0900hrs Rodolphe headed to the assembly point of the troops on the road to Lobsbann. The groups were organized according to their function – General Services-Engineers under Lieutenants de Mougins and Harispe; Artillery of the Ouvrage West under Captain Ducrot and Lieutenants Hulot, Hauer, Schertziger, Simon, Lefebvre and Monnen; Artillery of Ouvrage East commanded by Captain Zyromski. The entire column is led by Captain Barrier and Lieutenants Gillet, Angles, Faure, Coquart, Weisé, Piet, Skenazi. The marching order was given and one by one the crews passed in review, each column ordered 'eyes left' to give final honours to Commandant Rodolphe. The men were carrying all sorts of small pieces of baggage containing food, personal items and keepsakes from their time in the fort. Some of them have bicycles and musical instruments. The column marched off 30km to Haguenau where they arrived at 1900hrs. They were joined there by personnel from SF Vosges who arrived from Bitche.

Over the next few days Hochwald received a number of visitors, mostly from officers whose men were hit by the fort's guns. Most of the visitors were very courteous and saluted the French officers. A couple of Germans showed an arrogance and hostility towards the French guides and the French were told that the Germans would not put up with such rude behaviour and would correct the problem. On 3 July officers from 246 RA made a visit and Schwartz received a less-than-warm greeting from a Lieutenant Colonel. Vowinkel whispered to Schwartz that this is the commander of the group of artillerymen hit on 23 June between Pechelbronn and Surbourg. The shelling resulted in thirty-three wounded and the loss of a large number of horses. He was severely reprimanded for his action in leading the column to this location. Vowinkel must have had a word with the man because, later on, after a lengthy visit to the fort, the Lieutenant Colonel congratulated Schwartz on the precision of the guns. He wished Schwartz the best for himself and his family and hoped his captivity would not last long. At 1230hrs General Denecke visited. An honour guard of ten Germans and ten French render honours at the entrance.

On 4 July, the 246 ID departed for Landau. General Denecke wished the French good luck and a short captivity. During lunch a small man arrived and all of the Germans present at the table jumped up and said, 'Heil Hitler'. The visitor was General von Molo, commander of all German forces between Sarrebrück and the Rhine. On 5 July Hochwald received a visit from General Ritter von Leeb. A group of Luftwaffe pilots visiting the forts were shocked at the lack of damage caused by their bombs. Schwartz showed them the only significant damage – a broken thermometer on the outside of the cloche in Obs 06. The pilots told Schwartz that they dropped bombs of 50kg, 100kg, 500kg, 1,000kg and 1,500 kg and stopped because they ran out of ammunition. On that same day Schwartz finally departed for Haguenau.

The Maginot Line's Final Count

Of twenty-two artillery ouvrages (GO), two were sabotaged on 12 June in SF Maubeuge (Chesnois and Velosnes). The rest were left intact. Fermont, Schoenenbourg and Hochwald were heavily bombarded but all guns remained operational. Of thirty-one POs, La Ferté was taken on 19 May, Thonnelle sabotaged on 12 June, and Kerfent, Bambesch, Haut-Poirier and Welschoff surrendered. Twenty-five were in French control on 25 June, along with 130 casemates, sixty abris and dozens of observatories. Twenty-five thousand men left behind in the Maginot Line had been under siege since 16 June.

Part VI

Aftermath and Conclusions, July 1940 to the Present

Chronology July 1940 to the Present

27 June	The forts of the Maginot Line begin to surrender to the Germans. The handover is complete by early July.
Late November 1944	The US Seventh Army approaches the Vosges Mountains.
9 December	12th Armoured Division's CCA pushes through the former Maginot Line defences between Singling and Rohrbach.
11 December	100th Infantry Division attacks Schiesseck and Simserhof, capturing the forts after several days using a methodical approach to trap and kill German defenders inside the tunnels.
9 November	The 90th Infantry Division crosses the Moselle and moves down the Hackenberg ridge. Engineers drive the Germans out of Ouvrage du Metrich and some of the casemates to the south.
15 November	American troops are shelled by 75mm guns from Hackenberg. Artillery is brought in during the night to take out the guns. The Americans move on towards Germany.
1998	French First Army, after using it as a command post for several years, abandons Ouvrage du Rochonvillers.
June 2015	The French radar installation inside Ouvrage du Hochwald is deactivated. Hochwald is abandoned.

Chapter 22

Aftermath

French troops became prisoners of war shortly after the armistice. The Germans took possession of the Maginot Line. Several of the ouvrages were used for storage of war materials, some were used as underground factories. Equipment was removed for use in other German fortifications such as the Atlantic Wall. For the most part, the Maginot Line was silent for more than four years, until September 1944.

The United States Army and its allies launched two operations in 1944 that would have a later effect on the Maginot Line – the D-Day Invasion of June 1944 and Operation Dragoon on 14 August. Seventh Army landed on the southern coast of France on 15 August between Cannes and Le Lavandou. From there they headed north with the Free French Army towards Alsace and Germany. Seventh army was commanded by General Alexander Patch, Third Army by General George Patton.

By late November Seventh Army was fighting through the Vosges. It included XV Corps with 4th Armoured (replaced by 12th Armoured), 44th Infantry, 100th Infantry, 45th Infantry and 79th Infantry Divisions. 100th Infantry Division would move up the crest of the Vosges to attack the German centre between Frohmuhl and Ingwiller. With 44th Infantry Division on its left it would continue north towards the former Maginot Line. General Spragin's 44th Infantry Division was to strike north-east towards Siersthal, 4km west of Bitche, while two regiments of 100th Infantry Division headed for Bitche. The main, dual-division attack was to proceed on 3 December with the objective to break through to the Westwall but was delayed by a strong German defence in the rugged terrain.

The XV Corps offensive pushed off on 5 December. 12th Armoured moved between Singling and Rohrbach; 44th Division west of Siersthal through Holbach and 100th between Siersthal and Bitche to face the German 25th Panzergrenadier Division and 361st Volksgrenadiers. Meanwhile, 106th Regiment was in reserve.

VI Corps' 45th Infantry Division moved west of Woerth through Lembach (PO Lembach and Ouvrage du Four-à-Chaux) and Wingen, 103rd Infantry through SF Haguenau between Climbach (Ouvrage du Hochwald) and Rott. 14th Armoured moved past Ouvrage du Schoenenbourg towards Schleithal and Hatten. These units faced 245th and 246th Infantry and 21st Panzer Divisions.

On 5 December, 100th Division's 397th and 398th Regiments moved north without resistance as the Germans had pulled back. 324th and 114th Inf. Rgts of

44th Infantry Division also advanced quickly on 5 to 6 December. On 7 December defences in their path stiffened and they came under mortar and artillery fire. Bridges and roads were destroyed and booby-trapped.

On the same day, 12th Armoured's CCA advanced and on the 9th attacked towards Singling and Rohrbach (Ouvrage du Welschoff and Rohrbach), securing the former on 9 December and the latter the following day. The division passed through abandoned or lightly manned concrete defences of the former SF Rohrbach.

It took 44th Division's 71st Infantry Regiment until 11 December to take control of Siersthal. 100th Division, moving on the right, was still short of Bitche. The Germans decided to hold the Maginot Line forts of Bitche, thus threatening the U.S. Army flank. 44th and 100th Divisions were ordered to mount assault operations against the forts. The German choice was a good one: the Bitche Ensemble was fully capable of defending against an attack from the south.

The Germans could make use of some of the French fortress casemate guns (the turrets had been stripped for spare parts) and their defences were strengthened by artillery and mortars located north of the fortress line. 25th Panzergrenadiers defended Simserhof, Schiesseck and Otterbiel. 361st VG Div defended Grand-Hohékirkel.

The Americans planned to take out the forts one by one, beginning in the west. 44th Division led off the attack on Simserhof. The 71st launched the main assault with 324th Regiment in support. The going was slow for the 71st. They encountered stiff resistance from German artillery and mortar fire, combined with a German counter-attack from Freudenberg Farm. The next day the 71st captured some blocs between Simserhof and Schiesseck and were able to move

Bloc 8 of Ouvrage du Hackenberg. American troops from First Battalion, 71st Infantry Regiment were fired on from this bloc in December 1944. (NARA)

west to invest Simserhof from the east. The Americans used all the firepower at their disposal (artillery and tank destroyers) to pound the Simserhof blocs, while the 71st advanced its combat engineers towards the EM and EH. By the evening of 17 December, the engineers had entered the fort. A final attack on the interior was scheduled for 19 December but thankfully the Germans fled.

Meanwhile 100th Division's 398th Regiment launched its attacks on Schiesseck and Otterbiel on the 14th. They encountered artillery fire coming from the two forts. Corps and Division artillery, including 240mm pieces started a two-day bombardment, combined with aerial bombing. Later investigation revealed the artillery and airstrikes caused little damage.

On 17 December the 398th Regiment captured 'Fort Freudenberg' and the EM and EH of Schiesseck. Infantry-engineer teams proceeded to drop explosives down lift shafts, stairwells and ventilation shafts to pin the Germans in the lower levels. No attempts were made to descend below, only to seal off the fort and kill any Germans left inside. The fort was secured on 20 December and the Division moved on to Otterbiel.

The operation cost the 398th Regiment fifteen dead and eighty wounded. The lower casualty figures resulted from the decision to use firepower versus infantry assaults, as had been done at Fort Driant in Metz in October, where losses were significantly higher. Also, the Germans had begun to withdraw to the Westwall.

On the right, 45th Infantry Division took Lembach on 13 December. 103 Infantry Division moved through Climbach and reached Rott on the 13th. Further east 79th Infantry Division closed in on the Lauter and the German border. 14th Armoured cleared Riedseltz on 15 Decmber. The German border was crossed in the late afternoon and the Americans would hold there until the coming German Operation Nordwind, where the Americans lost all ground gained since 7 December, but it would be retaken for good in late January.

In September 1944 XX Corps of Patton's Third Army approached Étain, north-east of Verdun. The cavalry group headed towards Thionville to plot a crossing of the Moselle north of Metz. 7th Armoured was to bypass Metz and head for Germany while 5th and 90th Infantry Divisions invested the fortress city. This was not accomplished until November. The Americans were forced to reduce, one by one, the former German forts that held up the Third Army divisions. Prior to this, 90th Division tangled with 106th Panzer Brigade south of Aumetz. On 10 September 357th Infantry Regiment headed to Hayange, 358th Regiment to Angevillers and 359th secured Aumetz and the ground north and west including some unmanned bunkers.

Metz was invested and finally surrendered in early November. XX Corps was finally able to move on to Germany. On 9 November, in the early morning hours of darkness, 90th Infantry Division crossed the rain swollen Moselle River north of Thionville. The 358th Infantry Regiment stormed and captured Fort Koenigsmacker, an older German fort similar to those at Metz. The engineers blew through the wire with Bangalore torpedoes and advanced from bloc to bloc, driving the Germans from one end of the fort to the other where they finally gave up a couple of days later. On 11 November III/90th moved towards Métrich and the former ouvrage of the same name. Once again the engineers exercised utmost caution as they approached the blocs. While the main force moved past, a detachment stayed behind to seal up the fort to keep the Germans inside. The rest of the 357th Infantry Regiment moved around the interval blockhouses and casemates along the ridge, leaving teams behind to mop up. By the end of the day resistance at Métrich was broken.

The Germans made no serious attempt to mount a very strong defence in the former Maginot Line in this sector. They did not have the men or the guns. German reports indicate the presence of 58 officers and 218 men, a formidable force in a fully-functioning system, but at the time there were only fifty-one machine guns and sixteen larger guns in the fortifications.

On 15 November, after working its way along the ridges of the former Maginot Line of SF Thionville, at 0645hrs II/90th and III/90th approached Budling and were hit by German shells. Forward observers pinpointed the shells originating from 'Fort' Hackenberg. III/90th could not move. A platoon of M10 tank destroyers with 3in guns, moved to within 3,000m and fired directly at the casemate from where the firing was coming from. This was Bloc 8. The tank destroyers didn't cause any damage so the Americans switched to 8in and 240mm guns but they could not stop the Germans. During the night, M12 self-propelled 155mm howitzers were moved to within 2,000m and on 16 November the casemate's 75mm guns were finally neutralized. III/90th moved ahead to occupy the fort. The American army now moved east through the Maginot Line towards Germany. They encountered no more German resistance from the former forts of Lorraine.

Minor fighting took place in and around other sectors of the Maginot Line but nothing like the operations near Métrich or the bloc-by-bloc clearing of Simserhof and Schiesseck. 4th and 6th Armoured and 35th Infantry Divisions fought past Singling and Bining and Ouvrage du Welschoff. 20th Infantry Division fought through the works in the vicinity of Wittring and Achen. Army engineers identified them as Forts Wittring and Grand Bois. Casemate de Wittring was a simple CORF casemate with one JM/AC47, one JM, one cloche AM (25 AC and JM), two GFM B with FM. Grand Bois was a simple CORF casemate with one JM/AC47, one JM, two cloche AM, 2 GFM B.

After the Achen casemates capitulated, the 328th Infantry Regiment's Company K approached Wittring in mid-afternoon of 8 December. The casemate was surrounded on three sides by a factory put up by the Germans. Shells from a tank destroyer took out the 25mm gun in the mixed arms cloche. At dusk a sergeant ran up and tossed a grenade against the entry door but he was hit by machine-gun fire. The engineers placed dynamite by the door but it failed to knock it down. At dawn engineers placed 200lbs of explosives against the door and the steel

Americans standing in front of the personnel entrance, Ouvrage du Simserhof. (NARA)

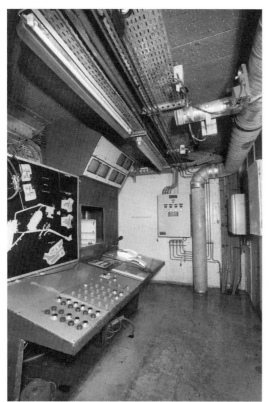

Security control room of Ouvrage du Rochonvillers. The entrances and barracks area of the fort were modernized for usage as a French army command post. (Dan McKenzie)

cracked, detonating ammuniton inside the casemate and killing the occupants. The attack on Casemate Grand Bois was much simpler. By the time the Americans moved in the Germans were gone. The Americans moved on towards the Sarre.

There is not much information on American occupation of the Maginot Line, other than curiosity and testing of weapons that would be used against the West Wall. Mostly, the Americans moved through the Line as their main objective was the West Wall and Berlin.

After the German surrender the French regained possession of the Maginot Line. It was used by NATO units until the 1960s. Rochonvillers was a French First Army command post until the late 1990s. In the 2000s it was in beautiful condition, but when the

French left it in 1998 it was vandalized and ruined inside. Hochwald served as a radar station until June 2015, when it was also abandoned, waiting for vandals. Some sites are still in use by the army for storage or the terrain for exercises. It is no longer used for its original purpose. The majority of the Line is empty, stripped of its equipment and weapons. In the 1990s the commander of the army at Metz ordered the entrances to be buried under mounds of soil in an attempt to keep visitors away – unsuccessfully, of course.

It is encouraging to see the number of ouvrages, casemates, blockhouses and shelters open as museums or in the process of being renovated. The list grows and grows and the Maginot Line has new life and hopefully a new reputation.

Chapter 23

Strengths and Weaknesses of the Maginot Line

The ouvrage showed its finest colours where the Line was the strongest. Its artillery capability was remarkable in terms of precision and speed of response to threats when support was requested. The principal weakness goes back to the beginning – the gap between planning and conception. Nowhere during planning was the Line intended to be left weak but in conception there was a combination of strong fortified sectors and those with limited or a practically non-existent capability of resistance when faced with a strong enemy attack. It can be compared in a certain way to the curtain wall made from different strengths of materials with the assumption that the enemy would never attack the weak areas or other obstacles could be placed in front of the weaker areas to stop the attack. Budget restrictions played a large part in that but were not in themselves the sole reason for the outcome.

The CORF planned a model based on geography, without regard for the financial implications. The model was based on the concept that natural obstacles were in themselves so formidable that the enemy would not attack there. This turned out to be a grievous error as those were the precise places the Germans attacked – Meuse, Sarre, Lower Vosges and the Rhine sectors. The Germans only attacked positions that were weakly defended in terms of artillery and fortifications. Once they broke through the main defences, the lack of depth left nothing to stop them from moving beyond and surrounding the rest of the Line.

The Maginot Line lacked depth, mostly as a result of the lack of funds. It was supposed to have a main line of resistance, consisting of large artillery forts and casemates, with a secondary line and anti-tank ditch to the rear. But only the main line was built, with a thin covering of advance posts and weak blockhouses.

The line did not have anti-aircraft capability, except for mobile batteries with no form of communication with the fort which was tasked with stopping a surprise attack. However, the 75mm turrets of Schoenenberg and Hochwald were adjusted to fire shell bursts at given heights that prevented German aircraft from accurately dropping their bombs.

Observations regarding the New Fronts:

- The conversion to mixed arms turrets was a regrettable decision and left the forts with no long-range artillery to fire on the approaches.
- The entire line from the North Sea to the Chiers River had miles of gaps.

- The casemates and blocks that defended the Line were of much lesser quality than the earlier CORF or even STG casemates.
- Only nine Maginot Line forts were built between the SF Escaut and Montmedy Bridgehead – Eth, Le Sarts, Salmagne, Bersillies, Boussois, La Ferté, Chesnois, Thonelle and Velosnes.
- All nine forts were surrendered or abandoned: five were captured – Eth, Les Sarts, Salmagne, Bersillies, Boussois; La Ferté was damaged and the crew killed by German pioneers; three others were sabotaged and abandoned as ordered on 13 June – Le Chésnois, Thonelle and Velosnes.
- The weaker frontier defences between the forts posed no obstacle for the Germans, who moved in behind the Line to attack them from the rear.
- PO Eth and the forts of SF Maubeuge were completely without long-range artillery, but nevertheless they put up a heroic defence. The forts of Maubeuge capitulated when the air inside became unbreathable and all the weapons were destroyed.
- La Ferté was the only fort attacked from the front and was the only fort of the Maginot Line taken in this manner.
- The field works were useless; only those at Monthermé put up a good defence. The line of blockhouses was easily taken.

Principal weaknesses of construction:

- Ventilation – the ventilators were so loud that telephone conversations were often inaudible. Of the forts that surrendered, the main cause was a fear of asphyxiation. The ventilation systems of all of the Maubeuge forts failed and the vent shafts were specifically targeted by German artillery, thus blocking the means of expelling the bad air.
- Some of the latrines were kept clean and odourless but the majority were not.
- Troop quarters were very cramped. Rooms made for twenty-four men were transformed to hold thirty-six with three-level bunks. The small space became like a crowded slum dwelling.
- Rubbish was often piled up in the corridors until such time as it could be taken outside.

Weapons:

- The weapons performed remarkably well; both infantry and artillery, with the exception of a handful of accidents:
  - Bursting of 75mm barrels.
  - Weakness of 135mm embrasures.
  - Explosion of 81mm mortars.

The concrete held up well against heavy bombardment, but it stood up very poorly against high-velocity 88s, and Pak 37s, especially against the rear facades, mostly because of the close range to which the Germans were able to bring up their guns and fire and because the walls were thinner and weaker there. While the concrete was reinforced with tightly-spaced steel rods, the shells eventually broke the rods and moved on to the next layer. This was a result of poor planning in thinking an attack by artillery from the rear would not take place. It was especially dangerous due to the lack of depth of the Line and the strong possibility that the Germans could get into the rear. The same scenario took place in 1914 at Liège, where they were struck from the rear where the concrete was thinner.

The steel used in the armour plating and in the cloches showed its weaknesses. It was the main target of the high-velocity guns. The turrets were much more resistant because they could be retracted. The cloches were the main handicap – the Achilles heel. They were crucial to observation but due to the necessity to see all around they stuck up like a sore thumb. The machine-gun cloches and observation cloches for periscopes did not suffer as heavily because of their reduced profile. The cloches GFM, AM and VDP were prime targets. The original cloche GFM was a poor design but was corrected in later models (GFM Type B). The number of cloches in the New Fronts was much higher, in some cases four cloches on one bloc, providing numerous targets. The episcopes were a prime target and caused several casualties when the glass was hit and the piece shattered. Photos reveal the number of shots fired by the Germans at the cloche embrasures and the damage done. While the cloche was being shelled, it was impossible for it to be occupied – it was like sitting inside a church bell while it was ringing and in some cases shells passed through open embrasures, killing the occupant.

The embrasures held up well and only suffered when the surrounding concrete was chipped away, dislocating the steel frame. A direct hit on the armour could further dislodge the concrete due to vibrations from the shock. The embrasures for machine guns were particularly problematic.

Museum of Ouvrage du Fermont. Left to right foreground: 75/33, 135mm and 81mm turrets. (Hans Vermeulen)

German Opinions Regarding the Maginot Line

Captain Von der Heide of the 246 ID visited Hochwald after the armistice. He commanded a squad that attacked PA 4. Three minutes after launching the attack his men were hit by shells from Schoenenbourg. On 20 June he was a passenger in a reconnaissance aircraft overflying the heavily-bombed Hochwald Ouest. He had happily reported its destruction. Von der Heide was absolutely shocked to see up close that the fort was still completely intact and operational.

Other German visitors were amazed at the scale of the underground complexes – the colossal galleries, electric trains, artillery blocs, the ease of manoeuvre of the turrets, the telephone system and the abundance of munitions and supplies. The M1 contained so many rounds that the visitors asked if the fort had fired any shots at all.

Captain Vowinkel of 246 ID visited Obs 07 and commented on the remarkable extended views from the periscope and that it was no wonder the shells fired on Schleithal-Oberseebach-Aschbach were so precise. The Germans were also very impressed by the French system of fire and observation. Their preconceptions and pre-war intelligence as to how it worked were wrong and they took copious notes during the French briefings.

During a visit to Bloc 7bis the Germans stated that the casemate resembled a clinic, everything was so clean, the guns greased, looking like they were new and had never been fired. The visit culminated with an excursion outside the bloc. The Germans could see the extensive damage done to the terrain by the Stuka bombs but were astounded by the lack of damage to the blocs. The ground was a mess, full of craters, but the three shining 75mm barrels protruded untouched from the embrasures.

A group of aviators visited on 5 July and could not believe the contrast between the inside of the fort and the devastation on the outside. They had dropped bombs ranging from 50kg to 1,800kg and it seemed to have been a complete waste of time.

Did the Maginot Line Fulfill its Role?

This is a difficult question and cannot be answered generally. The line must be examined function by function and only then can a final judgement be made. One cannot make a blanket statement that the Maginot Line was a complete success, but neither can one make the same statement that it was a complete failure.

The primary role of the Maginot Line was to prevent a sudden attack and to provide security to allow for the secure mobilization of troops. This role was fulfilled, but one must take into consideration that, during mobilization, the Germans were occupied in Poland and had no intention of launching a major attack on France.

The secondary role was, in the case of an enemy offensive, to be able to fight on favourable terrain and to force the enemy to the flanks where he would be forced to attack through Belgium. This role was fulfilled because the Germans did exactly that. The problem was that Gamelin also did exactly what the Germans wanted him to – abandon the north and advance into Belgium. Gamelin had a choice between a battle of movement on the Belgian plain or a battle of position on the Maginot Line, a choice between coming to the aid of allies or defending French territory. He chose the more dangerous action – to leave the safety of the forts to fight a mobile war for which the French were ill-equipped.

Detrimental effects of the command reorganization

At the end of 1939 the GQG made a regrettable decision to remove the notion of the 'Fortified Sector" as a command and control element and replace it with a hybrid organization that alternated between Army Corps and Fortress Infantry divisions and field army troops. A well-organized fortress system suddenly found itself dependant on field troops and under the authority of a local corps commander. In lieu of constituting the backbone of the position, the fortress became an auxiliary of the field troops since the forts had no prime role to play. If the battle took place along the fortified position it would have been on a pre-defined battlefield that left little initiative to the field troops. This resulted in disorganization and above all caused decisions to be made by officers with little knowledge of the potential of the fortifications.

This was not Gamelin's only mistake, since the Maginot Line missed another of its roles – the economy of force. In effect, the fortified line was conceived to be sufficient in itself, which permitted the deployment of a maximum number of divisions facing Belgium and consisted of a solid reserve. The French commander did not use this opportunity and the Maginot Line, rather than permitting an economy of force, on the contrary absorbed numerous divisions that were missing when the time came when they were needed most.

The Germans chose not to launch frontal attacks on the fortified position, even after the departure of the interval troops. They chose instead to carefully pick their way through the weakest spots (Sarre, Rhine, Vosges) and only when the field troops and some of the fortress troops had begun to pull out. The absence of infantry without a doubt led to this decision but a greater factor was the lack of French artillery to keep the German artillery pieces at a distance and allowed them to approach to within a short distance of the French blocs.

Missed opportunity

Among the worries expressed by the German high command, the most sensible concerned an eventual counter-attack from the Maginot Line against the German flanks. The operations taken against the PAL, for example, had no other purpose than to reduce the risk of such an attack against XIX Corps. These were legitimate worries but unfortunately without foundation. The French command at no time made use of the opportunities presented by and available from the fortifications to cut into enemy formations. A vigorous armoured attack on the flank of the Panzer divisions could have dislodged the German formations. At the least, the possibility could have made the Germans more cautious.

The unfortunate legacy for the Maginot Line is that it was not viewed apart from the defeat of France as a whole. In some respects, it was blamed for the defeat. However, blame can only be pinned on the commanders who made very poor decisions from the very beginning. The most unfortunate legacy of all is the missing history of the massive amount of fighting done by the fortress troops. Very few people know their story and it's time they did.

The Maginot Line was not a person but it became a personality – a French star that everyone wanted to see on the big screen. But it was only an inanimate weapon, like a tank or a ship or an aircraft; subject to the whim of the men who controlled its levers and switches. As a weapon, it worked marvelously, up until the very end.

Order No. 3
Fortress Artillery Group No. 3

Since September 1939 the fortress artillery has ceaselessly worked to perfect its combat preparation. It has done this with all of its heart and the difficult combat that it has participated in since 14 June has been severely tested.

Since this date it has been reduced by two-thirds and attacked at the same time on its flanks and from the rear. It has brilliantly faced this situation.

Informed day and night by vigilant observers it was able, despite massive aerial bombardments and shelling from heavy guns, to furnish at every moment, support to its infantry that allowed them to break up repeated enemy attacks.

It used aerial barrages to take the place of anti-aircraft guns.

It harassed enemy troop concentrations, observers, gun batteries and infantry columns.

It has, through rapidity, precision, violence and frequency of fire, preserved the Line of ouvrages and casemates and the Line of advanced infantry posts.

These brilliant results, recognized and admitted by the enemy, were the work of all: officers, NCOs, brigadiers, cannoniers, who, each at his post and with all his heart, has done all of his duty.

I thank them and tell them how proud I was to command such a force.

Whatever happens, all of the artillerymen of the fortress of the 'Lauter' can hold their heads up high.

They have held out until the end their proud motto: '*On ne passe pas*'.

From the PC of the Ouvrage du Hochwald, 25 June 1940
Chef d'Escadron Rodolphe
Commandant GAF3
Signed: Rodolphe

Notes

Introduction

1. A *Sous-Lieutenant* (Sub-lieutenant or second lieutenant) commands at the same level as a lieutenant, but is a more junior officer rank.
2. For example, Hochwald was used as a radar installation until 2015. Rochonvillers was First French Army headquarters until 1993; Camp de Bitche, with Ouvrage d'Otterbiel and Ouvrage Grand Hohékirkel on the property, is still an active military site.
3. *Faites Sauter la Ligne Maginot, On a Livré la Ligne Maginot* and *Offensive sur le Rhin*.
4. *Combats dans la Ligne Maginot*.
5. *La Veille Inutile*.

Chapter 1

1. In 1860, Savoy, along with the county of Nice, was annexed to France by a plebiscite, as part of a political agreement (the Treaty of Turin) brokered between the French emperor Napoleon III and King Victor Emmanuel II of the Kingdom of Sardinia that began the process of the unification of Italy.
2. He was looking much further ahead than would become reality.
3. The reason will be discussed later.
4. Fort de Moulainville and Fort de Vacherauville at Verdun.
5. Tricaud's full first name could not be found in any source.
6. 'Essai sur la fortification permanente actuelle par le Lieutenant-colonel du Génie TRICAUD', *Révue du genie*, December 1933.
7. Old Fronts 1929–1934.
8. The area between Longwy and Briey contained Lorraine's major iron ore deposits that produced about 17 million tons of iron per year prior to 1914. The ore is deep in the ground. It is called minette and carries 25 to 48 per cent iron. The ore from Briey was the richest with 36 to 40 per cent iron. Longwy was 25 to 40 per cent. Iron ore was extracted from deep shafts 200–250m in depth.
9. *Parcs mobile de fortifications* included equipment and construction materials to build field fortifications to give flexibility and depth to the defences.
10. There is no clear translation for this word other than 'work', like a work of art, which indeed it was. An *ouvrage* could just as easily have been called 'fort', but, very simply, it wasn't.
11. Term to be used throughout this book.
12. Using a telephone, radio or flares.
13. Major anti-tank works were built at Hochwald and Hackenberg. These consisted of concrete-lined ditches several metres deep, defended by casemates with machine guns and anti-tank guns. Anti-tank ditches were proposed at several other locations but were not built because of funding restrictions.

14. Ouvrages Pas-du-Roc, Roche-la-Croix, Rimplas, Mont Agel.
15. The locomotive from the depot pulled inside the fort. The munitions, stored in metal cases called 'caissons', were offloaded from the wagons and moved along metal monorails in the ceiling then inside the lift. At the base of the shaft, the caissons were loaded onto another set of wagons pulled by locomotive or pushed by hand.
16. This never happened during the Battle of France. It was suspected that German troops had entered the abandoned Bloc 1 of Ouvrage du Welschoff but they did not penetrate to the underground area. There was never a concerted attack inside an ouvrage.
17. Numbered, for example, 01, 02, 03, etc.
18. *Transmetteur d'ordres Doignon* – same principle as Carpentier but based on the use of a system similar to the TM32 telephone exchanges. Instead of a dial a small flap was opened indicating the order for the receiver box. This did not work well since vibrations in the blocs caused the shutters to open and close by themselves. They were replaced by the Carpentier devices. The Saint-Chamond Granat system was used after the war.
19. Officers and NCOs had a minimum of two years of local training prior to 1939.

Chapter 2

1. Billotte was killed in a car crash on 23 May 1940 and was replaced by General Georges Blanchard.
2. STG casemates were built in a number of configurations. Their level 2 protection was relatively strong, with one or two gun chambers for a 25mm or 47mm anti-tank gun and JM. Models were STG A: double blockhouse; STG A1: double with cloche; STG B: simple with a cloche; STG B1: simple with cloche
3. First name not found.
4. Small shelters, types A and B equipped with machine guns and FMs and types N1 and N2, version *droit, gauche, frontal* (d, f, g) for a machine gun or anti-tank gun
5. Fortified position equipped with a Renault FT tank turret armed with a Hotchkiss machine gun.
6. *Canon de 155 Grande Puissance Filloux*, designed during the First World War by Colonel Louis Filloux. A heavy artillery piece for a 43kg shell, muzzle velocity 735m/s and range of 19,500m
7. Pounded during the Battle of Maubeuge in 1914.
8. Blocs specific to this region.
9. Barbed wire, road barricades, trenches, redoubts.
10. First name unknown.
11. One artillery fort, two casemates, five observatories, twenty-four shelters and another twenty-three blocs of various types were cut in phase two. Two of the six artillery forts were constructed; the other four became infantry forts.
12. The older German forts of Guentrange and Koenigsmacker each had four 100mm turrets operated by 151 RAP.
13. On 22 April 1940 the 51st Division was detached from the rest of the BEF and placed under the command of the French Third Army. The division was stationed in front of the Ouvrage Hackenberg and escaped being surrounded with the rest of the BEF during the Battle of France.
14. SF Sarre until 27 October 1938; *Secteur Défensif de la Sarre* until 15 March 1940.
15. Three GO were included in the original plans but were not built.
16. *Ensemble* – an earlier term used to describe a grouping of fortified elements, such as the *Ensemble d'Hochwald, Ensemble de Bitche*, etc.

17. Shifted from the Army of the Alps in 1940.
18. Three GO and seven PO.
19. See Chapter 12 for specifics.
20. Thirty Type M2F casemates, about twelve Type M1F and four Type M2P
21. *Secteur Fortifié du Bas Rhin* – heavier and more powerful casemates generally identical in design; double flanking with a cloche GFM and often several cloches for JM.

Chapter 3

1. Bruge, *Faites Sauter*, p. 49.
2. Charged with guarding the border during times of peace.
3. Bloc equipped with a turret for two 75mm Model 1933 guns (Turret No. 217), weighing 265 tons with semi-automatic breech, the only one of its kind in Alsace. From the top of the outer surface of the roof to the foot of the stairwell was 41m, one of the longest staircases with 210 steps.
4. The GQG issued several alerts in April.

Chapter 4

1. Army Group A included 4 and 267 ID; Fourth Army with 87, 211 and 26 ID; V Corps with 28 and 251 ID; VIII Corps with 8 ID; XV Corps with 62 ID, 5th and 7th Panzer Divisions; II Corps with 12 and 32 ID; Twelfth Army with 9 and 27th ID; III Corps with 3 and 23 ID; VI Corps with 16 and 24 ID; XVIII Corps with 5th, 21st, 25th ID and 1st Mountain Division; the Von Kleist Group – see following note; Sixteenth Army with 6, 15, 26, 33, 52, 71 and 197 ID; XIII Corps with 17 and 34 ID; XXIII Corps with 58 and 76 ID.
2. Panzer Group Kleist included HQ Troops included two signals battalions, a Nebelwerfer regiment, three pioneer battalions, three artillery regiments; XIX Corps (Motorized) with four *Grossdeutschland* infantry regiments, heavy artillery, pioneer battalions, 1st, 2nd, 10th Panzer Divisions; XXXXI Corps with Luftwaffe Flak Regiment, 6th and 8th Panzer Divisions, 2nd Motorized Division; XIV Corps with 13th and 29th Motorized Divisions; Flak Corps with 101st, 102nd and 104th Flak Regiments
3. Army Group C included First Army (Generalfedlmarschall Erwin von Witzleben) with 197 ID; Hohe Kom.z.b.V.XXXVI with 246, 215, 262 and 257 ID; XXIV Corps with 60, 252 and 168 ID; XII Corps with 75, 268 and 198 ID; XXX Corps with 258, 93 and 79 ID; Hoh.Kom.z.b.V.XXXXV with 95 and 167 ID; Seventh Army (Generaloberst Friederich Dollman) included Hoh.Kom.z.b.V.XXXIII with 213, 554, 556 and 239 ID; XXV Corps with 557 and 555 ID and 6th Mountain Division; XXVII Corps with 218 and 221 ID.
4. 3 DLC included 5th Cavalry Brigade with 5th Hussar and 6th Dragoon Regiments; 13th Light Mechanized Brigade with 3rd Armoured Car Regiment, 2nd Dragoon Regiment, 3rd Divisional Anti-Tank Squadron with 25mm guns; plus two Artillery Regiments with 75mm and 105mm guns, 10th Division Anti-Tank Battery with 47mm guns, three Divisional Reconnaissance Groups, 1st Spahis Brigade, 2nd Company, 5th Infantry Tank Battalion with R35 tanks and 58th Infantry Division as of 13–14 May
5. Bruge, *Faites Sauter*, pp. 122–3.
6. Replaced by General Renondeau on 27 May 1940.
7. 128 and 139 RIF and a number of smaller groups and detachments; 20th Infantry Division including 128 RIF; 58th Infantry Division with 139 RIF.
8. Light cavalry units primarily from Tunisia and Morocco.
9. *Groupe de reconnaissance de corps d'armée/infanterie* (GRCA/GRDI).

10. Under General Freydenberg's Colonial Corps.
11. Under 56 DI.
12. Under 28 DI.
13. The Panhard 178 *Automitrailleuse de Découverte modèle 1935* was a 4x4 armoured car designed for the French cavalry. It had a crew of four and was equipped with a 25mm gun and a 7.5mm machine gun.
14. Behlendorf returned to command in November.
15. XIX Army Corps OOB.
16. Masson, p. 27.
17. Ibid., p. 29.

Chapter 5

1. The village of Villy was a defensive strongpoint with numerous small bunkers with machine-gun positions, trenches, etc.
2. Casemate Vaux-Dessus was an STG artillery casemate for a 75mm Model 1897/33 gun that flanked to the west.

Chapter 6

1. Included the 62nd Infantry Division, 5th and 7th Panzer Divisions.
2. Ninth Army was commanded by General Andre Corap; II Corps by General Jan Bouffet; XI Corps by General Julien Martin.
3. The CORF planned to build an ouvrage at Epine.
4. There is no historical or technical information in the archives concerning these *Maisons Fortes* in SF Haguenau. They no longer exist and appear on engineer maps only.
5. Located on D245 on the northern outskirts of Hatten.
6. Masson, p. 32.
7. Originally General Hanaut until 1 January 1940.
8. 28 ID included 7, 49, 83 and 28 IR, 64 Artillery Regiment, 28 *Panzerjäger* Bn, 28 Recon Bn and 28 Pioneer Bn.
9. The high-velocity 88mm Flak proved to be a devastating anti-tank and anti-fortifications gun during the war.
10. It is unclear which blockhouse this refers to. There were three blockhouses with the name Élesmes in the vicinity – A90 – Bois d'Élesmes Nord, B636 – Bois d'Élesmes and T19 and T20 BE Centre and Sud. Most likely it is A90 since this is directly behind La Salmagne.

Chapter 7

1. Bruge, *Faites Sauter*, p. 257.
2. Ibid., p. 260.

Chapter 8

1. This sector did not have the A, C, or X designation.
2. Located on the road over the Hochwald ridge, south of the ouvrage's combat blocs.
3. Blocs 8 and 9 were, respectively, the EM and the EH of Hochwald Ouest.
4. Rodolphe, p. 103.
5. The casemate was designated C24 but since it was also an observatory it was given the designation O-12.
6. Masson, p. 62.

Chapter 9

1. 1875–1951 – commander of all French field armies as of September 1939. After the collapse of the French Army after Sedan, Georges was sacked by Prime Minister Paul Reynaud and replaced by Weygand on 19 May 1940.
2. 1878–1966 – became Prime Minister on 21 March 1940. He resigned on 16 June 1940 after refusing to support an armistice with Germany.
3. Billotte was killed in a car accident on 23 May 1940. The army was reshuffled afterwards into four army groups, plus Seventh Army.
4. Seventh Army with I Corps (4, 25 Motorized Infantry Divisions), XVI Corps (21, 60 Infantry and 1 Light Mechanized and 9 Motorized Infantry Divisions); First Army with III Corps (2 North African, 1 Motorized Infantry Divisions), IV Corps (1 Moroccan Infantry, 15 Motorized Infantry), V Corps (101 Fortress Infantry, 5 North African, 12 Motorized Infantry, 2 and 3 Light Mechanized Divisions, General Prioux's Cavalry Corps,
5. XV Corps with 5th and 7th Panzer Divisions.
6. Bruge, *Faites Sauter*, p. 311.
7. Ibid.
8. Ibid.
9. First Army, with 215, 246 and 96 Divisions.

Chapter 10

1. *Artillerie Lourde sur Voie Ferrée* – Heavy railway guns.
2. Identified by Bruge as 31 BC.
3. Shelters made of logs.
4. Also referred to as Abri M12b.
5. The crew of the blockhouse who belonged to II/174 RMIF was ordered to retreat at 2100hrs but the position was already surrounded by the Germans. Tirbisch decided to stay and defend in place. On 14 June at 0500hrs R4B blocked the passage of 268 ID troops. A renewed attack at 0700hrs was also contained but the bloc succumbed to Pak 37 damage and surrendered at 1130hrs.
6. C12B was a MOM blockhouse for an anti-tank gun located on the Rother-Hubel hill (250m) south-east of the *Étang de Hoste Bas*; R6B was a MOM FM blockhouse built to defend the *digue de Hoste-Bas*, occupied by CM/6 of II/174 RMIF and commanded by Chief-Sergeant Bauer; MC8B, also designated Mc-27, was a STG simple casemate, type B, under S/Lt Morge
7. M113N, an infantry blockhouse with a Hotchkiss machine gun and FM guarded the dyke; C15N was a MOM blockhouse for an anti-tank gun on the opposite side of the road
8. The two blockhouses protected the dyke and the Hoste-Bas to Hoste-Haut road. M108N was a blockhouse for an anti-tank gun. The crew was from CM/2 of I/174 RMIF, commanded by Chief Sergeant Hilaire; R8B – Hoste Haut was also an MOM infantry blockhouse for FM, to protect the dyke. It was also part of CM/2 and was commanded by S/Lt Rudolph.

Chapter 11

1. Bruge, *Faites Sauter*, p. 4.
2. Ibid.
3. Masson, p. 75.
4. Ibid., p. 76.

5. Built by SOM Paris. This was an ensemble of two monocular periscopes in a single housing, one, with a magnification of 8, was the scope for direction while the second scope indicated the height of an object.

6. Welschoff received orders from Bourret of Fifth Army and Haut-Poirier from General Condé – Third Army.

7. Some suggested he was a German in disguise.

8. Two sources record that Kaupisch was commander of HK XXXI, but other sources show he was replaced by General Gallenkamp of 78 ID on 10 April 1940 after which Kaupisch joined the reserves.

9. XXXI Corps was in command of German troops in Denmark and took command of reserve divisions in France in June 1940 under Sixteenth Army, including 161, 162 and 183 ID.

10. Designated Ermitage Saint Quentin-C7, a CORF infantry casemate located south of Pracourt near the Bois de Tappe. The casemate was equipped with a JM/AC47, JM, cloche GFM A, cloche JM and two FM embrasures.

Chapter 12

1. The *bataillon de chasseurs pyrénéens* (BCPyr) was identical in composition to the *bataillon de chasseurs alpins* (BCA) except it lacked the ski scout platoon. This difference ended for the battalions of the 4th Half-Brigade when it was assigned to the Army of the Alps and a platoon was formed in each battalion from the SES left behind by the alpine infantry regiment that had moved north.

Chapter 13

1. True but the Italians had not yet signed.

Chapter 14

1. XVI Corps was assigned to guard SD Rhône and SF Savoie on 15 September but was quickly moved to the north-east on 27 September.

2. Scouting ski patrols.

3. 5, 6 Alpine Regiment, 2 Alpine Artillery Regiment.

4. General Hoepner's XVI Corps was moving in the Rhône Valley with the intent of getting behind the Army of the Alps.

5. Advanced post with seven blocs and one entry guarded the exits of Col de la Seigne; six blocs were casemates for FM, one for MG, one observatory and the entrance.

6. Twelve 75mm Model 1927, twelve 100mm Model 1917 howitzers, eight 20mm AA guns.

7. A blockhouse with three FM embrasures, plus several trench positions.

8. Infantry, artillery, mortars.

9. *Barrage Rapide*.

10. Anti-tank Monobloc with a *barrière rapide* to block the RN 90 from the direction of Italy. Equipped with a JM/AC47 to enfilade RN 90 and JM and FM to guard the uncompleted Versoyen anti-tank ditch. Crew included twelve men of 70 BAF under command of Adjutant Bernard.

11. Infantry ouvrage with one bloc for JM/AC47, two JM, one 25mm anti-tank gun; one NCO and 18 men commanded by S/Lt Bochaton. The mission was to interdict the access to Bourg St. Maurice with enfilading fire on RN 90.

12. Constructed between 1897 and 1910 and modernized by the MOM in the 1930s.

13. Wikimaginot – 71 BAF, Mary 81 BAF

14. Demouzon, pp. 94–5, cites S/Lt Cavin, four NCOs and twenty men from 10th Company of CAB 3 of 281 RI.
15. Blockhouse for MG and 25mm anti-tank gun, manned by four men of 10th Company of 281 RI.
16. One of two armoured batteries built on the plateau of Mont Cenis to defend the Susa Valley. The fort was equipped with four 149/35 A turrets.
17. Artillery ouvrage built on top of the Fort du Sapey. Five blocs: entry; Bloc 1 – 75/33 casemate; Bloc 2 – 75/33 casemate; Bloc 3 – Obs/VDP; Bloc 4 – two 75/29 casemate. Blocs 1 and 2 of Sapey were called Blocs Maurienne and Bloc 4 was called Bloc Fréjus due to the zones they covered.
18. Advanced post with five blocs; entry, observatory, two casemates for MG and FM, emergency exit bloc with FM.
19. Artillery ouvrage with five blocs and two entries: Bloc 1 – south-flanking casemate for two 75mm mortars; Bloc 2 – casemate for two 75mm mortars for frontal action; Bloc 3 – Obs/VDP; Bloc 4 – infantry casemate for two mortar cloches and one LG cloche; Bloc 5 – casemate for two 75/31 mortars and four 81 mortars.
20. Artillery ouvrage with four blocs, commanded by Chef d'Escadron Valat: Blocs Maurienne 1 – 75/33 howitzer, 2 – 75/33 howitzer; Bloc 3 – Obs/VDP; Bloc 4 – south-flanking casemate for two 75/29 gun/howitzers; mixed entry.
21. Four blocs: Bloc 1 – infantry casemate for mortars, GFM, LG; Bloc 2 – ObsVDP; Bloc 3 – casemate flanking Lavoir with two 75/31 mortars; Bloc 4 – frontal action casemate for four 81mm mortars.
22. The only engineer officer to command a Maginot Line ouvrage.
23. Equipped with two 8mm MG, twelve FM, two 60mm mortars.
24. 1st Superga Division.
25. Infantry AP with four blocs for FM and MG and two concrete positions for 60mm mortars. Mission was to guard the Col de la Vallée Étroite. Crew include forty men of 81 BAF under S/Lt Girard-Madoux.
26. Infantry ouvrage with two 'demi-forts': first – entry bloc, Bloc 1 – Obs/VDP; Bloc 2 – JM to enfilade the Valley of Fréjus. Second – entry with FM and bloc for emergency exit. The ouvrage was manned by 20th Company of 81 BAF with fifty-four men under Lt Desgrange. The mortar section was commanded by Lt Bégué.
27. Small AP with one MG, twelve FM, two 60mm mortars.
28. Three infantry blocs for JM and FM.
29. CORF artillery ouvrage with seven blocs and one entry (Bloc 1). Bloc 2 flanked the route de Montgenèvre with two 81mm mortars; Bloc 3 flanked the Vallée de la Clarée with two 75/31 mortars; Bloc 4 – Obs/VDP; Bloc 5 – observatory (not VDP cloche); Bloc 6 – casemate for JM; Bloc 7 – JM to flank route de Montgenèvre; Bloc 8 – part of the old Fort de Gondran Sud with four 95mm guns. Manned by 72 BAF for infantry and 11th Battery of 154 RAP for artillery and commanded by Captain Mandrillon.
30. Ten blockhouses with two Alpine shelters and one cavern shelter. The mission of the post was to cover the village of Montgenèvre, Bois de Sestrière and Col du Clot Enjaime. Manned by a company of 91 BCA under Lt Berthoux. Defences included FM and MG.
31. Four infantry blocs for FM, MG and 25mm anti-tank gun. In included a small sluice to create a flood zone in the Fond du Vallon. The ouvrage was manned by ninety-two men of 2nd Company, 72 BAF under Lt Renoux.
32. A small masonry battery built to protect Fort de l'Olive and used as a rifle position in 1940.

33. Gondran was more of an ensemble with five main components: Gondran A – barracks with six open-air artillery positions; Gondran B – same with three positions; Gondran C – same as B; Gondran D – a masonry redoubt with three gun positions; Ouvrage Gondran E – three blocs: Bloc 1 – entry; Bloc 2 – MG casemate; Bloc 3 – Observatory with a Cloche Digoin; commanded by S/Lt Gandemer with forty-two men from 72 BAF.

34. Small uncompleted infantry position with tunnels dug in the rock but no blocs. Commanded by Adjutant Béraud from 91 BCA.

35. Four CORF blocs – Bloc 1 entry; Bloc 2 and 3 were cloches Pamart modified for a FM 24/29 and 50mm mortar, Bloc 4 was a STG GFM A observation cloche. The ouvrage was mannded by fifty-two men of I/83 BAF, commanded by Lt Deloy.

36. Large artillery ouvrage with six blocs: Bloc 2 – 50mm mortar and FM to flank the access road; Bloc 3 same to flank the road leading from the forest; Bloc 4 – Obs/VDP; Bloc 5 – a very powerful bloc with two 75/31 casemate mortars, two 81mm mortars in the lower level and a 75/33 turret; Bloc 6 – Obs. The mission of the ouvrage was to flank Ouvrage de Saint-Ours Haut and cover the Col de Larche and the frontier zone. The commander was Captain Fabre of 162 RAP, with a contingent of 155 men from 162 RAP and 83 BAF.

37. Also Observatoire d'artillerie from the Séré de Rivières époque, with 150mm mortars. It was commanded by Lt Proal and men from 162 RAP.

38. Ouvrage de Saint-Ours Haut was a CORF artillery fort with five blocs: Bloc 1 – entry with approach defences; Bloc 2 – artillery casemate for 75/31 mortar and 81mm mortar; Bloc 3 and 4 – observatories; Bloc 4 – casemate for two 81mm mortars to cover the plateau of Mallemort, Ravin de Pinet and route de Viraysse. Commanded by Captain de Courcel with 233 men and eleven officers from 83 BAF and 162 RAP.

39. Small MOM post with five blocs for FM and MG, plus a mortar on top of Bloc 2. Thirty men and two officers from II/299 RIA were commanded by Lt Josserand (as of 12 June).

40. Planned for eight blocs, only four were completed. Bloc 3 – JM; Bloc 4 – JM and cloche FM/50mm and VDP; Bloc 6 – two 75/32 howitzters and one 75/31 howitzer. Ten officers and 216 men from 73 BAF and 162 RAP, commanded by Captain Gilotte as of 29 May.

41. Built by the MOM wth five blocs for FM and MG; twenty-one men from 73 BAF, commanded by Lt Delécraz.

42. Principally an observatory with four blocs for MGs, with twenty-seven men under the command of SC Joyeux.

43. Five blocs built by the CORF, commanded by Captain Toussaint with eight officers and 334 men. Bloc 1 – two 81mm mortars; Bloc 2 – platform for 81mm mortars in open air; Bloc 3 – MG cloche; Bloc 4 – two 75/33 howitzers and one 75/31 mortar in casemate flanking west; Bloc – two 75/33 gun-howitzers and one 75/31 mortar in casemate flanking east.

44. Artillery ouvrage with three blocs: Bloc 1 entry and FM/MG; Bloc 2 – two 81/32 mortars; Bloc 3 – two 75/31 mortars and two 81/32 mortars. Its mission was to inderdict the Vésubie valley and guard the exits to the Vallon de Gordolasque. The crew of 246 men and five officers, commanded by Captain Cardi, were part of 61 DBAF and 12th Battery of 167 RAP.

45. Large artillery ouvrage, the only one in the south with a 135mm turret. Six blocs plus mixed entry: Bloc 3 – 75/29 in casemate; Bloc 4 – four 81/32 mortars; Bloc 5 – 75/33 turret; Bloc 6 – 135mm turret; Bloc 7 and 8 – JM and MG and VDP cloche; Bloc 2 was not built. The crew included ten officers and 363 men from 85 BAF (40 DBAF) and 158 RAP, commanded by Chef de Brigade (CB) Cucchietti.

46. Two 75/31 in casemate (Bloc 2); four 81mm mortars in casemate (Blocs 2 and 3); one 75/33 turret (Bloc 3), with a crew of seven officers and 295 men from 95 BAF and 11th Battery of 158 RAP, commanded by Captain Lejeune.

47. Five blocs: two entries with FM, one observatory, two infantry blocs for MG, plus a number of small blockhouses, manned by five officers and twenty-seven men of 2nd Company of 76 BAF (Adjutant Chef Lanteri).

48. Six blocs: two entries (Blocs 1 and 2); Bloc 3 and 4 for MG; Bloc 5 – Obs; Bloc 6 FM. Forty men and four officers commanded by Lt Carmes.

49. The strongest ouvrage in the Alps with four blocs: Bloc 1 – entry; Bloc 2 (Casemate d'artillerie Sud) – two 75/31 mortars; two 81mm mortars; two 135mm lance-bombes; Bloc 3 (Casemate d'artillerie Nord) – two 75/31 mortars, two 81mm mortars; Bloc 4 – Observatory; Bloc 4 and 6 – FMs flanking north and south. The crew included 310 men and eight officers from 86 BAF and 8th Battery of 157 RAP, commanded by Captain Panzani.

50. Bloc 1 – entry with cloche LG and two 81mm mortars; Bloc 2 (Bloc de Barrage) – 75/29 casemate plus MGs; Bloc 3 – two 81mm mortars in casemate, two 75/29 in casemate. 354 men and eleven officers commanded by Captain Hugard.

51. Three entry blocs and four combat blocs: Bloc 1 – EH; Bloc 2 – vehicle entry; Bloc 3 – cable car; Bloc 4 – FM; Blocs 5 and 6 – 75/33 turret; isolated CORF Observatory Est de Mont Agel. Crew of seven officers and 194 men from 58 DBAF and 10th Battery of 157 RAP, commanded by Captain David.

52. Small post with JM interchangeable with 37mm anti-tank gun, FM. The post controlled a mine (*Dispositif de Mine*) at the intersection of the Route de Garavan. The post was manned by eight men and one officer from 95 BAF. The commander was S/Lt Charles Gros.

53. Today IME Bariquand Alphand.

54. Earthen infantry blockhouse defended by 2nd Coy 76 BAF

55. Collet du Pilon-Balmetta – five MOM blocs for observation and small arms, commanded by Adjutant Maurin. AP Baisse de Scuvion – observation post with two MG, five rifles, one mortar; four NCOs and twenty-seven men of 76 BAF; Adjutant-Chef Vignau. AP de Pierre Pointue – infantry post with five blocs: 2 entries, observatory, two MG casemates, plus several blockhouses; guarded the Mont Razet sector; five NCOs and twenty-seven men of 2nd Company of 76 BAF, AC Lanteri. AP de la Péna – three blocs for small arms and a number of shelters; manned by twenty-seven men of 2nd Company of 76 BAF under Adjutant Chef Olivier.

56. Two blocs including the entry: Bloc 2 with two 75/29 guns, two 81/32 mortars flanking right towards Castillon and Menton; men of 12th Battery of 158 RAP and 157 RAP plus infantry from 95 BAF. Twelve officers, forty NCOS and 277 men commanded by Captain Diné. Fort de Suchet was an older fort above the ouvrage and was equipped with old 155mm Mougin turrets.

57. CORF ouvrage with six blocs, defended by Captain Finidori. Bloc 1 – entry; Bloc 2 – two 75/31 mortars; Bloc 3 – casemate flanking north with two 75/29 howitzers and two 81mm mortars; Bloc 4 – JM, Mortar and Obs/VDP; Bloc 5 – JM and Mortar; Bloc 6 – two 81mm mortars in casemate.

58. Active CORF shelter with FM, defended by fifty-nine men under S/Lt Roman.

Chapter 15

1. Lt Choné, commander of Bloc 3, let Cattiaux know that he would not obey such an order as it would be a violation of his honour to do so.

2. Or *obus perforants* – anti-armour shells used primarily on naval vessels against coastal batteries or other heavily-armoured ships. The term was also used for armour-piercing shells of the Maginot Line.

3. Under XXXVII Corps, with 352, 404 and 689 IR and 246 AR.
4. Large artillery ouvrage with nine blocs plus two entries. Bloc 1 – MG turret; Bloc 2 – 75/33 turret; Bloc 3 – 75/32 turret; Bloc 4 – Obs VDP; Bloc 5 – casemate for 75/29, 135mm; Blocs 6 and 7 – 135mm turret; Bloc 8 – casemate flanking east for JM/37 and JM; Bloc 9 – MG turret. Crew included 782 men and twenty-six officers from 169 RIF and 151 RAP, commanded by Chef d'Escadron Guillemain.
5. RFM type 35 Mi for two MG.
6. CORF infantry casemate for JM/AC47, JM, FM, GFM A, commanded by Lt Klein with twenty-nine men.
7. Monobloc for two JM/AC37, two JM, MG turret, commanded by Lt Pobeau with two officers and seventy-seven men.
8. Ouvrage du Kobenbusch – seven blocs plus two entries. Bloc 1 – MG turret; Bloc 2 – JM and JM/AC47 casemate; Bloc 3 – Obs VDP; Bloc 4 – MG turret; Bloc 5 – 75R32 turret; Bloc 6 – 81mm mortar turret; Bloc 7 – casemate for three 75/32. Commanded by Commandant Charnal with fourteen officers and 513 men from 163 RIF and 151 RAP.
9. Ouvrage du Galgenberg – six blocs plus two entries. Bloc 1 (Casemate Nord-Ouest) – casemate for JM/AC47 and JM; Bloc 2 (Casemate Nord-Est) – same; Bloc 3 – MG turret; Bloc 4 – 81mm mortar turret; Bloc 5 – Obs VDP; Bloc 6 – 135mm turret. Fifteen officers and 430 men from 167 RIF and 151 RAP, commanded by Captain de la Teysonnière.
10. Ouvrage du Billig – seven blocs and one mixed entry. Bloc 1 – JM/AC47 and JM; Bloc 2 – MG turret; Bloc 3 – casemate for JM/AC47 and JM; Bloc 4 – 75R32 turret plus two 75/32 casemate; Bloc 5 – two 75/32 casemate; Bloc 6 – 81mm mortar turret; Bloc 7 – Obs VP. Crew of sixteen officers and 521 men of 167 RIF and 151 RAP, commanded by Commandant Roy.

Chapter 16
1. Making up what was known as the '*Ensemble de Biesenberg*'.
2. 215 ID (XXXVII Corps) – General Baptist Kniess – 380, 390, 435 IR, 268 AR.
3. 246 ID (XXXVII Corps) – General Erich Denecke – 313, 352, 404 IR and 246 AR.
4. 262 ID (XXIV Corps) – 462, 482 and 486 IR and 262 AR.
5. Battery 810 – 355mm Rheinmetal; Battery 820 – First World War vintage Krupp 420mm Gamma; Battery 830 – First World War vintage Skoda 420mm.
6. XXIV Corps – 457, 466 and 477 IR and 257 AR.
7. DCA – *Défense contre avions* – anti-aircraft. The turret guns were adjusted to fire at a high angle and the shells fixed to burst at certain altitudes. France did not otherwise have a strong anti-aircraft capability.
8. Destined to be ouvrages.
9. Should a second raid be necessary the aircraft had to return to Mannheim to refuel and to reload. This would cause a two-hour delay.
10. Junkers Ju-87 *Sturzkampfflugzeug* (dive bomber). Normal payload was one 250kg bomb under the fuselage and four 50kg bombs, two under each wing.

Chapter 17
1. OKH Reserve.
2. First Army, XXX Corps.
3. Identified by the Germans as *Panzerwerk* 230. Kerfent was *Panzerwerk* 240.
4. Also called C2 de Bréhain, it was a bloc adjacent to but not connected with the ouvrage. Work to connect the casemate to the ouvrage was started over the winter of 1939/40.

5. Another source says Hauptmann Amsberg.
6. Most likely Haie aux Mures 1 or 2, west of Bloc 2.
7. Casemate for JM/AC47, commanded by Adjutant Tilly.

Chapter 18

1. XXIV Corps, included 462, 486, 486 IR and 262 AR.
2. Austrian.
3. Double casemate with JM/AC47 and JM, cloche AM, cloche GFM B.

Chapter 19

1. XXIV Corps – 215 ID with 457, 466, 477 IR and 257 AR
2. Type RFM35 for frontal action built between 1935 and 1936 in Thionville sector for a 47mm anti-tank gun on a fixed carriage and one or two Hotchkiss 8mm Model 1914 machine guns.
3. Bloc 2 included an observation post designated Obs 09 that was attached to Ouvrage d'Anzeling,
4. Rodolphe, p. 144.

Chapter 20

1. Also designated O26 and attached to Simserhof.
2. Bruge, *On a livré la Ligne Maginot*, p. 242
3. Ibid., p. 243.
4. Ibid., p. 244.
5. Masson, p. 94.

Chapter 21

1. 'This slow silent procession in the semi-darkness of the galleries resembles the funeral of France …', Rodolphe, p. 76.

Bibliography

Bruge, Roger, *Faites Sauter la Ligne Maginot*, Paris: Fayard, 1973.

Bruge, Roger, *On a Livré la Ligne Maginot*, Paris: Fayard, 1975.

Bruge, Roger, *Juin 1940, Le Mois Maudit*, Paris: Librairie Arthème Fayard, 1980.

Cole, Hugh M., *United States Army in World War II, The European Theater of Operations, The Lorraine Campaign*, Washington D.C.: Centre of Military History United States Army, 1993.

Cole, Hugh M., *United States Army in World War II, The European Theater of Operations, Riviera to the Rhine*, Washington D.C.: Centre of Military History United States Army, 1993.

Demouzon, Laurent, *Les Fortifications Françaises Du Mont Cenis – 1890–1945*, Société d'Art et d'Histoire d'Aix-les-Bains, 2007.

Horne, Alistair, *To Lose a Battle – France 1940*, New York: Penguin, 1969, 1990.

Mary, Jean Yves, *La Bataille des Trois Frontières, Mai-Juin 1940*, Bayeux: Heimdal, 2012.

Mary, Jean-Yves and Alain Hohnadel, *Hommes et Ouvrages de la Ligne Maginot, Tome 1*, Paris: Histoire et Collections, 2000,

Mary, Jean-Yves and Alain Hohnadel, *Hommes et Ouvrages de la Ligne Maginot, Tome 2*, Paris: Histoire et Collections, 2001.

Mary, Jean-Yves and Alain Hohnadel, *Hommes et Ouvrages de la Ligne Maginot, Tome 3*, Paris: Histoire et Collections, 2003.

Mary, Jean-Yves and Alain Hohnadel, *Hommes et Ouvrages de la Ligne Maginot, Tome 4*, Paris: Histoire et Collections, 2009.

Mary, Jean-Yves and Alain Hohnadel, *Hommes et Ouvrages de la Ligne Maginot, Tome 5*, Paris: Histoire et Collections, 2009.

Masson, Claude-Armand, *La Veille Inutile*, Paris: Sercap, 1985.

OKH, *Denkschrift über die französische Landbefestigung*, Heeres, 1941.

Rodolphe, René, *Combats dans la Ligne Maginot*, Vevey: Klausfelder, S.A., 1973.

Rolf, Rudi, *A Dictionary on Modern Fortifications*, Middleburg: Prak Publishing, 2004.

Romanych, Marc and Martin Rupp, *Maginot Line 1940 – Battles on the French Frontier*, Oxford: Osprey, 2010.

Truttmann, Philippe, *La Muraille de France ou La Ligne Maginot*, Thionville: Gerard Klopp, 1996.

Wahl, Jean-Bernard, *La Ligne Maginot en Alsace, 200 kilomètres de Beton et d'Acier*, Steinbrunn-le-Haut: Editions du Rhin, 1987.

Wahl, Jean-Bernard, *Hochwald, une Forteresse en Alsace*, Ostwald: Les Éditions du Polygone, 1999.

Wahl, Jean-Bernard, *Il Était un Fois, La Ligne Maginot*, Colmar: Jérome, 1999.

Index

Page numbers in *italics* refer to illustrations